AF556697

The Economy of Bikaner State 1746-1828 AD

The Economy of Bikaner State 1746-1828 AD

Kanti Lal Mathur

First Published, 2016

ISBN 978-93-83723-09-6

Published by
LG PUBLISHERS DISTRIBUTORS
49, Gali No. 14, Pratap Nagar
Mayur Vihar Phase I, Delhi 110 091
Tel: 011 2279 5641 email: lgpdist@gmail.com

Leser Typeset at
Arpit Printographers, Delhi-92

Printed at
Sapra Brothers, Delhi 110 092

To
the memory of
my mother Smt. Vidya Devi
and father Shri Amarlal Mathur 'Pattanavish'
and also elder brother Shri Mukesh Mathur

Preface

The Mughal Empire occupies a significant place in Medieval Indian History as it bequeathed a rich legacy of administration, army, economy, society, culture, art and architecture. The Rajput chieftains of Rajputana who served the Mughals as *Mansabdars* for a long time, also contributed significantly to their success in providing unity and stability to the empire. Their intimate relationship and strong bonding helped each other. If the Mughals achieved success in expanding and consolidating their empire, the Rajput chieftains also rose to prominence and attained affluence. They could safeguard their *watans* and *jagirs* as well. Thus, the Mughal state proved to be a benefactor state for them.

But with the decline and dismemberment of the mighty Mughal empire in the mid-18th century and consequent separation of the Rajput chiefs from the Mughal empire created a different scenario in Rajputana. In the absence of the imperial protection the Mughal successive states had to survive on their own and manage their affairs on their own accord. It is, therefore, the conditions in Rajputana in the want of effective protection of the Mughals underwent substantial changes and the chieftains behaved as *de facto* rulers. They had to reformulate their principalities with their own resources fostering many changes in their administration, economy, taxation system and army structure exhaustively to survive. This transient phase of the post-Mughal era in Rajputana is the subject of desideratum in historical studies. The successive events testify that soon they had to submit to another imperial protection and subordination of the British in 1818 AD.

The present work is a humble attempt to study the economy of the erstwhile transient State of Bikaner which was a Rathore principality of Western Rajputana in the *Thar* desert. It also examines the changes and continuity in the Mughal successive state of Bikaner during the period 1746-1828 AD after being separated from the Mughal empire. It is worth examining its economy on various scores. The state of Bikaner with harsh desert conditions had survived for more than seventy years carrying an independent status. Moreover, it was, in its history a period of re-formation and re-organizing the state in the intervening phase of autonomy between the period of subordination of the two imperial powers of the Mughals and the British. Interestingly, it is also to see the after effects of the decline of the Mughal empire in its economy that despite some traces of increase in commercial activities and emergence of some towns as commercial centres, the general trend of the state economy showed a trend of decline and deficit to opt for another patronage under the British.

The study has largely been done through the contemporary unpublished archival source material forming mainly of the *Bahis*. These were to record state accounts, commercial transactions and details of the administrative and revenue systems, etc. These *Bahis* have been preserved in the Rajasthan State Archives, Bikaner. Since, hitherto these have scarcely been used, maximum exposure to them has been given through illustrations and statistical data and with an objective interpretation of evidences. Apart from it, other relevant source material has been gainfully utilized. All the sectors of the economy have been covered in ten chapters, the first and last being introduction and conclusions, others relate to agricultural economy, the taxation system, aspects of trade and commerce, *Mandi* system, prices, role and activities of commercial groups and the crafts and artisans in detail.

It was such an arduous a task to attempt on being the source material in a local dialect and in a distinctive form and also a complex theme, that mistakes of interpretation otherwise is possible despite my utmost care in this regard.

At the outset, I would like to place on record my deep sense of gratitude and whole-hearted thanks to my teacher and Supervisor Professor S. Inayet Ali Zaidi, Department of History and Culture, Jamia Millia Islamia, New Delhi, for his valuable guidance and encouragement, analytical approach to the subject and rational interpretation of the evidences which played a significant role in the formulation of this Doctoral Research work. My sincere thanks are also due to my respected teacher Professor Sunita Zaidi, Dean, Faculty of Humanities and Language, Jamia Millia Islamia, New Delhi for her inestimable help and suggestions throughout the work. I am also thankful to my respected teacher and M.Phil. Supervisor Dr. Aminuddin, former Professor and Head, Department of History, Government Dungar College, Bikaner for his guidance, minute corrections and encouragement all the time.

I seek pleasure in recording my gratitude to the authorities and staff of the following research institutions, archives and the libraries for allowing me to have an access to published and unpublished records. The Rajasthan State Archives, Bikaner; Anup Sanskrit Library, Lallgarh Palace, Bikaner; Maharaja Sadul Singh Museum and Library, Lallgarh Palace, Bikaner; the Zakir Husain Central Library, J.M.I., New Delhi; the Departmental Library of the History Department, J.M.I. New Delhi; the Central Library of Rajasthan University, Jaipur; and the Choupasni Shodh Sansthan, Choupasni, Jodhpur.

I also feel that it is my duty to acknowledge thanks to my colleagues and friends for their help in completing this work. Dr. Ahmed Ali, Department of Geography, very constructively helped me in drawing various maps in the work. Dr. A.K. Joshi, Department of English, deserves special thanks for checking the English text. Dr. N.K. Vyas, Department of Economics, Dungar College, Bikaner and Shri Kailas Khatri gave guidance in formulating the price indices. I express my sincere thanks to my friend Dr. Anjula Jain for her valuable suggestions at times. I am also highly obliged to Shri Rajendra Kumar Mathur and Shri Narendra Kumar Mathur and their families for their hospitalities, both in Delhi and Bikaner during my long stays.

I should mention warm thanks and appreciation to my friends, relatives and to my wife Chandrakala Mathur, daughter

Komal and Son Kapil for their cooperation, help and encouragement for this book without which it was not possible.

Finally, my sincerest thanks to Shri Rahul Saxena of LG Publishers Distributors who took particular care and keen interest in publishing my book and bringing it out in an excellent format.

Kanti Lal Mathur
Professor & Head
Department of History
Jai Narain Vyas University
Jodhpur (Rajasthan)

Contents

List of Maps and Graphs

Abbreviations

A.S.L.B.	:	Anup Sanskrit Library, Bikaner
e.g.	:	Exempli gratia
IHR	:	Indian Historical Review
PIHC	:	Proceedings of Indian History Congress
PRHC	:	Proceedings of Rajasthan History Congress
RORI	:	Rajasthan Oriental Research Institute, Jodhpur
RSS	:	Rajasthani Sodh Sansthan, Choupasni, Jodhpur
RSAB	:	Rajasthan State Archives, Bikaner
SMLB	:	Sadul Museum and Library, Lallgarh, Bikaner
SBLU	:	Saraswati Bhandar Library, Udaipur
viz.	:	Namely
Badi	:	Dark Moon
Sudi	:	Bright Moon

1

Introduction

The 18th century is considered to be significant in Indian history as many political changes and upheavals took place during it. It saw the collapse of the Mughal empire and then, with an apparent chronological gap in which transitional regimes intervened, the rise of the British power.[1] The Mughal empire which began to decline in the 17th century had ultimately fragmented till the second half of the 18th century.[2] This decline and disintegration led to many 'succession states' in India including Rajputana. Many contemporary provincial Mughal *subedars* and officers succeeded in founding their dynastic rule in the provinces of Hyderabad, Bengal, Awadh and in the Deccan. In Rajputana also the Rajput chiefs who had served the Mughal empire for a long time as *mansabdars* created the principalities of their own by simple acquisition of their *watan* (hereditary *jagir*) and other contiguous *jagirs* independently.[3]

The chief Rao Kalyan Mal of Bikaner, who after the foundation of the state in 1488 AD by Rao Bika, had joined the Mughal services in 1570 AD.[4] After serving for a long time (nearly 175 years), when the Mughal empire reached the verge of complete decline about the middle of the 18th century, they began to formulate their own erstwhile principality known as *watan jagir.* From the mid 18th century to 1818 AD they had to re-form and re-organise their state. But soon it had to opt for the subordination of the British East India Company in 1818 AD and the British became thier paramount power. Therefore, the period in itself from mid-18th century to the early decades of the 19th century (till the treaty of subordination with the British East India Company), a period between the two Imperial powers of the Mughals and the British, in the history of Bikaner was transitional and crucial in many respects and thus qualify legitimately as a subject of interest and study to assess the implications and developments in the economy of the state. The long association with the Mughal empire, as a part to it, was to have a significant impact upon its economy.

Some eminent scholars and historians of Indian history have been evaluating the implication of the decline of the Mughal empire for the 'succession states' in the political field, administration and economy and also interpreting the 18th century divergently.[6] According to one point of view the collapse of the Mughal empire led to political disorder and instability in the 'succession states'. The economy of these states also sustained an adverse impact like contraction of commerce and net loss in urban prosperity and there was no real economic growth in the era following the collapse of the Mughal empire.[7]

But contrary to it some are of the view that there was a general continuity in the economic process with certain changes and also with the disintegration of the Mughal authority, the political power shifted from the central authority to the regional potentates in these 'succession states'. So, instead of the 'Dark Age' it was a major shift of the policitical power or sovereignty. The economic process did not altogether break down but underwent some positive changes and registered growth and development.[8] It was the waning of the traditional social groups, and they were replaced by new social groups. Thus, it was not the complete decline of the Indian economy.

It would be rational to study on a more micro or regional level to test these versions. Unless studies of the history of the 'succession states' on the basis of the local archival resource material are not carried out, the composite and clear picture of the after effects of the collapse of the Mughal empire would not emerge. The attention of the scholars to study the economic history of the regional states in this perspective is lacking.

The present study is undertaken with the aims and motives to fill this gap partially, studying in detail, the 'changes and continuity in the economy of Bikaner state as reflected from the *Bahis* of the 18th and 19th century', more specifically between

1746 to 1828 AD.[9] The period is represented for the indigenous regime of Bikaner chief as an autonomous both internally and externally between 1746-1818 AD (I have taken upto 1828 AD as the regime of Surat Singh, the chief of Bikaner continues upto 1828 AD). Thus, the present study has the following aims and motives:

(i) It is to consider the developments and ascertain the changes in the economy as well as trace the continuation of the Mughal systems.
(ii) It would be a matter of interest to find out how the chiefs of Bikaner managed to survive, re-formed and re-organized their economy and created financial resources of their own.
(iii) And finally, consequent upon the detachment from the Mughal empire and also the collapse of the Mughal empire in itself, what implications did it bear for the economy of the state of Bikaner during the said period. Did it make any economic growth and progress or retarded virtually to conclude the treaty of subordination in 1818 with the British East India Company?

II

Although historical events are in a continuous process and cannot be reviewed in a pigeonholed period of time, nevertheless, it is perhaps legitimate to isolate the period 1746-1828 AD for the purpose of historical analysis and consider developments, in the economy from the point of view of the indigenous regime of Bikaner. Furthermore, this was dictated by the fact that the indigenous and contemprary primary source material was largely available from this period in the Rajasthan State Archives, Bikaner. Of greater importance in the primary sources are in the form of a number of *Bahis* which were created in the course of the official activities and record a variety of information regarding the economy, society, administration, constructional work and social ceremonies like marriages as well.

A *Bahi* literally meant an account book or a ledger book to maintain the income and expenditures of the state along with recording information regarding land grants, commercial transactions, taxes, wages, prices, social ceremonies and other general administrative and revenue orders.[10]

The practice of maintaining *Bahis* as an account book was presumably as old as the 13th century. The revenue records of the villages were used to be maintained in *Hindavi* language by the *Patwaris* during Allauddin Khilji's period which were called *Bihi* (*Bahi*) in *Tarikh-i-Firuzshahi* by Ziauddin Barani.[11] In Medieval Rajasthan the practice of writing *Bahis* was followed largely in the states also in the offices of traders and merchants.

The *Bahis* of Bikaner state have been categorized subject wise, and run in sequences, as is explicit from their captions, viz., *Kagad Bahis* (which record the administrative and revenue orders), *Kamthana-Bahis* (detail of construction works and wages), *Byav Bahis*[12] (details of social ceremonies observed during marriage, expenditures relating to it and prices of commdities purchased), *Sawa Bahis* (*Bahis* related to daily income and expenses), *Jagat Bahis* (commercial transaction and collection of *Jagat*, import/export of commodities), *Patta-Parwana Bahis* (assignments of land and exemptions in taxes), *Hasil Bahis* (details of collection of state revenue), *Khalisa Bahis* (details of actual land revenue and other taxes in *Khalisa* villages) and *Lekha wa Jama Kharch Bahis* (details of expenditure and income of sources). There are many other *Bahis* preserved and grouped in the State Archives Bikaner of equal importance. These *Bahis* however, pertain to the period from the 17th to 19th century,[13] but are mainly available from the 18th century onwards.

The large number of *Bahis* not only provide useful information on different aspects of the economy but are also significant, their being contemporary, unpublished indigenous archival source material. They contain the correct and objective state accounts of income and expenditure and unbiased descriptions of events and therefore can be relied upon and used for evidences.

However these have limitations of their own. Some of the

Bahis are missing in the sequences, while some are so brittle to be used, specially the *Hasil Bahis.* It is for this reason that it could not be possible to compute the annual state income or expenditure for even a single year. Sometimes, the information available is scattered, fragmented or missing and so is the statistical data. Further, these have been written in a style that *Mattras* and punctuation marks have scarcely been used. Owing to bad handwriting, often these become illegible. The script is *Devnagri* and dialect *Marwari.* At places, prevalent Persian and Urdu revenue terminology have been used while hundreds of local revenue terms of the area are also used therein. Even then, they have been of immense value for the study of the economy of the state and have largely been used.

The shortcomings of the *Bahis* are being supplemented by another categories of source material both contemporary and later contemporary.

Among them are some important and contemporary private collections of records. They include the *Bhaiya Records* and *Mohta Records* both preserved in the Rajasthan State Archives, Bikaner[14] and the *Lallgarh Collections of Bahis* in the custody of the royal household at Lallgarh Palace, Bikaner. They have been used in the study suitably and are of immense value.[15]

The non-archival type of source material like *Khyat* and *Baat* literature and *Tawarikhs* are of great value and have been consulted to fill in the gap of the *Bahis* after a careful scrutiny.

While using this source material, an analytical approach has been adopted. Maximum possible statistical data have been collected and tabulated to probe the change and continuity. Maximum examples from the *Bahis* and other sources have been used to substantiate the facts, comparative analysis have also been offered whenever required in the study. The important works of modern scholars on the subject have also been consulted and gainfully utilized.

III

The study consists of ten chapters, the first and last being the introduction and conclusion.

Since geography is an effective determinant in an economy, therefore, the physiography and economic resources of the state have been analysed in detail in the second chapter along with its bearing on the economy. The historical background with administrative changes and political developments have also been added to it in brief.

Chapter three deals with the 'Agricultural Economy'. The state being predominantly an agricultural economy, therefore, the various principal aspects of the agricultural sector, viz. the agricultural production, the land revenue, agricultural taxes and cesses have been critically discussed. Besides, the state's efforts at the rehabilitation of depopulated villages and the development of cultivation have been dealt with in detail.

The finance being an important ingredient of the desert economy, the fourth chapter has been devoted to deal with the non-agricultural sources of state income. While the desert state had very meagre resources of income, it is interesting to ascertain its various sources of income. More specially when it had to part—with the *Tankhwah-i-Jagiri* received from the Mughals, it attempted to generate the various indigenous alternative resources.

Chapter five deals with trade and commerce as it was of immense significance to this desert state and could prove a viable and alternative source for enhancing its income. Therefore, the aspects related to trade and commerce have been dealt, in detail viz. the trade routes, the internal and external trade, its import and export as well as the 'transit trade', the state policy towards trade and commerce has been discussed. The minting of the currency of their own was a significant feature in the economy of the state after the collapse of the Mughal empire. The coinages, its discounting and exchange have been discussed, and also the varying weights and the measurements have been mentioned in the chapter.

Chapter six deals with the *Mandis* (the commercial centres). A significant feature of the post Mughal economy was the *Mandi* system which developed prominently in the state. It has been analysed in detail with its functions and administration and with a focus on the *Shri Mandi Sadar Bikaner* during 1750-1800 AD.

In Chapter seven a comparative analysis of the prevailing prices of various essential commodities and the available prices of luxury items have been provided to ascertain the trends of prices through relevant price indices and graphs.

Chapter eight covers in details the social composition of the commercial groups of the state, its various categories and their activities and role in the commercial pursuits of significance.

In the last but not the least, the important sector of the economy was the crafts and artisans. The aspects of rural and urban-based craft production and the state's encouragement to the artisans' class, their wages and contribution have been discussed in Chapter nine in detail.

REFERENCES

1. Ali, Athar, 'The Eighteenth Century–An Interpretation', *IHR*, July 1978-January 1979, Vol. V, Nos. 1-2, pp. 175-86, Delhi, 1979.
2. Sarkar, J.N., *Fall of the Mughal Empire*, 4 Vols., *History of Aurangzeb*, III, Calcutta, 1916, pp. 283-364.
3. Habib, Irfan, 'The Eighteenth Century in Indian Economic History', *NIAS*, Wassenaar, Netherlands, June, 1993, pp. 50-85.
4. *Akbarnama*, Abul Fazal (Eng. Tr.) H. Beveridge, Vol. II, pp. 516-19. Ojha, G.H., *Bikaner Rajya Ka Itihas*, Vol. I, Ajmer, 1936, pp. 95-96, 155-56.
5. Ibid., Vol. II, pp. 399-401.
6. Singh, Chetan, 'Centre and Periphery in the Mughal State', *MAS*, XXII, 27, 1982, pp. 299-318, Cf. Habib, Irfan, op. cit., pp. 50-85; Ali, Athar, op. cit., pp. 175-86. Alam, Muzaffar, *The Crisis of Empire in Mughal North India: Awadh and the Punjab, 1707-48*, Delhi, 1986, pp. 41-318.
7. Habib, Irfan, op. cit., pp. 50-85; Habib, Irfan, *The Economic History of Medieval India: A Survey*, New Delhi, 2001, pp. 39-41.
8. Alam, Muzaffar, op. cit., pp. 41-42, 318.
9. During 1746-1828 AD in Bikaner Gaj Singh ruled from 1746-1787, Raj Singh (1787), Pratap Singh (1787) and Surat Singh from 1787-1828 AD.
10. Sita Ram Lalas defines the word *Bahi* as the account or ledger book to record the income and expenditure or the detailed accounts of the commercial transactions of the merchants and

traders. Lalas, Sita Ram, *Rajasthani-Hindi Sankshipt Shabdkosh,* Vol. II, Jodhpur, 1987, p. 190.

11. The word *Bahi* has been referred as *Bihi* earlier. In fact, in the Persian language the word *bha* is not used and being a local word it has been pronounced as *Bihi* but the correct pronunciation is *Bahi*. The 13th century revenue records of the villages were maintained in *Hindavi* language by *Patwaris.* See *Tarikh-i-Firuzshahi of Zia-ud-din Barani,* Cf. *The Comprehensive History of India* (CHI), Vol. V, (eds.) M. Habib and K.A. Nizami, PPH, 2nd ed. (Eng.), 1992, pp. 358-61.
12. *Byav* literally means marriage. At the occasion of any marriage in the royal household, the record of the social ceremonies observed during the marriage alongwith the expenditures incurred on cloth, ornaments and food-raw materials have been recorded in the *Bahis* termed as *Byav Bahis.*
13. See, 'A Descriptive List of Bikaner *Bahis*' (17-19 C), Part I, Bikaner, 1982, R.S.A., Bikaner.
14. See, The Descriptive Registers of the *Bhaiya Collection* and *Mohta Collection* in the Rajasthan State Archives, Bikaner.
15. See for details–The Bibliography. There are a number of *Bahis,* files and important published records in the personal custody of the Royal household, Lallgarh Palace, Bikaner.

2

Geographical and Historical Background

The geography is an effective determinant and plays a significant role in shaping the course of history in general and the economy in particular. It is more evident in the context of the erstwhile *Rathore* Principality of Bikaner[1], (established in 1488 AD[2]), and the territory comprised the *Thar* desert. Since, the state had suffered recurrently on account of its poor natural resources and harsh desert conditions, the economy of it, consequently, sustained stresses and strains under natural calamities. The dearth of the financial and economic resources, further deterred the progress.

Therefore, an analysis of the inheritance of nature of the area over which the state formed its limits and sustained for a long a struggle with nature is, in fact, not out of the question but more relevant to discuss.

The state takes its name from its capital city Bikaner i.e. the settlement or habitation (*ner*) founded by Rao Bika (1488-1504 AD)[3]. The antiquity of the tract is however, much older and was known as *Jangal desh.*[4] A reference to it is also available in the *Mahabharata.*[5]

Location and Extent

The area under the former state of Bikaner was the northern most part of *Rajputana*. It was the second largest state in *Rajputana* with an area of 23,317 sq. miles.[6] It was located between the parallels of 27° 12′ north and 30° 12′ north latitudes and 72° 12′ east and 75° 41′ east longitudes. The state was bounded on the north-west by Bahawalpur; on the south-west by Jaisalmer; on the south by Marwar; on the south-east by the Shekhawati area of Jaipur; on the east by Loharu and Hissar; and on the north-east by Ferozpur.[7] The territorial expanse of the state during 1746 to 1828 AD to which our study relates was much larger than to what Rao Bika (1488-1504), the founder of the principality, had initially carved out for himself than in our period of study it was ruled over by his successors Gaj Singh (1746-1787), Raj Singh (1787), Pratap Singh (1787) and Surat Singh (1787-1828). During this period, more territories in the north and north-west were added after defeating *Bhattis, Johiyas* and *Daodputras* and included finally *pargana* Bhatner (1804 AD), *pargana* Punia (1770 AD) and Anupgarh (1770 AD).[8] The state mainly comprised territories of the Mughal *Sarkar* of Bikaner (*Subah* Ajmer) and Dronepur (*Sarkar* Nagaur), Sidhmukh, Bhadag belonging to *Sarkar* Hissar and *Subah* Delhi.[9]

(1) THE ECOLOGY AND ECONOMY OF THE *THAR* DESERT

(A) Physiography

(i) Geographical Divisions

The state appeared to be an irregular polygon with many sides. It had its maximum length from village *Khakha* (खक्का) in the north to *Sarunda* (सारुंडा) in the south and the width from *Rampura* (रामपुरा) to *Ballar* (बल्लर) approximately 208 miles.[10] It's elevation varies from 400 ft. to 1200 ft. above the sea level and forms a significant part of the sandy plains of the country.

The whole state can be classified mainly into two geographical zones, viz.

(i) Western desert area (ii) North and Eastern semi-desert area.[11]

It can further be classified as per the land construction and distribution shown in Map 2.1.

(ii) The Land Construction and Distribution

Vagar or *Bagar*[12]

The southern and most part of eastern and some northern

portion is the part of vast sandy tract known as *Vagar* or *Bagar*. The area is not so fertile and has a small population.

Map 2.1: Physiography of Bikaner State

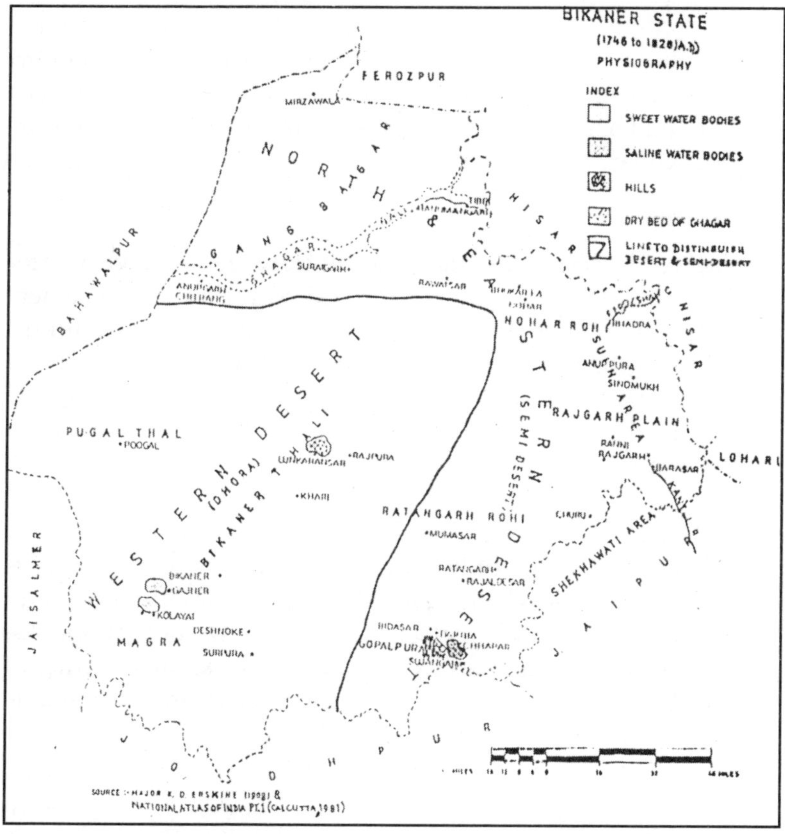

The *Thar or* Dhora

The north-west and a part of the north formed part of the great Indian *Thar* desert locally known as *dhora dharti* and arid zone of undulating sand hills and sandy plains.[13]

The *Thali* or *Pat*

In between the sand dunes the land is level and sandy in the western and central part of the state locally identified as *thali* or *pat*. This part has scanty rainfall and is more rugged but flatter (*pat*) than the *Thar*. A considerable portion of *thali* is barren and sparsely populated which even has the tendency of migrating to more fertile tracts during the years of famine and scarcity.[14]

Suin Area

While the north-eastern corner is the least infertile section of the state termed locally as the *suin* area as the surface area is a flatter and fertile plain.[15] The greater part of the *suin* area comes under Nohar, Bhadra and Rajgarh.

Nali Area

A tract of dry bed of seasonal *Ghaggar* from Hanumangarh (new name of Bhatner) to Anupgarh is called the *Nali* area, where once the river Ghaggar originating from Sirmur hills and flowed and joined the river Indus. It entered the state near *Tibi*. Now there is only a dry bed. But most of it becomes useless due to floods in the rainy season. The area is also identified as the *Ghaggar* area.[16]

Chitrang

The south-west part of Anupgarh in the west of the state is known as *chitrang* which is not at all fertile for cultivation and is known for its salinity or saltish land.[17] A part of land in the north-east of the capital city Bikaner is Lunkaransar, tract of brackish-water-land known locally as *kharipatti* and not suitable for cultivation and low quality of salt is produced.[18]

Magra

The southern portion of the state is rocky. It is arid and waste land containing approximately 2/3 rocky part and 1/3 of sand.[19] Comparatively it has fewer dunes, it is more dreary and desolate. It gives an impression of vast gravel plains with small sandy patches scattered throughout.[20]

Hills

The only rocky hill deserving the name are in the south at the tri-junction of Marwar, Jaipur and Bikaner, which seeks its maximum height at Gopalpura village is 600 ft. above sea level.[21]

The maximum portion of the surface of the region is covered with undulating sand hills of 20 ft. to 100 ft. height and the inter-dunal plains. The slopes of these sandhills, lightly furrowed by action of the winds, suggest the ribbed appearance of seashore.[22]

The general condition of Bikaner state was extremely dreary and desolate in the extreme. 'The region is a waste as the wildest part of Arabia' wrote General Elphinstone who passed through it in 1808 AD on his way towards Kabul.[23] But during and after the rains it wears a very different appearance becoming a vast green pasture land covered with the richest and most succulent grasses.[24]

(iii) Soils and Fertility

The greater part of the central, southern and western area was stretched out within an unproductive and scantily watered loose sandy soil and the capacity to hold water is the least. The fertility is the least.[25]

In *Magra* in the south, it is hard and rocky, extensively level and sandy soil and is fairly productive only under better rainfall conditions.[26]

The *chitrang* area was an extensive plain of hard level soil and also not suitable for cultivation due to excessive salt contents.[27] In the *Ghaggar* bed for its whole length from upper Anupgarh to Hanumangarh the soil is a hard loam which increases in hardness and consistency till the centre is reached. The admixture of clay increases as we go eastward. It has a yellow tinge and is known as *pili mitti*. It is fertile.[28]

Beyond the *Ghaggar*, in the north the land is more levelled and least sandy. The region improves in soil considerably varying from sandy loam to light clayey loams.[29] The area also consists of *tal*[30] suitable for cultivation. The portion of Suratgarh, upper Anupgarh, Mirzawala and Hanumangarh has such soil.[31]

The most fertile section of the state has been the north-eastern part of Nohar-Bhadra-Rajgarh. The soil is loam and clay and has good water holding capacity, and needs less rainfall. The double crops are grown in this part and it is the *suin* part. Therefore, the comparative population density and the numbers of villages are also comparatively higher than other parts.[32]

(iv) Water Resources: Rivers, Streams, Lakes, *Talabs* (Ponds) and Wells

There is no perennial river or streams, except the seasonal river *Ghaggar* (also called *Nali*) in the north-east and *Katli* in the east of the state. The former once flowed through the northern part of the state and joined the Indus,[33] but it is now dry, except in the rains, and even then the water rarely flows more than a mile or two, west of Hanumangarh; the latter enters into Rajgarh in the east from Shekhawati and runs only a few miles in the good rains.[34] Apart from these natural seasonal rivers, a small length of Firuzshah canal also reached the state. The waters of the Firuzshah canal built primarily, to irrigate Hissar Firoza in the 14th century by Firuzshah (1351-88 AD) entered the north-eastern corner of the state and terminated at Bhadra town. It was because of this channel being brought from the west Yamuna river, the desert tract could be irrigated in those days, the underground water level could considerably increase (upto 8 to 12 ft.) and crops like wheat and sugarcane could be obtained due to this man-made canal in the area.[35]

Obviously, it is interesting to note the impact of these water channels on the part of the desert tracts which is either covered by the streams, canals or seasonal rivers have increased in fertility, water level and had become the double-cropping area. It seems that the north and north-eastern part is therefore, more fertile in soil and production in the state.

The region had only two small fresh water lakelets formed by the drainage of the rocky country (called *magra*) in the south-west of the state. Both existed on the route to Jaisalmer from Bikaner. The first is at Gajner, 20 miles away and the other is Kolayat, 32 miles away from Bikaner. The waters of these two were used for drinking, bathing and for limited irrigation purpose for the produce of wheat and *sarson* (Mustard) in the catchment area.[36] The Kolayat is of a religious merit and an annual commercial fair is being organized there. It was a beautiful oasis amidst the vast expanse of arid desert.[37] The availability of water in these places facilitated to organize socio-religious fairs annually. These fairs became an important part of economic activity and a source of yielding revenues.[38]

Salt Lakes

There are two salt lakes also, one is at *Chhapar* (Sujangarh) in the sourth-east area and the other is at Lunkaransar in the north-east of Bikaner town. Both are shallow and a principal source of salt but salt produced by them was not good enough in quality in comparison to the salt produced at Sambhar lake (Jaipur).[39]

Wells and *Talaabs* (Ponds)

The wells and *talaabs* (locally known as *sar* also) were the traditional main sources of drinking water for animals and people and for limited irrigation. The underground water is available, notwithstanding the slight apparent difference in the level of the country at very varying depths (about 90 to 100 mtrs.) and of quality as unequal.[40] Wells of the southern part are comparatively deeper than the north and the north-east specially in the riverbeds. Therefore more wells are dug up in the dry beds of the rivers and apparently it tended the settlement to be denser in comparison to other parts.[41]

The people also largely depended on the water harvested from the rain and reserved in depression or *talaab* (ponds). The sites of villages are almost around a depression (known as *sar* locally) and often where rain water is collected.[42] In the desert area, water was a priceless source helping the mankind and livestock to survive. Due to its significance, the villages which were founded in the places where the water could be restored was known by suffixing *sar* with their names. For instance, such villages are Bidasar, Nathusar, Ghadsisar, etc. It is significant to point out that during the period of our study, the absence of the reference of *kundis* maintained in the *Baghichis* is conspicuous. The development of maintaining *baghichi*, the storage of water (*kundi*) was an essential segment. This concept seems to have developed later on. Later, the *Baghichi* became a point of social gatherings and ceremonizing rituals.

(v) Climate and Temperature

The climate has also been significant for settlement. Indeed it is the most influential geographical factor, in that it not only has direct effects through sun and shadow, heat, wind and rain, but indirect influence. The region has been characterized by harsh and dry climatic conditions of erratic rainfall, high wind velocity, intensity of heat, large temperature variations. Therefore, drought and famines are frequent. The summers have been very hot and winters very cold and dry in character.[43] Hot winds blow with great force in May-June and heavy sand storms frequently occur. The sun shines so powerfully that one is feared to travel in the mid-day. On the other hand, the cold in winter is generally intense and trees and vegetation are often, injured by the frost. In summer, the maximum daily mean temperature at capital is about 106.7 F/41.5°C with a minimum mean daily temperature is about 84.7 F/29.3°C but in winter, maximum daily temperature touches 71.8 F/22.1°C and minimum daily mean temperature comes to 41.3 F/5.2°C.[44] But for the whole state, the temperature touches up to 123 F/50.5°C in summers and sinks up to 31 F/0.5°C in winters.[45] Thus the low temperature causes dust storms and these are an essential part of the desert environment and very common during the summer.[46] This process brings the intensity of temperature low.

(vi) Rainfall

The trend of the average rainfall is generally decreasing while we proceed from south-east towards north-west. But the rainfall is erratic and scanty in general. The fluctuation in rainfall is crucial and leads to famines in the region and generally a famine is expected once in ten years in average and a drought once in four years in absence of the normal rainfall.[47] The annual rainfall for the whole state remains slightly under 10 inches varying from less than 6 inches in the north-west to over 14 inches in the south-east and east. About two-third of the rains is received in July and August. The heaviest fall in any one year was nearly 45 inches at Churu, in the south-east in 1892, while in 1885 less than half an inch fell at Anupgarh in the north-west and at Hanumangarh in the north-east.[48]

The marginal figures taken from the 1891 AD Census report for Rajputana[49] give the average annual recorded rainfall for the past 10 years show the trend of various places (period of years from 1866-67 to 1890-91)

Table 2.1 : Average Annual Rainfall of Places

Place	*Rainfall in Inches*	*Remarks*
Bikaner	10.2	The average rainfall for past 10 years in 1891 AD is 9.31 inches.
Lunkaransar	8.48	
Dungargarh	5.79	
Sujangarh	12.76	
Sardarshahar	7.26	
Ratangarh	9.57	
Churu	9.47	
Rajgarh	10.83	
Bhadra	13.55	
Nohar	7.83	
Hanumangarh	5.13	
Suratgarh	7.64	

Source: Census Report for Rajputana, 1891 AD, p. 3.

(B) Economic Resources

(1) Vegetational and Pastoral Resources

Trees

The vegetation cover is thin and Bikaner possesses no denser forests throughout and for the want of trees. The pattern of it largely depended upon its specific physiography. The commonest tree is the *khejra* (*Prosopis spicigera*), the pods (फलियाँ), bark (छाल) and leaves (पत्तियाँ) of which are eaten by cattle and, in times of famine, by the poor. The *jal* (*Salvadora oleoides*) and the *khair* (*Acacia catechu*) are available profusely in Suratgarh and Hanumangarh. The *babul* (Acacia arabica) is found on the sand hills in an extensive belt along the dry bed of the Ghaggar near Hanumangarh. A few *shisham* trees (*Dalbergia sissoo*) grow spontaneously near Sujangarh and *Ber* (Zizyphys jujuba), *Neem* (Azadirachta indica), *Pipal* and other varieties at capital and around places. The best timber produced is the *Rohira* (*Tecoma undulata*) around Ratangarh.[50]

Bushes

Of bushes, the most common is the *phog* (*Calligonum polygonoides*), its twigs and roots are used to support the sides of wells and supply material for huts, while its buds are eaten with butter milk and condiments, and its leaves by camels.[51] The *sajji* (*Salsola griffithii*) and *lana* (*Haloxylon salicornicum*) are important and valuable plants which grow plentifully in the firm soil north of the Ghaggar and in the south west of Anupgarh, when burnt, it yields and impure carbonate of soda, used in washing and dyeing cloth. The other deserving of mention are *Aak* or *Aakra* (*Caltropis procera*), the *Karel* (*Capparis aphylla*) and two spurges called *Thor* (*Euphorbia neriifolia* and *E. royleane*) which supply a juice of medicinal value.[52]

Grasses

Bikaner is famous for its large number of excellent grasses which grow even in a fair rainfall and forms one of the best grazing grounds in India. Among them are *Bhurat*[53] (*Cenchrus catharticus*). It is abundant in the southern half of the state and is brought out by a few early showers, is often plentiful in years of scarcity and its seed makes fair breed when ground. *Sewan* (*Eleusine feagellifera*) a rather tall grass and good for sheep; *Dhaman* is in the north and specially favoured by cattle. There are two other local varieties also, viz. *Ganthil* and *Kiu*. These grasses are used for both production of wool and *ghee* (milk fat). *Kiu* is available particularly near the banks of *Chhapar* lake in Sujangarh. Owing to the variety of grasses cattle rearing is a prominent occupation here and some famous species of them are available.[54]

(2) The Mineral Deposits

Some mineral deposits are also to be found in the state but mainly concentrated in the *magra,* i.e. rocky area in the south of the state. The fuller's earth (*multani mitti*), a greasy clay, used as soap and dyeing cloth, is quarried in larger quantity in south-west of Bikaner near Kolayat and is exported towards the Punjab. Gypsum is an another mineral found in abundance in best quality and largely available in Jamsar, Lunkaransar,

Dhirera near Bikaner. Excellent Redstone is found in Khari and Dulmera in north to Bikaner alongwith rougher stone known as *Rora*. References of copper deposits and its extraction are available at Biramsar and Dariba-Bidasar in Sujangarh. Other significant minerals of Bikaner are white clay, glass sand, grit and yellow ochre (रामरज-पीली मिट्टी).[55]

(3) Animal Wealth

Animal husbandry was a major economic activity and not only an adjunct to agriculture.[56] In this arid and semi-arid region, it was the larger sector of the economy next to the agriculture.[57] The region has a great variety of livestock, including some of the best breed of India.[58] The *Bhatner* buffaloes are said to be very good, as indeed, in all the cattle of that region.[59] Sheep of *Magra* breed, *Poogal* breed, *Nali* and *Bikaneri* breed are important for wool production.[60] Goats of Bikaner are also famous for milk and meat. It was only because of this wool and woollen products that Bikaner was popular in distant regions and its products reached there.[61] Bikaner breed of camel were also considered good in quality and strength and found a place in the export list. *Rathi, Pugal* cows and *Tharparkar* breads of cattle/cows were also popular in the region[62] for their milk and *ghee*. The western and southern parts of the state were dominated by the pastures[63] by the pastoral castes like *Johiyas, Bhattis, Raths* and others. Pasture lands were earmarked in almost every village to feed the livestock and satisfy the needs of fodder of animals.

Due to the animal wealth pastoral castes like *Bhattis, Johiyas, Raths* exclusively along with *Jats, Raibaries*[64] were earning their livelihood on the products derived from animals, viz. milk, *ghee*, milk products, wool, hair, bones, manure, skins and hides and sale of animals.

(4) People and Population

The inhabitants of the state comprised different castes, creeds and religions, and were engaged in many occupations, mostly of their parental inheritance. The state had Jats, Banias, Rajputs, Brahmins in large numbers[65], whom cultivation was a common occupation. There were also artisan castes. Apart from these castes there were numerous castes living in the state. They were *Chamars* (leather-dressers and village drudges), *Kumhars* (potters), *Khatis* (carpenters), *Kayamkhani* (Muslim of Rajput extraction)[66], *Nai* (barber), *Dhanak* (menial), Saiyad and others, *Rath* (Muslim of Rajput extraction), *Zargars* (Goldsmith), *Bairagi* (Vishnu worshippers), *Malis* (gardeners), *Dhobi* (washermen), *Gosain* (religious character), *Baori, Chhipa* (cloth printers), *Swami* (devotees of Mahadeo), *Khatris* (*banias*), *Fakirs, Kassabs* (butchers), *Raigers* and *Khatika* (leather workers), *Dammamis* (Muslim cattle drum beaters), *Mochis* (shoe makers), *Telis* (oilmen), *Gujars* (cattle rearing caste), *Bisati* (peddler), *Minas* (*chowkidars*), *Rangrez* (dyers), *Charans* (a caste of minstrels), *Kalals* (spirit sellers), *Lakhara* (workers in lac), *Ahirs, Darji* (tailors), *Lohar* (iron worker), *Chunapuz* (lime makers), *Maimar* (mason), *Sewak* (temple servant), *Sepoys, Bafinda* (weavers), *Sakka* (water carriers), *Niaria* (sifters of ashes obtained from gold and silver smiths), *Bhagat* (devotees), *Sikligar* (tin worker), *Bharbhunja* (cooks), *Kayath* or *Kayastha* (writer caste), *Kunjra* (green grocers), *Jattis* (Jain priests).[67] These artisan and professional castes suggest that the *Thar* desert society was a caste closed society. Though from some of the artisan castes like *Rangrez, Chunapaz, Kalal, Maimar* (a Persian idiom), *Sakka, Kassabs* etc., one can safely glean that the occupations discharged by these castes were an import-effect of the central Asian society[68] and this might have reached the desert through the *Sultanate* and Mughals where the chiefs of Bikaner were in service. Even in our period after detaching the *Rathore* Chief of Bikaner from the Mughals, the occupations and occupational castes continued to be a part of the desert society of Bikaner state. *Ustas*, the caste of painters also resided in the society, after being patronized by the chiefs in our period.[69]

In spite of the larger areas the population was very low, and the state usually had the problem of colonizing its villages. The state orders reflect the deficiency of man power in the state and it always exhorted upon to persuade and encourage more settlements in the state territories.[70] In the absence of statistical data it is difficult to provide the population figures for the period under study. Since no regular surveys of population were undertaken before 1881 AD, when the first census was done, only conjectures and estimation of population have been offered.

Capt. Powlett (1874) on the basis of numbers of houses and allowing 5 souls to each house arrives at the population figures of 2,90,710 and assumes that it must have been more than 3,00,000 souls in the state.[71] Col. Tod (1877) estimated a population of 5,39,250 for Bikaner and an average density 10 persons per sq.km. in 1877 AD.[72] Another estimation of populaion of state for late 17th century has been offered by some modern scholars as around 2,50,000 allowing 4½ souls per house (*guwadi*)[73]. This calculation is arrived-at on the basis of realization of *Dhunwa bhanchh*[74] (a hearth tax realized from each family). Notwithstanding, it is the rational apprach for the calculation of the population, it also, in fact, does not represent the real picture as many disabled, poor, bachelor and unemployed categories of people and some rehabilitated peasants were exempted from this tax.

In fact, the arid climate, shortage of water, and insufficient rainfall which led to recurrence of scarcity and famines in the state were some major deterrent in the growth of population[75]. In the event of such famines and scarcities larger numbers of people along with their livestocks usually migrated to other fertile adjoining areas, abandoning their houses, some time the entire of village was deserted.[76] Besides, many succumbed to the calamities. Thus, larger fluctuations in the population, at times, took place which severely affected the agricultural production and the economy as well.

The census of 1891 AD conducted for Rajputana provides the following population statistics for the state.[77]

1.	Population of Bikaner state in 1881 AD (as per census report)	5,09,021
2.	Population of Bikaner in 1891 AD	8,31,955
3.	Total increase in population	(+) 3,22,934
4.	Total population of Rajputana amounts to 1,22,20,342 in 1891 AD to which Bikaner's population was of %	6.81%
5.	Density per sq.mile	35.9

It is significant to note the substantial positive increase in the state population at the close of the 19th century and seems to have a cumulative impact of state's efforts in encouraging human settlements in villages largely, during our period of study.

Impact of Geography on the State Economy

With this desert physiography and the scarce economic resources a viable and strong economy could hardly be possible. It has naturally affected varyingly the economic condition in the state.

The agrarian pattern and conditions were tenuous despite agriculture being a principal occupation in the state.[78] The cultivation could not be extended to larger areas because of the scanty and erratic rainfall, dearth of irrigational facilities and the poor soils. The percentage of the cultivated area was very low in different areas.[79]

The *hasil bahis, lekha bahis* and *bhog bahis* preserved in the R.S.A., Bikaner evince that in the large part of the state only one *kharif* (*Siyaly*) crop could be raised and that too for the necessary consumption of food grain and not for commercial or cash crops.[80] The *rabi* (*Unalu*) crop was confined to the limited areas of north-eastern part of state. The other crops were possible only in five *chiras* (administrative division) and two *parganas* of the north-eastern belt, out of the total *chiras* and *parganas*.[81]

The cultivation was entirely dependent on the rainfall which was not only very low but varying as well (the average for the state was below 10 inches)[82]. It often failed resulting in the failure of crops and scarcity of fodder (despite being a good pasturages) water and grains which led to famines. The recurrence of such famines were frequent and often the *guwadis*[83] (rural settlement) had to migrate with families and their livestock to the more fertile areas for subsistence. The villages were often deserted completely.

These famines took a heavy death toll of the livestock and the people at a considerable scale migrated to the more fertile areas which affected the whole economy.[84] The state, in consequence, had to either suspend their collections of dues of *bhog* (land tax in kind) and *bhanchh* (other taxes in cash) from the villages or provide remission in large scales for consecutive years to retain the inhabitants in the villages. Therefore, collection of state dues in full was a persistent problem for the rulers.[85] It adversely affected the financial conditions and resulted in gross imbalance in the income and expenditure for which the state had to borrow larger loans.[86]

The number and nature of the settlement was also affected by the cropping pattern. The population was shiffting in nature and fluctuating in number in the arid zones of the south-west and central part where only the single crop of *kharif* was possible. It was more stable and denser comparatively in the north-eastern part of the state.[87]

The colonization pattern also largely depended on the character of the water supply, the good grazing grounds (i.e. availability of fodder in abundance), in river beds and the fertility of the areas. Therefore, the villages in the arid part of the state were far apart and very thinly populated in contrast to the north-eastern areas.[88] The numbers of the *khalisa* villages were greater in this fertile track.[89] The production and distribution of principal food crops of *bajra* and *moth* contributed to the variation in the regional settlement pattern.[90]

Due to larger grazing grounds there have been plenty of animal wealth and therefore a few castes, viz. *Raths, Jats, Johiyas,* etc. have resorted to the occupation of cattle rearing.[91] The popular breeds of cows-*Tharparkar, Rathi,* etc., sheep, goats and camels are available in abundance,[92] which can survive even in lesser intake of water but have played a significant role in the agrarian life and have been advantageous in the economy.

There have been a positive aspect of this geography as well. While it offered a security from the external invasions, it was strategically important being nearer to Delhi-Agra, the centre of political activities.[93]

Its location amongst the prosperous provinces around it was commercially advantageous to it.[94] The traders passed through with their merchandize in carrying their trade activities and paid off good transit duties to the state besides supplying the necessary articles of use.[95]

It is thus evident that the agrarian and settlement patterns were largely affected and the economy could not be more than an economy of subsistence and this can be termed as 'desert economy'. However, the income from agricultural sector was not sufficient enough for the state to survive. Before the re-formation of the state, the chiefs of Bikaner had income from the *jagirs* assigned to them outside their *watan* by the Mughal Emperors under whom they served. Thus, the state had to depend upon the alternative resources of trade and commerce.

(2) BIKANER STATE: A POLITICAL SUMMARY

An old name of the Bikaner region *Jangal Desh* denotes the 'No-man's Land' or it was wild forest. In a subsequent period, with a density of population in the Punjab some agricultural social groups seem to have immigrated to this *Jangal Desh*. It seems reasonable to conjecture that the *Jats* who moved from Sindh to the Punjab along with the Indus river and became sedentary agriculturists.[96] Sometimes in the subsequent period, the *Jats* who are known as aborigins in the region became the sovereigns in the region.[97] This is the reason that Rao Bika (1488-1504 AD) who founded Bikaner state in 1488 AD is known to have accepted *Tika* on his forehead from the Godara Jats.[98] It was the symbol of having sovereignty being delegated to Rao Bika. Later it has become customary with every succeeding Rathore chief of Bikaner state that he will receive the *Tika* on his forehead from a member of the Godara Jat family. This goes to suggest that it was a 'Social contract' between the Rathore chief and the local inhabitants. In assuming the sovereign power from the revenue yielding peasants' social groups, it was an assurance to them for protecting their lives and property from the invaders. In lieu of this protection, the inhabitants would pay the revenue.[99]

Apart from these *Jats* in the region, *Johiyas, Raths* and the *Bhattis*[100] were the other domiciles in the desert tract who led an agrarian and pastoral life and quarreled to each other and among themselves. The *Bhati, Sankhla* and *Parmar* Rajputs[101] were also among the inhabitants and had control over the small tracts of the desert.

Rao Bika (1488-1504 AD) and his successors continued to hold the region[102] and remained busy with the formation of Bikaner state.[103] The focus shifted from Bikaner to the centre when in 1570 AD Rao Kalyan Mal (1542-1574 AD) along with his son Rai Singh (1574-1612 AD) joined the Mughal services at Nagaur when Mughal Emperor Akbar was on his way to Ajmer and Lahore.[104] Rao Kalyan was bestowed with a *mansab* of 2000/2000 *sawar* and a *jagir*.[105] The chiefs of Bikaner continued in the Mughal services of the central government and rendered military services till the Mughal empire fragmented towards the middle of the 18th century. The ensuing list shows the names of the chiefs and their highest *mansab* in the Mughal service.

Table 2.2: Bikaner Chiefs and Their *Mansab* and Military Obligation in the Mughal Empire

S.No.	*Name of the Chief*	*Year of Receiving Highest Mansab*	*Mansab*
1.	Rao Kalyan Mal (1542-1574 AD)	1570AD	2000/2000[106]
2.	Raja Rai Singh (1574-1612 AD)	1605 AD	5000/5000[107]
3.	Dalpat Singh (1612-1613 AD)	1612 AD	2000/1000[108]
4.	Sur Singh (1613-1631 AD)	1631 AD	4000/3000[109]
5.	Karan Singh (1631-1669 AD)	1656 AD	3000/2000[110]
6.	Anup Singh (1669-1698 AD)	1695 AD	3500/4000[111] (1500 *Do Aspa Seh Aspa*)
7.	Swaroop Singh (1698-1700 AD)	1699 AD	1500/500[112]
8.	Sujan Singh (1700-1735 AD)	-	2000/1000[113]
9.	Zorawar Singh (1735-1746 AD)	-	1500/500
10.	Gaj Singh (1746-1787 AD)	1753 AD	7000/5000[114]

In lieu of the salary against their *mansab* equivalent *Tankhwah-jagir* were bestowed to them. The Mughal patronage (1570 AD onwards) ushered in an era of stability and growth of the economy as it afforded to pacify the disruptive forces and enemies to secure the principality (it was a *jagir* under Mughal administration).[115]

The process of growth and development continued under Rai Rai Singh (1574-1612 AD), Dalpat Singh (1612-13), Sur Singh (1613-31), Karan Singh (1631-69) and Anup Singh (1669-98) until the close of the 17th century, despite at times, some temporary displeasures[116] of the Mughal Emperors. However, the significance of Bikaner did not recede as such in the phase of temporary displeasure. Political conditions deteriorated with the gradual eclipse of the Mughal empire in the late 17th and the early 18th century and the chiefs as *mansabdars* owed only nominal allegiance to the Mughal Emperors. The next few decades (i.e. 1698-1744 AD) were noticeable for the internal disturbances, revolts and conspiracies of the subordinate *sardars* and the external incursions by Jodhpur state.[117]

The *Bhattis* and *Johias* recurrently rebelled and challenged the authority of the rulers. The *thikanedars* of Bhadra, Pugal and Churu and the *Bidawats* created problems. Above all, the entire 18th century was marked by the frequent incursions of the Rathores of Jodhpur by which the situation turned from bad to worse and kept the rulers entangled in solving the crisis in the absence of Mughal patronage.

Consequently upon, owing to the internal disturbances and disorder the economic retardation cannot be ruled out. More so, because of Bikaner chiefs had ceased to be the *Mansabdars* and sustained the loss of *Tankhwah-i-jagirs*.

The area of Bhatner and Hissar had also slipped from them. To add to their misfortune the issue-less Maharaja Zorawar Singh had died in 1745 AD leaving the successions to be decided in complete chaos.

The situation to some extent improved when Gaj Singh (1746-87), cousin of Zorawar Singh was selected as the heir-apparent in 1746 AD.[118] He not only consolidated his position soon but tackled the situation in the state with sternness. All conspirators and rebellious *thakurs* of Mahajan, Bhukarka and Churu were made to surrender. Bhattis of Bhatner were attacked twice and compelled to yield an annual tribute of Rs. 40,000 in 1773 AD.[119] It is worth mentioning that Gaj Singh was conferred a *mansab* of 7000/5000 *sawars* and *pargana* of Hissar by Mughal Emperor Ahmedshah.[120] He was bestowed with the rare privilege of minting coins in his name by Alamgir II.[121] This was the hallmark of the process of the decentralization and heading towards complete detachment from the centre. In fact, it also shows that the centre was not in a position to control the local chiefs. To replenish his dwindling finances, he began to re-organize his state economy. He encouraged agriculture, trade and commerce through remissions in taxes and inducements. When famine occurred in 1755-56 he made adequate arrangements to mitigate the distress of his subjects by providing employment through construction works.[122] Rajgarh was also founded by him.[123] So general conditions were improving in his tenure.

Surat Singh's regime (1787-1828) proved to be important in several respects. Many changes occurred in the politico-administrative and economic system of the state in the absence of the Mughal authority.

(i) It witnessed the complete detachment from the Mughal subordination and survived autonomously for a couple of decades, i.e. until 1818 AD.

(ii) Surat Singh extended the territories of the state in the north and west. He inflicted a crushing defeat on the *Johiyas* and *Bhattis* and constructed Suratgarh and Fatehgarh forts to garrison the contingent of the army.[124] Bhatner, another fort in the north, was annexed permanently in 1805 and renamed as Hanumangarh.[125] Advancing towards Anupgarh he conquered Meergarh, Jangarh, Maujgarh from the Daudputras in the Multan area in 1801 and also in 1802 Kangarh in lower Sindh. *Pargana* Phalodi was also acquired temporarily in 1807.[126] However, most parts thus conquered had again slipped from his control in the north-west frontiers, but the state could extend upto its fullest form and new frontiers.

(iii) The fighting between the house of Jodhpur and Bikaner continued and they were still pitched against each other[127] and formed a factor for accepting a subordinate relationship with the British East India Company in 1818 AD.

(iv) Surat Singh's excessive warfare and between 1809 to 1813 his heavy extortions enraged the nobility.[128] Financially, the state was not sound enough already, therefore, he extorted money through plundering, imposing fines and murdering his *thakurs*. With the result that in 1815 there was widespread rebellion.[129] The ousted *thakurs* recovered their estates, revaged the country, and defied the ruler. Amir Khan Pindari appeared on the scene in 1816[130], and the insurrection had become so serious that the Maharaja asked for British aid. A treaty of subordination with the British East India Company was concluded on March 9, 1818; and British troops entered the state, captured 12 forts and restored them to the ruler along with suppressing the insurgents.[131]

(v) Surat Singh's period was significant and in fact, due to his excessive warfare the state expenditure increased considerably. Consequently, he had to levy new taxes and increase the rates of some old ones to level the expenditures. This had such an adverse impact over the economy that the state had to arrange loans on a larger scale. When he died in 1828 AD, large sums were outstanding in the state from the debtors. The debtors were pressing hard to recover the same.[132] So, in financial matters the state from the very beginning to the conclusion of the treaty of subordination faced a course of fluctuations.

It is also worth mentioning that the chief of Bikaner had their subordinate chiefs and military warlords (known as *thikanedars* and *pattayats*) who served the chiefs in different capacities. These subordinate chiefs had owned sub-assigned territories (known as *thikanas* and *patta* land) in the state. For their assignment, they had hereditary claims while the warlords and the soldiers who served in their military contingents received assignments in lieu of their services. Before joining the Mughal services, the chiefs of Bikaner had *thakurs* and *sardars* (*pattayat*), who were expected to maintain a specific number of *chakars* (soldiers) and at the time of necessity they had to render the service to the chief. For instance, there were *thakurs* belonging to the *thikanas* and were expected to render military service, i.e. the *chakri* to the state as shown in the following Table 2.3.

Table 2.3 : Military Obligations (*Chakri*)[133] of the *Thakurs* and *Pattayats* to the Bikaner Chief

S. No.	*Year*	*Rathore Rajput*						*Non-Rathore Rajputs (Desi-pardeshi Thakurs)*	
		Bikawats		*Kandhlots*		*Bidawats*			
		No. of Villages	*No. of Sawars*	*No. of Villages*	*No. of Sawars*	*No. of Villages*	*No. of Sawars*	*No. of Villages*	*No. of Sawars*
1.	1668 AD	384	279	170	154	174	164	27	25
2.	1818 AD	460	482	308	318	228	272	101	156

The table evinces that when the Bikaner chiefs did not remain in the Mughal service, their demand for the *chakri* from their sub-chiefs, increased considerably and also they assigned the villages to the Rathores as well as non-Rathores. The non-Rathores have excelled in proportion in the list. This is worth noticing.

The chiefs while in the Mughal service maintained a military contingent as per the *mansab* assigned to them. In this contingent, the *thakurs* as well as others known as *pattayats* were included. The income received by the chiefs of Bikaner from the Mughals was shared with their *sardars*. These *sardars* were assigned *pattas* of land in lieu of their services rendered to the chief. The introduction of *Patta* assignments also came into vogue in the Rajput states after the coming of the Turks and Mughals to India. The *Patta* institution has similarities with the *Iqta* and *Jagir* institutions.[134] The assignment of *Patta* had become an integral part of the polity in all the Rajput states of Rajputana and this is also discernible and evident in Bikaner state. However, this system continued even after the detachment of the Rathore chiefs from the Mughals in the second half of the 18th century. Though, the chiefs of Bikaner could not establish *mansab* institutions as the Mughals had but certainly they had fixed the strength of *chakri* on each of their *sardars/pattayats*. Obviously, this *chakri* was determined as per the competence of the *sardar* and also corresponded to the number of villages assigned to a *patta* holder.

Like the Mughals, the Bikaner chiefs classified their state territories into the *Khalisa* land (land under direct control of

Map 2.2: Distribution of *Chiras* and *Pargnas* in Bikaner State

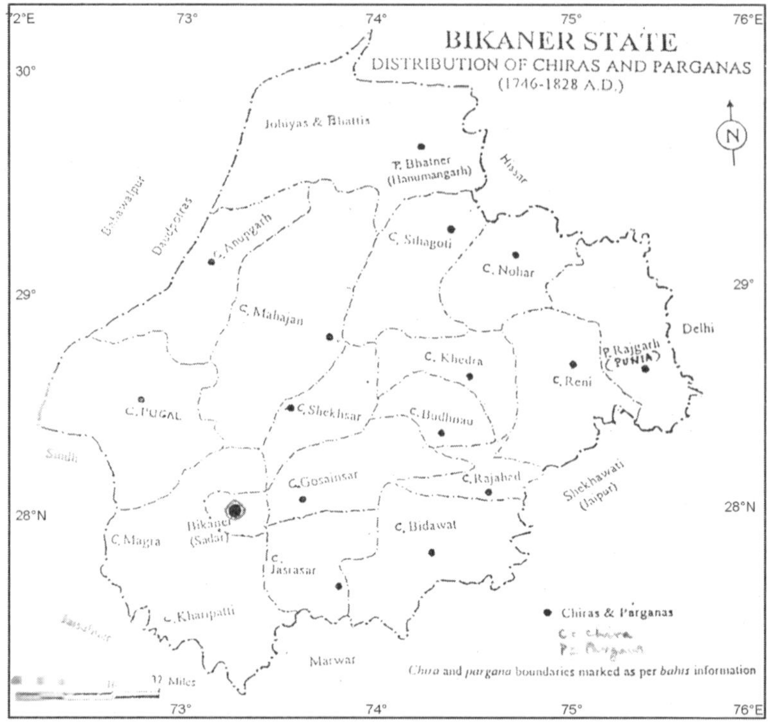

Source: Reports on the Administration of Bikaner State, 1934, Bikaner

Note : The boundaries of *Chiras* and *Parganas* have been drawn out on the information of *Kagadon Ri Bahi,* No. 13, V.S. 1861/1804 AD. *Kooch Muqam Re Kagadon Ri Bahi,* No. 1, V.S. 1886-98/1829-41 AD. *Marzaad Re Kagdon Ri Bahi,* No. 1, V.S. 1934/1877 AD and *Bahi Khalisa Re Gawan Ri,* V.S. 1826-30/1769-73 AD of the state wherein information regarding the villages *Chira*-wise and *Pargana*-wise are entered while issuing the notices and necessary orders and also mentioning details of the tax collections in the state.

ruler) *Patta* (assigned land to subordinate chief) and the *sasan* land (revenue free land given for religious purposes) during the period of re-organization of their state. The *Khalisa* resembled the Mughal *Khalisa* concept, whereas *Patta* and *sasan* resembled the *Jagir* land and *Madad-i-Maash* land respectively of the Mughal times.

The Bikaner archival records, specially the *Kagad Bahis* of the period under study have frequent references to various *chiras* and some *parganas*. A *chira* and a *pargana* were both administrative and revenue units. (Map 2.2)It seems that Bikaner chiefs reorganized and reframed their territory acquired in succession after the disintegration of the Mughal empire. The *Parganas* of their *Watan Jagir* and other contiguous *parganas* to *Watan Jagir* (which were usually assigned to them) were reconstituted into *chiras* in the second half of the 18th century. These *chiras* were framed considering the yield of revenue, geographical uniformity or administrative convenience. Thus, we see that during the state formation and recreation, the chiefs also reorganized and reconstituted their administative and revenue units and the system they adopted was influenced by the Mughal administration. (see enclosed map of *parganas and chiras*). However, this classification of *chiras* and *parganas* needs further and indepth study. The *chiras* may be similar in the *Dastur* circle (revenue unit) and *pargana* may be an administrative unit apart from its being a revenue unit.

REFERENCES

1. The Rathores of Bikaner were the descendants of Rao Bika (1488-1504 AD), who was the son of Rao Jodha and had come from Marwar. Ojha, G.H., *Bikaner Rajya ka Itihas* (Hindi) Part I, Ajmer, 1936, pp. 1-2.
2. Rao Bika, the founder of Rathore principality tried to establish his dominion initially at a place 15 miles west of Bikaner city called Kodamdesar in 1472 AD, but later shifted finally to the present location of Bikaner city in 1488 AD to avoid any confrontation with the *Bhatis* of Pugal. Ojha, G.H., op. cit., Part I, pp. 95-96.
3. The tradition says that '*Nera*' was the name of the owner of the site of Bikaner, who parted with it on the condition that his name should be included or linked with 'Bika', the founder and hence the name 'Bikaner'. Erskine, K.D., *Rajputana Gazetteer—Bikaner*, Chapter 1, 1972, p. 1; Tod, Col. James, *Annals and Antiquities of Rajasthan*, Vol. II, Reprint, Delhi, 1971, pp. 1129-30. In fact, '*Ner*' literally means habitation as it is reflected in the names of places like Bhatner, Gajner (in Bikaner), Sanganer, Jobner (in Jaipur). Gajner is a place near Bikaner city established by Maharaja Gaj

Singh (1746-1787 AD). It is also suffixed by *Ner* and was founded in the 18th century.

4. The features of the *Jangal desh* are defined in the classic work- *Sabdakalpdrum*, Part II, p. 529 as follows 'स्वल्पोदक तृणो यस्तु प्रवातः प्रचुरातपः । स ज्ञेयो जांगलो देशो बहुधान्यादिसयुतः ॥' ('where there is a shortage of water and grass, the abundance of wind, sunshine and grains should be identified as *Jangal desh*').
   In *Bhav Prakash* it is defined as follows— 'आकाश शुभ्र उच्चश्च स्वल्पपानीय पादपः । शमी करीर बिल्वार्क पीलू कर्के घुसकुलः ॥ .....देशो वातालो जांगळ स्मृतः' ('where there is a clear and bright sky, a dearth of water and trees and there grow only *khejra, beelv, aakra, peelu* and *ber* trees is called *Jangaldesh*'), *Bhav Prakash*, p. 529, These features testify to its existence in desert land. Cf. Ojha, G.H., op. cit., Part I, pp. 1-2.
5. The *Mahabharata* also records that *Jangladesh* in context with the other *Janapads* like *Kuru, Panchal* and *Madreya* of Janapad Age, 'तत्रेते कुरु स्रपांचाला शाल्वा माद्रेय जांगला', *Mahabharata, Bhishma Parv*, Ch. IX, *Sloka*-39. Cf. Ojha, G.H., op. cit., pp. 1-2.
6. Erskine, op. cit., p. 309; *Imperial Gazetteer of India*, Vol. VIII, Oxford, 1908, p. 202, provides us as 23,311 sq. miles whereas Capt. Powlett, P.W., in his *Gazetteer of Bikaner State* (1874), Bikaner, 1935, p. 91 slightly differs in area and mentions 23,500 sq. miles.
   Ojha, G.H. explains the difference saying that due to the addition of two villages in place of village Gunjal and three other villages in the south, the area of the state increased slightly in sq. miles. Ojha G.H. op. cit., p. 4 (footnote). The erstwhile state of Bikaner was second largest in Rajputana and sixth in India in respect of area. The area of these are as follows:

1.	Jammu & Kashmir	8,58,855 sq. miles
2.	Hyderabad	82,698 sq. miles
3.	Jodhpur	35,066 sq. miles
4.	Mysore	29,475 sq. miles
5.	Gwalior	26,367 sq. miles
6.	Bikaner	23,317 sq. miles

   Cf. : Singh, Karni, *The Relation of the House of Bikaner with the Central Powers*, Delhi, 1974, p. 1.
7. Capt. Powlett, P.W., *Gazetteer of Bikaner State*, pp. 91-92; *Imperial Gazetteer of India*, Vol. VIII, op. cit., p. 202.
8. Ojha, G.H., op. cit., Vol. II, pp. 47, 51-52, 78, 335.
9. The *Sarkar* of Bikaner under *Subah* Ajmer included the *Parganas* of Bikampur, Barsalpur, Pugal and Bikaner. The Bikaner *Sarkar*

comprised eleven *Mahals* and yielded a revenue of 47,50,000 *Dams*. *Ain-i-Akbari*, Abul Fazal, Tr. Jarrett, Vol. II, Reprint, Delhi, 1989, pp. 273-82. When the chiefs of Bikaner finally detached themselves from the Mughal empire, the territories of their *Watan jagir* remained in their possession. They also captured the contiguous *parganas* of Bhatner, Poonia and Beniwal in the north and north-east, over which they usually put their hereditary claims and remained with them as *Tankhwah-i-jagir* in lieu of the their salaries.

It is noteworthy that after 1818 AD the British East India Company took away in their possession 41 villages of Tibi (the fertile part near Bhatner) setting aside the claims of the Bikaner ruler as their territory. These villages were returned after 1857 AD to Bikaner rewarding the services rendered by the Bikaner ruler to the Company. Powlett, p. 79; Ojha, op. cit., Vol. II, p. 404.

10. Ojha, G.H., op. cit., p. 4.
11. Sharma, R.C., *Settlement Geography of the Indian Desert*, New Delhi, 1972, pp. 1-10. (Chapter-1, Nature of the Indian Desert); *Rajasthan District Gazetteer: Bikaner*, Jaipur, 1972, p. 1.
12. The word *Vagar* or *Bagar* resembles the Gujarati word *Vagada*, which means an area of forest and grasses with very thin population. Still the area of Banswara and Dungarpur is known as *Vagar/Bagar*. Ojha, G.H. op. cit., p. 5 (footnote).
13. Fagan, P.G., *Report on the Settlement of the Khalisa Villages of Bikaner State*, Bikaner, 1893, Ch. 1, pp. 1-2; Capt. Powlett, op. cit., pp. 91-92; Sharma, R.C., op. cit., pp. 9-10
14. Fagan, op. cit., pp. 1-2
15. Fagan, op. cit., pp. 1-2; Capt. Powlett, op. cit., pp. 91-92
16. Sharma, Dashrath, *Rajasthan Through the Ages*, Part 1, R.S.A., Bikaner, 1964, pp. 2-3; Sharma, R.C., op. cit., p. 7. The *Nali* locally means a drain. It is in fact, the tract of the old rivers of *Saraswati*, *Drasadvati* and *Hakra* and the beds have firm loamy soil. During good rains flood water spreads over this tract and often makes the land useless because of excessive water. It is also called *Ghaggar* plains and form a gently sloping area running from the north-east to west and south-west.
17. Fagan, P.G., op. cit., pp. 1-2.
18. Ibid.
19. Ibid., Capt. Powlett, op. cit., pp. 91-92.
20. Sharma, R.C., op. cit., p. 9.
21. Erskine, op. cit., p. 309, *Imperial Gazetteer of India*, p. 202, Powlett, pp. 91-92.

22. Ibid.
23. Ojha, G.H., op. cit., p. 5.
24. Capt. Powlett, op. cit., p. 95.
25. Fagan, P.G. had done an extensive survey of the area and has very vividly discussed the nature and fertility of soil in his report. See the report, op. cit., pp. 1-3; Sharma, Dashrath, op. cit., pp. 2-3.
26. Fagan, P.G., op. cit., pp. 1-2.
27. The *soda* is extracted after processing the *sajji* and the *lana* plants however, grown in abundance in the area. It is of some commercial value. Fagan, P.G., op. cit., pp. 1-3.
28. Ibid.
29. The majority of the *Khalisa* villages were located in the north-eastern part. Out of the total 654 *Khalisa* villages, 438 were in Suratgarh zone (north), 147 in Reni (east), whereas in Bikaner there were only 49 villages. The area is more fertile and even with less rainfall the *kharif* (*siyalu*) and *rabi* (*unalu*) crops were possible. The arable (zarayati layak) land was more compared to other regions of the state. Fagan, P.G., op. cit., pp. 1-3, 5-6.
30. *Tals* are the fertile plains and are occasional between sand ridges and contain soil admixture of loam and clay. These *tals* are preferred for cultivation as (i) it has firmer soil and is not easily carried away by winds (ii) the rainfall sinks deeper in the surface than the sides of the ridges from which it drains off. (iii) And it is easier to plough on the level *tals* than the sloping ridge. Fagan, P.G., op. cit., p. 4.
31. The soil in the northern part of Anupgarh is light loam and known locally as *Baggi* and in Hanumangarh's north upto Hissar is yellowish loam known as *Kathi*. Fagan, P.G. op. cit., p. 3, Ojha, G.H., op. cit., p. 12.
32. Ibid.
33. Ojha, G.H., op. cit., p. 6.
34. Capt. Powlett, op. cit., p. 92.
35. Shams Siraj Afif, *Tarikh-i-Firuzshahi*, ed. Wilayat Hussain, Calcutta, 1891, pp. 127-29, Cf. Abha Singh, 'Irrigating Haryana : The Pre-Modern History of the Western Yamuna Canal', *Medieval India-1, Researches in History of India (1200-1750)*, ed. Irfan Habib, Delhi, 1982, pp. 51-52 (see for the details). Ojha, G.H., also mentions that only upto 20 miles inside Bhadra, the waters of this canal reached. Ojha, G.H., op. cit., pp. 6-7.
36. Capt. Powlett, op. cit., p. 92.
37. Ibid.
38. Ibid.

39. The salt produced from both lakes is of very inferior quality, valued at about half the price of *Sambhar* salt. Powlett, op. cit., p. 92.
40. Capt. Powlett, op. cit., p. 93; Ojha, G.H., op. cit., p. 10.
41. Ibid.
42. Ibid.
43. Ojha, G.H., op. cit., p. 9; Sharma, R.C., op. cit., pp. 10-11.
44. *Rajasthan District Gazetteer: Bikaner*, Jaipur, 1972, p. 14.
45. Ojha, G.H. op. cit., p. 10.
46. Ibid.; Sharma, R.C., *Settlement Geography of Indian Desert*, pp. 10-11.
47. Sharma, R.C., *Settlement Geography of Indian Desert*, p. 14.
48. Fagan, P.G., op. cit., pp. 4-5; *Imprial Gazetteer of India*, op. cit., p. 204.
49. *Census of India, 1891, Vol. XXVI, Rajputa*na, Part I, Lt. Col. Abbott, Calcutta, 1892, Bikaner, p. 3; Fagan, P.G. op. cit., pp. 4-5.
50. Fagan, P.G., op. cit., p. 2; Capt. Powlett, op. cit., p. 94.
51. Ibid.
52. Capt. Powlett, op. cit., pp. 94-95; Erskine, op. cit., p. 31.
53. Mughal Emperor Aurangzeb often used the word *Bhuratia* for Maharaja Karan Singh when he was offended with him as recorded in the Persian *Tawarikhs*. Cf. Ojha, G.H., op. cit., p. 14. However if reflects the popularity of this grass.
54. Ibid., Fagan, P.G., op. cit., p. 10.
55. Capt. Powlett, op. cit., pp. 92-93, 109-110.
56. Sharma, R.C., *Settlement Geography of Indian Desert*, pp. 35-40.
57. Ibid.
58. The state was rich in livestock not only numerically but also in quality, *Techno-Economic Survey of Rajasthan*, Jaipur 1963, p. 48.
59. Powlett, p. 106.
60. Ibid.
61. *Jagat bahi-Oon re Lunkara ri bahi*, No. 53, V.S. 1844 and *Sawa Bahis Mandi Sadar Bikaner*, No. 2, V.S. 1802-04, R.S.A., Bikaner, testify to the fact. The region is one of the principal regions of sheep rearing in India. It has also affected the rural landscape by the existence of sheep enclosures and wool markets etc., Sharma, R.C., op. cit., p. 40.
62. Sharma, R.C., op. cit., pp. 35-40.
63. Ibid., Powlett, p. 106.
64. *Raibari* is the name given to a class of Hindus who are acquainted with the habits of camels. They teach the country-breed *lok* camel so to step as to pass over great distances in a short time.

Ain-i-Akbari, Abul Fazal, (Eng.Tr.), H. Blochmann, 2nd ed., Delhi, 1965, pp. 155-56.

65. Ojha, G.H., op. cit., Part-I, pp. 18-22; Capt. Powlett, op. cit., pp. 97-98.
66. Jan kavi, *Kayam Khan Raso*, ed. and pub., Jaipur, 1953, p. 11; see for detailed study, Zaidi, Sunita, 'The Qayamkhani Shaikhzada family of Fatehpur-Jhunjhunu' *PIHC*, Hyderabad, 1978, pp. 412-425.
67. Ojha, G.H., op. cit., Part 1, pp. 18-22; Capt. Powlett, op. cit., pp. 97-98.
68. Siddiqqi, I.H., 'Social Mobility in the Delhi Sultanate', *Medieval India-1, Researches in the History of India (1200-1750)*, (ed.) Irfan Habib, Delhi, 1992, p. 23. See it for details.
69. *Parwana Bahi*, Bikaner, V.S. 1800-1900, RSA, Bikaner, *Ustas* received patonage from the Bikaner Chief in the form of land, services and *Rozgar* (employment).
70. *Kagdon ri Bahi*, No. 1, V.S. 1811; No. 2, V.S. 1820, R.S.A., Bikaner. These *bahis* do contain number of references in the testimony to it in the *choot-ra-kagad*.
71. Capt. Powlett, op. cit., pp. 96-97.
72. Col. Tod, *Annals and Antiquities of Rajasthan*, Oxford, 1920, Part II, p. 1164.
73. Devra, G.S.L., *Rajasthan ki Prashashnik Vyavashtha*, Bikaner, 1981, p. 2.
74. *Dhunwa Rokad Bhanchh Bahi*, No. 88, V.S. 1750/1693 AD, Bikaner *Bahis*, R.S.A., Bikaner. Cf. Devra, G.S.L., op. cit. p. 2
75. Sharma, R.C., *Settlement Geography of the Indian Desert*, pp. 52-53.
76. Famines and droughts are very common to the state. It is famous saying here that after every 10 years on an average a famine occurs and scarcity is recurrent every fourth year.

    Kachhawa, O.P., *Famines in Rajasthan*, Chapter-Famines in Bikaner; Jodhpur, 1988: *Rajasthan District Gazetteer: Bikaner*, Jaipur (1972), pp. 142-48. However, the first severe famine of which we have records in the history of Bikaner occurred in 1755-56 AD followed by famines in 1868-69, 1891-92, 1896-97 and 1899 AD The famines were recurrent even before the recorded years.
77. *Census of India, 1891, Vol. XXVI, Rajputana*, Part I, Lt. Col. H.B. Abbott, Calcutta, 1892, pp. 3, 6, 16.
78. Agriculture, despite poor natural resources has been the principal occupation with the animal husbandry. Fagan, P.G. op. cit., pp. 5-10.
79. The highest average of land under cultivation in the area was

34% in the eastern *Pargana* Bhatner (Hanumangarh) and lowest 3% in the Anupgarh *Chira* (Administrative division). Fagan, P.G., op. cit., pp. 6-7. Fagan's estimation is based on the *Khalisa* villages. The average of cultivated area for state is estimated as 15%. Cf. Devra, G.S.I., 'Registani Kshetra Mein (Bikaner state) Krishi Yogya Bhoomi wa Uska Vargikaran', PRHC, IX Kota, 1976, p. 38.

80. *Khalsa Gawan re Hasil ri Bahi*, No. 101, V.S. 1761; *Hasil re Lekhe ri Bahi*, No. 23(a), V.S. 1773-75; *Khalisa Gawan re Hasil Bhog ri Bahi*, No. 19, V.S. 1827, *Bikaner Bahis*, R.S.A., Bikaner. Devra, G.S.L., Cropping Pattern and Rural Settlement in Bikaner State (1650-1700 AD), PRHC, (Bikaner session, 1984), Vol. XIV, Jodhpur, 1986, p. 219.
81. The *Parganas* were Bhatner, Punia, and *Chiras* were Nohar, Reni, Bhadra, Gandheli and Rajgarh. Devra, G.S.L., op. cit., pp.127-30.
82. See table of rainfall referred in this chapter.
83. *Guwadi* is a local term used in both senses, i.e. for family and the locality as well.
84. The fluctuation in the number of cattle was considerable and a glance at the following figures of livestock would substantiate the fact. However, the data relates to a later period–

Year	Sheep & Goats	Bullocks, Cows, Buffaloes
1896	2,49,294	2,25,741
1898	3,38,763	1,35,995
1899	1,63,328	38,766
1900	1,41,187	51,515

At times not less than 75% of the cattle have to be moved out of the tract owing to the scarcity of water and fodder.

Cf. Singh, Karni, *The Relations of the House of Bikaner with the Central Powers*, Delhi, 1974, p. 5.

85. See *Chhoot ra kagad, Kagdon ri bahis*, No. 2, V.S. 1820; No. 3, V.S. 1827; No. 8, V.S. 1849; No. 13, V.S. 1861; No. 19, V.S. 1870; Rampuria records, R.S.A., Bikaner.
86. The imbalance and difference in income and expenditure has been studied for Bikaner *Mandi* and a research paper was presented during the Indian History Congress at the Calicut session, 1999. Mathur, Kanti Lal, 'Pattern of Income and Expenditure of Bikaner *Mandi* during the Second Half of the 18th Century', PIHC, Calicut Session, 1999 (Abstract Published), p. 1165.
87. Devra, G.S.L., op. cit., pp. 219-20.
88. Ibid.
89. Fagan, P.G. op. cit., p. 1.
90. Devra, G.S.L., op. cit., p. 219-20.

91. Powlett, op. cit., p. 95.
92. Ibid., op. cit., pp. 106-7.
93. Singh, Karni, op. cit., pp. 6-8.
94. Ibid., p. 10.
95. Sharma, G.S., *Marwari Vyapari*, Bikaner, 1988, pp. 20-23.
96. Col. Tod, *Annals and Antiquities of Rajasthan*, Vol. II, op. cit., pp. 1124-26.
97. The *Jats,* who formed the seven different sub-castes amongst themselves ruling predominantly in the central and eastern part of the state, were (1) Punia of Ludi (2) Godara of Sheikhsar (3) Sihag of Suin (4) Sohua of Dhansia (5) Kaswa of Sidhmukh (6) Beniwal of Raisalana and (7) Sarans of Bhadag. However, some other minor castes of *Bhadu, Bhukar, Kalehar, Nen* and *Jakhar* also ruled in separate entities. Sidhayach Dayaldas, *'Dayal-Das-ri-Khyat'*, Part II (Pub.) (ed.) Dashrath Sharma, Bikaner (1948), pp. 5, 7-10, 51-54; Powlett, op. cit., pp. 2-4.
98. Col. Tod, *Annals and Antiquities of Rajasthan*, Vol. II, pp. 1128-29; Munshi Devi Prasad, *Rao Bika ka Jeevan Charitra*, p. 19, Cf. Ojha, G.H., op. cit., Part I, p. 299.
99. Ibid.
100. The *Johiyas*, identified as the descendants of the *Yodheyas*, inhabited the territory of the north to the *Jat* occupied areas. Where *Raths* (Muslim pastoral nomadic tribe) and *Bhattis* (converted Muslim of *Bhati* Rajputs) shared the area with them. The *Bhattis* fortified themselves in Bhatner. Sidhayach Dayaldas, *Dayal-Das-ri-Khyat*, Part II (Pub.) (ed.) Dashrath Sharma, Bikaner (1948), pp. 5, 7-10, 51-54; Powlett, op. cit., pp. 2-4.
101. Towards the south-east were settled in those days, the Rajputs known as *Mohils* and the area as *Mohilwati.* The *Mohils* have been regarded as *Chouhans*. Another important Rajput clan which inhabited this tract, was *Sankhla* (*Parmaras*) occupying a portion around *Janglu* village. The area to the west and north-west of the erstwhile state of Bikaner was under the possession of the *Bhati* Rajputs who had the strong principality of Pugal. All these social groups used to quarrel with each other and among themselves. Das, Sidhayach Dayal, *Dayal Das ri Khyat*, Part II, (Pub.) (ed.) Sharma, Dashrath, Bikaner (1948), pp. 5, 7-10, 51-54; Tod, Col. James, *Annals and Antiquities of Rajasthan*, Vol. II, Oxford (1920), pp. 1165-66; Ojha, G.H., *History of Rajputana*, Vol. V, Part I, Ajmer (1939), p. 70; *Bikaner Rajya ka Itihas*, Part I, Ajmer, 1936, pp. 69-74.
102. *Dayal Das ri Khyat*, op. cit., pp. 3-5; Ojha, G.H., *Bikaner Rajya ka Itihas*, Part I, pp. 90-100.

103. *Dayal Das ri Khyat* (Pub.), Vol. II, pp. 11-12, 27-29, 38-39; Tod, Col. James, op. cit., Vol. II, p. 1146; Powlett, Capt. P.W., op. cit., p. 4; Ojha, G.H., op. cit., pp. 111-17.
104. *Akbarnama,* Abul Fazal, (Eng.Tr.), H. Beveridge, Vol. II, pp. 516-19. *Muntkhab-ut-Tawarikh*, Badaoni, (Eng. Tr.) Low, Vol. II, p. 137. Ojha, G.H., Part I, op. cit., 155-56.
105. *Ain-i-Akbari*, op. cit., Vol. I, p. 373, Ojha, G.H., op. cit., Part I, p. 197-200.
106. *Ain-i-Akbari*, Abul Fazal, (Eng. Tr.) Blochmann, Part I (1873), Calcutta, p. 356.
107. *Tuzuk-i-Jahangiri* (Eng. Tr.) Rozers and Beveridge, Vol. 1, p. 1. *Massir-ul-Umara,* Shahnawaj Khan, Part I, p. 360.
108. *Massir-ul-Umara,* op. cit., Part I, p. 362.
109. Ibid.
110. Ibid., Part II, p. 286.
111. Ibid., p. 289-91.
112. Ibid., Part II, p. 291.
113. Ali, M. Athar, *The Mughal Nobility under Aurangzeb*, Bombay, 1966, p. 246.
114. *Farman* of Mughal Emperor Ahmedshah dtd. V.S. 1810 *Shrawan Sudi* 5/3 August 1753 AD, 'A Descriptive List of *Farmans, Mansoor* and *Nishans*', Bikaner, 1962, p. 101; Ojha, G.H., Part I, p. 336.
115. *Ain-i-Akbari* Abul Fazal, (Eng. Tr.) Blochmann, Vol. I, p. 373. Col.Tod, *Annals and Antiquities of Rajasthan*, op. cit., pp. 1130-33; Devra, G.S.L., *Rajasthan Ki Prashashnik Vyavastha* (Hindi) Bikaner, 1981, p. 10.
116. Ojha, G.H., op. cit., pp. 184, 188, 247.
117. Maharaja Anup Singh's reign (1669-98) was followed by the weak successions of Swaroop Singh (1698-1700), Sujan Singh (1700-35) and Jorawar Singh (1735-45). The period was marked by the internal dissension among the *Mutsaddis* (aristocracy), disturbances by the *Bhattis, Johiyas* and *Raths* and the revolts of Churu and other *Thakurs*. Also the Rathores of Marwar under Ajit Singh, Bakht Singh and Abey Singh attacked Bikaner during the period. The absence of the Bikaner rulers from Bikaner because of services in the south in the Mughal army created further problems. Ojha, G.H., op. cit., pp. 292-295, 302, 317-18, Devra, G.S.L., op. cit, p. 11.
118. Ojha, G.H., op. cit., p. 323.
119. Ibid., pp. 326, 342-43, 345-48.
120. *Farman* of Mughal Emperor Ahmedshah, dtd. V.S. 1810 *Shrawan Sudi* 5/3 August 1753 AD; A Descriptive List of *Farmans, Mansoor*

and *Nishans*, Bikaner, 1962, p. 101; Powlett, Capt. P.W., op. cit., p. 61; Ojha, G.H., op. cit., pp. 335-36.
121. Ojha, G.H., op. cit., pp. 335-36.
122. Ibid., pp. 342-43.
123. Ojha, G.H., op. cit., p. 350.
124. *Dayal Das ri Khyat*, (pub.), op. cit., pp. 313-17; Ojha, G.H., op. cit., pp. 368, 375-77; Devra, G.S.L., op. cit., pp. 11-12.
125. *Dayal Das ri Khyat*, op. cit., pp. 313-17; Ojha, G.H., G.H., op. cit., p. 378.
126. Ibid.
127. Though Surat Singh, to procure *gaddi* and recognition for himself against his minor nephew Pratap Singh, who was the legitimate heir, collaborated with the chief of Jodhpur by paying Rs. 1,00,000 and got a recognition (*tika*) of succession for himself. In spite of this, the conflict between the two houses continued. Agrawal, Govind, *Churu Mandal ka Shodhpurna Itihas*, Ajmer, 1974, p. 237; Powlett, Capt. P.W., op. cit., p. 73.
128. Agrawal, Govind, op. cit., p. 237; Ojha, G.H., op. cit., p. 393.
129. The *Thakurs* of Churu, Bhadra, Dadrewa, Jasana, Rawatsar, Birkali alongwith ruler of Sikar and *Bhattis* and *Johiyas* jointly revolted against the ruler in 1815 AD Ojha, G.H., op. cit., p. 395.
130. Ojha, G.H., op. cit., 396-97.
131. Ibid., pp. 398-99, 402-03.
132. *Kagad bahi*, No. 34, V.S. 1885/1828 AD; Agrawal, Govind, *Potedar Sangrih ke Aprakashit Kagzat*, Bikaner (1976).
133. Source- This statistical information is from Devra, G.S.L., *Rajasthan Ki Prashashnik Vyavastha*, Bikaner, 1981, p. 79.
134. Sharma, G.D., *The Rajput Polity*, (*1638-1749 AD*), New Delhi, 1977, pp. 118-59.

3

Agricultural Economy

Though the erstwhile state of Bikaner was located in the *Thar* desert and had desert ecology agriculture was the principal occupation of the inhabitants.[1] The state usually attempted to extract the maximum possible revenue from the agricultural sector. Being pre-dominantly an agricultural economy, therefore an attempt has been made in this chapter to study and analyse aspects of the agrarian economy.

(1) AGRICULTURAL PRODUCTION

The agricultural production in the state was not uniform and certain and had large variations at places in the state territory. It was mainly dependent on the rainfall; that is why, in the absence of adequate rainfall famines and scarcities frequently occurred and had an adverse impact on the agricultural production.[2] In the *Thar* region, the rainfall was already scanty and low; the irrigation was not at all possible through wells owing to the deep underground water level.[3] As such, the cultivation was sparse and precarious and entirely depended on good rainfall. Only the single *Kharif* crop was possible in most parts of the state.[4] The other crops of *Kharif* (*Siyalu*) and *Rabi* (*Unalu*) could only be grown in the north and north-eastern part of the state in the areas of Suratgarh, Rajgarh, Nohar, Bhadra, Reni, Churu and Bhatner (Hanumangarh).[5] Suratgarh and Hanumangarh were part of the *Nali* area (the river-bed of Ghaggar) and therefore, were comparatively more fertile. The remaining part of the state mainly comprised the zone of the single *Kharif* crop.

(a) Extent of Cultivated Land

It is very difficult to ascertain the exact area under cultivation during the period under review. The contemporary sources and the *Bahis* do not provide us the exact figures of the total land over which agriculture was done.[6] Besides, there are some problems in ascertaining it.

Firstly, the region was prone to famines and droughts and during the natural calamities emigration outside the state of the peasantry was large.[7] Col. Tod records that 1/3 of the populaion migrated during famines.[8] So, the cultivated area was frequently subjected to changes.

Secondly, due to lack of irrigational facilities large areas of cultivable land remained uncultivated. The *Kagad Bahis* contain many *Kagads* (directors) asking the peasants to cultivate and bring more fallow land under the plough.[9]

Thirdly, the numbers of the *Khalisa* villages fluctuated due to assignments.[10]

Lastly, the detail of the cultivated area of the *Jagir* land is missing in the *Bahis*[11]. For these reasons we cannot determine the exact extent of land under cultivation.

The state also made efforts to encourage the agricultural population to increase the cultivation and bring fallow land under the plough through providing concessions and inducements.[12] The *Choudharies* were asked to rehabilitate the migrated cultivators and attract new ones from the neighbouring states to settle in the villages.[13]

However, the later contemporary sources like the gazetteer and settlement reports provide us with some ideas about the cultivated area to which scholars tentatively adhere to.[14] The report of Fagan's settlement of 1893 AD for the *Khalisa* villages of the state points out that the average area under cultivation of the state was 15 per cent and varied greatly from 35 per cent in *Pargana* Bhatner (Hanumangarh) to only 3 per cent in *Chira Anupgarh*[15]. It is interesting to note that these variations in regard to the volume of production are due to the quality of soil and different conditions of physical geography.

(b) The Crops

The *Kharif* crop consisted only of *Bajra* and *Moth* on a large scale[16] and others being *Gawar, Jawar, Moong* and cotton sparsely grown in the state.[17]

The *Rabi* crop consisted of wheat and barley confined to the north-eastern parts and a portion of *Chira Magra* adjacent to the capital.[18] The agricultural produce in Bikaner was mainly food crops for local consumption. Production of cash crops were negligible. The agricultural products were as follows:

Bajra was an important *Kharif* crop and was extensively grown in the entire state and in larger proportions in Nohar and Bhadra as it had become the staple food of the people.[19] Under the desert's favourable conditions, *Bajra* grows and ripens quickly. It was the first crop to be sown in the middle of June and August but if the crops is sown after the end of July (*Pachhet*) the yield of the grain would be poor.[20]

Moth was another important agrarian product in addition to the grains, the stalks, the leaves and the pods supplied good fodder for camels.[21] It did best in the light soil and was usually sown upto the end of August. It was grown in equal proportion to *Bajra* in Nohar and Bhadra in the eastern part of the state.[22] *Sawa Bahi Reni* of 1758 AD records that the state realized 71 maunds of *Moth* from Reni in 1758 AD.[23]

Gawar was also sown in every part of the state at the end of September. The grain stalk and broken grain pods are used as fodder cattle[24]; specially if is boiled in water and given in *Banta* (mixture of *Gur* and *Khal* with pulses) to animals like cows and buffaloes to obtain quality of milk and *ghee.*

Jawar or great millet was not commonly sown in the area as it required a rather stiff soil and better irrigation.[25] It was generally sown later than *Bajra* and took a longer period to mature. Its stalks (*Karbi*) supply good fodder for cattle and is usually grown in Suratgarh, Nohar and Bhadra.[26]

Til (Sesame) was a valuable crop and did well in the loam soil of Suratgarh and parts of the north-east region.[27] It could be sown up to the middle of August and was grown for the edible oil which was extracted by the village *Telies* (oil pressurers).[28]

Wheat–In the sandy soil of Bikaner a small quantity of wheat was produced. It had to be imported from Kota, Multan, Sindh,[29] Nagaur and Jodhpur. However, in the northern fertile part of the state wheat was grown but was confined to the dry *Nali* bed of Ghaggar.[30] The largest proportion of *Rabi* cultivation was found in *Pargana* Bhatner, Nohar, Bhadra, Suratgarh and also in the few villages of *Chira Magra*.[31]

Barley was produced in the villages of Rajgarh, namely Dokuwa, Berasar, Ludi and Hammirwas in the *Rabi* crop. We come across an estimated figure (*Jama*) of barley produced for Rajgarh. It was 1,320 maunds and out of which 220 maunds were realized in land revenue in 1798 AD.[32] In the village Hammirwas 13 maunds were realized by the state in 1808 AD.[33]

Gram was also an important *Rabi* crop and was produced in a limited proportion in Bhatner, Suratgarh, Nohar and Bhadra. When it was grown mixed with barley it was called Bejhr. *Moong* was also sparingly grown in *Chira* Reni, Khedra and *Pargana* Rajgarh.[34]

Cash crops were negligibly produced in the state. Tobacco of low quality was produced in Rajgarh[35] but did not cater to the local requirements and therefore, had to be imported mostly from Malwa, Kota and Sindh.[36] Cotton on a minor scale, was also produced in the Ghaggar belt and also in *Chira* Magra.[37]

(2) THE INCOME FROM AGRICULTURE: THE LAND REVENUE

(a) The Components of the Land Revenue

In Bikaner the income from agriculture formed a considerable part in the sources of the state's income.[38] The land revenue and taxes/cesses had essentially offered an important linkage between the agriculture producers and the ruling classes, i.e. the surplus appropriators.

Under the Mughals, the land revenue formed a considerable portion of the fiscal component borne out by the peasants. It was essentially appropriation of a state share[39] called in the Persian terminology by different names such as *Khiraj* or *Māl*. Besides the *Mal,* there were other levies as well and they were termed and grouped under the head *Māl-o-jihat* and *Sair-i-jihat*[40] which could be either in cash or kind. Similar to the Mughal system of land revenue, we find that in the local terminology as mentioned in the revenue records of Bikaner the land revenue was comprised of the following three components [41]:

(i) The *Bhog* (synonymous to the *Mal*)
(ii) The *Rokad Raqams* and
(iii) The *Bija Raqam*

The collection of all these three components by the state were collectively termed as *Hasil* and this *Hasil* has been further sub-divided into *Hasil bhog*, which was realized in kind and *Hasil-Rokad-Bhanchh,*[42] which was realized in cash[43], constituted in all, the state share or the land revenue.

(i) The *Bhog*[44] was the original land tax collected in *Jinsi* (kind) as per the prescribed rates of state share from the total produce.
(ii) The *Rokad Raqams*[45] (tax realized in cash) were the cash collections of taxes, over and above the *Bhog*. This was the general realization prevalent in all the methods of land revenue assessment without exception. This realization was made not on an individual peasant but the village as a unit considering the economic condition of the village concerned.
(iii) The *Bija Raqams*[46] (other taxes in cash) included the administrative expenses incurred at the time of collection of the *Bhog* and the *Rokad Raqam* as explained above. These *Raqams*[47] in the form of taxes were transferred to the peasants and the latter paid the amount to the state including the perquisites/ *rozgar* (*lawazima*) of the revenue officials, etc. It is interesting to note that the term *rozgar* is also used for such kind of payments. From the perusal of the sources, a difference is made between the *lawazima* and the *rozgar*. *Lawazima* is to be paid in addition to the officials' salary. But the term *rozgar* (employment) is used for these payments which were made to the persons whose services were sought on a contractual basis.

(b) Methods of Assessment of Land Revenue

The process of land revenue collection consists of broadly two parts, i.e. 'assessment' and 'collection' of land revenue. In the revenue terminology assessment is called *Jama* and whatever has been actually realized is called the *Hasil*. That system is considered to be the best, wherein *Jama* and *Hasil* are equal but it rarely happened.[48] In Bikaner the terms of *Jama* and *Hasil* used frequently in its revenue manuals signified both stages of operation, i.e. 'Assessment' of land revenue as well as its 'Actual Collection'.[49]

The *Hasil Bahis*[50] and the *Kagad Bahis*[51] reveal that various methods of revenue assessment were in practice over here, because of various factors, viz. nature of territory, fertility of land[52], the caste and the condition of the peasant but very frequently, peasants have been addressed by the names according to the method through which they paid the state share and taxes.[53] For example, the *Asami* of the *Kunta* system was termed as *Hali* and his payments of land revenue as *Dez;* likewise *Asami* of 'per plough method', i.e. the *Halgat* system as *Pasayati* and his payments also as *Halgat* and the peasants cultivating land on a contract basis were called *Muqati, Boliyar* (cultivating land on agreed terms) or *Baghru* (tiller of fallow land on contract), etc.[54]

The following were the various methods of the land revenue assessment prevailing in the state.

(i) *Kunta or Kankut*

The most popular and widely prevalent method of land revenue assessment was the *Kunta* or *Kankut* (*Kan* means grain and *Kut* means estimation) applied in Bikaner.[55] This method involved the estimation of crop rate per bigha[56] in consultation among *Asami, Huwaldar*[57] and other village level officials. In case of difference, the expert opinion of the *Sohna*[58] (the assessor) was obtained. Whenever the *Asami* dissented and did not accept the assessment he could appeal to the higher authorities including the ruler.[59] The *Sohna* had a preferential say in determining the crop rate,[60] even then, the difference of opinions persisted regarding estimation if any, the actual sampling of per *bigha* of crop was taken into consideration and then the crop rate was decided. Subsequently, the area under cultivation was measured and thus the total estimated production was arrived at and the state share determined.

The system was less expensive to the state because it did not involve many revenue officials as well as it saved time in assessing the land revenue. Moreover, assessment was made, to a great extent on the actual produce and the damage to crops, if any, was equally shared by the state and the peasantry.[61]

(ii) Halgat System

Halgat was another method of land revenue assessment in the desert part of the state and income derived under this system was known as *Halgat* income. In the desert area because of the frequent shifting of sand dunes measurement was not possible.[62] Besides, cultivation of crops was not uniformly estimated. Under these circumstances the counting of the ploughs was the determining factor in the land revenue assessment.[63] As for example, if a peasant used a single plough known as *Ekaliya Hal* in his field with an ox or with a camel or if, a peasant had a double plough which was termed as *Doleda Hal* with two oxen or two camels then the rates would be higher in the latter case.[64] Usually, it is supposed that one plough (*Hal*) is deemed equivalent to 5 *bighas* of land.[65]

Under this system there were two types of peasants. One was an ordinary peasant and the other was a peasant enjoying privileges. This privileged category of peasants has been designated as *Pasayati*[66] in the *bahis*. The question arises who were these *Pasayatis* enjoying privileges. Our revenue records show that Brahmins, Rajputs[67] and Sahukars, i.e. persons belonging to the higher strata of society were called *Pasayatis*. Sometimes the *Patwari* of a village, military personnel and revenue official and occasionally some menials were granted the *Pasayati* privileges because of services they rendered to the state.[68] If anybody under this system would bring new land under the plough the due *Hasil*, i.e. land revenue or taxes/cesses were not realized. In village *Gudawas* in 1770 AD such exemptions were granted to Darbari Sarup Singh, Natho Nando,

Sahebo Gaur, Chaker Sarup Singh, Nathio and two menials on their ploughing new land in that village.[69] The *Bahi Halgat Re Hasil Ri* of 1752-65 AD shows that in the year 1752 AD the land revenue accruable under this *Halgat* system was collected through a *Muqata* (*Ijara*) in the state. The *Muqata* was let out on Rs. 3,001.[70]

(iii) Bighedi System (Land Revenue on Bigha Basis)

Another system known as *Bighedi* was in practice in the *Chiras* of Reni, Nohar and Sihagoti and Pargana Punia in the north-east and the eastern part of the state where land was comparatively more fertile.[71] In order to realize a maximum possible land revenue the cultivable land was measured after every third year[72] and the land revenue in cash was calculated on the basis of *Bighas* which was known as *Bighedi*. This system of land revenue was adopted for both the harvest of *Rabi* and *Kharif*.[73] Rupees 507 and *Annas* 10 were collected in Rajgarh in 1793 AD under this system.[74]

The important aspect of this method was that the *Bighedi* which was fixed after measuring the land, was normally, not to be changed or altered before the next measurement, i.e. after three years. Therefore, a peasant could be at a loss in case of the land under plough would reduce.[75]

(iv) Muqata or Boliyar

There was a general practice in the state to lease out (on farming) a land or village by its owner to an individual, the right to cultivate it on a lump sum amount and on the agreed terms for a particular period of time. Generally, it was called an *Ijara* in Mughal terminology, *Muqata* at local level and the person taking the lease was called *Muqati*, or *Boliyar*.[76] The word *ijara* is also used in our sources but very rarely.

In either case the *Jama* (the estimated land revenue) along with the taxes if any, of land in question was to be paid to the state by the *Muqati/Boliyar*.[77] In addition, *Malba* (a tax for village development) cess was to be paid by the *Muqati* either to the state or to the land owner.[78] Such *Muqatas* were obtained by those who intended to settle down in a village or lived temporarily were termed as *Nawa*.[79]

(v) Miscellaneous Methods

There was yet another system, in use in some parts of Bikaner. *Bhint-ki-bhanch*[80] was one of them under which land revenue was taken on the number of residential houses or the number of *Guwadi*[81] (family) in the western part (*Chira* pugal). *Dhatoi*[82] was another method, in which some fixed amount was realized tri-annually.

While assessing the total *Jama* of a village either *Khalisa or Jagir* village, the *Rokad Raqams* (the other taxes) were also separately assessed. These were to be taken at the time of realization of the land revenue. For example, this was done in the case of *Khalisa* village Barjogsariya and Giwarsor[83] and a village Bisorasar, given in *Jagir* in the year 1770 AD.[84] These systems prevailing in the *Khalisa* (directly administered territory by the ruler) territory were also, more or less in practice in the sub-assigned villages, i.e. the villages asigned by the chiefs in his state, either to his relative for subsistence, or to his subordinate feudals in lieu of their military services, or granted in charity, i.e. the *Sasan* villages. These were locally called the *Patta* villages or *Jagirs* and their holders as *Pattayat* or *Jagirdars.* Such sub-assignments were largely made out by the chiefs, more specially, when they were the independent chiefs after the detachment from the Mughals. The systems which were in practice during the 18th century, continued to be in vogue till the early 19th century as mentioned in the *bahis.*

(c) Systems of Land Revenue Collection

From the archival records pertaining to Bikaner state it is evident that no uniform system of collection was in vogue throughout the state. Besides, different systems obtained in the *Khalisa* area and the *Jagir* (assigned) area.

In the *Khalisa* territory two officers, namely *Huwaldar*[85] and the *Daroga*[86] were made responsible for collection with the help of village level intermediary officers, i.e. the *Choudhary,*[87] *Patwari*[88] and *Sohna.*[89] They were also assisted by the *Amin*[90] and *Potedar*[91] (*fotedar*) so that proper accounts were maintained with regard to the land revenue collections.

In the *Khalisa* area two systems of collection were simultaneously, operating known as (i) *Huwala-Soapa* system and the (ii) *Muqata* system. In the former system, certain villages were assigned to the *Huwaldars* on a fixed remuneration and certain conditions to be followed. The remuneration would be paid to the officer only when his due collection was completed within the stipulated time. In the latter case, i.e. of *Muqata*, the work of land revenue collection was to be auctioned to the highest bidder on certain conditions. For instance, in 1770 AD. *Muqata* was auctioned to Parihar Daulat Ram of the work of land revenue collection of village Nakodarsar for Rupees 151; with a condition that he would maintain the numbers of the peasantry in the village.[92] Likewise, in 1781 AD the *Muqata* of the taxes *Korad, Ghas-charo, Charo sehtero,* and the income of *Halgat* was let out to Dannoni Gumani Ram, Daga Hatthi Ram and party for *Chira Reni* in the year 1781 AD.[93]

The bid amount was to be paid to the state and the difference between the two, i.e. the actual realization and the bid amount was appropriated by the bidder or *Muqati* as his profit. Sometimes, the state realized the bid amount in anticipation of the realization[94] and sometimes, the due amount was paid to the state in instalments.[95] This system of *Muqata* had become so popular that *Huwaldars* used to work as *Muqatis*.[96] During the same period in Bengal also the revenue officials by taking the collection of land revenue on *muqata* emerged as very powerful *zamindars*. This was a profitable business. The state also resorted to pay-off the state loans to its creditors by way of such assignments.

It is significant to note the state requirements, i.e. the need of money could not be met by the usual income. Therefore, the state had to fall in prey to the moneylenders and the state mortgaged the collection of land revenue of a particular village to the *Mahajan* in lieu of the loan taken from him. Thus, the peasants were left to the mercy of the *Mahajan*.

The due land revenue of village *Bandlo* for the year 1770 AD was mortgaged to Acharya Jagnath for the recovery of his loan to the state and the state issued order to the concerned to pay the land revenue to Acharya Jagnath instead to the *Bhogta* of the village.[97] Likewise, the due *Hasil* of village Seruna was mortgaged to Damami Daftari Meghraj in the year 1770 AD.[98] The state issued directions to the villagers to help in the realization of dues of the land revenue to such state-debtors.[99]

In the *Jagir* areas, the *Jagirdars* or the *Pattaholder*, as it is generally called in the state, and the *Bhumias*[100] had their own officials, viz. *Kamdars* and *Gumashtas* (agents) to realize the land revenue from their area. The amount collected in *Jagir*, in relation to the *Bhog* part was appropriated by the *Pattedar* and the amount of other taxes were shared by the state and the *Pattedar* with the help of their respective officers. In the *Bhom territory*, the *Bhumias* (the hereditary right holders) were supposed to pay only the *Bhombab,* i.e. the quit-rent to the state and the rest of the collection from the peasants was taken over by them. Thus the *Bhombab* was a symbol of accepting the subordination of the ruler. It seems that the state was quite conscious and cautious about the increasing and unbearable burden on the peasantry therefore, from time to time the state had given specific directions with regards to safeguarding the interest of the peasantry at the time of the collection of land revenue. The state had clearly directed all the officials and the concerned not to realize, over and above, the fixed land revenue.[101] Peasants from the *Khalisa* territory were not allowed to go to the *Jagir* areas without permission. In the year 1789 AD the village Devidaspura' (*Chira* Nohar) was assigned in *Jagir* to *Khuwas* Hindumal Chhajer. The peasants of Nohar were not allowed to cultivate the land in Devidaspura. If anybody violated the instructions and cultivated the land in that village then the land revenue of that cultivator, as mentioned in the order, would be realized by the officials of *Khalisa* territory instead of the officials of *Jagirdar*.[102] They were also instructed to extend cultivable area and to bring fallow land under cultivation.[103] The peasants should not be ejected as far as possible.[104] The grantees of *Betalab patta* (tax exempted grantee) and the *Sasan* (tax free land) were not to be taxed at all.[105]

Despite the state's effort not to exact over and above what has been sanctioned, it is inherent in the system of *Muqata* (farming of land revenue collection) that those who were the highest bidder; they would demand more than what the peasant was supposed to pay. This difference was the profit which accrued to the highest bidder. Similar consequences should have emerged from the *girvee* system. This led to the exploitation of the peasants. Though the state was wary and concerned about the welfare of the peasantry but it had its own compulsions because of deteriorating financial conditions. The state was stringent enough in realizing the state dues. Its officials seized the villages temporarily and after recovering the dues released later. We find references of such seizure and release in the *Bahis*, some villages of *Chira* Jasarasar were under *Attak* (seizure) for the recovery of dues of taxes *Korad, Bhuraj* and *charo-Sehtaro*.[106]

(d) Payments of the Land Revenue

The land revenue was realized in kind as well as in cash. The *Bhog* part was realized in kind[107] which was immediately sold out and as per the prevailing market prices[108] the other taxes and cesses were collected in cash from the peasants.

For this, in Bikaner a number of coins of different denominations, viz. *Rupiya, Annas, Taka* and *Dam* were used. The *Rupiya* was always a silver coin and the others were of copper. It was the speciality that these coins were also called by the names of the rulers under whose regime the coins were minted.[109]

(e) The Rate of Land Tax and its Economic Pressure on the Peasantry[110]

Regarding the rate of the land tax and its economic pressure we have been provided with the following two types of evidences in the revenue records of Bikaner:

(a) Statistical evidences recorded in the *Hasil Bahies* of the state.[111]

(b) The administrative instructions and orders passed at intervals regarding the land revenue system, compiled in the *Kagad bahis*.[112] The state's attitude towards the peasantry as well as various concessions and remissions granted on exigencies have been recorded in them.

We know from these evidences that in Bikaner, similar to the Mughal system, the rates of land tax varied under different systems of assessment, and also differed as per the caste and conditions[113] of the peasants along with the fertility of the land.[114] This difference also occurred on the *Rabi* and *Kharif* harvests and on the cash crop or food crop as well.

During the Mughal period, the *Zabt* system could not be implemented in Bikaner due to certain limitations[115] but many other indigenous systems as have been discussed, were in vogue and we may examine the rates prevailing under them separately.

Under the *Kunta* or *Kankut* (estimation of grain) system during the period of the Mughal hegemony, the rate of land tax was either 1/7 or 1/8 or 1/10 of the total produce which gradually increased up to 1/5. At the close of the 17th century along with the above rates 1/3 (Tihaliya) and 1/4 (Chauhatiya) rate depending upon fertility of land, were levied.[116]

We encounter in records that when the chiefs of Bikaner detached themselves from the services of the Mughals the rates did not differ substantially as the state continued to levy land tax at the rate of 1/5 or 1/6.[117] Only once, the state did try to enhance it by 1/2 (*Adhiya*)[118] around V.S. 1851-52/1794-95 AD both in *Khalisa* and *Jagiri* areas, but it was resisted by the peasantry. We have some references available regarding opposing the *Adhiya*. In village Rangdesar, the mother of the choudhary complained to the ruler that it was not possible for her to pay the *Adhiya*. So she was exempted of it by the state. Likewise, wife of choudhary Sukha of village Sheikhsar complained of incapability of paying the *Adhiya* and was exempted later by the states. Likewise complaints of inability to pay the *Adhiya* was received from villages Masaroo, Foga and Mudsar. Peasants of these villages showed their inability to pay the *Adhiya*.[119] However, the state gave exemptions to some peasants but continued to levy taxes up to 1813 AD.

A concessional rate of 1/4 to 1/7 was allowed to the higher strata of society (i.e. Rajputs, Brahmins and *Sahukars*)[120] The village *Choudhary* was enjoying the *Nankar land* (exempted land) besides the *Pachotara,* i.e. 5 per cent of the land revenue of his village was kept by him as his share.[121] *Choudharies* enjoyed some more concessions. *Dhunwa* tax was not levied on them.[122] Likewise, *Bhogta* (term used for *Jagirdar* in the *Bahis* as he appropriated the *Bhog*) was exempted for his *Gharuwala Hals*, i.e. personal cultivation.[123] It is also interesting to note that under the *Halgat*, the rates varied on deploying single or double ploughs which were known as *Ekaliya* and *Doleda* ploughs respectively[124] and the land revenue was realized in cash.

During the latter half of the 18th century we encounter varying rates for *Halgat*. In 1760 AD we find the following rates in *Bahi Halgat Ri*, No. 1, 1760 AD (V.S. 1817-RSAB).

Table 3.1: Rates of Halgat Available in 1760 AD[125]

S.No. (1)	*Type & No. of Plough* (2)	*Animal Deployed* (3)	*Rate per Plough* (4)
1.	Single (Ekaliya)	One-Ox	Rs. 3
2.	Double (Doleda)	Two-Ox	Rs. 4
3.	Single (Ekaliya)	One-Camel	Rs. 5
4.	Double (Doleda)	Two-Camel	Rs. 6

However, we see a considerable increase in the rates in 1781 AD than the rates cited above. We find in village *Khedado* a *Muqata* for *Halgat* was given to a Jat *Muqati* for Rs. 15 and Rs. 20 for single and double ploughs respectively.[126] In the very next year in that village the rates quoted above were reduced by fifty per cent due to famine conditions.[127]

This considerable increase might be due to the fact that the income of *Halgat* was often let out on the *Muqata* (let out on contract) for its realization and *Muqatis* might have been responsible for such an increase as they used to appropriate over and above the sanctioned *Jama* of land revenue.[128]

However, it is well known that the realization of tax varied from caste to caste. The higher castes like Brahmins, Rajputs and *Sahukars* who were termed *Pasayati* were enjoying concessional rates. This concession was of either Re. 1 in rate or up to the limit of 50 per cent of prevailing rates.[129] It is interesting to note that the Mughal administration had accepted the local traditions prevailing in western and eastern Rajasthan to realize land revenue at concessional rates. The distinction based on the castes was not a departure of the practice prevailing in ancient Indian society according to the *Dharmashastras*. By giving this privilege to the upper castes, it was easy for the state to realize the revenue from the lower castes of the peasantry without any protest. Thus, we do not find any change in the social attitudes of the Mughals and the Rajput rulers towards the upper and the lower strata of the society.

In the fertile part of the state, i.e. the north-eastern part where the land tax was realized on the measurement of the land and in cash on the basis of *Bighas* was known as *Bighedi*.[130] The rates pertaining to the latter half of the 18th century onwards ranged from Rs. 3 to Rs. 8 per 100 *bighas* of land.[131]

The *Muqati* or *Boliyar* (a tenant under contract with the owner of land) paid a lump sum cash amount as the land revenue to the state. The rates depended on the system in which it was applied, such *Muqatas* are similar to the *Bil-muqata* or *Ijaras* of the Mughal administration frequently adopted to collect the land revenue in the late 17th and 18th century. In the sub-assigned *Patta* villages or *Jagiri* areas the rates of land tax did not differ substantially under these systems of land revenue assessment.

In order to ascertain the scale of revenue demand in 'kind' and 'cash' we had a sample survey of the data of some 15 villages of *Chira* Jasarasar (near the capital, Bikaner), the statistical details of which are available in the *Bahi Khalisha Re Gawan Ri*–V.S. 1853/1796 AD.[132] (available in R.S.A., Bikaner) and the results are shown in the following tables.

Table 3.2: Scale of Revenue Demand in Grain (*Bhog*) under *Kunta* in theYear V.S. 1853/1796 AD

Total Quantity ('Kunta') (1)	*Raiyati's Share (Peasants' Share)* (2)	*State Share as 'Bhog'* (3)	*Remarks* (4)
Mds.-Seers 28,758-01	*Mds.-Seers* 23,583-30	*Mds.-Seers* 5,174-11	Aggregate state share comes to 17.99% i.e. 18%

Table 3.3: Revenue Demand in Cash (Taxes/cesses) under *Kunta* in the Year V.S. 1853/1796 AD

Total amount collected (Rs) (1)	*'Rokad-Rakam' (Taxes)* (2)	*'Badi Bhanch'* (other tax)* (3)	*Remarks* (4)
14,368.00 (100%)	6,429.00 (44.75%)	7,939.00 (55.25%)	The amount has been rounded off to the nearest rupee.

* *Badi Bhanch* was a common term for three taxes collectively realized, viz. *Dhunwa*, *Pagh* and *Ango*.

It is evident that the state share in kind under *Kunta* does not exceed 18 per cent of the gross produce, but the additional cash demand was also significantly high.

While examining the rate under various methods, we see that the rates of land tax have gradually increased but more specially after the mid-18th century. However, it still did not increase substantially. Perhaps the state could understand the limitation of the peasants paying capacity and the limited prospects of the agricultural growth in the state.

But the economic pressure on the peasantry was certainly mounting high on the ground that many new taxes and cesses were imposed with the continuation of the older ones. Their rates were also revised in the second half of the 18th century and which continued up to the early 19th century. So, the increase in number and volume of the cash taxes increased the overall demand on the peasantry.

For example, *Rukhwali-Ri-Bhanch* (Protection tax) was imposed in 1794 AD by Surat Singh (1787-1828 AD). Initially it was realized at the rate of Rs. 2 per family, later on was realized at the rate of Rs. 10 per family in the year 1800 AD.[133] The *Dhunwa* tax (tax on each hearth of a family) was an old tax and realized from all. Initially it was collected per *Guwadi* (family) @ Re. 1 later on increased to @ Re. 1 and *Takka* 25.[134] Likewise *Kiyadi*, i.e. a tax on each house was levied in 1788 AD @ Re. 1 and *Anna* 4 was raised to Rs. 2 per house.[135] *Khusali* was another tax realized for the cause of protection and welfare by Surat Singh on the occasion of the invasion of Bhatner in 1804-06 AD Many *Habubs* (name of the cesses to meet the exigency), viz. *Hala Ri Bhanch* (tax on plough) *Sal-Siledi* (tax from the menials), etc. were recovered.[136] These taxes were also applied in the *Jagiri* areas along with the *Khalisa* areas. Sometimes the people resisted paying them and left the village in resentment. There are various such *Kagads* in the *Kagad Bahis* for verification.[137] The Jat *Asamis* of village Dulchasar approached the Darbar in 1770 AD and complained that the taxes/cesses were not being realized as per the old rates as well as new cesses were being demanded by the officials[138] Likewise, the peasants of Sihag community opposed the excess demand and left the village Bhadlo.[139]

Moreover, Surat Singh also realized the *Chakri* (the military services) from his *Jagirdars* in cash for the first time in 1794-95 AD[140] @ Rs. 50 per Sawar initially and later on it increased to Rs. 100 per Sawar around 1800 AD.[141] In fact, while in Mughal service, the chiefs of Bikaner, as a *mansabdar* had to render military services according to his *Sawar* rank and in order to meet his military obligations he had asked his *Thikanedars* (Feudals) to maintain certain military contingents called *Chakri* in the *Bahis*.[142] Subsequently, with the collapse of the Mughal state the chief ceased to function as a *mansabdar*. Now there was no need of the military contingents of his *Thikanedars,* i.e. the *Chakri*. In this changed situation the chief converted this *Chakri* (Military Service) into cash, i.e. the *Thikanedars* were now to pay in cash at a fixed rate to the state in lieu of their *Chakri*.[143]

There were many other exactions in the name of *Neota*[144], *Nazar* and the *Peshkashi*[145] from *Jagiri* areas and obviously this cash demand was transferred by the *Thikanedars* to the peasants, thereby increasing the pressure of an increased amount by way of taxes over the peasantry. We find that the peasants of a *Jagiri* village Ghatiyal made a loud protest against the *Pattayat* for various exactions levied upon them.[146]

Thus, the overall burden on the peasantry in the other territories, i.e. the *Khalisa* and *Jagiri* increased substantially after the mid-18th century.

The substantial increase in cash demand in the second half of the 18th century and early 19th century needs to be explained.

It was the outcome of two significant reasons. One, the income of the *mansab* of chiefs of *tankhwa-Jagir* which formed a significant part in the state's total collection of revenue had now ceased to come after the decline of the Mughal empire. This loss of their income caused a deficiency of finance. Secondly, the absence of the strong Mughal protection led the chiefs to be involved in many disputes with the nobility as well as the neighbouring states; which ebbed their large finance, more specially during the period of Surat Singh (1787-1828). He not only incurred a heavy amount in the pacification of the restive nobility but also in undertaking military expeditions and encounters against the principality of Jodhpur and others. To recompensate and recoup the loss and to meet the increasing expenditure, Surat Singh imposed some new taxes as well as increased their rates.

The state's demand (both *kind* and *cash*) collectively resulted in a situation which had the maximum economic pressure on the peasantry and is evident from the fact that:

(a) The state dues of taxes in villages remained pending. This *Baqaya* (pending amount) of taxes also fairly increased. A manual speaks that in 1752 AD the *Baqaya* of taxes was Rs. 3,486 and it increased in 1757 AD to Rs. 10,933.[147] The accumulation of the *Baqaya* and thereby a gap between in *Jama* and *Hasil* indicates[148] that the peasantry was heavily burdened and its paying capacity had been exhausted to a considerable extent.

(b) The peasantry had to owe loans from the *Mahajans* or *Sahukars* of village at higher interest rate after mortgaging their harvest in advance to pay the state dues.[149]

(c) Pressed hard for the state demands or for the private loans the migration of peasantry from the villages also took place. But the state did mollify their move or dissuaded them by assuring certain concessions in realization of taxes. The state also deferred their dues or asked the private debtors not to press for their loans in order to keep the cultivation unaffected.[150]

This burden was largely shared by the traditional agrarian

castes of Jats, Malis and Bishnois while the higher strata of society were enjoying privileges in the form of concessions and exemptions. It is explicit from the sample survey of data of village Somadsar in the year V.S. 1802/1745 AD[151] is given below:

Table 3.4 : Differential Incidence of *Hasil* from Various Categories of Peasants

Village/ Year	*Peasant*	*Total no./Hasil (Rs.)*	*% of the total Hasil*	*Burden/Economic Pressure Per Head (Category-wise) (in Rs.)*
(1)	*(2)*	*(3)*	*(4)*	*(5)*
Somadsar	1. *'Dezhali'*	(23)/328	56.36	14.26
V.S.1802/	2. *'Pasayti'*	(17)/105	18.04	6.18
1745 AD	3. *'Muqati'/ 'Boliyar'*	(54) 149	25.60	2.76
Total		(94)582	100%	

In the above mentioned chart column 5 shows a considerable discriminative burden, e.g. a *Dezhali* paid Rs. 14.26 while a *Pasayati* and a *Boliyar* paid only Rs. 6.18 and Rs. 2.76 respectively; and more than 50 per cent of the total realization is borne out by the *Dezhali* category of peasants.

(3) TAXES AND CESSES

The chiefs in Bikaner had realized different taxes and cesses with different nomenclature to meet their economic needs in the prevailing conditions. These were realized either in kind or cash. To compensate the services rendered by some officials certain perquisites were also levied on the peasants. Cumulatively, these were termed as *Rokad Raqams* (amount realized in cash), *Bija Rakams* (other amounts), *Lawazima* (Perquisites/Remuneration of officials), *Takini* (customary charges), etc. Some of them were levied on an individual basis and some were levied per village considering it a unit.[152]

From various *Bahis*, viz. *Hasil Bahis, Habub Bahis, Lekha-wa-Jama-Kharach-Ri-Bahis, Sawa Bahis* and *Kagad Bahis* we know the nature, kind and volume of the agricultural taxes and cesses.[153] They are as follows:

(i) Rokad Raqams

We know from the *Bahi Dhunwa-Desprath-Ri* of 1753 AD and *Bahi Khalisa Re Gawan Re Hasil Ri* of 1751 to 1760 AD[154] of Bikaner Records that following other cash taxes classified under *Rokad Raqams* were realized from the villages considering a village as a unit.

Dhunwa was however a part of the *Rokad Raqam* but levied from an individual family (*Guwadi*) on its each hearth. The general rate was Re. 1 per hearth of a *Guwadi*.[155]

Deshprath was a tax on animals. It was realized @ Anna 4 per animal.[156]

Shri Thakur Ji– Re. 1 to 2 per village was charged for maintenance of the local temples.[157] ***Gusain ji*** was a tax for religious persons in a village levied @ Re. 1.[158]

Mela-Phargati– These were two separate taxes, viz. (a) *Hakim-Ro-Melo,* i.e. perquisite of *Hakim* and (b) *Khazanchi-Ri-Phargati,* i.e. the remuneration of the cashier for clearing the account.[159]

Korad– The leaves of *Moth* and *Til* are locally known as *Korad* and were used as fodder for horses. Initially villages had to provide such fodder to the royal horses, later on, it was converted into cash @ Re. 1 to Re. 2 and *Anna* 8 lump sum per village and continued to be known by the same name.[160]

Bhuraj was a tax for storage expenses for procuring grains in village @ Re. 1 or 2 depending on the volume of the grain to be stored.[161]

Jakiro was another tax for the firewood used by the rural population in the village @ Re. 1 per village.[162]

Charo-Sehtero (lit. – good quality grass) was a tax for the expenses of *Sewan ghas* (grass) to be provided to the state animals @ Re. 1 to Re. 2.[163] We have income figures of this head of some *Chiras* in the year 1752-1753 AD.[164]

Table 3.5: Incidence of Income from *Charo-Sehtero* from *Chiras*

S.No. (1)	*Year (V.S./AD)* (2)	*Chira* (3)	*Amount Collected (in Rs.)* (4)
1.	1809/1752	Villages of 'Magra' and 'Desh' Bikaner	105.00
2.	1809/1752	Chira Jasarasar	116.00
3.	1810/1753	Chira Gosaisar - Misc. villages	106¾.00

The table shows that a significant amount was collected from this source.

Ghas-Charo tax on ordinary grass @ Re. 1 per village. There are some more cash taxes under the *Rokad Raqam* as enumerated in the *Bahi Dhunwa Desprath-Ri* of 1753 AD as under–

Jhal was a tax for using the useful trees in the village.

Asami was a tax presumably, on the cultivator or labourers.

Dulo-Choplano was a tax for expenses of paper and ink used for maintaining accounts of the village.

Qanungo-Kharach was a levy on the name of *Qanungo*.

Talaba was charges for the corespondence done by the state to recover the dues and sending reminders.

Gai-Ro-Gobar was the tax for collecting the cow dung to be used in storage of the grain or maintaining the *Kaccha* houses in villages.[166]

We have been provided in the above cited *Bahi* the estimated *Jama* of these *Rokad Raqams Chira*-wise for the year V.S. 1810/1753 AD.[167]

Table 3.6: *Jama* of the *Rokad Raqams Chirawise* for the Year 1753 AD

S. No. (1)	*Name of Chira* (2)	*Estimated 'Jama'* (3) *(in Rs.)*	*Remarks* (4)
1.	Gusaisar - Radbi	1,720	
2.	Reni	2,998	
3.	Magra - Kharipatti	2,642	
4.	Jasarasar	1,978	The '*Hasil*'

5.	Khedaro	2,367	figures for these *Chiras* are not available
6.	Sihagoti	950	
7.	Nohar	573	
8.	Sheikhsar	1,016	
9.	Bidahad	2,751	
10.	Rajahad	1,875	
	Total	18,870	

The estimated *Jama* shows that the *Rokad Raqams* had a significant impact in the *Jama bandi* of the land revenue in the state.

(ii) Bija Raqams, Lawazima and Takini

Apart from the *Rokad Raqams* there were some more miscellaneous agricultural taxes and cesses entitled as *Bija Raqams, Lawazimas* and *Rozgars* (employment of the revenue officials) and *Takini* (cutomay charges) borne by the peasantry or rural population in *kind* or *cash* as under:

***Seri* or *Sehri*:** A cess in kind, as its literal meaning suggests, that one seer per *maund,* i.e. 2.5 per cent[168] was levied by the state or *jagirdar* in acknowledgement of its proprietary rights.[169] Sometimes, as the records mentions it was levied @ *Takka* 1 per *maund* on grain and *til.*[170]

Tali (Threshing floor) was the place where grain was stored by the cultivators before the sharing of crops by the state for payment of revenue. In village Jodhasar (V.S. 1747/1690 AD) it was levied @ 10 per cent of total *Kunta,* i.e. 32 *seers* at the *Kunta* of 08 *maunds*[171] as a charge for using the floor.

Kath (lit.-wood) a charge for wood (presumably firewood) @ 2 *seers* to 4 *seers* per *maund.*[172]

Shri Thakurji was a levy in kind for offering to local deities in temples @ ½ *seer* to 1 *seer* per *maund.*[173]

Khunta was fodder expenses of the animals of the revenue officials employed in the realization work.

Sirawan was refreshment charges of the revenue officials.

Huzdar was expenses of the revenue collecting officials.

Dera-Kharch was staying charges. These were levied in *kind.*

Bhog-Bhado After realizing the land revenue in kind (*Bhog*) it was carried to state storage and *Bhog-Bhado* was charged for it (i.e. the carriage expenses). Rates for carrying the grains varied according to the quantity of grains and distances covered. Therefore, the rates varied from *Pargana* to *Pargana*. In village Udarasar in V.S. 1810/1783 AD the *Bhog-Bhado* was realized in cash @ Re. 1 per 11 *maunds* of grain and thus Rs. 24 and *Annas* 4 in all, was collected for the 267 *maunds* of grain.[174]

Ghughri was a kind of preparation with boiled wheat/*Bajra*. There was a levy in kind known as *Ghughri* in *Khalisa* and *Jagir* villages[175] which was later converted into cash. Rupees 5 were charged for 33 *maunds* taken from village Jodhasar in VS 1810/ 1743, while the official realized the assessed land revenue.[176]

Sukhado-Khichdo was a levy for supply of food or grain to the army passing through a village. It was also charged to provide food to revenue officials visiting villages for assessment work. *Sukhado* was charged @ 1 to 2 *Takkas* per *maund* grain.[177]

Grazing Tax The tax for grazing animals in pasture land was known as *Paan charai* and levied @ Rs. 5 for a camel, Re. 1 for an ox and also for a cow and four *annas* for a goat. A lump sum of Re. 1 was levied in *Jagir* villages where it was termed as ***Bhunga. Singoti*** was another tax (sale of horned cattle) collected @ Re. 1 per 14 sheep.[178]

Kiyali **or** ***Dhadat*** (weighing tax) was another tax for weighing the grain of *Bhog* for both harvests by the weighmen while collecting the land revenue.[179]

Rukhwali Ri Bhanch was another tax for protecting their harvest and their family against any untoward loss caused by the way.

Officials'* levy** - Apart from the above mentioned taxes there were certain cash levies which were taken from the villages later on to be spread over among the cultivators to meet the expenses of the revenue officials termed in the *Bahis* as *Lawazimas* (perquisites) and *Rozgar*. ***Bahi Khalisa Re Gawan Re Hasil Ri of 1850 AD mentions that Rs. 202 and *annas* 4 were realized as the *Lawazima* and *Rozgar*. These were of the following nature– ***Kunta Ri Kambal*** (blanket for assessor), ***Lekhania-Ro-Lawazimo*** (scribe's expenses), ***Sohna-Ri-Minai*** (measurement charges of *sohna*) ***sohna-Ro-Rozgar*** (remuneration of *Sohna*) ***Dibri*** (Expenses for drinking water of officials),[180] etc.

Malba[181] was another cess charged from the peasantry for the general expenses of the village. The collection from this cess was pooled with one fund which was used primarily for the development of the village and other sundry expenses. It seems from the ***Kagad Bahi*** for 1794 AD that *Malba* cess was recognized as a privilege of aboriginal Jats in their villages but in other than Jat areas the state realized it.[182] The Jats were authorized to collect *Malba* @ Re. 1 and *Takka* 1 per cultivator in village Devsaria in 1804 AD over and above, the land revenue.[183]

(4) RELIEF MEASURES AND CONCESSIONS: REHABILITATION OF PEASANTRY IN THE DEPOPULATED VILLAGES AND EXTENSION OF CULTIVABLE AREA OF LAND

The *Jama* and *Hasil* had never been equal, the reasons are obvious. The *Jama* was assessed during the harvesting period and the *Hasil* was realized after the harvesting. Agriculture depends on nature's generosity and frugality, but in the case of this state, *Hasil* always fell short tremendously because the state consists of desert area where rainfall used to be low and scarce. Since the state had frequent famines and scarcity, it had to resort to relief operations as well as grant concessions while realizing the land revenue and taxes from the peasants to deter and combat the eventualities of the following nature:

(a) **Natural calamities** such as famines and drought; scarcity, invasions of locusts, or pests due to which there was a complete or partial failure of crops in the state.[184]

(b) **Man-made calamities** like destruction of crops during military campaigns, raids or setting the village on fire by enemies. The conditions were further aggravated or intensified by these artificial factors or unsettled political conditions.[185]

In any of these calamities the agriculture production suffered and as a consequence, the peasantry had to migrate with their livestock for livelihood to more fertile regions.[186]

There are ample examples in various *Kagad Bahis* pertaining to the period 1754-1828 AD describing these remissions and concessions classified under the caption *Chhoot-Ra-Kagad*. They describe the nature and quantum of the concessions granted on the occasions discussed above. These were provided to either individual peasants or granted in general to a village or the *Chira* (an administrative unit consisting of a group of villages) as a whole, depending on the needs.[187]

Famine and scarcity conditions in Bikaner region (a tract of *Thar* desert) are fairly frequent as it has to depend for production of food grain and fodder (even for drinking water), on the erratic rainfall there being practically no other means of irrigation.[188] On an average, a famine may occur in ten years but local scarcity is a common feature at least every four years.[189] The distress is also caused by the invasion of locusts and pests sometimes. Such conditions are relieved only by temporary migration for the livelihood.

The first recorded severe famine occurred in 1754-56[190] during the times of Maharaja Gaj Singh which was followed by successive famines in the years 1763, 1783 and in 1796 AD[191], as they have been referred- to in the *Bahis*. Famines have also occurred in the years 1834 and 1849 AD[192] However, no details of these famines and scarcities are available in the records except the concessions and remissions in the respective years.

It was natural for the rulers[193] of the state to adopt certain relief measures during the calamities and afer it certain ameliorating steps in this connection. They have been analysed in the following manner:

(i) Relief Measures During the Famines and Scarcity

The centres for distribution of food and fodder called *Sadavarat* were organized by the state and employment was provided to many people in construction work. In 1754-55 Maharaja Gaj Singh had done so and the city wall of Bikaner was constructed[194] under this project.

The state dues of the land revenue and other taxes for the current year were either suspended or postponed or realized at reduced rates considering the severity of the calamity. In village Leghasar, Rs. 15 was exempted out of Rs. 75 in 1754 AD[195] and in the *Pargana* Punia the total *Jama* was exempted except the dues of *Khed Kharach Ri Bhanch* (a military tax)[196] for one year. In 1774 AD a village Bukansar which was assigned to Prem Singh Sahabsinghot in *Patta* was totally exempted from any realization.[197] Likewise, it was ordered for village Atbhomdesar that the dues would be recovered only when it was possible to realize.[198] The overall reduction in taxes was often limited up to ½ or to ¼ of the dues. Such exemptions are available in the *Bahis*.[199]

The arrears of the state dues were also postponed to the future dates. For instance, the dues for the village Upani were suspended for one year in 1770 AD.[200] Orders were issued in 1774 AD to defer the arrears up to the following year for villages Mahalsar, Sahwa, and Nohar.[201]

The *Mahajans* and *Sahukars* who had given private loans to the peasants were also dissuaded not to realize their loans during the calamity. Orders to this effect were issued for villages Asrasar in 1754 AD[202], village Norangdesar in 1763 AD[203] and for villages Likhmidessar, Himmatsar, Madawas, Del, Zalimsar and Dhatdi in 1770.[204] Similar orders were also issued for villages Kharde, Bukansar, Qasba Noher, Kolasar and Sawai.[205] In any attempt on the part of creditors to forcefully realize the debt or confiscate the belongings of any peasant in lieu of his debt, the state extended full protection to such cases and did not allow to do so.[206]

It is a general pattern throughout the period that whenever there was a famine or scarcity the prices of food articles went up.[207] In order to meet such contingencies and keeping in view the purchasing power of the peasantry and other affected people, the state followed a definite procurement policy and imported food grain and other essential items from the neighbouring states and for this the merchant were granted concessions in *Jagat*. For instance, the concession of 50 per cent *Jagat* was provided, in the year 1783 AD to the grain merchants of Malwa, Harauti and Mewar[208] and also of Nagaur.[209] They were asked to expedite the supply.

Although, *Begar* (compulsory service without any payments) was a general feature in the state. But under an adverse condition no *Begar* was to be asked for by the officials. The *potters* of Nohar were exempted from giving the *Begar* due to their poor condition in 1774 AD.[210] Likewise in the famine-affected village Kesardesar no *Begar* of food or fodder was to be taken by the state officials.[211] This shows that during the famine and after it, the demand of *Begar* was forbidden in the affected villages.

(ii) Reliefs and Concessions During Man-Made Calamities

Owing to the recurring disturbances of Raths, Johiyas and Bhattis and some feudal subordinate chiefs as well as the external attacks over Bikaner, particularly after mid-18th century, the political situation in the state was not satisfactory and the instances of loot, dacoity and raids were very common, which equally contributed to the destruction of cultivation and a loss to some extent. Such instances of man-made calamities are recorded in the *Bahis* and the state had to offer concessions and remissions in such instances. For instance, the dues of *Dhunwa tax* was exempted to half in village *Nenasar* (*Chira* Khedra) in 1774 AD[212] and in village *Jhonjhni* (*Chira Reni*) in *Rokad Raqams* for their being attacked.[213] The state dues were completely remitted in village Baradhwas since its was looted in 1774 AD. Also, total dues of the state of Rs. 481 were exempted in village Gusaisarbado in 1783 AD due to plundering in the village.[214]

(iii) Reliefs and Concessions After Famines and Other Calamities

After the visitation of famines or drought there has been a period of normal rainfall but it was found that the peasantry was so incapacitated that they were not in a position to use the good monsoon, because they had neither the ploughs nor cattle nor any money to purchase seeds. In order to provide strength to them, *Taccavi* loans were usually granted by the Mughals without interest, the Bikaner rulers also followed the same. They provided interest-free loans to the peasantry, so that they could purchase seeds, ploughs, etc. Also, no *Jagat* was charged from peasants on the imported grains (seeds) for sowing or for domestic use. The *Jagat* was completely exempted to the peasants of Gajsinghpura[215] and to the peasants of Jasarasar[216] on importing food grains for sowing and consumption respectively in 1763 and 1804 AD.

In fact the relief measures and tax reductions were planned in such a manner that it would help the peasants in their distress and to safeguard its own interests. The state help in different ways were aimed at the following:

(a) Encouraging the rehabilitation of villages.

(b) Encouraging the extension of cultivable area of land. The state made all efforts to achieve these goals.

(iv) Efforts for Rehabilitation and the Extension of Cultivable Area of Land

It is reported in the *Bahi* that if any one in the state suffered harm due to any reasons, he would receive compensation.[217]

New villages were founded in order to promote agricultural work and in order to ease the problem of employment. At the same time, obviously this was done with a purpose to enhance the state income.

To encourage the settlements, people were assured that they would be given tax reduction and protection, and this is how the number grew.[218] It was in this connection that for Anupgarh it was decreed that methods be developed to colonize 84 villages.[219]

Owing to famine and other reasons such as lack of security and peace many village were depopulated. This affected the income of the state. It was the policy of the state that depopulated or under populated villages should be restored to their original positions. For this the village *Choudharies*, *Bhogtas* and *Jagirdars* who undertook such tasks of rehabilitation of a village were granted various privileges from the state. Besides, a *Nankar* land (rent-free land) a *choudhary* was authorized to 5 per cent deduction (*Panchotra*) of total revenue to retain with him while collecting the revenue.[220] They were also granted rent-free pasture land. A *Bhogta* was allowed exemptions on his *Gharuhal* (personal plough).[221] The state also conferred the *Zamindari* rights to certain *Aasamis* in order to increase the agricultural population in villages. They were supposed to attract their relatives and other kinsmen to come from other adjecent states and live in the village to help increase cultivation. In 1827 AD, as many as 28 *Asamis* of village Hardesar, and Bhonipura, Bakusar (*choudhary* Mewaram Dewoni and Jeevan Sadani and others) were conferred *Zamindari* rights in such villages. They paid the state Rs. 325 as *Nazrana*, and in lieu of this they realized some traditional cesses such as *Dhol*, *Tikawani*, etc. from the inhabitants of their villages.[222]

Likewise, in order to rehabilitate the deserted villages, those who had left their villages decades earlier were encouraged to resettle in their original villages. The state tried to restore the same agricultural land which they had left years ago. The exemptions in taxes were also given to them which varied from the total exemptions to partial exemptions, so much so that they were exempted from paying tax for life. The term used for it was *Sadamad* (perpetual). For instance, in 1797 after 40 years families of 8 *Asamis* who came from Nagaur to live again in their original village Rajedu were granted permanent exemption of half the plough-land-cultivation perpetually (*Sadamad*) along with remission in *Dhunwa* tax to 2 *Asamis* of the families for ever.[223] In certain cases such concession were enjoyed by a few people up to three generations.[224] In order to increase the agricultural population we find that those offenders who were declared *Barothia* (sent out of state) and penalized were being exonerated and were rehabilitated. *Rawat* Bhinv Singh and his sons and grandsons who were declared *Barothia* were allowed to resettle in the village Kolasar in 1794 AD. Interestingly enough, one Jat peasant who had become *Beragi* or *Sadhu* and left cultivation of land was again put to cultivation work. However, he was exempted from the *Dhunwa* tax along with a concession in the land revenue. Instead of 1/6 part of land revenue 1/7 was realized from him.[225] Peasants living in the newly settled villages were not charged tax on pasture land and they were free to choose any system beneficial to them for the payment of land revenue.[226]

Total exemptions of taxes like *Dhunwa, Halgat, 'Korad', Charo, Ghas and Deshprath* was granted in the newly colonized villages like Sarupdesar and Raitudo for two years, i.e. for the years 1802 AD and 1803 AD.[227] The same exemption was also given to those who settled in Rajgarh, a newly established town by Gajsingh.[228]

Reduction in taxes was also available to those villages which were economically weaker on any account. Village Navalsari (*Chira* Reni) was given a reduction of Rs. 22 and *Annas* 12 in its *Jama*.[229]

Although, the desertion of villages were normally deterred by the state[230] but in calamities, people deserted them. For instance, village Khiyali *Pargana* Punia when completely deserted due to famine was granted complete exemption of *Dhunwa* tax for three years from 1800 to 1802 AD.[231]

The rulers also showed concern for the poor and menials to settle down on land.[232] Special care was taken to rehabilitate certain professional castes like *potters*, oil pressers, and carpenters in the village as they were an essential part of the village society. Concessions were also given in 1770 AD to *Kumhar*, *Teli* and *Suthar* when they were rehabilitated in village Radbi.[233]

On the partial failure/damage of crops due to certain reasons in any village the *Jama-Bandi* (assessment of land revenue) of that village was reduced.[234] For instance, the *jamabandi* of village Molisar, Motsara (*Chira* Rajahad) was revised in 1783 AD for it was partially deserted. The *Jamabandi* was reassessed for Rs. 37 to be realized from these village. This shows that the state was cautious enough to realize the dues in the pecuniary conditions in villages.

To augment the state income in a fertile area near a pond, the state sometimes resorted to force the peasants to cultivate crops which need good irrigation facilities. In village Chandasar, the state enjoined upon the peasants to grow wheat, gram and barley.[235]

Certain relief measures were granted to those peasants who repaired the old wells or helped with the construction of a new well in the village. The state provided Rs. 50 as financial aid to Sukhoni Jeevan in village Berasar in 1805 AD who ventured digging up a new well for drinking water.[236] Likewise, Chauhan Jeevan who dug up a well in a piece of land of village Beechhwal near Bikaner in 1780 AD was granted a portion of land and then onwards that area was to be known as a village Jeevandesar in his name.[237] In case of excess realization the state ordered a refund or adjustment towards other due taxes.[238]

It was enjoined upon *Pattedars* (assigness) that if someone suffered damage from a theft they would have to compensate him for the harm done or the village would be transferred to *Khalisa* (crown land) if he himself had failed. On the officials of *Khalisa* villages it was enjoined that if they treated cases incorrectly they would have to pay compensation for this from their own pockets. If an official died, monetary compensation would be given to the members of his family and if they had no means of earning their livelihood, subsistence would be provided for them. In case of death an official was survived by offspring, he was employed in the government service.[239]

These efforts of the state suggest that the state was very keen to increase the population of the villages and thereby increase the size of land accruing more revenues under the plough. The granted exemption and concessions were also motivated to extend the cultivation on more fallow land in the desert.

REFERENCES

1. Nearly 76.4% of the population were engaged in agricultural and animal husbandry. Fagan, P.G., *Settlement Report of the Khalisa Villages of Bikaner State*, Bikaner, 1893 AD, p. 5, R.S.A., Bikaner.
2. Kachhawah, O.P., *Famines in Rajasthan*, Jodhpur, 1988, pp. 146-75.
3. The underground water level was as deep as 300 ft. to 400 ft. below the surface level. Ojha, G.H., *Bikaner Rajya ka Itihas*, Part I, Ajmer, 1939, p. 10.
4. *Basta Khalisa Gawan Ra*, No. 2, *Hasil Bahis*, V.S. 1810/1753 AD, R.S.A., Bikaner.
5. Fagan, P.G., op. cit., pp. 6-7.
6. *Khalisa Gawan ri Hasil Bahis, Basta* No. 1 and 2; and *Kagad Bahis* do not provide details of the total cultivated areas. See *Hasil Bahis*, V.S. 1807 to 1817, and *Kagad Bahis* No. 1 to 7, V.S. 1811 to 1840 and Nos. 10 to 15 V.S. 1854 to 1866, R.S.A., Bikaner.
7. Kachhawah, O.P., op. cit., pp. 146-75.
8. Col. Tod, *Rajasthan ka Itihas*, (Hindi Tr.) (ed.) Keshav Thakur, p. 53.

Tod has mentioned that during Surat Singh's tenure (1787-1828) number of villages were reduced.

9. *Kagad Bahi*, No. 34, V.S. 1885/1828 AD.
10. *Khalisa Gawan ri Hasil Bahis, Basta* Nos. 1-3, V.S. 1807-1870, R.S.A., Bikaner.
11. Ibid.
12. *Chhoot Ra Kagad* (Papers of Remission) have been appended to almost all *Kagad Bahis* pertaining to the period record the exemptions and remissions in the land revenue and other taxes and cesses. For instance, see *Kagad Bahi*, No. 1, V.S. 1811; No. 3, V.S. 1827; No. 5, V.S. 1838; No. 9, V.S. 1851; No. 12, V.S. 1859, R.S.A., Bikaner.
13. *Kagadon Ri Bahi*, No. 11, V.S. 1857/1800 AD.
14. Sharma, R.C., *Settlement Geography of the Indian Desert*, Delhi 1972, p. 30; Statistical Extracts, Rajasthan, 1965, pp. 18-19.
15. Fagan, P.G., op. cit., pp. 6-7.
16. Ibid., pp. 3-6.
17. *Bahi Hasil Re Lekhe Ri*, V.S. 1748/1691 AD; *Bahi Pargana Ri*, No.1, V.S. 1749-57/1692-1700 AD, R.S.A., Bikaner.
18. Fagan, P.G., op. cit., pp. 3-6.
19. Ibid., pp. 3-6, 7-8.
20. Ibid., pp. 7-8; Erskine, *The Western Rajputana States Residency and The Bikaner Agency*, Allahabad, 1908.
21. Fagan, P.G., op. cit., pp. 7-8.
22. Ibid.
23. *Sawa Bahi Mandi Reni*, No. 1, V.S. 1815/1758 AD, R.S.A., Bikaner.
24. *Bahi Hasil Re Lekhe Ri*, No. 7, V.S. 1748/1691 AD, R.S.A., Bikaner.
25. Fagan, P.G., op. cit., pp. 7-8; *Rajasthan District Gazetteer, Bikaner*, Jaipur, 1972, p. 132.
26. Ibid.
27. Ibid.
28. Ibid.
29. *Sawa Bahi Mandi Sadar Bikaner*, No.16, V.S. 1827/1770 AD, f 48(b); No. 22, V.S. 1837/1780 AD, f 32(b); Col. Tod, op. cit., p. 225.
30. Fagan, P.G., op. cit., pp. 7-8.
31. *Bahi Hasil Re Lekhe Ri*, No. 7, V.S. 1748/1691 AD *Bahi Pargana Ri*, No.1, V.S. 1749-57/1692-1700 AD.
32. *Sawa Bahi Rajgarh*, No. 8, V.S. 1855/1798 AD, f.22(b).
33. *Sawa Bahi Rajgarh*, No. 11, V.S. 1865/1808 AD, f. 103.
34. *Rajasthan District Gazetteer, Bikaner*, p. 130.
35. Ojha, G.H., op. cit., p. 13.
36. *Sawa Bahi Mandi Sadar Bikaner*, No. 16, V.S. 1827/1770 AD, f.48(b);

No. 22, V.S. 1837/1780 AD, f.32(b); Powlett, P.W., *Gazetteer of Bikaner State*, Bikaner, pp. 150-51.

37. *Sawa Bahi Mandi Sadar Bikaner*, No. 3, V.S. 1805/1748 AD, f.63; *Bahi Hasil Re Lekhe Ri*, V.S. 1748/1691 AD.
38. For the period 1669-1693 AD during Anup Singh's reign (1669-1698 AD) the average per year land revenue including taxes/cesses comes to Rs. 1,54,024 (as Rs. 38,50,605 in all has been realized for 25 years) and it is quite a significant collection. For detail see the table of the total land revenue realization in the state during 1669-1693 AD appended at the last folio of the *Bahi Khalisa wa Pargana Re Jama Jod Ri*, V.S. 1726-50/1669-93, No. 99, Bikaner Records, R.S.A.B.
39. Habib, Irfan, *Agrarian System of Mughal India*, Bombay, 1963, p. 190; *The Cambridge Economic History of India*, Vol. I (1200-1750 c.) (ed.) T.R. Choudhary and Irfan Habib, Hydrabad, 1984, p. 235.
40. Ibid.; Siddiqi, N.A., *The Land Revenue Administration under the Mughals (1700-1750 AD)*, Bombay, 1970, pp. 41-42.
41. These components of Land Revenue have been shown in the *Bahi Khalisa Wa Pargana Re Jama Jod Ri*, No. 99, V.S. 1726-50/1669-93 AD, RSAB.
42. *Bhanchh* is a local term used for a cess or cesses realized by the state at times. For example, for the construction work in the fort of Bikaner a *Bhanchh* called *Shahar Koṭe Ri Bhanchh* was realized. Also, *Sahukari Bhanchh* was an annual cess on the merchants, traders and *Sarrofs* as well. Lalas, Sita Ram, *Rajasthani Hindi Sanskshipt Sabdakosh*, Vol. II, RORI Chopasani, Jodhpur, 1987, p. 280. *Bahi Haboob Ri*, V.S. 1851-53/1794-96 AD, Bikaner Bahiyat, RSAB.
43. *Hasil Bahis* of the state under various captions pertaining to different years (1700-1828 AD) have shown the *Jama* and the *Hasil* figures and the further sub-division of the land revenue under *Hasil Bhog* and *Hasil-Rokad-Bhanchh* see the *A Descriptive List of* Bikaner *Bahis*, Part I (17-19 c.) 1982, pp. 1-61 RSAB.
44. The *Bhog* has been defined as the land tax of the state share on the agricultural production. See Lalas, Sita Ram, *Rajasthani Shabdkosh*, Vol. III, Jodhpur, p. 3445; Sharma, G.N., *Social Life in Medieval Rajasthan*, 1st edition, Agra, 1968, p. 297. In Rajasthan the word *Bhog* is deemed at par with the Sacred *Bhog* (offerings) to the God. The *Raja* has been considered by the peasantry in the Indian political philosophy as at par with the God, Therefore, a first-share of its produce is offered to him. The *Bahis* of the state also use this term for the state share. See for detail definition

Khyat, No. 1, December, 1994, Marubhumi Sodh Samsthan, Dungargarh (Bikaner, Rajasthan) (ed.) B.L. Bhadani, p. 104.

45. *Bahi-Dhunwa-Deshprath Ri*, No. 68, V.S. 1810/1753 AD; *Lekha Bahi*, V.S. 1814/1757 AD; *Bahi-Khata-Khazana-Sadar*, V.S. 1852/1795 AD; Devra, G.S.L., *Nature of Incidence of Rokad-Raqam in the Land Revenue System of Bikaner State (1650-1750 AD)* P.I.H.C., 1976.
46. Ibid., *Bahi Khalisa Re Gawan Re Hasil Ri*, V.S. 1808-17/1751-1760 AD, *Basta* No. 2, Bikaner Records, R.S.A.B.
47. These cash collections were ultimately spread to the peasants village by village by the choudhary.
48. In the year 1794 AD in the Village *Gusaisar Bado* the difference between the *Jama* and *Hasil* was of 351 *maunds* of grain, *Kagad Bahi* No. 9, V.S. 1851/1794 AD f. 38, and *Kagad Bahi*, No. 3, V.S. 1827/1770 AD f. 12.
49. *Bahi Khalisa Re Gawan Re Hasil Ri*, V.S. 1808-17/1751-60 AD op. cit, Also see *Jama-Bandi-Ra-kagad* in various *Kagad Bahis* No. 2, 8, 11, op. cit., Bikaner Records, R.S.A.B.
50. *Hasil Bahis* are one of the important series of revenue collection in the state, preserved in the Rajasthan State Archives, Bikaner (RSAB)for the period 17th to 19th century. These *Bahis* contain peasants wise/village wise/*chira* wise (Revenue unit) details of statistics of the land revenue. See A Descriptive List of Bikaner *Bahis*, op. cit., pp. 1-61.
51. *Kagad Bahis* are another important series of *Bahis* wherein state orders pertaining to various administrative aspects including land revenue have been mentioned. 'The *Jama Bandi Ra Kagad*, The *Chhoot Ra Kagad, Sanad Aur Likhat Ra Kagad, Prachun Kagad*, including others are useful papers appended in the *Bahis*. See A Descriptive List of Bikaner *Bahis*, op. cit., pp. 120-38.
52. *Kagad Bahi*, No. 3, V.S. 1827/1770 AD records thus ''थांहरे तीजे हेसे री जमी छै .... हेसो तीजो रो ओईडो (खरच) देजो वा. हेसो तीजो री धुवां रकमां लागै छै सु चुकाय देजो।'' (Your land pertains to one-third part..... you pay expenses and *Dhuwa* amount at the one-third rate as well).
53. *Kagad Bahi*, No. 3, V.S. 1827/1770 AD, f. 31,. RSAB.
54. *Kagad Bahi*, No. 4, V.S. 1831/1774 AD, and No. 5, V.S. 1838/1781 AD, f. 48.
55. The word *Kunta* has been very frequently used in the *Kagad Bahi* and the *Hasil Bahis*. See, for instance, *Kagad posh sudi*-1, *Kagad Bahi*, No. 5, V.S. 1838/1781 AD, f. 6.
56. Sharma, G.N., *Rajasthan through the Ages*, Part II (1300-1761 AD). Bikaner, 1990, p. 314 (17a).

57. Literally, *Huwaldar* was a local term. He was one whom responsibility of anything been handed over, hence called *Huwaladar*. The word has been many times mentioned in the *Bahis*. As per his functions, it is clear that a *Huwaldar* was primarily an official made responsible for the realization of the state revenue. There were two categories of *Huwaldar*–one, has been called *Daftar Ra Huwaldar*, obviously he was to manage the office. The other one has been called *Thod Ra Huwaldar* (*Thod* means source of income) means he was responsible for collecting the state revenue, i.e. the income of specific source.
58. *Sohna* was a revenue official, considered an expert in estimation of the crop rate or total yield in the field. He used to estimate by conjecture the production of crop in a field.
59. The Jat *Asamis* of Village Seruna had complained against the excessive assessment to the ruler in the year 1789 AD. *Kagad Bahi*, No. 8, V.S. 1846/1789 AD f. 9. (कूतो मारे अकरो मांडियों छै। ने कूंतो सुणायो न छै सु गांव बीसताल छै) (The *Kunta*, i.e. the assessment has excessively been entered. It was not conveyed even. So, the village was deserted.) Another complaint was made to the ruler by the choudhary Thakursi of village Gusaisar against the higher assessment in the year 1794 AD *Kagad Bahi*, No. 9, V.S. 1851/1794 AD, f. 38.
60. *Kagad Bahi*, No. 4, V.S. 1831/1774 AD, f. 31.
61. Siddiqi, N.A., op. cit., pp. 50-52.
62. Sharma, G.C., *The Administrative System of Rajputs*, New Delhi, 1979, p. 31.
63. Ibid.
64. *Bahi Halgat Ri*, V.S. 1817/1760 AD Basta No. 1. *Ekaliya Hal* meant tilling of the land once either horizontally or vertically, but *Doleda Hal* meant tilling of the land twice horigentally and vertically in both directions. Obviously, The production in the desert would be higher this way than the former tilling method.
65. Incidentally, a *Parwana* of 1796 AD while allotting a piece of land to a carpenter Ram Chand in village Kodamdesar records as "*Bighas 200 consisting of 40 ploughs*". This shows that 1 plough was equivalent to only 5 *bighas* of land. *Parwana* dtd. *Jyesth Sudi* 4, V.S. 1853, *Parwana Bahi*, No. 4, VS 1800-1900, Rampuria Records, RSAB. Whereas, G.C. Sharma, (*The Administrative System of the Rajputs*) mentioned that 1 plough was equivalent to 50 to 60 *bighas* of land. B.L. Bhadani also mentions that in Marwar also one plough consisted of 50 *bighas* of land as *Muhnot Nensi* has quoted it in his *Marwar Re Paregna Ri Vigat* (Part 1, p. 395) Cf. Bhadani,

B.L., *The Peasants, Artisans and the Entrepreneurs*, Jaipur, 1999, p. 214. (footnote)

66. *Pasayati* word has been used for a privileged category in our records. See *Kagad Bahi*, No. 4, V.S. 1831/1774 AD, f. 31; *Parwana Bahi*, V.S. 1800-1900/1743-1843 AD f. 232. But, in Wilson's Glossary of Revenue terminology the words like *Pussaita* and *Pasethi* have been defined varyingly. *Pussaita* means-a rent free land allotted to the different orders of village servant (In Gujrat) or for religious purpose and for *Pasethi* means the head cultivator of a village. See the Glossary, p. 405. Lalas, Sita Ram explains it as an assignee of a land on concessional rates in lieu of his services to the state. *Rajasthani Hindi Sankshipt Sabda Kosh*, Part-II, Jodhpur, 1987, p. 48. In Marwar also the same terminology *Pasayati* is used. See Bhadani, B.L., op. cit., p. 123 (footnote).
67. Land Revenue from Bhati Sultan Singh and his Rajput *Chakars* were exempted. Kagad., dtd. *Bhadwa sudi* 12, *Kagad Bahi*, No. 3, V.S. 1827/1770 AD *Parwana Bahi*, No. 4, V.S. 1800-1900, V.S. 1885, First *Asadh Sudi* 6, f. 233.
68. *Patwaris, Sohnas*, military personnel or some menials were granted the *Pasayati* privileges. *Parwana Bahi* Bikaner V.S. 1800/1743 AD, p. 232.; *Kagad Bahi*, No. 4, V.S. 1831/1774 AD ff. 25, 31.
69. *Kagad Bahi*, No. 3, op. cit., *Kagad* dtd. *Asoj Badi* 14.
70. *Bahi Halgat Re Hasil Ri*, No. 67, V.S. 1809-22/1752-65 AD.
71. *Bahi Pargana Punia Re Hasil Ro Lekho*, No. 123, V.S. 1884-87/1827-30 AD; *Bahi Punia Re Pargana Ro Khato*, No. 76, V.S. 1824/1767 AD.
72. *Bikaneri Bigha* was 1/36 part of an acre. The measurement of land was done by a unit known as *Dori* of twenty *Hath* (and arm-length). *Kagad Bahi* No. 4, V.S. 1831/1774 AD, f. 19.
73. *Kagad Bahi* No. 11, V.S. 1857/1800 f. 91; No. 15, V.S. 1866/1809AD.
74. *Sawa Bahi*, Rajgarh No. 8, V.S. 1850/1793 AD.
75. Fagan, P.G., *Report on the Settlement of the Khalisa Village of Bikaner State*, Bikaner, 1893.
76. *Bahi Khalisa Re Gawan Ri*, V.S. 1827/1770 AD *Habub Bahi* V.S. 1851/1794 AD; See *Kagad Asadh Badi* 12, *Kagad Bahi*, No. 9, V.S. 1851/1794 AD f.40.
77. *Bhaiya Collection*-letter *Asadh Sudi* 10 V.S. 1872/July 16th, 1815 AD, RSAB, *Bhaiya*, Nathmal and Jethmal Mathur were brothers and served the state on important positions as revenue officials. Their correspondence and records have a historical significance for the period under study. Their collection is preserved in the Rajasthan Archives, Bikaner and captioned as *Bhaiya* Records.

78. *Kagad Bahi* No. 3, op. cit., ff. 26, 34; No. 16, VS 1867/1810 AD, f. 26.
79. *Habub Bahi*, V.S. 1851/1794 AD.
80. *Khalisa Gawan ri Bahi*, VS 1812/1755 AD; *Bhaiya Collection*-Letter dtd. February, 10, 1821 AD; Fagan's Settlement Report, p. 19.
81. *Guwadi* is a local term which has been used for a family of a peasant. The locality where families of the same caste usually lived was termed as *Guwad* (locality). The word *Baas* has also been used for a *Mohalla* in villages of Bikaner.
82. *Kagad Bahi*, No. 4, V.S. 1831/1774 AD, f. 39, 47; Col. Tod, Vol. II, op. cit. p. 161.
83. *Kagad Bahi*, No. 3, op. cit., p. 67.
84. Ibid., f. 68.
85. *Huwaldar* was an official discharging the functions as revenue official was entrusted with the work of land revenue realization on a certain remuneration. Some *Huwaldars* also worked on the salary basis, see *Huwala kagad, Kagad Bahi*, No. 2, V.S. 1820/1763 AD, ff. 2-10.
86. *Daroga* was a police official to assist *Huwaldars* in his work.
87. *Choudhary* was a revenue-cum-administrative official in the village. He was responsible for collecting the revenue as well as enforcing the state orders. He offered an important linkage between the state and the rural population.
88. *Patwari* was a village official, next to the *Choudhary* and enjoyed state recognised hereditary assignment. His main function was to maintain the land records of village and assist in the work of assessment as well as realization.
89. *Sohna* was a land revenue assessor.
90. *Amin* was responsible for the revenue assessment.
91. *Potedar* was a *Khazanchi* or incharge of the state treasury.
92. *Kagad Phagum Badi* 8, *Kagad Bahi*, No. 3, op. cit., f. 24.
93. *Kagad Asoj Badi*-13, *Kagad Badi*, No. 5, V.S. 1838/1781 AD, f. 44.
94. See *Huwala Kagad, Kagad Bahi*, No. 2, 3, 8, 11, op. cit.
95. Ibid.; *Kagad Bahi*, No. 4, V.S. 1831/1774, f. 29.
96. Fagans, P.G., *Settlement Report of Bikaner*, pp. 14-17.
97. The *Bhogta* was the assignee of land or village, He was termed as *Bhogta* because he enjoyed the *Bhog* i.e. land revenue. *Kagad* Asoj *Badi*-5, *Kagad Bahi*, No. 3, op. cit., RSAB.
98. *Kagad, Kartik Sudi*, 3, *Kagad Bahi*, No. 3, op. cit., RSAB.
99. *Kagad, Asoj Badi*, 5, *Kagad Bahi*, No. 3, op. cit., RSAB.
100. *Bhumias* were the hereditory right holder of land and their land was called *Bhom*. *Bika, Bidawat* and *Kandhlot* Rathors alongwith

Bhatis and *Johiyas* were enjoying such *Bhom* rights. They paid only quit-rent to the state known as *Bhombad*.

101. *Kagad Bahi*, No. 2, V.S. 1820/1763 AD ff.2-3, *Kagad Bahi*, No. 4, op. cit., f.44.
102. *Kagad Bahi*, No. 8, V.S. 1846/1789 AD, f.2.
103. *Kagad Bahi*, No. 2, op. cit., ff.2-3, No. 4, op. cit., f. 44.
104. *Kagad Bahi*, No. 11, V.S. 1857/1800 AD, f. 89, 208; No. 23 V.S. 1874/1817 AD, f. 159. The state used to issue orders directing the *Huwaldars, Muqatis* as well as *Jagirdars* that they should encourage, the cultivation, by inhabitating the new agrarian communities (i.e. new *'Guwadis'*) in the villages and also the peasants should not be ejected from their land.
105. *Kagad Bahi*, No. 8, *Chhoot Ra Kagad*, V.S. 1827/1770 AD.
106. *Kagad Bhadwa Sudi*, 15, *Kagad Bahi* No. 13, V.S. 1861/1804 AD.
107. The state insisted upon the Brahmins of village Jhajhu to pay the land revenue in to cash. *Kagad* dtd. *Kartik Sudi* 3, *Kagad Bahi* No. 3, op. cit., f. 11.
108. *Bahi Khalisa Re Gawan Re Hasil Ri, Basta* No. 2, V.S. 1807-1817/ 1750-1760 AD.
109. Webb, W.W., *Currencies of the Hindu States of Rajputana*, pp. 45-63; Sharma, G.S., *Marwari Vyapari*, Bikaner 1988, p. 24.
110. A Research paper was presented in the Rajasthan History Congress, Jodhpur session, in February, 2001. Mathur, K.L., The Rate of Land Tax and its Economic Pressure on the Peasantry during the Second Half of the 18th Century, PRHC, Jodhpur, Session, 2001, pp. 36-42.
111. A Descriptive List of Bikaner *Bahis*, op. cit., pp. 1-16.
112. Ibid. pp. 120-38.
113. *Kagad Bahi*, No. 9, V.S. 1851/1794 AD f.51.
114. *Kagad Bahi*, No. 3, op. cit. The land in the state was generally the desert land, but even then as per its type and productivity and the irrigational facilities the rate of land tax also differed accordingly. For example Rs. 2 was levied, per *Hal* (plough) cultivation on the *Banjar* (Barren) land, and Rs. 3 for *Mazrua* (i.e. ordinary land but comparatively better than *Banjar*) was levied, likewise Rs. 4 or 5 was realized on the irrigated or more productive land called as *Chahi* and *Beri* land in the *Halgat* system in 1755 AD. See *Bahi Khalisa Ri* No. 1, V.S. 1812/1755 AD, Bikaner. It is also to be noted that one who attempted to cultivate new lands for the first time, encouragement was provided to him by applying a concessional rate or full exemptions in land revenue. *Kagad Bahi*, No. 3, *Asoj Badi*-14, and *Kagad Bahi*, No. 9, op. cit. f. 40.

115. Most of the region of Bikaner state comprises desert and it completely depended on rains for the crops. Being uncertainty of rains and the desert soil the *Dasturs* were not formulated. Probably due to these reasons the *Zabt* system was not implemented in this region.
116. *Gaon-Jodhasar-Re-Hasil-Ro-Lekho-Hasil Bahi,* V.S. 1747/1690 AD.
117. *Kagad Bahi,* No. 5, V.S. 1838/1781 AD, f.44.
118. *Kagad Bahi,* No. 9, V.S. 1851-52/1794-95 AD, ff. 25-26.
119. *Kagad Magh Sudi* 10, *Kagad Bahi,* No. 13, V.S. 1861/1804 AD f. 188. It is interesting that the peasants began to hide their produce of grain in the pits to abstain from the *Adhiya.* A peasant did hide 60 *maunds* of *Bajra* in village Bigga to abstain from *Adhiya. Kagad Bahi* No. 17, V.S. 1867/1810 AD. This shows that it had some adverse bearings on the peasantry. *'Kagad Bahi'*, No. 16, V.S. 1866/ 1809 AD, f. 18; No. 19/1, V.S. 1870/1813 AD, f. 73.
120. *Bahi Gaon Jodhasar-Re Hasil Ro Lekho,* op. cit., also see *Chhoot-Ra-Kagad, Kagad Bahi,* No. 3 & 4, op. cit.
121. *Kagad Bahi,* No. 11, V.S. 1857/1800 AD, f. 137.
122. *Jama-Bandhi-Ra-Kagad, Kagad Bahi,* No. 8, V.S. 1846/1789 AD.
123. *Prachun-Kagad, Kagad Bahi,* No. 5, V.S. 1838/1781 AD f. 44.
124. *Bahi Halgat Ri,* Basta No. 1, V.S. 1817/1760 AD.
125. Ibid.
126. *Kagad Bahi,* No. 5, V.S. 1838/1781 AD, f. 20.
127. *Jama-Bandhi-Ra-Kagad, Kagad Bahi,* No. 6, V.S. 1839/1782 AD f. 18. (Village Khedado).
128. The Jats of village *Jatawas* in the year 1774 complained in the *Darbar* against the *Muqati* that he was demanding more than what was already fixed as land revenue from them. *Kagad Bahi,* No. 4, op. cit., f. 44.
129. *Kagad Bahi,* No. 9, V.S. 1851/1794 AD, f. 51.
130. *Bahi Paragna Punia Re - Hasil Re Lekho Ri,* No. 123, V.S. 1884/1727 AD.
131. Ibid.
132. *Bahi Khalisa Re Gawan Ri,* V.S. 1853/1796 AD. These villages are (1) Jasarasar (2) Gajroopdesar (3) Atbhomdesar (4) Saloodo (5) Jeglo Ro Bas (6) Sizkau (7) Penchu Ro Bas Hakima Ro (8) Masuri (9) Likhmisar (10) Kilonsar (11) Kisturdesar (12) Radbi Subhaghdesar (13) Biggo (14) Tejrasar (15) Jakhasar.
133. *Kagad Bahi,* No. 11, V.S. 1857/1800 AD, f. 26.
134. *Habub-Bahi,* V.S. 1831/1774 AD, *Kagad Bahi,* No. 22, V.S. 1873/ 1816 AD
135. Ibid.

136. Ibid.
137. See *Kagad Bahi*, No. 20, V.S. 1871/1814 AD, ff. 222-30. No. 21, V.S. 1872/1815 AD, ff. 66-71, 103-108; No. 13, V.S. 1861/1804 AD, No. 15, V.S. 1866/1809 AD, as well. The letters of Bhaiya Nath Mal, the *Huwaldar* of Nohar of year V.S. 1871-72/1814-15 AD also reflects that villages were being deserted due to the excessive burden of taxes during the period, see Bhaiya Nathmal's Letters-*Bhaiya Records*, Rajasthan State Archives, Bikaner; Col. Tod. (Part II, pp. 1182-83) also testify that population of the region was decreasing. Consequently, in the year 1816 AD. Surat Singh withdrew these taxes/cesses except *Rekh* on Jagirdars and *Rukhwali Bhanch*, See *Kagad Bahi*, No. 22, V.S. 1873/1816 AD, ff. 191-92.
138. *Kagad Bahi*, No. 3, op. cit., *Kagad* dtd. *Kartik Badi* 2.
139. Ibid. f. 13, *Mingsar Sudi* 5.
140. *Kagad Bahi*, No. 8, op. cit., '*Prachum Kagad*'.
141. *Kagad Bahi*, No. 11, V.S. 1857/1800 AD.
142. *Prachum Kagad, Kagad Bahi*, No. 8, op. cit.
143. Ibid.
144. Tax for marriages in the Royal Family called *Neota, Kagad Bahi*, No. 3, op. cit., ff. 39-40. *Bhaiya Record, Neota Letters*, 1803/1806 *Basta* No. 2.
145. *Nazar* was a charge given on the occasions of marriage, birth or Coronation etc.; whereas *Peshkashi* was levied by the superior from his subordinate on assignment of an office or for inception of a new business by a trader or businessman, *Bahi Peshkashi Ri*, V.S. 1817/1760 AD, V.S. 1860/1803 AD.
146. *Kagad Bahi*, No. 3, op. cit., f. 34.
147. *Bahi-Chira-Re Bharti-mein-Khat Baqi Teri Vigat*, V.S. 1809-13/1752-56 AD.
148. Devra, G.S.L., *Rajasthan Ki Prashashnic Vyavstha* (Hindi), Bikaner, 1981, p. 202. The percentage of gap was upto 15.33% in the second half of the 18th century.
149. Singh, Dilbagh, 'Peasant's Indebtedness in the State of Bikaner (1887-1943 AD)', PRHC, VII Session Pali, 1974 refer to the practice of owing loans from the *Bohras* and *Sahukars* in their exigencies.
150. *Kagad Bahi*, No. 3, op. cit., dtd. *Kartik Sudi-2; Margshish Sudi-5*, *Kagad Bahi*, No. 4, V.S. 1831/1774 AD, ff. 62-63; *Kagad Bahi*, No. 6, V.S. 1839/1782, f. 50.
151. *Bahi Halgat Ri*, V.S. 1802-07/1745-50 AD.
152. *Bahi Khalsa Re Gawan Ri*, V.S. 1810/1753 AD, *Basta* No. 2.
153. See A Descriptive List of Bikaner *Bahies*, Bikaner, RSAB.

154. *Bahi Dhunwa Despath Ri*, No. 5, VS 1810/1753 AD; *Bahi Khalisa Re Gawan Ri Hasil Ri*, VS 1808/1751 to 1817/1760 AD; *Basta* No. 2, Bikaner Records, RSAB.
155. *Bahi Dhuwa Ri*, V.S. 1786/1729 AD, No. 90, Col. Tod. Part II, p. 1157. *Bahi Dhunwa-Deshprath Ri*, - V.S. 1810/1753 AD, No. 68.
156. *Bahi Khalisa Gawan Ri*, *Basta* No. 2, V.S. 1809/1751 AD
157. Ibid.
158. Ibid.
159. Ibid.
160. *Bahi Khalisa Gawan Ri*, V.S. 1809, 1810, 1817, *Basta* No. 2.
161. An indigenous system of procuring the grain in a pit or clean flat surface properly covered by cow dung or mixed with sand, so as to retain the grains for longer time, *Bahi Khalsa Re Gawa Ri*, *Basta* No. 2, V.S. 1810/1753 AD
162. *Gaon Kalu Re Hasil Ro Lekho*, *Bahi Khalisa Gawa Ri*, *Basta* No. 2, V.S. 1808/1751 AD
163. *Lekho-Charo-Sehtero-Desh-Ro-Gawan Aur-Futkar-Gawan Ro*, *Bahi Khalisa Gawa Ri*, V.S. 1809-10/1752-73 AD, R.S.A., Bikaner.
164. *Bahi Dhunwa Desprath Ri*, V.S. 1810/1753 AD, No. 68.
165. Ibid.
166. Ibid.
167. Ibid.
168. Nensi-*Vigat*, op. cit., Part I, p. 159; Wilson's Glossary, p. 474.
169. Sharma, G.C., op. cit., p. 126; It was identical to *Serino* of Eastern Rajasthan, See Singh, Dilbagh, *The State, Land Lords and Peasants*, Delhi, 1990, p. 123 (Appendix-I). Sharma, Dashrath, *Lectures on Rajput History*, p. 147, says that it was 2 *seers* per *maund*.
170. *Bahi Gaon Jodhasar Re Hasil Ro Lekho*, No. 15, V.S. 1747/1690 AD
171. Ibid.
172. *Bahi Khalisa Gawan Re Hasil Ri*, V.S. 1810/1753 AD, f. 2.
173. *Bahi Khalisa Gawan Re - Lekho - Budhnao-Ro*, V.S. 1810/1753 AD, 7 *Seers* were realized from the village.
174. *Village Udarasar Ro Lekho - Bahi Khalisa Gawan Ri*, V.S. 1810/1753 AD
175. Lalas, *Rajasthani Hindi Sankshipt Sabdkosh*, Vol. I, Jodhpur 1986, p. 341.
176. *Bahi Gaon Jodhasar Re Hasil Ri*, op. cit.
177. Ibid.
178. *Kagad Bahi*, No. 10, V.S. 1854/1797 AD; No. 14, V.S. 1864/1807 AD, ff. 275, 294.
179. Wilson's Glossary, p. 272. In Eastern Rajasthan it was paid to *Kayal* (Weighman) when the grains was sold to merchant. The

rate of taxation was Rs. 10 per hundred rupees worth of grains sold. Gupta, S.P., *The System of Rural Taxation*, P.I.H.C., 1972, p. 285.

180. *Bahi Khalisa Re Gawan Ri-Lekho Gaon Rovanio Ro*, V.S. 1907/1850 AD *Basta* No. 3, Bikaner records, RSAB.
181. A Hindi word for all payments from the village fund, apart from the land revenue and so including the perquisites of the various officials and the 'village expenses', is *Malba*. See Wilson's Glossary, op. cit., p. 324. This term has been quoted in the state *bahis* very frequently, e.g. *Kagad Bahi*, No. 9, V.S. 1851/1794 AD; No. 13, V.S. 1861/1804 AD. In the Mughal documents also the term *Malba* has frequently been used signifying, in general, the officials' private exactions from the villages. Cf. Habib, Irfan, *Agrarian System of Mughal India (1556-1707 AD)*, 2nd ed., OUP, New Delhi, p. 154 (f.n.).
182. *Kagad Bahi* No. 9, V.S. 1851/1794 AD
183. *Kagad Bahi* No. 13, V.S. 1861/1804 AD, *Bhadwa Sudi* 6, RSAB. For further details see my research article pub. in *The Jats: Their Role & Countribution to the Socio-Economic Life and Polity of the North & North-West India*, Vol. 2 (ed.) Vir Singh, Originals, Delhi, 2006, entitled *A Note on the Malba Cess in the 18th Century Bikaner State*, pp. 227-36.
184. There are descriptions of these eventualities in the *Kagad Bahis*, for examples see *Chhoot Ra Kagad*, '*Kagad Bahi*' No. 1, V.S. 1811/ 1754 AD, No. 2, VS 1820/1763 AD, RSAB.
185. The period from 1745 to 1818 AD was predominantly the period of instability, revolts, disturbances, attacks and interferences due to lack of strong and effective Mughal protection.
186. See for detailed features of geography of the Bikaner state - chapter: Geographical and Historical Background.
187. *Chhoot Ra Kagad*, *Kagad Bahis* No. 1 to 7, V.S. 1811; to1840; No. 9 to 11, V.S. 1851 to 1857; V.S. 1872; No. 26, V.S. 1877; No. 34, V.S. 1885, RSAB.
188. (i) See chapter Geographical and Historical Background.
     (ii) *Report on the Administration of Bikaner for 1936-37*, p. 1, RSAB.
     (iii) Erskine, *Rajputana Gazetteer*, Vol. III A, p. 309.
189. Gahlot, J.S., *Rajasthani Krishi Kahavaten* (The Meteorological Wisdom of Rajputana) Introduction, Jodhpur, 1941, p. 1. A couplet for famine is famous in Bikaner as under:
     ''पग पूगल धड़ कोटड़े, उदरज बीकानेर। भूलो चूको जोधपुर, ठावो जैसलमेर।''
     ("My (Famine) feet remain in Pugal (a part of Bikaner), my head in kotada (Marwar) and my belly in Bikaner, And sometimes, I

(Famine) can be found in Jodhpur but Jaisalmer is my permanent residence.").

190. *Kagad Bahi*, No. 1, V.S. 1811/1754 AD; Erskine, op. cit., pp. 354-55.
191. The famine of 1783 and 1796 AD are respectively known as *Chalisa* (Famine of V.S. 1840) and *Trepania* (Famine of V.S. 1853); Sharma, G.N., op. cit., p. 346.
192. Erskine, op. cit., pp. 354-55.
193. These rulers were Gaj Singh (1746-1787), Raj Singh (1787), Pratap Singh (1787), Surat Singh (1787-1828) and Ratan Singh (1728-1851 AD).
194. *Chhoot-Ra-Kagad, Kagad Bahi*, No. 1, V.S. 1811/1754 AD; Erskine, pp. 354-55.
195. *Kagad Bahi*, No. 1, V.S. 1811/1754 AD, *Kartik Badi* 5.
196. Ibid., *Falgun Sudi* 6.
197. *Kagad Bahi*, No. 4, V.S. 1831/1774 AD, f. 44., *Posh Badi* 14.
198. *Kagad Bahi*, No. 6, V.S. 1839/1782 AD, f. 55.
199. *Kagad Bahi*, No. 1, V.S. 1811/1754 AD, *Kartik Bahi* 12.
200. *Kagad Bahi*, No. 3, V.S. 1827/1770 AD, f. 11.
201. *Kagad Bahi*, No. 4, V.S. 1831/1774 AD, f. 28.
202. *Kagad Bahi*, No. 1, V.S. 1811/1754 AD
203. *Kagad Bahi*, No. 2, V.S. 1820/1763 AD, *Asoj Badi* 8.
204. *Kagad Bahi*, No. 3, V.S. 1827/1770 AD, f. 27.
205. *Kagad Bahi*, No. 4, V.S. 1831/1774 AD, ff. 44, 52, 56; *Kagad Bahi*, No. 5, V.S. 1838/1781 AD, f. 43.
206. *Kagad Bahi*, No. 5, V.S. 1838/1781 AD, f. 43.
    Kagad Bahi, No. 4, V.S. 1831/1774 AD, f. 56.
207. Powlett, P.W. writes in his *Gazetteer of Bikaner* that 'during the famines of 1868-69 AD, the prices of grains in Bikaner gradually went up to 6 seers the rupee and there was little difference between the prices of the different kinds; just before the famines *Bajra* was 35 *seers* (British) and *Moth* at 45 seers. The people consider that a famine has begun when *Bajra* is at 15 seers', p. 108.
208. *Kagad Bahi*, No. 7, V.S. 1840/1783 AD, *Mingsar Badi* 7.
209. *Kagad Bahi*, No. 6, V.S. 1839/1782 AD, *Vaisak Badi* 3.
210. *Kagad Bahi*, No. 4, V.S. 1831/1774 AD, f. 52.
211. *Kagad Bahi*, No. 9, V.S. 1851/1794 AD, f. 21, *Kartik Sudi* 7.
212. *Kagad Bahi*, No. 4, V.S. 1831/1774 AD, f. 6, *Asoj Sudi* 13.
213. *Kagad Bahi*, No. 4, V.S. 1831/1774 AD, f. 6, *Kartik Badi* 3.
214. Ibid., f. 7., *Kagad Bahi*, No. 7, VS 1840/1783 AD, f. 21. *Mingsar Badi* 11.
215. *Kagad Bahi*, No. 2, V.S. 1820/1763, *Magh Sudi* 15.

216. *Kagad Bahi*, No. 13, V.S. 1861/1804 AD, *Sawan Sudi* 6.
217. *Byav Bahi* V.S. 1889/1832 AD, *Lekha Va Jama Kharch Ri Bahi*, V.S. 1896/1839 AD, RSAB.
218. *Kagad Bahi*, No. 34, V.S. 1885/1828 AD
219. *Kagad Bahi*, No. 50, V.S. 1900/1843 AD
220. *Kagad Bahi*, No. 11, V.S. 1857/1800 AD, f. 137.
    Kagad Bahi, No. 3, V.S. 1827/1770 AD, f. 27.
221. *Kagad Bahi*, No. 11, V.S. 1857/1800 AD, ff. 123, 140, 141.
222. *Bahi Kagdon Ri*, No. 33/1, V.S. 1884/1827 AD, f. 176 (a).
223. *Kagad Bahi*, No. 10, V.S. 1854/1797 AD, f. 99.
224. *Chhoot Ra Kagad, Kagad Bahi* No. 1, V.S. 1811/1754 AD, *Posh Sudi* 5.
225. *Kagad Bahi*, No. 1, V.S. 1811/1754 AD
    Kagad Bahi, No. 7, V.S. 1840/1783 AD, f. 11(b), f. 13.
    Prachoom Kagad, Kagad Bahi, No. 9, V.S. 1851/1794 AD f. 34, *Jyestha Sudi* 14.
    Kagad Bahi, No. 10, V.S. 1854/1797 AD. The Bahi contains ample instances of returning of *Guwadis* (Families) to their native villages even after 40-50 years. They were restored their *Khets* (Fields) as well as house to live in as far as possible alongwith the remission in taxes. They were asked to increase the land under plough and further concessions would only apply, *Kagad Bahi* No. 11, V.S. 1857/1800 AD, ff. 137, 138.
226. *Kagad Bahi*, No. 3, V.S. 1827/1770 AD, f. 6.
227. *Kagad Bahi*, No. 11, V.S. 1857/1800 AD.
228. *Kagad Bahi*, No. 10, V.S. 1854/1797 AD, *Asadh Badi* 6.
229. *Kagad Bahi*, No. 3, V.S. 1827/1770 AD, *Mingsar Sudi* 1.
230. *Kagad Bahi*, No. 7, V.S. 1840/1783 AD, f. 34; *Kagad Bahi*, No. 12, V.S. 1859/1802, f. 131.
231. *Kagad Bahi*, No. 11, V.S. 1857/1800 AD *Vaishak Badi*, 11.
232. *Kagad Bahi*, No. 50, V.S. 1900/1843 AD.
233. *Kagad Bahi*, No. 3, V.S. 1827/1770 AD First *Asadh Sudi* 1.
    Kagad Bahi, No. 12, V.S. 1859/1809 AD.
234. *Kagad Bahi*, No. 1, V.S. 1811/1754 AD; *Asoj Badi* 2 and 4, and *Kagad Bahi*, No. 5, *Kagad Bahi*, No. 7, V.S. 1840/1783 AD, *Kagad Bahi*, No. 11, V.S. 1857/1800 AD *Jama Bandi Ra Kagad*.
235. *Kagad Bahi*, No. 11, V.S. 1857/1800 AD, f. 90.
236. *Kagad Bahi*, No. 13, V.S. 1863/1806 AD, *Phalgun Badi* 4.
    Kagad Bahi, No. 3, V.S. 1827/1770 AD, f. 9(a).
237. *Parwana Magh Badi* 7, V.S. 1837/1780 AD, *Parwana Bahi* No. 4. V.S. 1800-1900, RSAB.
238. *Kagad Bahi*, No. 11, V.S. 1857/1800 AD, f. 286.
239. *Kagad Bahi*, No. 8, V.S. 1846/1789 AD, No. V.S. 1900/1843 AD.

4

The Non-Agricultural Sector: Sources of Income

The state participation in economic life of the people has existed since the beginning of the formation of the state. The state took a keen interest in the economic activities of the people. Besides, the agricultural sector, the state encouraged the trade and commercial activities, so that, its income could increase and moreover it would bring prosperity to the people. The sufficient income of the state and the economic prosperity of the people were considered the hallmark for a good state.

By joining the Mughal service in 1570 AD[1], the chiefs of Bikaner flourished along with the expansion of the Mughal empire in terms of political and economic powers.[2] But when the Mughal empire declined and disintegrated during the 18th century, it gave birth to some new succession states in the second half of the 18th century and the chiefs of these states (including Bikaner state) created their own political and fiscal infra-structures.[3] But the Rajput chiefs who had already their own states, however, managed to survive during the eclipse of the empire. It would be particularly interesting to gauge how the chiefs of Bikaner re-organized their economy and finances during the later 18th and early 19th century period (1746 to 1828 AD)[4], when they were neither the Mughal *Mansabdars* nor received any income from the centre.

During the process of recreation of the state after the detachment from the Mughal services[5] chiefs realized numerous taxes and cesses, over and above the land tax to meet their needs from traders and merchants, the professional groups and artisans. The state also derived income from its *jagirdars* and officials, religious fairs and fines and penalties. The mines and mineral products were also significant in the economy. Therefore, in this chapter an attempt has been made to analyse the sources of income from the non-agricultural sector.

Non-agricultural Sources of Income

The non-agricultural income can be classified into two following categories–

(1) Commercial Income

(2) Non-Commercial Income

Evidences of these two categories of income are mainly available in the *Sawa Bahis* and *Jagat Bahis* of various *Mandis* and *Chowkis* and also from the *Kagad Bahis* pertaining to the period of study.[6]

(1) Commercial Income

The commercial income of the state was mainly collected at the various commercial centres of the state located at towns and known locally as *Mandis*[7] (marketing centres). The outposts (*Baharli chowkis*) were situated at the bifurcations of the internal routes and the *Bholawanias*[8] deputed in villages also collected the commercial income which ultimately reached the *mandis* headquarters. It is seen that a widespread network of *Chowkis* and *Mandis* over the various trade routes in the state and the bordering villages had come into being in the latter half of the 18th century for the collection of commercial revenue in the form of different taxes, duties and cesses levied upon the movement of merchandize.[9]

The commercial income accruing to the *Mandis* and *Chowkis* can further be divided as per their nature into two following categories as under–

(i) *Jagat* Income[10]

(ii) Income other than *Jagat* (other taxes)

The amount collected from these two categories of commercial income are mentioned separately in the *Bahis*, therefore, it is convenient to understand and analyse them.

(i) *Jagat* Income

The *Jagat* formed an important part of the commercial income at *Mandis* and *Chowkis*. The word *Jagat*, which is a corrupt form of *Zaqat*, was a common term evolved for tax or duty realized on *Nekal* (export), *Pesar* (import) taxes and *Vahtivon* (duties on transiting goods through the state territory).

(a) *Nekal* (export) and *Pesar* (import) Taxes

The goods which were exported from a village, town or state were called *Nekal* (export), and goods which were imported in village, town or state were known as *Pesar* (import). These were the taxes realized on carriage of goods for sale from one town, or state to another town or state. The rates generally differed on the commodities. Essential goods like *gur*, sugar and grains were exempted for carrying on the occasion of marriages etc.[11] Rawat Hathi Singh was exempted from *jagat* on the occasion of marriage in his family in 1774 AD[12] We find the following rates of *nekal* and *pesar* taxes in the state in 1774 AD.

Table 4.1 : The *Jagat* Rates of *Nekal* and *Pesar* in *Mandi* Nohar in 1774 AD[13]

Sr. No. (1)	*Commodity (2)*	*Unit of Carriage (3)*	*Pesar or Nekal (4)*	*En route (5)*	*Applicable Rates (6)* Rs.	As.	Takka	Dam
1.	*Kiryana* (Grocery)	One camel load	*Pesar*	-	2	13	1	19
			Nekal	-	2	8	1	12
2.	*Aal*, and *kharki*	-do-	*Pesar*	-	2	1	4	25
			Nekal	-	2	8	1	12
3.	*Gur*, Sugar (Bura)	-do-	*Pesar*	-	1	2	0	0
			Nekal	-	1	0	0	0
4.	*Kut* (grind), *chob, sunth, kadu, harde*	-do-	*Pesar*	North	2	7	0	37
		-do-	*Nekal*	-	1	2	0	37
5.	*Dowti* (Cloth)	-do-	*Pesar*	*Desh* area	1	14	3	25
			Nekal	-	2	8	0	0

Contd...

Contd...

6.	*Khand* (sugar)	-do-	*Pesar*	-	2	4	3	25
			Nekal	Northern area	2	10	0	0
7.	Tobacoo	-do-	*Pesar*	Northern area	1	14	0	0
			Nekal& Pesar	*Desh*	1	8	3	25
8.	Fine cloth	One camel load	*Pesar*	-	2	8	6	25
			Nekal	-	2	0	5	12
9.	Rice	-do-	*Pesar*	-			8	25
			Nekal	-			11	37
			Nekal	Churu			13	49
10.	Wheat	-do-	*Pesar*	Northern area			7	0
11.	Gee & oil	-do-	*Pesar*	*Desh* Region			3	0
12.	Grains (*dhan*)	-do-	*Pesar*				3	0
13.	Salt	-do-	*Pesar*	-			3	49
			Nekal	Northern area			3	25
14.	*Moonj*	-do-	*Pesar*	-			10	12
			Nekal	Northern area			12	25
15.	*Til* (Seasame)	-d0-	*Pesar*	Northern area			6	6
			Pesar	*Desh* region			6	6
16.	*Lac Ratti*	One cowri	*Nekal*	-				31
17.	Indigo	-do-	*Pesar*	Northern area			6	6
			Pesar	*Desh* area			6	6
18.	*Sajji*	-do-	*Nekal & Pesar*	*Desh* area			5	6
			Nekal & Pesar	Northern area			5	12
19.	Cotton (*khari Dowtia and khalsi*)	-do-	*Nekal & Pesar*	-		12	1	0

Note: The rates in general were revised after granting a concession of 25% on old rates applicable in Nohar.

Table 4.1 evinces that the *Jagat* rates for the essential items like wheat, grains (*Dhan*), salt, *ghee*, oil, rice, *sajji* and *moonj* were kept low to encourage regular and smooth supply in the state. In 1809 AD when there was a short supply of the grain and the new crops of grains were being brought into the market of Bikaner, the state applied distinctive tariffs for the old and new grains and also the *Nekal* and *Pesar* as shown in Table 4.2 below.

Table 4.2 : Distinctive Tariffs for Grains in the State in 1809 AD[14]

Sr.No.	*Nekal/Pesar (Per camel load)*	*Rate for the Old grains Rs.*	*As.*	*New grains Rs.*	*As.*
1.	*Pesar* within the state territory	1	4	0	12
2.	*Nekal* out of the state territory	2	0	1	4

When the supply of grains were improved the following revised rates were applied as under–

			Rs.	*As.*
1.	If sold in territory	per camel load	0	8
2.	If carried to Ratangarh	-do-	0	12
3.	If exported out of territory	-do-	1	4

This shows that the state was conscious enough of the maintenance of the essential goods and therefore, regulated the tariffs according to the supply and scarcity of any essential goods and accordingly changed the rates of *nekal* and *pesar*.

Likewise, in 1819 AD village Agnao was newly founded and to facilitate the village various goods were needed to be imported/exported from Sindh to Bikaner and vice versa. The state enforced a concessional rate structure of *Nekal* and *Pesar* for the need as per the Table 4.3 below.

Thus, it is evident from the tables that the rates of *Nekal* and *Pesar* were altered and also regulated in exigencies and essential concesions. as required, were granted to meet the specific needs. The flow of goods in a particular direction was maintained and also restricted so as to maintain the prices.

Table 4.3: Concessional Tariffs of *Nekal* and *Pesar* for Village Agnao in 1819 AD[15]

Sr. No.	*Commodity*	*Weight*	*Nekal or Pesar*	*Rates*	
				Rs.	*As.*
(1)	*(2)*	*(3)*	*(4)*	*(5)*	
1.	*Sajji, multani mitti*	*1 camel load*	*Nekal Pesar*	1	
2.	Cotton, dry fruits, *bandedo* (packload), iron	-do-	-do-		8
3.	Tobacco, *sindhi* salt, alum, *sakud, majith*, salt	-do-			6
4.	Wheat, grain (*dhan*), *hirmich*	-do-	-do-		3
5.	Rice	-do-	-do-		4
6.	Silk, cosmetics, ivory, brass and bronze	-do-	-do-	1	4
7.	Cloth, pepper, wet fruits	-do-	-do-		12
8.	*Asafoetida*	-do-	-do-	1	2
9.	Horse	1 horse	-do-	1	0
10.	Camel	1 camel	-do-		5
11.	Indigo	1 camel load	-do-	1	12
12.	*Ghee*	-do-	-do-		10
13.	Oil	-do-	-do-		6
14.	Common salt	-do-	-do-		1¼
15.	*Moonj*	-do-	-do-		1¼

(b) *Vahtivon* (Transit duty)

This duty was realized on carriage of goods by traders through the state territory. It usually varied at places in the state. It was a fee for the protection which the states provided to the traders. It was also known as *Rahdari*. The rates of transit duty in Bikaner on different articles was usually charged per camel load.

We find quoted in the *Bahi* in 1750 AD to be applied for the various routes passing through Bikaner from Rajgarh to Marwar and Jaisalmer as per the following table 4.4.

Table 4.4: Rates of *Vahtivon* in 1750 AD in the State[16]

Sr. No. (1)	Commodity (2)	Unit (3)	Rates of transit duty Rs. (4)	As. (5)
1.	Kiryana	one camel load	3	12
2.	Gur, sugar	-do-	1	12
3.	Rice	-do-	1	8
4.	Sheep, goats[17]	per 100 animals	7	8

Important commodities as mentioned below were transported from Sindh and Bahawalpur towards Delhi, Hansi and Hissar through Suratgarh-Anupgarh and Hanumangarh routes. So, the state realized the following rates of transit duty (*vahtivon*) on the route as under in 1824 AD as per table 4.5.

Table 4.5: Rate of *Vahtivon* (Transit Duty) in 1824 AD in the State[18]

Sr. No.	Commodity	Unit	Total Rs.-As.	Transit Duty for Suratgarh Rs.-As.	Anupgarh Rs.-As.	Hanumangarh Rs.-As.
(1)	(2)	(3)	(4)	(5)	(6)	(7)
1.	*Kiryana* (grocery)	1 camel load	6-0	1-0	3-0	2-0
2.	*Asafoetida*	-do-				
	(i) first quality		12-0	2-0	6-0	4-0
	(ii) second quality		5-8	1-0	2-12	1-12
3.	Dry fruits	-do-	7-0	1-4	3-8	2-4
4.	*Chintz* cloth	-do-	7-0	1-4	3-8	2-4
5.	Horses	1 horse	7-0	1-4	3-8	2-4
6.	Camel/mare	1 camel/mare	5-0	1-0	2-8	1-8
7.	Silk, ivory, indigo	1 camel/ load	12-0	2-0	6-0	4-0
8.	Sugar, *gur*	-do-	3-4	0-8	1-8	1-4
9.	Sakud	-do-	3-0	0-8	1-8	1-0

Thus, the rates of these two tables, if matched, it will evince that the rates had considerably increased for the *Vahtivon* in the state. The state made a concerted effort to enhance its income by all means including the *Vahtivon*.

Additional Transit Duty

We find that an additional duty was also sometimes realized from traders for a *chowki* or a *mandi*. In the year 1797 AD such duty was realized (rates not quoted) for *Reni chowki* at the *Rajgarh mandi* while traders passed through Nagaur.[19] Also, when Ratangarh *mandi* was being newly established, an additional transit duty for exporting grains towards the Rajaldesar route was recovered from the *sahukars*. The *sahukars* resisted it and requested for its withdrawal; and it was withdrawn in 1810 AD.[20] The *sahukars* were also sometimes subjected to pay the expenses for any construction work. For construction of fortress in Ratangarh, a tax was realized in 1814 AD @ *Anna* 1 to 4 from traders.[21] This shows that the state did try to extract the contingent expenses also from the traders as far as possible.

Concessions and Exemptions in *Jagat*

The state granted partial and full exemption in taxes and duties to *sahukars* on many occasions. We find that 1/4 exemption in *jagat* was provided to Mian Syed Husain in 1804 AD.[22] Also Sarwar Din who settled in Anupgarh in 1774 AD was granted a concession of 1/5 in *jagat* if he engaged himself in import and export of commodity.[23] The *charans* of Sinthal Mewa Ram Sarupo etc. were granted a 1/2 the rate of importing grains, cotton and iron in 1804 AD.[24] The *Nayak* of Baladia (*Banjara*) Mansingh was granted a concession of Rs. 2 per 100 oxen of salt and other items to be carried into Lunkaransar, Reni, Nohar, Bhadra and Rajgarh via Bikaner from Sambhar and other places.[25] The prominent *sahukar* of the state Mirza Mal Potedar was exempted 50% of *jagat* on *nekal* and *pesar* of grains.[26] In the event of exigencies like famines or calamities full exemption was granted. In village Jeevandesar everything was destroyed due to fire and therefore, full exemption in taxes and duties were granted in 1797 AD.[27] The same concession was provided to the newly colonized villages.[28]

Some of the *sahukars* and *jagirdars* were granted a share in the collection of *jagat* revenue. In Ratangarh Vyas Moji Ram was assigned a share of 6 *dams* per camel load of grains received in *mandi*.[29] Likewise, *Jagat* Singh was allotted a share in the transit duty of Reni and Rajgarj @ 1 *takka* on certain consumable items in 1813 AD[30] presumably to honour their services. It seems that the state granted concessions and exemptions to those traders and merchants (i) who imported needful commodities like grains, salt, cotton and iron, (ii) who agreed to settle down in the state territory and also engaged in the export/import business. So that the state might earn more income. (iii) such privileges were also extended to commercial magnets of the state like Mirza Mal Potedar who was the respected business man of the state and had multifarious commercial activities.

Thus, the state enforced taxes and duties of varying rates and regulated them as per needs. The necessary concessions and exemption to some of the merchants and traders were also provided to encourage commercial activities in the state.

Apart from the *Jagat* realization, the state also realized some other following mentioned charges along with *Jagat* on goods. They are as under:

(c) Kiyali

Kiyali was a weighing charge which was realized from traders at the time of weighing the goods. The state appointed weigh men called *Kayals* or *Tolawatiyas*, who were authorized to weigh the goods and realize this tax called *Tolai* or *Kayali*. The rates also differed on commodities.[31]

(d) Moharno

It was a fee for putting a seal (seal is locally called *Mohar*) on the consignment papers of the transiting goods in certifications of the receipt of payments of due *Jagat* at the checkpost. In Bikaner it was realized along with the custom duty (*Jagat*) on the goods passing through the *Pargana*. It was levied at four checkposts, viz. Sodwa, Pithod, Rajaldesar and Hardesar.[32]

(e) Panchayati

It was another cess realized along with the *Jagat* on the checkposts for the *Panchayat* of the village[33] soliciting the Panchayat's decisions.

(ii) Income Other Than *Jagat* (Other Taxes)

Besides, the collection of *Jagat* income there were many other taxes which were realized and credited into the account of *Mandis and Chowkis*. They are explained below:

(a) Taxes on Dalals and Speculators: The State realized a tax from *Dalals* (brokers) and *Satorias* (speculators). The *Dalals* who dealt in various commodities such as groceries, fodder, woollen and cotton clothes, precious metals, animals-camels and horses, moveable and immovable property.[34] The *Satorias* (speculators) executed *Saudas* (oral transactions) on the fluctuations of the prices of opium (*Afim ka sauda*) or the possibility of rains (*Meh ka sauda*).[35] The state permitted them and realized a tax from *Dalals* and *Satorias* known as *Dalali* and *Sauda* respectively. With the expansion of the commercial activities in the state during the latter 18th century *Dalals'* activities had increased and the state could earn a good income.[36] For instance, Rs. 2,089 was realized in the year 1795 AD in Suratgarh by the state.[37]

(b) *Parkhai tax*: *Parkhai* (testing of purity of coins) was a tax realized from the goldsmith and the *sarrafs* who usually tested the purity of coins and gold and silver. The state often authorized this work to the highest bidder and earned the lump sum amount.[38]

(c) Rupota tax: It was a tax on the shopkeepers and on the camel dealers. Rs. 2 was charged monthly from every shopkeeper as *Rupota-ki-Chungi*. Rs. 1,320 *Annas* 4 were realized in Bikaner in this head of income in the year 1747 AD.[39]

(d) *Mapa*: *Mapa* was a sales tax imposed on articles sold in the market being brought by merchants from within and outside the state. From the grain dealers the state realized the *Mapa* known as *Dhan-ri-Chauthai*.[40] The state was very particular in realizing this tax.[41] The income from this head in *Chira* Jasarasar was Rs. 24,966 in the year 1790 AD. The high income in Jasarasar was because the grain merchants of Marwar were hiding their grains in the villages of Bikaner adjacent to Marwar fearing the raids of the Marathas at the close of the 18th century. The state could realize the *Chouthai* from them. Therefore, it had become an important source of income for the state.[42] The income of

Mapa also accrued from the sale of other articles as well.

(e) *Chungi Bichayati Mal Ri*: It was a tax realized from the *Bichayati* merchants (retailer) who sold their goods by displaying them on the pavements of the market.[43]

(f) *Rut-Ri-Chhadami*: It was a tax realized from the merchants dealing in cotton (*Rut*) in *Mandi*. Rs. 45 were collected from this tax in *Mandi* Bikaner in 1782 AD.[44]

(g) *Hundawan*: It was a tax from those who were doing business of issuing, executing and discounting *'Hundis'* (Bills of exchange) and earning *'Hundawan'* as commission.[45] Rs. 180 and *Annas* 8 were collected in year 1746 AD for this head of income.[46]

(h) *Jokho-ri-Chouthai*: It was a tax on those who were engaged in insurance business of transiting goods.[47]

(i) *Ghadat Sajji*: It was a tax on those who manufactured and sold sajji (alkaline)[48] in the state.

(j) *Chouhate-ri-Bhanchh*: It was realized from the traders and merchants for the security and maintenance of the markets.[49] Rs. 351 was realized in 1758 AD in *Mandi* Reni.

(j) *Pani-Peev Ra*: It was a tax on using water by men and animals and the maintenance of the water reservoirs like *Talab* (pond), wells or other water sources. Rs. 29 and *Annas* 4 were collected in Rajgarh in 1771 AD.[50] It was also realized from the traders. We find that a *Qatar* of *Gusains* paid Rs. 3 for 4 days stay in Rajgarh.[51] In Bikaner *Ghadsisar Re Talab Ri Bhanchh* was charged for its construction and maintenance and Rs. 88 and *Annas* 10 were realized in 1799-1800 AD[52] in Bikaner.

(l) *Income from Melas (fairs)*: The state organized religious fairs such as *Kolayat Mela* of Kolayat, *Goga Meri Mela* near Nohar, *Gajner Mela* of Gajner, *Ganesh Mela* in Bikaner. The traders from distant places brought and sold animals and various other items of need and the state earned good income through levying taxes on them. Rs. 1,495 *Annas* 11 were realized in 1822 AD from the Kolayat Mela in the *Mandi* Bikaner.[53]

(m) Income from Pokhan (mines) and Nauda (salt pits): Income also accrued from the mining and sale of stone, *Multani mitti* (Fuller's earth) and on the salt production. The state usually gave on *Muqatas* (*Ijaras*) to the highest bidding merchants for these mines and earned a fixed income. A *Muqata* for *Multani mitti* was given to a merchant in 1767 AD for Rs. 6,524 and *Annas* 8 for a period of three years. Likewise, Bidasar copper mines was bid out for Rs. 41,011 in 1763 AD. Production of salt at Chhapar salt lake and Lunkaransar from the salt pits was also a useful source to the state.[54]

(n) Bhada (Rent): Revenue also accrued from the rent of the state owned shops, buildings and the stands in fairs. For instance, Rs. 111 and *Annas* 6 in 1828 AD and Rs. 107 in 1786 AD were realized as *Bhada* (rent) in Rajgarh by the state.[55] Income under this source was also accruing in Bikaner, Suratgarh and Ratangarh *Mandis*.

(o) Taxes on Various Professionals and Artisans: The person engaged or employed in various professions or occupation were required to pay an annual tax to the state which ranged from Rs. 2 to 10 and was known by different names according to the name of particular occupations as under–

'Chejara-Ri-Karni Lag'[56] (tax from mason), *'Chungaroh-Ri-Bhatti Lag'*[57] (tax on lime workers), *'Teliyon-Ri-Ghani'*[58] (tax from oil pressers), *'Nihariyon-Ro-Niharo'*[59] (tax on *Nihariyas* who extract gold and silver from its dust), *'Girat Bilowna Ro'*[60] (tax on milkman), *'Aal-Re-Mate-Ra'*[61] (tax on dyers), *'Sut-Jat Ra'*[62] (tax on *meghwal* leather workers), *'Daru-Ri-Bhatti-Ra'*[63] (tax from wine distillers or *Kalals*), *'Bansole-Ri-Bhanchh'* (tax from carpenters), *'Luharon-Ri-Bhanchh'* (tax from iron smith), *'Kohar-Ri-Bhanchh'* (tax from *Malis* and *Sakka* community), *'Sal-Siledi'* (tax from menials), *'Kansera-Ri-Bhanchh'* (tax from makers of metal wares), *'Juwariyan-Ri-Bhanchh'* (tax from the players of dice). Towards the close of the 18th century during Surat Singh's period even *Brahmins* and Rajputs were also subjected to pay the taxes called *Brahmino Ri Bhanchh* and *Rajputon-Ri-Khed Kharach Re Bhanchh* respectively. Surat Singh did not spare any occupational caste from levying this *Bhanchh*. From the Barbers and *bairagis* (Vishnu worshipers) this *Bhanchh* was also realized, called *Naiyon Ki Bhanchh* and *Bairagiyon Ki Bhanchh* respectively. Although, *Bairagis* were religious saints but had enough accumulated wealth. They often gave loans to the state in need. Therefore, the state realized *Bhanchh* from them also.[64]

Sahukari Bhanchh: It was realized annually from all merchants, traders, *sarrofs* and moneylenders. Its rate was not fixed but was realized from the *sahukars* taking into consideration the financial condition of a *sahukar*[65]. During Gaj Singh's time in Bikaner in 1749 AD Rs. 721 *Takka* 3½ were realized from *Oswal, Maheshwari* and *Multani Sahukars*[66] and in 1751 it was realized Rs. 615 *Annas* 12 Takka 4 Dam 37 from Bikaner.[67] Surat Singh demanded heavy lump sum amount of this *Bhanchh* from *sahukars* as *Tees Hazari* (Thirty thousand) *Saath Hazari*[68] (Sixty thousand) and *Do Lakh Ki*[69] (Two lakh) the amount later to be spread over among the *sahukars* of the state. The *sahukars* in general resented this *Bhanchh* and often, many of them along with their kinsmen took shelter in Deshnoke (a sanctum place of deity Karniji) near Bikaner to abstain it.[70] Consequently, the state had to liquidate their dues of *Bhanchh* to recall and resume their business.[71]

(2) NON-COMMERCIAL INCOME

The following were the important non-commercial sources of income (other than land revenue):

(a) *Nazar* and *Peshkashi*

Nazar was a token of gift called *Nazrana,* which was to be paid by every *Jagirdar* and official and even the common people had to pay some amount to the ruler at the occasion of marriage or birth of a prince or on the coronation ceremony of the ruler.[72] A peasant had also to pay *Nazrana* according to his land revenue assessment.[73] Whereas, the *Peshkashi* was a charge realized by thr ruler from *Jagirdars* on their resumption of *Jagir,* on assignment of a new *Jagir,* from the subordinate officials on the assignment of new offices, from the traders/merchants on their initiation of new business.[74] The *Choudharies, Patwaris, Mutsaddis* (administrative officials), *Hazurias* (personal attendants) paid it while receiving the *sanads* or *parwana* of their respective appointment.

Since, the Mughal Emperors used to resume the *Jagirs* of their noblemen at the time of their death and bestow it again on their successors whenever they pleased.[75] The Rajput rulers were conversant with this practice being their subordinate *mansabdars*, now followed this practice in their chiefdom while they detached from the Mughals. They realized its importance as a source of income and applied it in their own territories and levied *peshkashi* from subordinates to enhance the income and also to establish the supremacy over the *jagirdars*.

But there were no fixed rates for *Peshkashi* and was arbitrarily realized by the state as per the status and capacity of a payee. The levy normally ranged between Rs. 1,000 to Rs. 10,000.[76] But during the later 18th century it was made a regular levy and was realized not only from payees referred above, but also from the traders and common people of the state. Therefore, it became a significant part of the state income. Maharaja Surat Singh levied *Peshkashi* from his *Jagirdars* with very high rates.[77]

A *Jagirdar* of the state in whose family *Bandhan* ceremony had been performed had to pay a sum equal to his one years income of his *Jagir*. But the *Jagirdars* who had been exempted from the *Rekh* had to pay one-third of the income of their *Jagirs*. There was also a category of *sardars* who were exempted form paying *Peshkashi*.[78]

Consequently, the income of *Peshkashi* increased substantially in Surat Singh's time as evinced from the following figures below–

Income of Peshkashi[79]

Sr. No.	*Year*	*Rs.*
1.	1757 AD	33,554
2.	1795 AD	59,093
3.	1803 AD	2,03,717

It is noteworthy that the income accruing from the *peshkashi* was very significant from 1757 AD to 1803 AD. If we assume income of Rs. 33,554 realized in 1757 AD as 100%, it increases by 176.11% in realizing Rs. 59,093 in 1795 AD and further increases by 344.73% in 1803 AD for Rs. 2,03,717. It is a net increase in percentage by 607.13% in 1803 AD as compared to the collection of 1757 AD.

(b) Military Taxes

Although the state's military needs were usually satisfied by the feudal armies under their military obligation (*Zamiyat Chakri*) in lieu of their assignment of *Jagirs;* but, at times, as we find mention of various military taxes in the *Bahis*, being imposed and realized to meet the eventual needs of the state. However, some of them later became the regular taxes.

Maharaja Gaj Singh (1746-1787 AD) realized *Khed Kharach Ri Bhanchh* or *Fauj Kharch*[80] @ Re. 1 and *Annas* 4 per house.[81] It became a regular tax and in 1809 AD during Surat Singh's period (1787-1828 AD) realization under this levy was Rs. 11,347.[82] As in 1809 AD it was realized with increased rate of Rs. 20 per house due to Marwar's invasion of Bikaner.[83]

To meet some protective obligations Surat Singh imposed *Rukhwali Bhanchh* (Protection tax) in 1794 AD.[84] In his times, military expenditures increased due to his expeditions and pacification of *Raths, Johiyas* and *Bhattis* in the north and north-west, which intermittently created internal disturbances in to the state.

Initially, *Rukhwali Bhanchh* was realized @ Rs. 2 per house in 1794 AD both in *Khalisa* and *Jagir* area but in 1800 AD it was realized with an increased rate of Rs. 10 per house.[85]

Also, while Surat Singh led an expedition against Bhattis in 1804 AD and snatched Bhatner permanently from them he imposed and realized *Khoosali* tax @ Rs. 1 per house to cover the expenses of war;[86] presumably from the richer people as its name signifies. He also introduced and realized in 1809 AD *Oothan Ri Bhanchh* to maintain the royal camel corps.[87]

Moreover, considering the excessive military needs and reducing his dependency over the *thakur's Zamiyat* (army) *Chakri*, he converted this *Zamiyat Chakri* into cash levy in 1794 AD.[88] He realized this *Chakri* initially @ Rs. 50 per *Sawar* from[89] the *thakurs* and termed as *Ghora Rekh*. Later, the rate of this *Ghora Rekh* was also raised upto Rs. 100 per *Sawar* in 1800 AD and Rs. 46,143 were realized from the *Jagirdars* or *Pattayats*.[90]

Some miscellaneous levies were also realized to meet out the contingent expenses. As mentioned in the *Bahis* they wee *Tan Bakshi Ro Kot*[91] (*Lawazima* of *Tan Bakshi* @ Re. 1 per village), *Thana*

Ri Bhanchh (expenses of the *Thanas* to maintain law and order), *Sipayon Ri Bhanchh* (levy from the army men of the ruler).[92]

Thus, the realization under military taxes were increased considerably in the late 18th and early 19th century period due to excessive military activities of the rulers. The conversion of the *Zamiyat Chakri* into cash levy established the fact. The resentment of *thakurs* against the state's administration was obvious. Surat Singh also revised the rates of old military taxes and imposed new ones. The economic pressure of these taxes ultimately fell on the common people. The *Jagirdars* also shifted this burden on to their public of jagirs.

In 1809, when Marwar attacked Bikaner, Surat Singh realized *Fauj Kharch* from all Brahmins of the state and that too with sternness, at the following rates—Saraswat Brahmins Rs. 10, *takka* 10 per *guwad*. Pareekh and other Brahmins Rs. 20 *takka* per *guwad*. The directions were issued that if anybody who refused to pay this demand would not be provided water in the village and he should be expelled from the village. This shows that Surat Singh had felt the exigency.[93] The Choudharies of various villages of Ghadsisar, Rinsisar, Bikamsar, Panchoo, Amarsar, Paatemdesar complained of excesses in 1809 AD.[94]

(c) *Neota*

Neota (invitation) was an invitation tax realized on the occasion of any marrige in the royal family from all castes. It was realized @ Rs. 2 per family both in the *Khalisa* and *Jagir* areas. Rs. 552 were collected in 1750 AD from Bikaner city.[95] However, it was not a regular tax but a casual one.

(d) *Gaiwali* Income (Heirless Property)

Property of a deceased person who had no inheritors was forfeited by the state and was called *Gaiwali* or *Gaimal*. When Bikhania Juhari died in 1781 AD without any successor his property worth Rs. 1,048 and *Annas* 9 were forfeited and paid into the state treasury.[96]

(e) *Khola* Tax

It was a tax or a fee charged by the state from a person adopting a male child as his inheritor (successor). Rs. 370 was collected from Rajgarh of *Khola* tax in 1804-05 AD.[97]

(f) *Dharti-Ri-Chouthai*

The state realized a fee for registration of the transactions of land and building @ 1/4 of the cost of the property sold or a quarter share of the sale proceeds. Rs. 204 and *Annas* 13 were realized in 1799 AD in Rajgarh[98] under this head.

(g) Fines

Income also accrued to the state from various offences, like *kasoor,*[99] i.e. a fine on failing to perform the assigned duty *Gunehgari,*[100] i.e. a fine on committing any unlawful offence and *Farohi,*[101] i.e. income from offences not specified in the above categories. Such income was deposited in the state treasury.

(h) *Reeth*

It was a tax on the remarriage called *Nata* or remarriage of the widow which the state recognized on payment of tax @ Rs. 2 per case.[102] The taxes for *sari* and *sehra* (*sari* for bride and *sehra* for bridegroom) and *Dhol* (charges for drum beating in marriage) were also levied at the rate of Rs. 2 per marriage.[103]

(i) Income from Mints (*Taksal*)

Minting of silver coins of *Rupya* and *Takka* and *Dam* of copper had started during Gaj Singh's period (1746-87 AD).[104] The state allowed the *sahukars* to get their coins minted for their own use. The state charged Rs. 2 and *Annas* 8 for minting of 100 rupees coins.[105] The state also gave on *Muqata* (*Ijara*) the work of minting to the highest bidder and thereby earned from the *Taksals*. It was given on *Muqata* to Kochar Anadu, son of Balchand in 1810 AD.[106] The state earned Rs. 466 *Annas* 8 in 1764 AD from the *Taksal*.[107]

(j) *Talbana* and *Lawazimas*

Talbana was a fee charged for expenses for serving notices in the state when dues were outstanding. Also for summoning the concerned in the *Darbar*.[108] *Lawazimas* were the office tax, realized to maintain the expenditures of the officials. Whereas *Davotari-Panchotari* was a fee for filing a suit in the *Darbar's* court or fee initiating a case in the *Panchayats*.[109]

(k) Income from *Karkhana* (Royal Establishment)

Like the Turks and Mughal ruling classes the Rajput rulers also maintained their *Karkhanas* (royal establishment). These *Karkhanas* primarily met the requirements of the ruling family but the surplus production was marketed in *Bazar*. The items manufactured were carpets, shawls, *pagris*, medicines, small carts, swords and daggers, arms-ammunitions. The surplus items were sold in the market and the income was realized by the state. Rs. 1,381 was earned in 1805 AD by the state.[110]

(l) *Habubs* (cesses levies in exigencies)

To compensate or to meet the emergent expenditures this *Habub* was levied.[111] There were many taxes like *Kiyadi* (tax on houses) *Qile Ri Bhanchh* (tax of fort) *Saal Siledi* (tax from menials) were levied during the times of Gaj Singh and Surat Singh to meet the exigencies.[112]

(m) Levy from the Officials

The *Nazrana* and *Peshkashi* paid by the various officials and administrative classes was turned into regular levies by Surat Singh and was known as the following names[113]—*Kamdaron Ki Bhanchh*, tax from *Kamdars*,[114] *Hazurian Ri Bhanchh*, tax on personal attendants of the ruler, *Choudhar Bab* and *Patwari Bab* were respectively levies upon *Choudharies* and *Patwaris* of villages. Surat Singh also levied occasionally tax from the *Huwaldars* as *Huwaldaron Ki Bhanchh* and from soldiers of army as *Sirbandhiyon Ki Bhanchh*.[115]

(n) *Bidawaton Ri Bhanchh*

The Bidawats were Rathore and the descendants of Bida, the brother of Rao Bika (the founder of Bikaner). Bida had carved out for himself a territory of Chhapar and Dronepur, the south-east Bikaner called Bidawati.[116] Bidawat Rathores, the *Jagirdars* of Bikaner, did not accept the sovereignty of the descendants of

Bika, the chief of Bikaner and defied them. Therefore, there were no freindly relations with Bidawats and the rulers. In 1759 AD Gaj Singh went to Bidasar and imposed a *Bhanchh* (a cess) on Bidawat *thakur*[117], which was called, *Bidawaton Ri Bhanchh* and it continued to be realized even during Surat Singh's time. Surat Singh, against whom many *thakurs* of Bikaner were antagonistic, realized this *Bhanchh* with sternness and at increased amounts. The demand under this *Bhanchh* reached upto Rs. 50,693 in 1809 AD during Surat Singh time.[118]

(o) *Phirangiyon Re Sartan Re Bhanchh*

When in 1818 AD Surat Singh concluded a treaty of subordination with the British East India Company, the visits of the English officials increased in the state, also the use of English army for pacification of revolts/expeditions by the chief also entailed additional expenditures to the state. Therefore, in order to compensate this expenditure Surat Singh realized a new *Bhanchh* of this name @ Re. 1 Takka 2 per *Guwadi* in the state.[119]

Therefore, it is evident that a variety of taxes and cesses were realized by the state to mobilize the financial resources in absence of the foreign income, the income received as *mansabdar* in lieu of their salary (*Tankhwah-i-Jagir*). Consequently, the ultimate pressure of this *Bhanchh* was borne by the subject in *Khalisa* and *Jagir* areas. *Jagirdars* also shifted their economic burden over to their subjects in *Jagirs*. The frustrated and financially constrained *Jagirdars*, therefore, also revolted due to their income being reduced. Apart from it, they realized many taxes in their areas which the state usually realized in *Khalisa*.

It is worth mentioning that while *Jagirdars* as discussed earlier had to pay many levies to the chief, he could, in his *Jagir* areas, collect all taxes and fees except *Chouthai* on sale of land by state, tax on *Khola* (adoption), *Gaival* property, *Qila Bhanchh, Choudhar Bab* and fines imposed on criminals or offenders.[120]

(3) SALT AND MINERAL PRODUCTS

Salts and mineral resources formed an important part of the desert economy as they supplied raw material of some industrial value as well as the state gained income from them. Some minerals and salt were produced in the state which were generally given on *Muqata* for a fixed period at predetermined rates.[121] The following were the salt and minerals available in the state:

(a) Stone

It was chiefly excavated from Khari and Dulmera near Bikaner, the capital city; and was also exported to the neighbouring areas.[122] The red stone of Khari was excellent in quality for the construction work. The Dulmera red stone was soft and fine with pleasing sheds and suitable for carving work. The Bidasar stone was specially suited for roof slabs as it was not so soft as the Dulmera stone.[123] It was used for construction of buildings at local level. Besides, rough stone known as *Rora* was quarried near Bikaner. Sand stone and lime stone of Sujangarh was also used in construction of houses in Sujangarh.[124]

(b) Copper

Copper was another mineral found in the territory. During the period of Gaj Singh (1746-87). Copper was discovered in 1753-54 AD at Dariba-Bidasar in Sujangarh and was extracted afterwards. Powlett says that the mine was not economically viable but the *Bahis* continue to mention the production of copper from the mines and these were given on *Muqatas*. Thus, it shows the significance of this metal.[125] We find in the *Kagad Bahi* of 1763 AD that the excavation of copper ore in Dariba-Bidasar was bid out to Shah Jagroop Gujarmal Bardia for Rs. 4,101 for one year.[126]

(c) Gypsum and Lime

These were also among the mineral wealth of Bikaner found and excavated in abundance around Bikaner and the *Chira* Magra, largely used for plastering buildings. Lime was also available in the Sujangarh area.[127]

(d) Mulatani Mitti (Fuller's Earth)

It was a well known greasy clay used as soap for hair wash and for dyeing clothes. It was quarried in large quantities in south west of Bikaner from village Madh and Kolayat and its contiguous area.[128] It was exported to Sirsa, Sindh and Multan as well as to Rajputana states.[129] The quarries of *Multani Mitti* was a good source of income to the state. We find that *Sawa Bahi Mandi Bikaner* of 1780-81 AD mentions that the excavation work was bid out on *Muqata* for Rs. 9,003 to Chauhan Jiwan for three years in 1780 AD.[130]

(e) Salt

It was chiefly produced at Chhapar (Sujangarh) and Lunkaransar[131] (Bikaner) but it was bitter in taste and of low quality. Generally, it was fit for tanning of leather and other antiseptic purpose; it was used by the poor people[132] *Sawa Bahi* Lunkaransar mentions that in 1830 AD Rs. 18 was incurred for preparing salt pits at Lunkaransar suggests that salt was being produced.[133] The work of salt production was often let out on *Muqata*. It was on *Muqata* for Rs. 521 in 1780-81 AD.[134] However, the salt production in Bikaner was neither fit for production nor was sufficient to cater to the needs of the local people.

(f) *Sajji* (locally called *Khar*)

It was found in Pugal, Anupgarh and the north of Ghaggar in Bikaner.[135] It is evident from *Sawa Bahi* Suratgarh of 1803 AD that the traders of Ajmer generally took away *sajji* from Suratgarh in lieu of tobacoo and salt which they brought from Ajmer to Suratgarh.[136] In 1847 AD a camel load loaded of *sajji* could be purchased in Rs. 4.[137] The *Jagat* was levied @ 1 *Anna* per camel load only. The *Bahi* of this year quotes that in 1840 AD Rs. 47 and *Annas* 8 towards *Jagat* were collected at Suratgarh *Mandi*.[138] A *Rath* trader carried 206 *maunds* of *Sajji* from Pugal to Bikaner.[139]

The state generally preferred to let out mining and manufacturing work of minerals and salts to the highest bidder called *Muqati*.[140] The chief aim was to earn the maximum possible revenue from these resources. However, the mineral resources were neither properly explored nor was any apt policy formulated to improve the quarries. Thus, the *Muqatis* did not work for the improvement of the mining resources. Hence, the state could also earn through whatever natural resources were available in the state through the *Muqatas*.

REFERENCES

1. *Akbarnama*, Abul Fazal, (Eng. Tr.) H. Beveridge, Vol.II, pp. 516-19; *Muntkhab-ut-Tawarikh*, Badaoni (Eng. Tr.) Vol. II, p. 137.
2. Initially in 1570 AD Kalyan Mal, the chief of Bikaner got a *mansab* of 2000/2000 *sawar* from Akbar, the Mughal Emperor, and later Rai Singh, the successor of Kalyan Mal was assigned the *mansab* of 4000/4000 *sawar* which was subsequently raised to 5000/5000 in 1605 AD by Jahangir on his accession. Raja Rai Singh had the privilege of administering governorship of the Punjab (1581), Burhanpur (twice in 1586 and 1605-06 AD), Surat (1593), received in *Jagir*-Merta, Nagore (1561) *Pargana* Nadiad (1596) Junagarh (1597), Shamshabad-Nurpur (1605) Sirsa, Hansi and Hissar. Besides, suitable *mansabs* and honours were granted to his nobles and relatives. He enjoyed a significant status and military obligations in the Mughal empire. The successors of Rai Singh till Gaj Singh (1746-87) enjoyed a significant place in the empire. See for details of *mansab* of chiefs of Bikaner Table 2.3 in Chapter-'Geographical and Historical Background.'
   Ain-Akbari, Abul Fazal, (Eng. Tr.) Blochmann, Vol. I, Calcutta, 1867, p. 358. Also see Karni Singh, *Relations of the House of Bikaner with the Central Powers*, New Delhi, 1974, pp. 59, 61-62.
3. The states of Hyderabad, Avadh, Bengal, Mysore and so in Rajputana including Bikaner states behaved as an independent states.
4. However, the chiefs of Bikaner owed a nominal alligiance to the Mughal Emperor but were the *de facto* rulers in their territory during 1746-1818 AD. They were busy in managing their affairs and creating new avenues of financial resources as the income which they previously received from the Mughals as *Mansabdars* had then ceased.
5. The chief of Bikaner were free from the Mughal services and ceased to be their— *Mansabdars* in its sense in the second half of the 18th century onwards.
6. *Sawa Bahi* (*Sian-Bahis*) which are part of the Rampuria collection in Bikaner Archives, implied the ledger or day book in which daily receipts and disbursement are entered; it is sometimes applied to a journal or diary in which state orders are also

appended. Wilson, H. H., *A Glossary of Judicial and Revenue Terms of British India*, 2nd ed., New Delhi, 1968, p. 481.
Jagat Bahis (Corrupt of *Zaqat*) formed a part of the *Bikaner Bahiyat* preserved in Bikaner Archives and record details of taxes and cesses along with the commercial transaction. The *Kagad Bahis* are the administrative manuals mainly but often record the rate-structure of the taxes in general. They are very significant collection of Rampuria section. See, A Descriptive List of Bikaner *Bahis*, Part I (17-19 C) Bikaner, 1982, pp. I to XIII, 78-119, 120-188 and 142-173 respectively.

7. A separate chapter has been contributed to study the '*Mandis*' and their functioning.
8. *Bholawania* was a person to whom the state had deputed in village on a certain remuneration and had entrusted to him the responsibility to collect commercial revenue from the merchandize passing through his village. *Jagat Ri Bahi*, No. 92, V.S. 1869/1812 AD, ff. 1-10, R.S.A., Bikaner
9. See Chapter *Mandis*. Also *A Descriptive List of Bikaner Bahis*, op. cit., pp. 78-119, 142-173, R.S.A., Bikaner.
10. *Jagat* is an idigenously assigned term for combined income of custom and transit duty. In *Islam Zaqat* is a religious tax while in Rajputana it changed its connotation and became a secular tax known as *Jagat*, i.e. transit and custom duty. Hence, *Jagat* is a vernacular corruption of *Zaqat*. Wilson, H.H., op. cit., p. 482. The officer-in-charge who realized it was called as *Jagati* or *Jagatiya* or *Jagatidar*. Lalas, Sita Ram, *Rajasthani-Hindi Sankshipt Sabdakosh*, Vol. II, RORI, Choupasni, Jodhpur, 1987, p. 1032.
11. *Kagad Bahi*, No. 6, V.S. 1839/1782 AD *Baisakh Sudi* 1, Rampuria records, R.S.A., Bikaner.
12. *Kagad re Nakal Bahi*, No. 4, V.S. 1831/1774 AD., f. 63, *Chhoot ra Kagad*, R.S.A., Bikaner.
13. *Nekal re Kagdon ri Bahi*, No. 4, V.S. 1831/1774, ff. 26-28.
14. *Kagad Bahi*, No. 15, V.S. 1866/1809 AD, f.61, R.S.A., Bikaner.
15. *Kagad Bahi*, No. 25, V.S. 1876/1819 AD, ff. 107-08, *Bhadwa Sudi* 11.
16. *Jagat Bahi Bikaner*, No. 81, V.S. 1807/1750 AD, R.S.A., Bikaner.
17. *Kagad Bahi*, No. 14, V.S. 1864/1807 AD, f. 275.
18. *Kagad Bahi*, No. 30, V.S. 1881/1824 AD, f. 9-10, R.S.A., Bikaner.
19. *Kagad Bahi*, No. 10, V.S. 1854/1797 AD, f. 51.
20. *Kagad Bahi*, No. 16, V.S. 1867/1810 AD, *Shrawan Sudi* 6.
21. *Kagad Bahi*, No. 20, V.S. 1871/1814, f. 116.
22. *Kagad Bahi*, No. 13, V.S. 1861/1804, *Bhadwa Sudi* 4.
23. *Kagad Bahi*, No. 5, V.S. 1838/1774 AD, *Sanad* papers, f. 30.

24. Ibid., *Baisakh Sudi*, 5.
25. *Kagad Bahi*, No. 5, V.S. 1838/1781 AD, *Chhoot ra Kagad, Bhadwa Badi* 11.
26. *Kagad Bahi*, No. 20, V.S. 1871/1814 AD, *Kartik Badi* 2.
27. *Kagad Bahi*, No. 10, V.S. 1854/1797.
28. *Kagad Bahi*, No. 30, V.S. 1881/1824 AD, f.1(a).
29. *Kagad Bahi*, No. 15, V.S. 1866/1809 AD, *Chetra Sudi* 12.
30. *Kagad Bahi*, No. 19/1, V.S. 1870/1813, *Shrawan Sudi* 6.
31. *Jagat Bahi Bikaner*, No. 81, V.S. 1807/1750 AD, Bikaner Bahiyat, R.S.A.B.
32. *Sawa Bahi Mandi Sadar Bikaner*, No. 2, V.S. 1802-04/1745-47 AD, ff. 1-2, R.S.A.B.
33. Ibid.
34. *Bikaner Re Talke Ri Mandi Ro Jama Jod Ri Bahi*, (*Jagat Bahi*), No. 43, V.S. 1840/1783 AD, ff. 2-3. *Shri Mandi Re Jama Kharach Ri Bahi*, No. 54, V.S. 1846/1789 AD, ff. 2-3, *Sawa Bahi Mandi Sadar Bikaner*, No. 39/(b), V.S.1877-80/1820-23 AD, f. 9(a), R.S.A., Bikaner.
35. Powlett, op. cit., p. 145; Sharma, G.S., *Marwari Vyapari*, p. 31.
36. *Shri Mandi Re Golak Ro Lekho*, No. 61, V.S. 1855/1798 AD, ff. 1-2, R.S.A.B.
37. *Sawa Bahi Suratgarh*, No. 1, V.S. 1852/1795 AD, f. 148. In *Suratgarh Mandi* Rs. 2,089 in all were realized in the year 1795 AD from *Dalals* as per the following details:

Sr. No.	*Dalals* dealing in the commodity	*Dalali* realized by the state, Rs. - *Annas*
1.	Weighing work	1,099 - 8
2.	*Ghee* (Milk fat)	704 - 8
3.	Wool	200 - 0
4.	Hundi work/insurance	50 - 0
5.	Camel sale	35 - 0
	Total	2,089 - 0

38. *Sawa Bahi Mandi Suratgarh*, No. 8, V.S. 1896/1839 AD, f. 60; No. 10, V.S.1909/1852 AD f. 147.
39. *Sawa Bahi Mandi Sadar Bikaner*, No. 2, V.S. 1802-04/1745-47 AD, No. 39(b), V.S. 1877/1820 AD; *Sawa Bahi Rajgarh*, No. 83, V.S. 1861/1804 AD ff. 2-3, R.S.A.B.
40. *Dhan-Ri-Chouthai* was a tax in kind from *Sahukars* and 1/5 of this *Chouthai* was shared by the *Jagirdar* of the respective area. During a famine it was to be realized at a concessional rate.
Sawa Bahi Rajgarh, No. 9, V.S. 1860/1803 AD, *Kagad Bahi*, No. 1,

V.S. 1811/1754 AD.

41. *Dhan-R-Chouthai Ri Bahi*, V.S. 1847/1790 AD, V.S. 1874/1817 AD, Cf. Devra, G.S.L., op. cit., p. 179.
42. *Dhan-Ri-Chouthai Bahi*, V.S. 1839/1782 AD, R.S.A.B.
43. *Sawa Bahi Mandi Bikaner*, No. 17, V.S. 1829-30/1782-83 AD, f. 22(b).
44. Ibid., *Lekho Rut Ri Chhadami Ro, Sawa Bahi Mandi Bikaner*, No. 2, V.S. 1807-10/1750-53 AD; No. 8, V.S. 1815-16/1758-59 AD, R.S.A.B.
45. *Chithi Khaton Ri Bahi*, No. 6, V.S. 1869/1812 AD.
46. *Bahi Sri Karkhane Re Basat Ro Saho*, V.S. 1821/1764 AD, Sadul Museum and Library, Lallgarh Palace, Bikaner.
47. *Kagad Bahi*, No. 20, V.S. 1871/1814 AD, f. 61.
48. *Sawa Bahi Anupgarh*, No. 5, V.S. 1834-35/1777-78 AD, No.11, V.S. 1885-88/1828-31 AD, R.S.A.B.
49. *Sawa Bahi Reni*, No. 1, V.S. 1815/1758 AD, f. 29.
50. *Sawa Bahi Rajgarh*, No. 1, V.S. 1828/1777 AD, f. 34.
51. Ibid., No. 8, V.S. 1852/1795 AD, f. 115.
52. *Sawa Bahi Mandi Bikaner*, No. 29, V.S. 1856-57/1799-1800 AD, f. 160(a).
53. *Sawa Bahi Mandi Bikaner*, No. 28, V.S. 1847-48/1790-91 AD, ff.176 (b), 177, No. 29, V.S. 1856/1799 AD, f. 52 (b), No. 39(b), V.S. 1878-79/1821-22 AD.

    Fairs had occupied a significant place in the rural society. Initially, they had started with religious identity around holy places but later on they had acquired economic characters. Gradually, fairs became centres of cultural-cum-economic activities. The rulers saw these fairs as a source of revenue and levied taxes on the goods sold there and took a keen interest in organizing them as well as inviting the merchants and traders from distant places to participate in transactions.
54. *Bahi Sri Mandi Re Khato Teri*, No. 12, V.S. 1818/1761 AD ff. 5-6; *Shri Mandi Re Jagat Ro Sawo*, No. 48, V.S. 1843/1786 AD, f. 3; *Muqata Kagad, Kagad Bahi*, No. 12, V.S. 1859/1802 AD, *Sawa Bahi Sujangarh*, No. 4, V.S. 1887-94/1830-37 AD.
55. *Sawa Bahi Mandi Sadar Bikaner*, No. 3, V.S. 1805/1748 AD, f. 97; *Sawa Bahi Mandi Rajgarh*, No. 2, V.S. 1831/1774 AD, f. 11(a); No. 1, V.S. 1828/1771 AD, f. 176.
56. *Sawa Bahi Sujangarh*, No. 6, V.S. 1905/1848 AD, f. 283.
57. Ibid., No. 7, V.S. 1909/1852 AD.
58. *Sawa Bahi Lunkaransar*, No. 4, V.S. 1890/1833 AD f. 46.
59. *Sawa Bahi Mandi Sadar Bikaner*, No. 20, V.S. 1833-34/1776-77 AD, f. 15(b).
60. *Sawa Bahi Anupgarh*, No. 15, V.S. 1910/1853 AD, f. 72.

61. *Sawa Bahi Rajgarh*, No. 8, V.S. 1852/1795 AD, f. 115(a).
62. *Sawa Bahi Rajgarh*, No. 2, V.S. 1831/1774 AD, f. 49(b); No. 9, V.S. 1860/1803 AD, f. 210.
63. Rs. 2 per *Bhatti* were charged and Re. 1 from a new distiller. *Sawa Bahi Rajgarh*, No. 9, V.S. 1860/1803 AD, f. 232(a).
64. *Kagad Bahi*, No. 15, V.S. 1866/1809 AD, f. 34.
65. *Sawa Bahi Mandi Sadar Bikaner*, No. 3, V.S. 1806/1749 AD, *Bhadrapad Badi* 13. *Sahukaron Re Bhanchh-Ri-Bahi*, No. 159, V.S. 1866/1809 AD, *Bikaner Bahiyat*, Bikaner, *Kagad Bahi*, No. 15, V.S. 1866/1809 AD, f. 19.
66. *Sawa Bahi Mandi Sadar Bikaner*, No. 3, V.S. 1806/1749 AD.
67. Ibid., No. 4, V.S. 1808/1751 AD.
68. *Kagad Bahi*, No. 14, V.S. 1863-64; f. 131(b).
69. *Kagad Bahi*, No. 15, V.S. 1866/1809 AD.
70. *Kagad Ri Bahi*, No. 15, V.S. 1866/1809 AD, ff.9, 19, No. 16, V.S. 1867/1810 AD, ff. 18-19, R.S.A., Bikaner.
71. For instance, in the year 1829 AD the following *Sahukars* had gone to Deshnoke in protest and to abstain from the *Bhanchh*. The state then issued a declaration that in future no excessive *Bhanchh* would be levied from them and should resume their business. Therefore, the state reduced their *Bhanchh* as per list below:

Sahukar	Due *Bhanchh*	Reduced *Bhanchh*
1. Kothari Roopchand Kapoor Chand	Rs. 52 p.a.	Rs. 10p.a.
2. Siponi Luno	Rs. 25 p.a.	Rs. 6 p.a.
3. Surana Jeetmal	Rs. 71 p.a.	Rs. 16 p.a.
4. Daga Uttam Santo	Rs. 15 p.a.	Rs. 6 p.a.
5. Daga Megha	Rs. 12 p.a.	Rs. 8 p.a.
6. Daga Chatu Kirato	Rs. 21 p.a.	Rs. 10 p.a.
7. Daga Hindu Cheno	Rs. 15 p.a.	Rs. 8 p.a.
8. Golecha Zorawar	Rs. 15 p.a.	Rs. 6 p.a.
	Rs. 226	Rs. 70

The state issued there eight orders on *Posh Badi* 4 in V.S. 1886, *Bahi Qooch Muqam Re Kagada Ri*, No. 1, V.S. 1886-98/1829-41 AD R.S.A.B.

72. *Kagad Bahi*, No. 3, V.S. 1827/1770 AD, ff. 53-55.
73. *Bahi Talab Tayara Ri*, V.S. 1866/1809 AD, f.77, Cf. Sharma, G.C., op. cit., p. 115.
74. Cf. Devra, G.S.L., *Rajasthan Ki Prashashnik Vyavastha*, Bikaner, 1981, p. 171.
75. Sarkar, Jadunatha, *Mughal Administration*, p. 162.

76. *Patta Bahi*, No. 3, V.S. 1704/1647 AD, *Bahi Peshkashi Ri*, V.S. 1814/1757 and V.S. 1860/1803 AD.
77. *Kagad Bahi*, No. 8, V.S. 1851/1794 AD.
78. Ojha, G.H., Vol. II, op. cit., pp. 618-19.
79. Cf. Devra, G.S.L., op. cit., p. 173.
80. *Hasil Bahi*, V.S. 1831/1774 AD; Sharma, G.C., op. cit., p. 137, Wilson in his glossary explains *Khed Kharach* as expenses towards maintaining elephants' army. p. 284.
81. *Bahi Hazur Re Khed Ri*, No. 208, V.S. 1803/1746 AD, *Bikaner Bahiyat Kagad Bahi*, No. 2, V.S. 1820/1763 AD; No. 14, V.S. 1863/1806 AD, f. 133, Rampuria Section, R.S.A.B.
82. Cf. Devra, G.S.L., op. cit., p. 176.
83. Ibid., *Bhaiya* Records, letter dtd. *Jyestha Sudi* 2, V.S. 1866 (16th May, 1809), *Basta* No. 2, R.S.A.B.
84. Tod, op. cit., Vol. II, p. 1159, Munshi, Sohan Lal, *Towarikh Raj Shri Bikaner*, Bikaner, p. 302.
85. *Kagad Bahi*, No. 14, V.S. 1863/1806, AD, f.196, No.20, V.S. 1871/1814 AD, f. 322; Jain, Anjula, *Rukhwali Bhanchh*, PRHC, Bikaner Session, Jodhpur, 1986, pp. 92-99.
86. Tod, op. cit., Vol. II, p. 131.
87. *Bahi Talab Tayara Ri*, V.S. 1866/1809 AD, R.S.A.B.
88. *Parchoon Kagad, Kagad Bahi*, No. 8, V.S. 1851/1794 AD.
89. Ibid., No. 10, V.S. 1854/1797 AD.
90. Ibid., No. 11, V.S. 1857/1800 AD, *Bhaiya* collection-*Bahi Khazana Ri*, V.S. 1866/1809 AD, R.S.A.B.
91. *Bahi Talab Tayara Ri*, V.S. 1866/1809 AD.
92. *Bhaiya* Collection - *Bahi Khazana Ri*, V.S. 1866/1809 AD.
93. *Kagad Bahi*, No. 15, V.S. 1866/1809 AD.
94. *Kagad Bahi*, No. 16, V.S. 1867/1810 AD, R.S.A.B.
95. *Sawa Bahi Mandi Sadar Bikaner*, No. 4, V.S. 1807-10/1750-53 AD, f.91(b); *Sawa Bahi Rajgarh*, No. 1, V.S. 1828/1771 AD, f.1(a), *Mandi Re Jama Re Khata Ri Bahi*, V.S. 1809-13, R.S.A.B.
96. *Sawa Bahi Mandi Sadar Bikaner*, No. 22, V.S. 1837-38/1780-81 AD, f 31(b).
97. *Sawa Bahi Rajgarh*, No. 5, V.S. 1847/1787 AD, ff.68-70; No. 10, V.S. 1861-62/1804-05 AD, f.41(a); *Sawa Bahi Mandi Sadar Bikaner*, No.2, V.S. 1802-04/1745-47 AD.
98. It has been called *Zami-Chauth*, i.e. 1/4 cost of land in the *Bahis*. *Sawa Bahi Mandi Sadar Bikaner*, No. 29, V.S. 1856-58/1799-1801 AD, f. 111(b); *Sawa Bahi Rajgarh*, No.10, V.S.1861/1804 AD, f.35(b).
99. *Sawa Bahi Mandi Sadar Bikaner*, No. 5, V.S. 1810-12/1753-55 AD.
100. Ibid., No. 10, V.S. 1821-22/1764-65 AD, No.2, V.S. 1804/1747 AD,

f. 27, Rs. 35 were recovered from the *Jagatidar* of Bhainisar as penalty as he did not maintain the account.

101. *Sawa Bahi Mandi Sadar Bikaner*, No. 9, V.S. 1818-21/1761-64 AD
102. *Reeth Ra Kagad, Kagad Bahi*, No. 3, V.S. 1827/1770 AD, ff. 67-70, *Sawa Bahi Rajgarh*, No. 1, V.S. 1828/1771 AD, f. 3(a)
103. *Sawa Bahi Mandi Sadar Bikaner*, No. 10, V.S. 1821-22, No. 28, V.S. 1853/1796 AD, f. 5, Rs. 83 and *Annas* 4 were realized for *Byav Ri Sari Ra* in Bikaner in 1796 AD
104. *Kagad Bahi*, No. 1, V.S. 1811, *Jyeshtha Sudi* 5; No. 2, V.S. 1820/1763 AD; Sohan Lal, op. cit., pp. 267-68.
105. Web, W.W., *The Currencies of Hindu States of Rajputana*, 1893, (Hindi Tr.) Mayank, Mangi Lal, *Rajputana Ke Hindu Rajwado Ke Sikke*, Jodhpur, pp. 69-82.
106. *Kagad Bahi*, No. 16, V.S. 1867/1810 AD, *Shrawan Sudi* 1.
107. *Bahi Sri Karkhana Re Basat Re Jama Kharach Re Sahe Ri* (*Bahiyat Rokad Khata*), V.S. 1821/1764 AD, Personal collection, Maharaja Bikaner, Lallgarh Palace, Bikaner in Sadul Museum and Library. I have consulted and used some *Bahis* from the collection.
108. Rs. 10 *Annas* 8 were collected as *Talbana* from Lunkaransar in 1832 AD *Sawa Bahi Lunkaransar*, No. 1, V.S. 1889/1832 AD, f. 28.
109. *Sawa Bahi Sujangarh*, No. 6, V.S. 1904/1847 AD, f. 147.
110. Cf. Devra, G.S.L., op. cit., p. 180-81.
111. *Bahi Habub Ri*, V.S. 1851-53/ 1794-96 AD, *Bahiyat* Section, R.S.A., Bikaner.
112. Ibid., *Kagad Bahi*, No. 14, V.S. 1863/1806 AD, *Kartik Badi* 11.
113. *Sawa Bahi Mandir Bikaner*, No. 2, V.S. 1804/1747 AD, f. 27.
114. *Sawa Bahi Rajgarh*, No. 10, V.S. 1861/1704 AD, f. 42.
115. *Bahi Peshkashi Ri*, V.S. 1860/1803 AD.
116. Ojha, G.H., op. cit., Vol. I, pp. 101-02, 345-46.
117. Ibid., pp. 345-46.
118. *Kagad Bahi*, No. 15, V.S. 1866/1809 AD, f. 379. *Bahi Khata Khazana Sadar*, V.S. 1852/1795 AD.
119. *Kagad Bahi*, No. 25, V.S. 1878/1821 AD *Chetra Sudi* 1, f. 1.
120. Rajvi, Amar Singh, *Medieval History of Rajasthan*, Vol. I, West Rajasthan, Bikaner, 1992, Chapter - Bikaner.
121. *Kagad Bahi*, No. 2, V.S. 1820/1763 AD, *Asoj Badi* 1, R.S.A.B.
122. Erskine, op. cit., p. 211; Powlett, pp. 92-93.
123. Powlett, p. 92-93.
124. Ibid., p. 142.
125. *Kagad Bahi*, No. 2, V.S. 1820/1763 AD; Lal, Munshi Sohan, p. 367, Powlett, pp. 109, 141, Erskine, p. 211.
126. *Kagad Bahi*, No. 2, V.S. 1820/1763 AD (*Huwala Kagads*), *Bahi Sri*

Karkhana Re Basat Re Sahe Re, V.S. 1763-64, Sadul Museum and Library, Lallgarh Palace, Bikaner.

127. Powlett, p. 142; Erskine, p. 110, *Rajasthan District Gazetteer: Bikaner,* Jaipur, 1972, p. 160.
128. Powlett, p. 93; Rajasthan District Gazetteer, p. 160. It gave employment to 25 persons, as Powlett reports, who received three *Annas* a camel load. More than 2,000 camels loaded of this *mitti* were exported in a year. 'Fuller's Earth and Its Uses', Bikaner Bulletin, Vol. 6, No. 6, Bikaner, January, 1949, p. 10.
129. Tod, Vol. II, p. 161; Erskine, p. 211.
130. *Sawa Bahi Mandi Bikaner,* No. 22, V.S. 1837-38/1780-81 AD, R.S.A.B.
131. Ibid.
132. Erskine, p. 211; Powlett, p. 142.
133. *Sawa Bahi Lunkaransar,* No. 1, V.S. 1887/1830 AD, f. 11.
134. *Sawa Bahi Mandi Bikaner,* No. 22, V.S. 1837-38/1780-81 AD, f. 7.
135. In about 20 villages of Anupgarh area *Sajji* was an important article of manufacturing. It was only a special product of *Raths* after animal rearing in Anupgarh. Erskine, p. 211; Powlett, p. 136.
136. *Sawa Bahi Suratgarh,* No. 3, V.S. 1860/1803 AD, ff. 48-49.
137. *Sawa Bahi Anupgarh,* V.S. 1904/1847 AD, f. 92.
138. *Sawa Bahi Suratgarh,* No. 8, V.S. 1897/1840 AD.
139. *Jagat Bahi,* Bikaner, No. 81, V.S. 1807/1750 AD, R.S.A.B.
140. Sohan Lal, op. cit., pp. 364-67.

5

Trade and Commerce

Significance of Trade and Commerce in Bikaner

Trade and commerce occupy an important place in the economy. It had a conspicuous significance for the desert state of Bikaner during the second half of the 18th and 19th century due to various reasons. First, the geographical location of Bikaner offered some important linkages with many trade-routes passing through from the north-west to the rest of the country. As the map shows (Fig. 5.1) it connected Sindh and Multan to Delhi and Agra via Anupgarh, Suratgarh and Rajgarh;[1] and via Bikaner to Marwar, Pali,[2] Jaipur[3] and the southern provinces.[4] The traders could traverse through with merchandize and the state could earn by levying duties upon it.

Secondly, being stretched out in the desert it had a limited fertile area and so was the production to export at a limited scale but it needed at the same time various items for local consumption and use. Therefore, there existed potentialities of trade and commerce by fulfilling the demand of the required goods in the state by the traders. They could, in turn carry out the available indigenous production with them. We find that items like cloth, luxury items, gur, sugar, opium, tobacoo, horses and foodgrains were brought into the state from different directions; while wool, woollen items, Multani Mitti (Fuller's earth), sajji, etc., were sent out from the state.[5]

Map 5.1: Trade Routes, *Mandis* and *Chowkis*

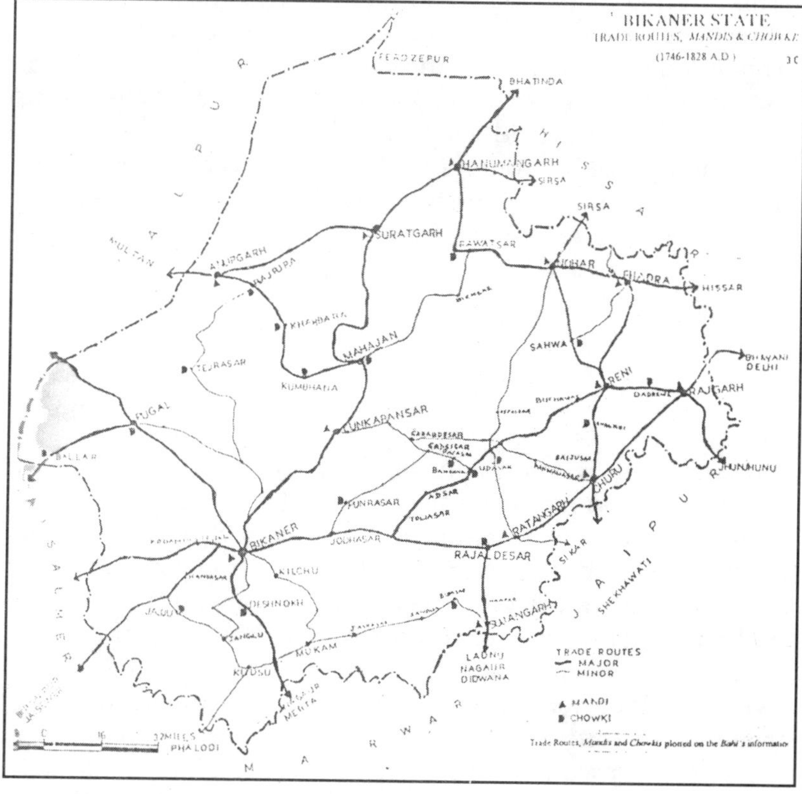

Lastly, by concentrating on trade and commerce in the state more finance could be generated through it and thus deficiency of irregular and insufficient land revenue could be made up.[6] So, the trade and commerce assumed greater importance during the period under review.

(1) TRADE ROUTES, TRANSPORTATION AND COMMUNICATION

(a) Trade Routes

The geographical location of the erstwhile state of Bikaner in Rajputana has influenced its history to a great extent as Bikaner is situated in the *Thar* desert.[7] However, it is surrounded by provinces like Sindh-Multan, Delhi-Agra, Gujrat-Malwa etc. This affected its economy and many trade routes in different directions passed through Bikaner.[8] These external routes were connected to the hinterland through minor internal routes also, which created a network of the trade routes in the state during the period of study and is shown in Map 5.1.

The epigraphic sources of the 10th-13th century establish, routes connecting various towns of Rajputana with those of Bikaner and its region.[9] As for example, one such trade route passed during the 12th and 13th century from Yoginipura (Delhi) to Gujrat via Reni (Bikaner region)[10]; another from Dipalpur to Sambhar via Chhapar, Dronepur and from Bhatinda to Ajmer via Pallu of Bikaner state.[11]

Not much is known prior to the establishment of the Rathore principality of Bikaner over the region in 1488 AD (V.S. 1545), but after collaboration with the Mughals from 1570 AD and owing to its characteristic strong centralized nature, the trade activities grew[12] on restoration of law and order and the pacification of the local turbulent elements in the state.[13] Further, the agro-industrial development which had already begun from Sultanate period and continued during the Mughal period, witnessed the commercial traffic in the state as well as in the whole of Rajasthan. This led to the establishment of some commercial centres in the state.[14] As the Map 5.1 shows that these centres were inter-connected with each other through various routes over which the traders, armies and the officials frequently traversed. Pugal, Rajgarh, Churu and Bikaner were such centres which were witnessing commercial traffic.[15]

The Mughal highway of Delhi-Marwar-Pali also passed, through a branch, from Rajgarh-Reni-Churu-Ratangarh-Sujangarh of the state.[16] The links between Delhi and Multan-Sindh had also established via Bikaner. Further, traders of Central Asia brought horses and dry fruits in abundance and carried to South via Bikaner. In short, a viable contact of Bikaner had been established with the external regions through various routes and some towns had, therefore, developed commercial significance in the early 18th century.

The process of growth in the trade routes did not stop

further even in the late 18th and the early 19th century. After the decline of the Mughal empire during the second half of the 18th century, the native rulers were desperately organizing their financial resources, specially, through trade and commerce. They provided various exemptions, security and inducements in many ways.[17] This resulted in the enlargement of area of commercial activities and the opening of new routes as well. This is evident from the increase in the numbers of *Mandis* in various towns and subsidiary *Chowkis* (known as *Baharli Jagat Chowkis*) which cropped up and developed in the vicinity of the towns and also in the remote area of the villages of the state. The realization of *Jagat* (the custom duty) income from these centres also testify to the fact. Gradually, the more fertile and primary producing areas and the areas of rich mineral deposits, linked-up with the collecting and distributing centres of towns. This led to a network of external and internal routes over the region which continued till the early decades of the 19th century. The major changes and retardation in the commercial significance of these traditional routes was the development of the second half of the 19th century.[18]

The *Kagdon ri Bahis, Sawa Bahis* and the *Jagat Bahis* of Rampuria collection of Bikaner state records,[19] preserved in the Rajasthan State Archives, Bikaner are of paramount importance to know about the major routes connecting Bikaner with distant regions of India; the inter-connecting routes of various commercial towns and capitals of Rajasthan with those of Bikaner and also the minor linkages of the countryside connecting its towns and capital.[20] These state *Bahis* record the movements and transaction of traders in and around the state. The otherwise informations related to routes have often been discussed in these *Bahis*. The details of the routes available in these *Bahis* are as follows:

(i) External Trade Routes Connecting Bikaner with Various Regions of India[21]

(1) Multan to Delhi

This route passed through Anupgarh, Suratgarh, Hanumangarh (Bhatner), Nohar, Reni and Rajgarh in the state and joined Delhi through Bhiwani. At Hanumangarh it forked for Bhatinda in the north and for Sirsa-Hissar in the east.

(2) Delhi to Marwar-Pali

Another significant external trade route through which commodities of the northern and eastern India reached the state passed through Rajgarh, Churu, Ratangarh, Rajaldesar and Sujangarh in the state and ultimately joined Marwar-Pali via Ladnu and Deedwana. It has also bifurcations on Rajgarh for Jhunjhunu and on Churu and Ratangarh for Jaipur and Sikar (Shekhawati) which further connected the towns of eastern Rajputana.

(3) Multan to Marwar-Pali via Bikaner

This trade route was important enough because the north-western region was connected through it with the southern provinces. It passed from Anupgarh, Rajpura, Kharbara, Kumbhana, Mahajan, Lunkaransar, Bikaner and Deshnoke in the state and connected Marwar-Pali via Merta and Nagaur. At Mahajan it bifurcated for Suratgarh to join again the Multan-Delhi route in the north and Bikaner in the south. Thus providing a straight way from Bhatinda to Marwar via Hanumangarh, Suratgarh and Bikaner.

(4) Jaisalmer to Delhi via Bikaner and Reni

One more lengthy route passed from Jaisalmer to Delhi via Bikaner, Jodhpur, Toliasar, Bandhnao, Buchawas, Reni and Rajgarh in the state to Delhi. It also connected Delhi via an alternative route passing via Rajaldesar and Rajgarh in the state.

(5) Sindh to Bikaner

Sindh was also connected with Bikaner via Ballar and Pugal. At Pugal it branched off for Bahawalpur also and through Bikaner it reached Marwar-Pali.

These routes clearly show that Bikaner was well-connected with various provinces of India in all directions. A trader could enter the state from four sides, i.e. from Rajgarh in the east, Pugal and Anupgarh in the west and Bikaner in the south and

Bhatinda in the north. Thus, these towns were entrepots and gateways to the state and the external trade could be done through these towns, besides, the traders could meet each other at these places.

(ii) Internal Trade Routes to Connect the Towns and External Routes of the State:[22]

The state *Bahis* also record the small linkages between a town and main routes which offered convenient and shorter connections to each other. The following were some internal link routes:

(1)	Bikaner to Sujangarh	:	via Kilchu, Muqaam, Jasarasar, Sandwa and Bidasar
(2)	Bikaner to Phalodi	:	via Janglu-Kudsu
(3)	Bikaner to Barsalpur	:	via Nal, Chandasar'
(4)	Anupgarh to Bikaner	:	via Rajpura and Tejrasar
(5)	Anupgarh to Pugal	:	via Rajpura and Tejrasar
(6)	Mahajan to Rawatsar	:	via Biramsar
(7)	Bhadra to Reni	:	via Sahwa
(8)	Reni to Churu	:	via Chalkoi and Saijusar
(9)	Nohar to Ratangarh	:	via Aspalsar and Udasar
(10)	Lunkaransar to Churu	:	via Garabdesar, Kanwaliasar
(11)	Lunkaransar to Ratangarh	:	via Garabdesar and Udasar
(12)	Jhajhu to Nagaur	:	via Janglu and Kudsu

It is significant to note that there were some alternative routes to various long distance trade centres and it offered the traders the options to choose as per their need and less probable risk. It is learnt from the records that the traders preferred the routes of Bikaner state instead of Shekhawati to avoid comparatively more risks and incidences of taxes.[23]

The Difficulties and Insecurity of Travelling Over the Trade Routes

The animal-based journey entailed a comparatively longer time to cover the difficult path of the *Thar* desert, as the caravans had to procure sufficient water and fodder provisions for their beasts of burdern. The routes were also not often smooth and wide to pass through conveniently. The caravans lost their way in the desert very often. Their journey was slow on account of the fact that usually the trade routes passed through the human settlements, no matter, it may have to cover a longer distances. The severe climatic conditions and scarcity of water added to their difficulties. The normal speed of caravans for trade, twenty miles was a good day's journey. The official *Harkara* or *Kasid* (messenger) moved faster and could cover some thirty-five miles a day; the express messenger might take a little lesser time.[24]

In spite of all the possible arrangements and efforts, the trade routes were, in general, not safe during the 18th century and specially in the latter half of it and in the first half of the 19th century. References of the theft, loot, seizure and dacoity of the caravans' goods by some unruly tribes, thieves, *Barothias* (expelled) and *Dhadayaitis* (raiders) and also by some disgruntled and refractory *Jagirdars* as well, are often quoted in the state *Bahis* of the period. For example, in 1797 AD a caravan of the merchant of Bikaner carrying *Pashmina* and cotton cloth from Bittod to Bikaner was looted by Kamardi Khan and his gang near Rajpur.[25] In 1802 AD Seth Kewal Ram Baheti and Bulaki of Bikaner, while carrying goods from Bikaner to Bahawalpur had been looted near Pugal.[26] Likewise, in 1806 AD when two camels of Sultan Bidal of Multan carrying cloth from Multan to Bikaner were looted by Rawal Jalim Singh near Kangarh. Also, in the year 1777 AD two caravans comprising sixty-four camels of the merchant of Pali carrying cotton, lead and ivory goods from Pali to Rajgarh were seized by Shekhawat Prithvi Singh and Dhiraj Singh near Nawalgarh.[27]

The above mentioned examples explain that the routes were not completely safe. Castes like Bhattis and Raths[28] living in the vicinity of the routes in the north and north-west part of the state were also antagonistic to the state and always indulged in looting activities. Often, the local *Jagirdars* in disgust, seized the goods of the merchants while passing through their territory. Some gangsters were also playing havoc with the traders, who had their own paraphernalia. Some disgruntled *Jagirdars* styled as *Barothias*[29] blocked the routes as a mark of their protest. Later, during the second half of the 18th and in the first half of the 19th century the routes were more unsafe on account of mounting dissatisfaction and the rebellious attitude of the *Jagirdars* due to the oppressive hand and excessive warfare activity of Maharaja Surat Singh (1787-1828 AD). He exacted heavy amounts in *Peshkashi* and *Nazrana* from them and reduced them to insignificant military and political figures. The resources of *Jagirdars* were decreasing and mostly felt financially strangulated. Consequently, they took recourse to the disrupting and looting activities out of their anguish.[30]

However, the state committed to reorganize the dwindling financial resources, did not shirk its duties and made necessary arrangements for protection of the traders' caravans. The state issued necessary directions to the officials of *Jagat* check-posts and the *Jagirdars* concerned to ensure the safe passing of traders from their respective territory.[31] Also, they were asked not to harass them in any way.[32] The *Kasids* (messengers) were sent in advance to escort the *Katars* of camels and *Balads* (herds of oxen carts) carrying goods. The armed personnel were deputed on the important junctions.[33] If the traders suspected any plundering ahead, the state provided armed escorts to help them reach their destination. However, the state charged the expenses and fee for it called *Badarki*.[34]

Compensation and Relief

Even, if the goods looted by dacoity or seized by *Jagirdars*, the state was instrumental in recovering the snatched goods. The state, by negotiation with the owner of goods, charged ¼ of the cost of the lost goods from the owner as expenses of exercise. The kind of revenue is termed as *Chauthai ra Jama* in the *Bahis*[35]. *Sawa Bahi Rajgarh* of 1782 AD quotes such example that when Rao Lunkaran Guman Singhot plundered a merchant who was on his way to Churu from Rajgarh with goods, the state did help in recovery of the snatched goods which was later, handed over to that merchant.[36]

The traders themselves, were conscious and took the precautionary measures of their own for such untoward incidents of loot. They usually moved in caravans (groups) and often, kept with them their own armed guards. Whenever, they sensed any danger, they would either stop at a safer place or alter their route or seek the state help to avert the danger.[37]

The *Charans* played an important role in their safety. They became the carriers of the merchandize of the merchants for traversing in the insecure trade routes. Merchants used their services to protect them against the nobles. The sacred character of the *Charans* overawed the lawless Rajput chiefs, other dacoits other dacoits and *Charans* were held high in society.[38] It is only because of this mounting insecurity that the insurance business became more popular in the state. Traders opted for the consignment of the goods under insurance cover.[39]

(b) Transportation

The 18th and 19th century transportation in Bikaner region was carried out mostly through camels and bullocks. The camel, better known as the *ship of the desert* was the fastest, most convenient and suitable means of transportation of goods and passengers. Bullocks or bullock-carts were another commonly used important means. The group of camels and oxen have been referred to as *Katar* and *Balad* and *Kataria* and *Baladia* respectively to their carriers in the state *Bahis*.[40] Elephants, horses, chariots and palanquins were restricted to the use of royalty and nobility only. Of course, traders of Kabul and Qandhar dealt in horses and brought fruits, dry and wet on their back.

The *Rebaries*, the professional expertise caste in camel husbandry were the principal carriers of commercial goods, in the area. The state and traders both hired their services for their ends.[41] Besides them, *Banjaras* were another significant community and most commonly used to carry commodities like salt, grain, rice, wheat and other grocery items from one place to another in oxenload whose number varied from 200 to 1,000 on an average. The state often honoured them with *Siropaos* and *Paghs* for their services. Sikhs known as *Diwana Fakir* were operating as transporters on the trade route of Bhiwani to Bikaner-Marwar and Bikaner to Bahawalpur route. Muller Brahmins also adopted the same profession on the routes leading to Jaisalmer and Punjab. The significance of *Charans* and *Bhats* had already been established owing to their respectful status in the contemporary society. They not only offered their services on payments but also, often indulged in trade activities.

Their significance increased profusely in the period of study when routes had become more insecure due to frequent incidents of raids and plunders. But in the presence of *Charan*, the loot and dacoity was not at all easy. The *Charans* and *Bhats*, as Col. Tod writes, took advantage of their sacred character to be the general carriers of goods in the country.[42]

(c) Communication

The communication system in Rajasthan had a long course of history from the system of letters being delivered as a courtesy by the wayfarers, travellers and the traders in their way of journey to the systemised and regular postal services. In Bikaner state, during the period of study an indigenous and government owned postal and communication system was working to cater to its aministrative, military and commercial needs. The *Sawa Bahis* of the period of Bikaner record the expenditures incurred recurrently in the different towns of the state as *Uthon ro Bhado* (camel rent) and *Kasidon ri Kasidgi*[43] which explains and testifies to the prevalent postal system and the payments made to them. The *Kasids* covered the distances through camels and horses to every part of the state territory and beyond it as well. In the rural areas public announcements were the popular means to convey the official orders and notices/declarations.

The terms *Kasids, Harkaras, Jasoos* and *Baniyo* used in the *Sawa Bahis*[44] of the period explicitly signifies with types of mesengers for different ends, viz. for transmitting important messages/orders, carrying money or *hundis* or collecting secret information from the required areas. The confidential and express letters were sent through the quicker camel posts. We encounter in the *Bahis* that the Brahmins, Jats, Rebaries carried the letters to the different places.[45]

Both regular and irregular postmen/messengers were kept in service after ensuring their honesty and diligence. Either, they were paid a monthly salary or remuneration for work, which depended on the number and weight of papers and the distance travelled by them.

This remuneration was generally paid by the recipient of the letters specially mentioned in the letters. Deductions of

Kasoor (default) from the payments were made out on their short services.[46] The traders also continued to be instrumental in carrying the posts of various places. Often, the big houses of traders kept their own network of the postal system, all over, to avoid delay and fulfil their own purposes.

But the transportation services were very slow, expensive and cumbersome as well. The growing insecurity over the trade routes, further increased their difficulties along with the routine limitations of fodder and water. However, with the expansion of the trade routes network in the period, and construction of some mortar roads in some parts in the north-west (Anupgarh) improved the services in that area.[47]

(2) NATURE AND PROCESS OF INTERNAL AND EXTERNAL TRADE

The commercial activities within the state were carried out in many ways. However, the needs of the rural areas were mostly met through mutual exchange of agricultural produce and services; thereafter, the surplus reached the deficit areas for sale by some peasants for procuring the necessary domestic items from towns. The state also often sold its realized revenue-grain for cash. For instance, in 1758 AD the *Modi-Khana* (a state department to manage raw food material for the royal household) sold 71 *mounds* of *moth* realized in revenue, in the *mandi* of Reni for Rs. 83 As. 8 @ 3/4 *maund* for Re. 1.[48] In 1766 AD the state sold revenue grain in Nohar and encashed Rs. 79 *As* 1 and *Takka* 3.[49] And also in 1847 AD it sold 86½ *maunds* of *Sajji* for Rs. 31 *As* 7 collected through *chungi* @ 25 *seers* per camel load in Anupgarh market.[50] The traders and merchants also procured the indigenous production while transacting for their supplied goods. They had their storages in villages. Traders Banthia Santokhi had his storages of grains in village *Biko-Jogsaniya* and after paying the *chouthai* tax to the state, he was allowed to transport his grains from the village to the *mandi*.[51] Similarly, Choudhary Khusala had his one hidden storage of *Moth* consisting of 93 *maunds* in village Likhmidesar.[52] Parakh Khusal Chand Anop Chand had storage of 1,000 *maunds* grains in village Toliyasar in 1804 AD, who was allowed to transport to *Mandi* Bikaner only after paying the due '*Chouthai Dhan ki*' (a tax on sale of grains) to the state.[53] These large storages of grains by the traders, sometimes hidden storages also, indicates two things-one, that the traders used to purchase the grains at the crop site and also merchants' capacity to hold grain for the time being; perhaps in order to sell at the appreciated prices or wait for high prices. Secondly, the hidden storages also indicate the merchants' bargaining capacity.

Moreover, various items which were not available in Bikaner had to be imported from the adjoining producing areas to fulfil the needs of the people.

All this necessitated trading as well as commercial activities within and from outside the state. It can be classified and analysed under (a) The internal trade and (b) The external trade.

The *Jagat Bahis* and *Sawa Bahis* of different *chowkis* and *Mandis* record transactions and movements of commercial classes and also the collection of *Jagat*. Through them we can infer the nature and the pattern of internal and external trade.

(a) The Internal Trade

Nature and Process of the Internal Trade

The internal trade here includes the trade in villages and towns as well as among the towns within the state. In villages the items of routine and daily consumption of life mostly satisfied within itself by the village merchants, known by different local names as *Bania, Bisaiti, Mahajan, Bohra* or *Sahukar*.[54] They used to stock all the necessary articles of consumption and use the regular scale in their own house godowns.

The *Pheriwala* (pedlars) termed in records as *Pothia*[55] with their packload of useful domestic items like cloth, salt, gur, ironware, grocery, spices, etc. also moved from village to village and sold the items.[56] A noticeable feature recorded in the sources shows a culture of bargain metality.

Sawa Bahi Mandi Churu of 1771 AD records that Lachho Agrawal *Pheriwala* of Jasarasar village carried 5 camels of *til* (seasame) from Churu to sell them in adjoining villages.[57] A *pothia* of village Kaklasar (*Chira* Sihagoti) brought 7 *poths* (packload) of wheat from Jaitpur to *mandi* of Churu for sale in the month of *Magh* in V.S. 1828 (1771 AD)[58] Likewise, a *Jagat Bahi* of 1808 AD mentioned that Heerji Agrawal, *Pheriwala* of Ratangarh carried one half of camel load of grocery goods for sale to the nearby village[59] and also Shivdan *Pheriwala* of Sujangarh in the territory carried three-fourth load of gur from Sujangarh to the adjoining villages.[60] A *Pheriwala* (peddler) Begani Bijai Ram of village Bidaṣar was allowed exemption upto 50 per cent in *Jagat* for his goods to be carried from *Ratangarh Mandi* and to be sold in villages of Bidasar in 1807 AD[61] Why the exemption of 50 per cent was given to the *Pheriwala* is not clear from the sources.

The major needs of the villagers were fulfilled in the seasonal fairs and festivals known as *Mela-magarias*.[62] People usually bought cattle and other animals, articles of domestic and agricultural use and the seasonal items therein. They awaited these fairs very eagerly for finding variety and competitive markets.[63] The state took an active interest in organizing them. The state not only invited the traders to participate in them with their goods but also gave exemptions in the local taxes to attract at large scale. During the period some religious-cum-commercial fairs were organized in the state. These were Kolayat mela, Gajner mela, Gogamedi mela, Muqaam mela. More *melas* on a smaller scale were organized at a local level. Powlett mentions some local *melas* of Bikaner city.[64] These fairs yielded revenues to the state. Revenue collection of Kolayat fair is shown in the following table.

Table 5.1: Income of Kolayat Fair

S.N.	*Year V.S./AD*	*Income pertains to days*	*Fair income Rs. - Annas*
1.	1847/1790[65]	11	1,278 - 5
2.	1848/1791[66]	13	3,314 - 8
3.	1856/1799[67]	11	2,759 - 4
4.	1878/1821[68]	16	811 - 13
5.	1879/1822[69]	12	1,495 - 11

Likewise, we do come across some *melas*[70] but the state income is not known to us.

The small markets of towns surrounded by the villages and the *mandis* of bigger commercial centres were also convenient places where varied commodities were bought and sold.[71] The surplus agricultural produce was disposed of by the *zamindars* and some farmers after carrying it to the markets of these towns and cities. Merchant Madan Lunia of village Hardesar carried ½ camel load of grain from Hardesar to Ratangarh *mandi* for sale in 1808 AD[72] Also, Soma Jat of village Aspalsar carried 3/4 camel load of grain (*Bajra*) and a Jat farmer brought 3½ camel load of grains for sale to the *Churu mandi*.[73] From *Sawa Bahi Rajgarh Mandi* of year 1823 AD we know that during two months of *Bhadrapad* and *Kartik* of V.S. 1880 Rs. 889 were collected at the *mandi* office of *Jagat* from villages from such direct sale by the farmers and *zamindaras*.[74]

The *Hatwalas* (shopkeepers), *Bichhayatis* (the pavement dealers), *Adhatiyas*[75] (commission agents) and *dalals*[76] (brokers) along with the traders were all to play a role of their own in the commercial activities of towns and cities.

The *Hatwalas* (both wholesale dealers and retailers) sold their goods at competitive rates to the consumers. However, they procured the goods from the producing areas through the *Adhatiyas* (commission agents), *Dalals* (brokers) and often *Hatwalas* themselves procured the produce directly from the villages. They held their storehouses of agricultural productions in the villages.[77] *Sawa Bahi Churu Mandi* of 1771 AD mentions that a merchant Har Roop Mehta of Nohar imported from Churu via Bhaironsar 1½ camel load of *kiryana* and Bijai Chand Kothari ½ camel load of *mehandi* and 1¼ camel load of *kiryana* (grocery) through an *Adhatiya*.[78]

The *Katarias*[78] and *Baladias*[80] who usually procured goods for traders and merchants also disposed of the goods in the markets or villages and procured other local items for further sale.[81] The *Banjaras* were sometimes hired for transportation of goods and other articles of the army of the state and were paid rent per ox.[82]

The *Bichayatis* (pavement sellers) carried on their trade in an easily accessible spot in the town market and sold items like grains, pulses, groceries, spices, cloth, wares, etc., at retail prices to the consumers. It seems that the *Bichayatis* paid a substantial amount of *jagat* to the state. We find that when a *Muqata* (*Ijara*) of income accrued of *Bichayatis* of market Bikaner was let out to a merchant Begani Umed in Rs. 14 for one month of *Posh* in 1807 AD. Soon this *Muqata* was revised for Rs. 451 for one month and the *Muqata* (*Ijara*) was given to Agrawal Sewa Ram Tomada Ram of Jhunjhunu at increased rates.[83] *Bichayati* traders from outside the state also participated in sales in the state.[84] *Sawa Bahi Mandi Sadar Bikaner* of 1748 AD and 1750-53 record some *Bichayatis* of Bikaner city as Pema Rampuria, Man Das, Jiwan Das, Ajbi Ram, and Gulab Mehta who usually sold their goods in the *Mandi* of Bikaner.[85] *Bichayati vyoparis* procured their goods from the producing areas and sold them in the adjoining villages.[86]

Thus, the shopkeepers, *Bichayatis*, and the *Pheriwalas* actively participated in the running of the domestic or internal trade. They contributed in transportation of commercial goods from the countryside to the towns and from towns to the bigger commercial centres through retail or wholesale transactions.

The small commercial towns served as the nodal-points between the countryside and the big commercial centres as the agrarian production of the hinterland reached *mandis* via these towns.[87] Towns of commercial significance were inter-linked with each other.[88] For example, Pugal and Anupgarh in the west were well-connected with Bikaner and Suratgarh,[89] Rajgarh, Churu, Reni, Ratangarh and Sujangarh were linked to each other and likewise, Nohar, Bhadra with Hanumangarh as it is visible in the map of the trade routes (Fig. 5.1).

The different artisans, craftsmen and specialized workers were concentrated in separate localities or streets in the towns.[91] *Telis* (oil pressers), *Chungar* (lime workers), *Kumhar* (potters), *Suthars* (carpenters) and *Luhars* (iron smiths) used to sell products at their own houses in the towns to the consumers. The state seemed equally concerned to encourage and take care of the artisans and craftsmen. The oil pressers (*Telis*) of Lunkaransar were given all assurances in 1809 AD that no excesses in taxes would be repeated in future, so they should stay in the village.[92] In bigger towns there were some specialized commodity markets. Such as *Dhan phad* (market of foodgrain), *Pattipera* (market of stone slabs), *Bakra mandi* (market of goats) and *Halwaiyon ki gali* (sweetmakers' locality), etc. Such localities based on the professional castes can be discerned from the Sultanate and the Mughal period.

The *Kiryana* (grocery), woollen products like *Lunkaras* (blankets), foodgrains, til, salt, sugar, gur, multani mitti and sajji, iron implements, leather buckets and cloth were some items of local trade as transaction of these items are mostly recorded in the *bahis*.[93] *Kiryana*, cotton, sugar,*gur* were frequently carried on the way from Anupgarh to Bikaner and Churu to Ranehar via Kumbhana.[94]

The local traders were also encouraged by way of exemptions in taxes to transport goods from one place to another. We find that a *Charan* trader of village Sinthal Mewa Ram Sarupa Karni Danoni was granted 50 per cent exemption for carrying cotton, iron, etc. to *Mandi* Bikaner in 1804 AD.[95] Traders who used to carry grain, ghee and oil to Hanumangarh from Mahajan they were granted 50 per cent exemption in *jagat* in 1806 AD.[96] So, the local trade seems to have developed steadily in the state and the activities of different commercial groups were increasing.

Dalals (Brokers)

Business in towns was also carried on with the help of a *Dalal* (broker) who finalized the transactions by charging his commission from the seller and the purchaser.[97] Thus, they played a pivotal role in the transactions in the bigger markets of towns and cities. The *Dalals* who worked as the commission agents procuring and selling the agricultural produce on commission in the wholesale market of *mandis* were identified as *Adhatias*. The *Sawa Bahis* of *Mandi Sadar Bikaner* and *Mandi Churu* record the activities of these *Dalals*.[98]

Seru *Dalal* sold 20 camels of Baloch Mal Bux in the fair of Kolayat and paid Rs. 6 and *Dam* 25 as *Jagat* to *Churu Mandi*.[99] From this it can be inferred that Seru *Dalal* in addition to working as *dalal*, also participated in the trade activities. The *Dalals* who could afford to buy goods themselves, traded independently.

These *dalals* dealt in commodities like cloth, animals, wool, immovable property, precious metals, grains, luxury items, etc.[100] The state gave due permission for it and levied the tax on brokerage known as *Dalali*. An annual tax on these *dalals* were also levied known as *Dalalon-ri-bhanch*.[101]The profession of *dalali* was becoming very popular in the state as *dalals* could earn lucrative profits and the profession continued to be popular till the early 19th century.[102]

(i) The External Trade

Nature and Process of the External Trade

There are sufficient evidences of trade relations of Bikaner with the other states of Rajputana[103] available in the *Kagad bahis* and *Jagat bahis* during the period. The state of Bikaner was well-connected through its trade routes to the commercial centres of Nagaur, Marwar, Pali, Jaipur, Kota, Udaipur, Ajmer and Jaisalmer. Sufficient goods of these states were brought into the state and exchanged with the articles available in Bikaner by the traders of these states.[104]

Raja Ram Daga, Gokul Chand Daga, Ratansi Dammani, Khetsi Shab Khusal Juhar, Sri Krishan, Asa Bhat and Devi Dan Godhi were among the traders who extensively traded between Bikaner and Nagaur, Nohar, Churu, Jaisalmer, Jaipur and Marwar. The state also invited and asked some big traders to settle down in the state and granted land for shops.[105] Balkishan Fatehpuria had his shop in Nohar and he was facilitated land in Mahajan qasba and in Ratangarh for shops and a house for his *qabila* (kinsmen) to initiate intra-state trade.[106]

There were various articles being brought from various states of Rajputana into Bikaner, and in exchange local production found their way to these states.[107]Bullocks, ashgandh, salt, foodgrains, wheat, pulses, cotton, precious metals and jewellery, asafoetida, *Khar* and alum were the items mainly brought into and sajji, multani mitti, sugar candy, camel, wool, woollen fabrics, *lunkaras* (blankets) were sent to these states.[108] The rates of *Jagat* on import and export were also controlled and revised from time to time, it is clear from the transactions of some *sahukars* of Ratangarh. When Agrawal Har

Bhajan Shiv Kishan Sawansukho, Sewa Ram Khemka imported foodgrains and groceries into Rajgarh, Ratangarh and Churu from Surajgarh and Hansi in 1810 AD and were immediately exported to Jaisalmer and Marwar. The following rates were effective:

Grocery (kiryana)	:	Rs. 3½ per 1 camel load
Gur, Sugar	:	Rs. 1¾ per camel load
Rice	:	Rs. 1½ per camel load

These rates were effective both on *Adhat* (goods procured through middle men) and *Gharu* (without *Adhat*) goods.[109]

The major trade routes lying in the desert regions were frequently in use by the traders of Sindhi-Multan, Delhi-Agra, Gujrat-Malwa, and other provinces[110] and continued to be used even after the establishment of the Bikaner state in the desert in 1488 AD. The rulers of Bikaner adopted a policy of encouraging the traders to pass through the state territory and earn transit duty. The *farman* of Akbar to Rai Singh dated April 25, 1592 AD is a testimony to the fact.[111] Under a considered trade policy of the rulers in the second half of the 18th and early 19th century, they continued the encouragement policy afresh.

The Baluch and Pathan traders of Sindh were asked to bring dry fruit, horses, asafoetida and cloth to Bikaner instead of going to the eastern direction, i.e. towards Delhi-Agra.[112] To boost the trade, merchants and traders from Sind were encouraged to participate in the trade of Bikaner state.[113]

Consequently, productions of these provinces briskly came into the state and needs of the state were fulfilled. Camels and horses, dry fruit, spices, paper, scents, cloth, opium, tobacco, indigo, wheat and rice, pashmina and saffron were sent to the state; and in turn sajji, *khar, multani mitti*, wool, *lunkara*, leather items, iron, swords, handles, matchlocks, goats and sheep, ivory bangles, *ghee*, camels were sent to these provinces. Rajgarh of Bikaner was the place where commodities of different provinces and regions reached.[114] *Khazanchi* Harnarain of Delhi who used to pursue trade-commerce in Bikaner *Mandi* was granted ¼ exemption in *jagat* as a token of encouragement for intra-state trade.[115]

Some of the traders were exclusively doing long distance

trade and widely traded between the provinces. For instance, Gopal Das Khatri, Sant Ram Khatri and Bhinv Das Arora were some of the traders in Bikaner who traded with Multan.[116] Traders of other provinces like the Punjab, Gujrat and Malwa were also requested to send required goods.[117]

Apart from these traders, *Dalals* and *Banjaras* played an important role in the long distance trade. the *Banjaras* were specially instrumental in the transportation of long distance trade.[118] They usually, apart from carrying other required items, transported salt and grains to the deficit areas. The salt was brought from Sambhar and Deedwana and the grains from Kota, Marwar, Sindh and other producing areas into the state. The long distance trade of the period was backed by a well-developed system of finance and credit. The use of *Hundis* or bankers' drafts was widespread. There was also an organized system of insurance against risks of loss in transit and other risks.[119] The commercial credit was available to the merchants and traders from *Sahukars, Bohras* and *Sarrafs*. They also helped to transfer their money at the desired places through their agencies. *Hundiyan Kiwi Teri Bahi* of 1669 AD records several examples of *Hundis* being sent to other places. Also cases of insurance cover are available on the transportation of the merchandize.[120]

(3) DIFERENT COMMODITIES OF TRADE AND THE TRANSIT TRADE

As I have discussed earlier that the state then was located at the cross roads and enroute to prosperous provinces of the Punjab, Multan and Sindh, Gujrat-Malwa and Delhi-Agra. It was considered significant[121] for the transit trade and useful for the trade of different commodities. The caravans of the merchants and traders largely used the routes of the state from different directions and therefore, its various bordering towns like Rajgarh,[122] Churu, Sujangarh, Bikaner,[123] Pugal, Anupgarh and Bhatner had emerged as important trading centres[124] and traders met each other at these places.

The traders not only supplied various goods to meet the local needs but also in exchange took away the indigenous production out of the state for sale. This resulted in the growth of the imports and exports and accelerated the trading activities as well as the transit trade.[125] The necessary state protection and incentives further encouraged the caravans to pass through the state territory and also the supply of necessary goods.[126] Therefore, the exchange of commodities could be done sufficiently and commercial growth and development could be generated. The details of consignments of *Nekal* (export), *Pesar* (import) and *vahtivon* (transit) of goods[127] as well as the payments of *Jagat* (custom duty) have been recorded in the *Jagat* and *Sawa bahis* of *chowkis* and *mandis* (trade centres).[128] Whereas, the *Kagad bahis* and *Byav bahis* provide ample light on the export/ import and transit trade during the period under study.[129] With the help of these archival *bahis* the details of export, import and transit trade may be analysed as under:

(a) Exports from Bikaner (*Nekal*)

Although, the production in this desert state was meagre and limited but whatever, was available, after meeting the local needs, was sent out of Bikaner as an export to the deficit areas. We have reference of a receipt of Rs. 130 as *Nekal* (export) *Jagat* in Rajgarh in 1782 AD.[130]

*(1) Categories of Commodities of Export (*Nekal*)*

The items being exported as described in the state record,[131] may be classified into two categories below–

(a) Those items which were locally produced and exported,and (b) Those important items which found their way into the state territory first and then sold or carried out of Bikaner for the benefit of the traders.

(a) In the first category, as is shown in the table that the state exported the agricultural production of *bajra,moth, til* in case of a good crop; otherwise, the same foodgrain had to be imported in the drought and lean seasons. The state was famous for its wool and woollen productions of *lunkaras* (blankets), cloth, carpets and shawls. The state was equally important for turbans, ivory bracelets, sugar candy, iron goods like swords-blades, match locks, daggers, iron lances and the handles of swords of high quality. Industrial goods like Fuller's earth (*multani mitti*), *khar*, salt and *sajji*, and animals like sheep and goats, camels and products derived from them like *ghee*, skin and hides were the items of export. The wooden saddles for camels called *pallans*[132] and the *chhagals*[133] (winnowing device) were also sent outside.

(b) In the second category, items which were imported into the state first and then exported had two distinct characteristics:

(i) Some items like dry vegetables, onions, paper, grocery, red chilly, sindhi salt, dry fruit, horses, pashmina wool, opium and tobacco were imported for commercial purposes. The traders who had surplus commercial capital invested in the storage of items and exported them when they fetched better or higher prices.

(ii) Some items in the form of raw material were imported and after reproducing and remanufacturing into new items, were exported. For instance, gur and sugar candy was manufactured here. Thus the main market of Bikaner state played the role of an emporium on a smaller scale.

The following table evince the export and distribution of different commodities of either categories from Bikaner:

Table 5.2 (ii) Commodities of Export from Bikaner[134]

S.No.	*Place where sent*	*En route*	*Commodities*
1.	Sirsa	via Bhatner (Hanumangarh)	*Multani mitti*, wool, *sajji*, *til*, ivory bangles with golden thread work, *bajra*, *moth*, *Chhagal* and sugar candy
2.	Rewari	-do-	Tobacco[135]
3.	Delhi	via Rajgarh	*Sajji*, sugar candy, woollen cloth, *multani mitti*
4.	Multan	via Anupgarh	Woollen blankets (*lunkaras*), wool, woollen cloth,

Contd...

Contd...

			shawls[136] sugar candy, iron, *kori* (unwashed cloth), indigo, sugar, *gur*, turmeric, dry-ginger and nutmeg (जायफल)
5.	Sindh	via Pugal	Grains, *til*, guwar, oxen, camel[137] (female) *ghee*[138], gum, wool, woollen cloth, *sajji*, sugar candy, indigo *gur*, sheep and goat.[139]
6.	Bahawalpur	via Anupgarh	Camel[140]
7.	Burhanpur	-	*Gur*, turmeric
8.	Nagaur	via Deshnoke	Woollen cloth, dry fruit, *sajji*,
		via Jhajhu	*sindhi* salt, alum,[141] camel, nutmeg (जायफल) Fuller's earth (*multani mitti*) paper (*dasta*) aniseed (सौंफ), dry ginger, sugar candy, *til*, oil cake (खल) and lac[142]
9.	Jodhpur	via Bikaner/ Sujangarh	*Multani mitti, bajra, moth, dry fruits*, sugar candy, *kachri* and *khelra* (dry vegetable) oil cake(खल) *siwal* cotton, wool, *til*, *ghee* and *sajji*[143]
10.	Jaipur	via Bidasar	*ghee*, grains, *til*, cotton, cloth, salt[144], *multani mitti*, sugar candy, wool, woollen cloth, *sindhi* salt,horses, blankets[145]
11.	Kota	-	*Sajji*, sugar candy, wool, camel, *multani mitti*
12.	Udaipur	via Bikaner	Horses, sugar candy, *sajji*, dry fruit
13.	Jaisalmer	via Barsalpur	Sugar candy, lac bangles, camel
14.	Phalodi		Camel, wool, woollen cloth, lac, sugar candy, dry fruit
15.	Ajmer	via Ratangarh	*Til*, *sindhi* salt, *multani mitti*[146]
16.	Pali	via Bikaner via Rajaldesar and Sujangarh	Indigo, *bandedo* (packload) tabacco.[147]

(b) Imports in Bikaner (Pesar)

As already stated, the production was not enough in the state. Although, sometimes the foodgrain like *bajra, moth* and *til* were supplied to the neighbouring areas in the event of good production, but shortage of the foodgrains on account of famine and scanty rainfall was very common. Whenever the state felt scarcity the export of foodgrains was banned. In 1802 AD such a ban was issued.[148] It had to be imported from neighbouring states to meet the essential needs of the masses besides some routine items. Exceptions of half of *jagat* was granted to traders of Udaipur, Marwar and Kota[149] to encourage the supply of necessary foodgrains in need.

The needs of the costlier items like horses, cosmetics, jewellery, cloth-silk and cotton, grocery and brass wares and arms ammunitions were in great demand by the richer sections of merchants, feudals and the ruling classes. The demand was also satisfied by importing such items.

These important items found their way into the state from different areas and directions. From Sindh and Multan through Pugal and Anupgarh came in horses, dry fruit, wheat, rice, sugar,tobacco, *sindhi* salt, *ghee*, iron, wooden legs of cots, wooden lintens (शहतीर), wheels and carts and silk.[150] Whereas the eastern provinces of India sent *gur*, tobacco, indigo cloth (silk and cotton) through Reni and Rajgarh of the state.[151] Metalwares, cloth, grocery, ivory, *ker-sangri* (vegetables of desert areas), paper, chilli were imported from Marwar, Nagaur and Phalodi.[152] Jaipur was the chief source of Sanganer printed cloth, silk thread, cosmetics[153] (मणिहारी) and the precious metals. The opium and tobacco, wheat and pulses were brought to Bikaner mainly from Kota and Ajmer.[154]

On comparative study of the commodities of imports and exports we are inclined to feel that the commodities of imports were larger than the exports. Moreover, the nature of the commodities imported shows that the state had to pay more in importing items like horses, cloth both silk and cotton, precious metallic wares, arms, cosmetics, sugar and opium and other luxury items. Comparatively, the exported items were

Table 5.3: Import of Various Commodities[155]

S.No.	*Place from goods imported*	*Commodity*
1.	Sirsa and Rewari	*Ghee*, wheat, tobacco[156]
2.	Bhiwani	Sugar, *gur*, rice
3.	Delhi	Silk, cloth, chintz cloth, indigo, sugar, variety of turbans, paper, iron[157]
4.	Burhanpur	Variety of *Paghs*
5.	Agra	Cloth
6.	Sikarpur	Horses, dry fruit, *asafoetida*
7.	Amritsar	*Pashmina*
8.	Multan	Dry fruit, wheat, tobacco, asafoetida, cotton *lehange*, wet fruit, chintz, lac, perfumes, rogan and saffron[158]
9.	Sindhi and Dera Gazikhan	Wheat, rice, silk, dry and wet fruit, *sindhi* salt, horses, tobacco, turmeric, *asafoetida*, cotton, gum, carpets, spices, betal nuts, *gugal*, camel, indigo[159]
10.	Jehanabad	Rice[160]
11.	Gujrat	Cloth, black pepper
12.	Jaipur	Sanganeri cloth, silk, precious stones and metals, Burhanpuri and Hyderabadi cotton, antimony, scent of roses, ivory, coconuts, paper,[161] etc.
13.	Sambhar and Deedwana	Salt[162]
14.	Ajmer	Tobacco, Indigo, *kimkhab sarees*[163]
15.	Kota	Tobacco, opium, wheat, gram, indigo
16.	Jodhpur	*Pagris* (turbans), *khas* fans, marble stone, chilli, cotton, brass utensils
17.	Pali	Spices, cloth, coconut, foreign, *pagris*, rice, golden and silver wares, *gota kinari*
18.	Nagaur	Chilli, cumenseed (जीरा), oxen, dry vegetables, cotton, scabbards of swords.[164]
19.	Daulatabad	Paper[165]
20.	Jaisalmer & Kishangarh	Alum, tobacco, dry fruits, *asafoetida*, silk and silk cloth, *hirmach*, gum, *kasumba*, *aal* and camel[166]
21.	Mewar (Udaipur)	Horses[167]
22.	Bombay & Calcutta	Cloth, coconut and betelnut

cheaper, therefore, the balance of trade does not appear to be favourable to the state. Still the transit trade was significant for the state.

The transactions and movements of traders as recorded in various *Jagat Bahis* evince that traders from different areas of northern India entered into the state territory through its routes and brought in large quantities of goods from outside. Such goods reached the consumers of towns and its hinterland.[168] Towns were well connected with the hinterland. For instance, messengers frequently traversed the routes from Reni town to its villages like Nurawna, Gorkhan, Hardesar, Hansiawar, Dadrewa, Jhanghni which informs travellers about the safety of routes. When the local needs were meted out they used to carry them out to other places. They also exchanged the local production over here in the process. However, limited quantities of indigenous goods reached outside.[169] The local traders and merchants were also encouraged by the state in it.

The process of exchange and commercial activities during the second half of the 18th century intensified and it is manifested in these evidences: (i) The description of various routes in the *Jagat* and *Kagad Bahis*, interlinking connections of towns and hinterland and the heavy trafficking of traders on them signify the expansion of such activities. In the process some new linkages were also traced.[170] (ii) During the period the growth of various commercial centres, establishment of commercial *mandis*[171] and *chowkis*[172] and appointments of village *Bholawanias* in large numbers to collect the *jagat* also testify to the fact.[173]

But owing to some difficulties and factors, this export-import business and commercial activity of traders might have hampered the progress in the early 19th century. The insecurity of routes on account of plundering and dacoities by the *Dhadvis* (raiders or plunderers) and *Barothia* enhanced the difficulties of trafficking the goods.[174] Surat Singh's military activities and also his extortions from the *sahukars* had an adverse impact. The system of *hundis* and insurance must have eased out these difficulties and helped them favourably. Merchants took to the work of *Dalali* and *Muqatas* which was considered to be a profitable business. However, the insecurity over trade routes and general political disturbance had an adverse impact on the trading activities.

(c) The Transit Trade

The contemporary descriptions show that the transit trade of Bikaner was equally important. It assumed significance as it augmented influx or transit of commercial goods from distant places. It was a good source to the state income from the transit duty termed locally as *Vehtivon* (the Rahdari). It enhanced the commercial significance of Bikaner around and strengthened trade relations with the neighbouring states and traders.

George Thomas in his military memoirs has confirmed that the transit trade for Bikaner was very profitable to it and sometimes it earned good profits.[175] In Suratgarh *Sawa Bahi* of 1823 AD mentions that it earned Rs. 2,085 on camels and wet fruit from transit duty.[176] In the favourable conditions and suitable encouragement from the state to the traders, the income from *Vahtivon* (transit duty) could reach upto Rs. 1,00,000 in 1848 AD which formed 1/3 of the state's total receipts.[177] References are available of neighbouring relations based on commercial interests. The Nawab of Multan wrote a personal letter to the Bikaner ruler in 1778-79 AD to exempt duty on horses of his traders. The traders were given some concession and only Rs. 150 was taken.[178] The traders were also treated well in the state. Routes from Bahawalpur to Sirsa via Bikaner were improved and looked after as the activities of the merchants was brisk over it. Rs. 1,881 was earned in V.S. 1906/ 1849 AD.[179] Minor loans to Multani traders and others and instances of state honouring these inter-regional traders are not lacking in the records.[180] We have the reference of the state providing petty loans to Multani traders of Rs. 1,026 As. 14 in 1748 AD in Bikaner. Also Sarup Chand Banthia was given Rs. 50 and Jaith Mal was given Rs. 20 as a loan, which was later recovered with an interest of Rs. 2 and *As*. 8 in Reni in 1766 AD.[181] But they were also penalized for their misconduct.[182] On quarrelling by Multani traders with the insurance dealer certain Banthia of Bikaner for compensation of the lost goods in 1750 AD, the state imposed a penalty on the Multanis and Rs. 500

including penalty were realized from Multanis in Bikaner.[183]

The commodities crossing the borders of the state were mainly horses and camels, dry fruit, opium, cloth, foodgrains, salt and precious stones. We find that the horses and camels being the most important out of them, which were supplied from Sindh and Multan to Rajputana, specially to the eastern and the southern states of it.[184] All the Rajput states of Rajputana as well as the south were good markets for the best breed of horses.[185] The state realizing the importance of the demand of horses took special care of the Pathan, Mughal and Balooch horse traders and issued directions to its officials not to harass them or realize undue *jagat* from them at the check posts. Instructions were provided to extend the necessary help to them.[186] Pathan Nasroo Khan, Mal Khan and others carried 347 horses from Dera Gazikhan to Jaipur and paid Rs. 1,452 As 11 and Dam 31 as transit duty in Bikaner in 1748 AD.[187] Likewise, *Sawa Bahi Bikaner* mentions that in 1770 AD Pathan Adu Khan and Kikhar Khan paid Rs. 34 As. 8 for the camels being taken to Deccan from Sindh.[188] The Pathan and Mughal traders of Dera Gazikhan (Sindh) paid Rs. 6,919 for their 1,340 horses and 300 colts while passing through Bikaner towards Deccan.[189]

Table 5.4: Commodities of Transit Trade in Bikaner

S. No.	*Producing/ distributing centres*	*Transited commodity*	*Destination/ consuming places*
1.	Dera Gazikhan/ Sindh	Horses, ponies, dry fruit[190]	Jaipur
		Camel[191]	Deccan
		Horses, tobacco[192]	Delhi
		Horses[193]	Nagpur
2.	Multan[194]	Camel[195]	Mundwa (fair) (Marwar)
		Sulphur, opium, camel, cloth cotton	Marwar
3.	Bahawalpur	Cloth, camel[196]	Sirsa
4.	Jaipur	Camel, iron, sugar, gur, navsadar[197]	Jaisalmer
		Silk thread, indigo,oxen	Sindh

5.	Jaisalmer	Horses	Jehanabad
		Horses[198]	Karuali
6.	Nagaur	Oxen[199]	Multan
		Red chilly, cotton[200]	Marot (Sindh)
7.	Pali (Marwar)	Gur, alum, grocery, sugar[201]	Fatehpur
		Dry fruit, bandedo[202] (packwood of eatables and spices)	Sindh

However, the state was equally keen regarding other commodities of the transit trade. We find some more references of other commodities such as dry fruit, silk, *pashmina* being crossing the territories from different directions. The transited commodities have been shown in Table 5.4.

The table shows that the traders passed through the territory from its different corners and transited goods sent to the deficit areas. Therefore, transit trade was of immense significance during the period.

(4) STATE: TRADE AND COMMERCE

The state *Bahis* testify that the rulers of Bikaner showed keen interest in the growth and development of trade and commerce during the period of the second half of the 18th and early 19th century.[203] They encouraged the traders and merchants through various measures, induced them with remissions in taxes and duties. They were also facilitated by protecting their goods.

The loss of the Mughal protection as well as the *Tankhwah-i-Jagiri* income after the decline of the Mughal empire, had put the state into manifold difficulties. It was exposed to external attacks and internal distrubances[204] and thus faced financial exigencies on account of the growing military expenditure, running of the state administration as well as maintenance of the royal household.

Therefore, Maharaja Gaj Singh (1746-87 AD) and Surat Singh (1787-1828 AD) both attempted to enhance their income from the indigenous sources like trade and commerce, a viable alternative left to them. The following were some methods and measures through which they manoeuvred to achieve their goal under a policy of encouragement and promotion of trade and commerce.

To keep them in good humour, the state honoured both local and foreign traders and merchants with *Pagh-pagris* (turbans), *Siropaos* (robe of honour), *Thirmas* (Shawls) and *Motiyon-ro-chowkdo* (a golden ornament embedded with jewels). It was a kind of encouragement to the commercial class.[205] For instance, a *pagh* was bestowed to merchant Maya Ram Tater of Churu in 1765 AD.[206] *Thirmas* were given to *sarrofs* of Sujangarh costing Rs. 60. The *sarrofs* were Roopchand, Agrawal Mun Ram, Fatehpuria Siwal Das and Jajodia Kishan Ram.[207] A *motiyan ro chowkdo* was bestowed on Seth Mirza Mal Potedar of Churu in 1827 AD.[208]

Traders and mechants were also invited to attend the royal court on celebrations of Diwali, Holi, Dussehra and such festivals.[209] A *Sahukar* (moneylender) was granted an honorarium of Re. 1 per day for the days he stayed in Bikaner.[210]

Besides patronising the local *Sahukars*, the state administration requested the foreign traders and mechants to carry on their trade, convey their goods through the routes of the state, so that it might earn transit duty. The traders were assured full protection and help of the state.[211] Moreover, the state instantly permitted the external traders for the trade. A camel trader Qader Bux of Bhatner was permitted to trade in Bikaner.[212] *Sahukars* of Hansi and Fatehabad were requested to send their goods to Rajgarh, Churu and Bikaner. All assistance was assured to them.[213]

To accelerate the commercial activities, traders and merchants of the neighbouring states and provinces were invited to come and settle in the state, open their shops and initiate business.[214] Traders were also invited to participate in the fairs of the state with commodities of distant places.[215] In response many traders and merchants came and initiated business in the state. Mirza Mal Potedar of Ramgarh, Shah Dewa Ram Ganga Bishan of Sikar and Shah Snehi Ram Jai Gopal of Agra were asked to open shops at Ratangarh in 1804 AD and having full trusts in the state support.[216] Also, Lohia Jeevan Ram Juhari Mal were given land for constructing six shops and two residential houses in Ratangarh in 1804 AD by the state.[217] Agrawal Harakh Chand was provided a shop in Lunkaransar.[218]

Shops and markets were also constructed in various commercial centres to facilitate merchants with the rental shops. References of such shops and markets are available in Rajgarh, Suratgarh, Ratangarh and Bikaner *mandis*.[219] The state collected *Bhada* (rent) of these shops.[220] In Rajgarh Rs. 107 in 1786 AD and Rs. 111 and *As*. 6 in 1828 AD were realized as *Bhada* (rent).

Facilities of petty loans were made available to the merchants. On occasions, they were extended loans on interest. For example, Multani traders were paid such loans on their demand.[221] Traders Sarup Chand Banthia was given Rs. 50 and Jaitmal was given Rs. 20[222] and later it was recovered with interest of Rs. 2 and *As*. 8 in Reni in 1766 AD.

Besides this financial assistance, the state stood surety for the traders and played an effective role in recovering their debts and in solving the various disputes amicably involving traders and merchants. However, it charged for its role.[223] It also entertained grievances pertaining to taxes or duties or otherwise. We see when Seth Bhomu of Rajpura raised an issue of *Chouthai* of grain (a tax on sale of grain) it was entertained and decided satisfactorily.[224] Also whenever *sahukari bhanchh* (annual tax on businessmen) realized some of the merchants resisted and deserted to Deshnoke (a sacrosanct place of deity Karani Mata near Bikaner). Later, they were persuaded by the state with some relief in tax.[225]

The traders were induced by granting partial or full exemption in taxes or duties. The *Chhoot ra Kagad* (remission papers) appended in almost all *Kagad Bahis* speak of the exemption of taxes and duties to the individual merchants or to villages as a whole.[226] The previous dues of *jagat* of Khatri traders and others at Kumbhana[227] village were exempted completely.[228] *Potedar* Chaturbhuj Jinda Ram Juhari Mal of Churu and Harnarain of Delhi, Ajodhya Prasad of Agra were among some of the prominent *sahukars* who enjoyed exemption in duties and taxes.[229] They were exempted from half the *jagat* on *nekal* (export) and *pesar* (import) of grains in the state.[230] Moreover, to earn the goodwill of the merchants exemptions were made on importing of goods or grains for the personal consumption on marriage or for feasts.[231]

In the event of unnatural calamities like fire, the traders and inhabitants of the whole village were exempted from all tariffs. Village Jeevandesar was exempted in 1797 AD in such an eventuality.[232]

The *Katars* (caravans of camels) and *Balads* (caravans of Banjaras' bullocks) carrying merchandize were provided with sufficient fodder, water and lodging facilities. Likewise, instructions were conveyed to the concerned officials.[233]

We see instances of providing the escort facility by the state to the traders. When the traders with their *Katars* reached the border of the state the escort immediately rushed to welcome them and escorted them to their desired destinations. For this service a tax was charged and it was known as *Badarki*.[234] Mention has been made in the *Kagad Bahi* of 1813 AD that merchants carrying grains and other goods from Bikaner to Barasalpur and from Barsalpur to Bikaner were escorted on each trip and were charged *Annas* 5 per camel load. Daga Panna, an official was appointed specifically for keeping the accounts of it.[235]

A *thana* was also created on the way from Sindh to Bikaner for the security of those who brought grain from Sindh. The cost of running that *thana* was borne by those traders.[236] Rs. 7 was realized in Nohar mandi as *Badarki*[238] in 1765 AD.

Every kind of protection was provided. In case they suspected any trouble on the way or a route, armed guards were provided by the state to escort them safe and sound. The gummen were provided whenever it was requested.[238]The like orders were issued to the officers and the *Jagirdars* of the state.[239] We find Rs. 14 and *Annas* 8 were realized in Rajgarh in 1883 AD for escorting Pathan traders upto village Bhensli.[240] In 1797 AD when a *katar* from Phuleda was on its way to Bikaner and a loot was suspected near Pugal (a place in the west of Bikaner) the officials were directed to escort them upto their destination and gunmen were also sent from Bikaner for the same.[241] Likewise, on the request of a certain Johri of Jaipur while he was on his way to Bikaner was escorted with gunmen and officials of the *Parganas* lying between Bikaner and Jaipur were instructed to ensure his safe journey.[242]

In case of a theft or plundering of merchandize in transit the state made all its efforts to recover it. There are many references available of recovering the stolen or plundered property/goods. In 1805 AD. A *katar* of Juhari Mal Agrawal was looted near Bikaner and the material was sold, the state recovered Rs. 139 from the dacoits and gave the money to Juhari Mal Agrawal.[243]

Sometime, the state compensated for the stolen or plundered goods of the traders in the state. We have such instances as well. The *Bajra* weighing 405 *maunds* of Potedar of Churu Juhari Mal Jinda Ram was looted at Ratangarh. The state paid Rs. 361 cash as compensation to the firm of Churu.[244] Likewise Rs. 150 was given to a *Sahukar* in Nohar for the goods belonging to him was mis-conveyed to Mohd. Hussain Bhati.[245] In the year 1765 AD when Tater Maya Ram conveyed a *katar* laden with brass and lead from Churu to Pithod it was stolen by miscreant Mamoodo at village Mehlusar. The state immediately blocked the traffic and recovered the material and handed it over to the owner.[246] The state did realize the 1/4 cost of the recovered property involved in loot or theft. Rs. 90 *Annas* 12 were recovered as the cost of labour put in recovery of the lost goods in 1771 AD in Rajgarh.[247]

The state administration was equally vigilant for their convenient journey throughout the state territory. It issued repeated instructions at times to its officials deputed on various positions in *Parganas, Chowkis* and *Mandis* for not realizing undue and not to harass them in any way and they should arrange all facilities for traders.[248] Whatever exemptions were provided, copies of such directions were sent to the officials for execution. So that, the grantee might be benefited at the other end and allowed to enjoy the exemption unhampered.[249]

Special privileges were given to some most reliable commercial magnets like Seth Mirzamal Potedar of Churu. He was allowed to keep his own agents in the state to watch his interests and accounts.[250] The *Rozgar* was paid to them by the state. Rs. 91 was paid for two agents for a 6 month period @ Rs. 15 per month[251] in Anupgarh. Also, no defaulter could be arrested if he took shelter in the *Haveli* of Seth Mirzamal in

Churu or elsewhere in his custody.[252] Perhaps this was a rare privilege granted to any merchant. Respect for this house is also evident from such a right. He was accorded special honour and gifts while departing from the *Darbar* (court).[253] He was also sometimes requested to reach the *Darbar* to confer with the ruler.[254]

The state paid enough attention towards the *vyaparis* and *sahukars*. The state borrowed larger loans from them. Seth Mirzamal loaned Rs. 4,00,001 through a *Hundi* in 1827 AD against the various sources of the state income to be mortgaged with him for repayment. The right to realize the same was handed over to him.[255] There were some other *sahukars* who used to extend loans to the state. For instance, Rs. 400 was lent to the state for construction work in Bikaner in 1797 AD[256], and it was to be adjusted from the *jagat*. These loans were usually adjusted against the due *jagat* in *sahukars* or were repaid in instalments or a *thod* (source of income) was assigned for realization.[257]

Roads, *talabs,* wells and shops were constructed to facilitate the commercial traffic. The *qasba* Anupgarh was fast growing as a commercial centre. Therefore, the road from Anupgarh to village Balochiya and village Dabjal, and *talabs* (tank) and wells were constructed in Anupgarh in 1844 AD.[258] Wells were also dug in Lunkaransar in 1770 AD.[259]

This shows that rulers followed a policy of giving encouragement and promotion to enhance the commercial traffic in the state. Consequently, it earned through trade and commerce. Besides, they must have thought of safeguarding the state authority and interest in the given condition by creating a supportive group of merchant class. Through this support they could counter the insurgent and restive nobility of the state. This affluent class of merchants could stand by the state and extend financial support to it. However, we do not come across any evidence suggesting state monopoly over any commodity. The state did not indulge in trade directly or monopolized any trade activity as such a practice followed by Mughal emperors and princesses.[260]

(5) CURRENCY AND MINTING; EXCHANGE AND DISCOUNTING

There are evidences that the metallic currency was in use in the Bikaner area in the early medieval period.[261] The Mughal Emperors minted and circulated Imperial *Rupaya* and *Dam*[262] in the Empire including Rajput states.[263] They considered it a prerogative of the sovereignty and guarded it[264] and did not allow the Rajput chiefs to mint their own coins in their respective *watan jagirs*. But in the *suba* of Ajmer, the imperial mints functioned in Ajmer, Nagaur, Ranthambhor, and Sambhar. The minting of coins of the Rathore chiefs in Bikaner as well as the whole of Rajputana started in the second half of the 18th century.[265] It was a development in the monetary system of Bikaner which suggests a process of becoming an independent state and re-formation of state in the 18th century.[266] The *Furrukhsahi* rupee was in circulation before the minting of coins started in Bikaner.[267] It seems that the Mughal power being weak, allowed the regional chiefs to strike the coins in their own states but it was to be done with due permission of the central power.

In Bikaner, a Mint was established for the first time in 1754 AD during the time of Maharaja Gaj Singh (1746-87 AD) with the permission of Emperor Alamgir II.[268] *Kagad Bahi* of 1754 AD mentions that Sahej Ram and Mansa Ram Brahmins were appointed in 1754 AD by the chief of Bikaner to strike silver coins in the Bikaner mint.[269]

W.W. Web observes that the silver coins were struck during Gaj Singh's time but only after the year 1759 AD, the first year of Shah Alam's reign and in his name (in Persian) on one side of the coins was struck, and which continued upto 1859 AD.[270]

Different rulers adopted a special device to distinguish their own coins from others. This was done by means of diffeent symbols marked on the coins. Gaj Singh's coins bore a symbol of *Pataka* or *Dhvaja* (*flag*) and Surat Singh's coin had *Trishul* (Trident) on them; and *Kirnia* (a Turban star) for Ratan Singh's currency.[271]

W.W. Web observes that only silver and copper coins were struck by the rulers and not the gold coins. However, both *Nazri* (specially fine and of full weight) and ordinary rupees were issued.[272] But, G.H. Ojha maintained that the gold *mohars* were also minted and were found in the state treasury by him.[273] Our evidence also strengthened Ojha's findings. There is a mention of the gold *mohars* in the *Byav Bahis* and other *Bahis*. The value of these gold coins (*mohar*) were equivalent to the metal. These *mohars* were generally given in *Juhari*[274] (honours/gifts) to the recipients and for ceremonial purposes.[275]

The silver coins of smaller denominations of half and quarter were not minted till Surat Singh's time, i.e. after 1828 AD.[276] The silver coins were known by the respective names of the rulers and the name preceded the word *Shahi* as Gajshahi and Surat Shahi.[277]

The weight of the *Gajshahi* coins was 174 grains in which 167.47 grains were pure silver. They stood in good shape and were considered to be the best in Rajputana.[278]

The copper coins were also struck and varied from 115 grains to 117 grains.[279] Powlett and Web both maintained that the copper coins were not struck at the Bikaner Mint but elsewhere.[280] It is found that the mint of Bikaner has frequently been referred to the *Bahis* as '*Rupe ri Taksal*' ('*Rupe*' meant silver) in the records.[281] Therefore, it seems possible that the copper coins might have been struck elsewhere in the state.

Besides these coins, other coinage known as *Shahjahani, Karanshahi, Farrukhshahi, Chehrashahi, Calkatia* and coins of other states were in vogue in the state. References to these coins have been mentioned in the account manuals.[282] We find that transactions were to be made in specific currency while issuing or discounting *Hundis* or seeking loans through a *Khat* (loan agreements) by the state.[283]

The *Sawa Bahis* of *Mandis* and the *Jama Kharach ri Bahis* have references of copper coins as *Takka, Paisa, Dam* and *Adhela*. These were small denominations of the copper coins commonly used in Bikaner.[284] For instance, a *Shahjahani Rupiya* had value of 18 *takka* 25 *dams* (i.e. 18½ *takkas*) in 1697 AD.[285] The *Chehrashahi* rupee consisted of 24 *takkas*[286], whereas a *Gajshahi* had value of 14 *takka* 31 *dams*.[287] The variation in these coins in vogue generally depended on the following factors. Fistly, apart from the difference in weight in an individual coin it also differed in the ratio of silver and alloy due to which the coin differed in intrinsic value. On the fluctuation of the silver prices it could also vary in value. Secondly, due to the persistent use of the coins they depreciated in weight and metallic value which after a testing of weight and value a *sarraf* determined the exchange value in *Takka* and *Dam*. Moreover, they were issued from different mints hence, the coins (*Shahjahani*, *Farrukshahi* and *Gajshahi*) differed in exchange value.

The following tables would evince the difference in the weight and ratio of silver with alloy in a silver rupee due to which the exchange value differed. Another table shows the respective weight of the copper coin.

Table 5.6: Weight and Ratio of Alloy in the Silver Coins[288]

Coins	*State*	*Rulers & Year of Minting*	*Weight in Grains*		
			Gross	*Alloy*	*Silver*
(1)	*(2)*	*(3)*	*(4)*	*(5)*	*(6)*
Gajshahi	Bikaner	Gaj Singh (1759 AD)	174.00	06.53	167.47[289]
Bijaishahi	Jodhpur	Bijai Singh (1780 AD)	176.40	06.50	169.90
Jharshahi	Jaipur	Ishwari Singh (1748 AD)	175.00	N.A.*	N.A.
Gumanshahi	Kota	Guman Singh	171.17	N.A.	N.A.
Chittori	Mewar	-	169.57	34.26	135.31

* N.A. = Not available

Table 5.7: Weight of the Copper Coins[290]

Coins *(1)*	*State* *(2)*	*Weight in Grains* *(3)*
Gajshahi	Bikaner	115-117[291]
Jharshahi	Jaipur	262-280
Gumanshahi	Kota	275-278
Dhabhushahi	Jodhpur	310-320[292]

Tables 5.6 and 5.7 show that the silver contents were reasonably good, but the copper coins of Bikaner had less weight

than the others, the reason may be understood in the difficult and irregular supply of copper from distant places like Calcutta to Bikaner.[293]

The mint of the state was located at Bikaner city and was run by a set of officials.[294] Instead of issuing coins it kept merely the *sikka* or dye minted the coins after purifying the metal.[295] The copper was received from Calcutta[296] and also from Dariba Bidasar in Sujangarh.[297]

The officer in charge was called *Huwaldar* and under whom other subordinate officials worked on a monthly salary.[298] Contractual services of *Daroga* and *Sarrofs* were also kept to help its running.[299] We are informed of the following salary structure of the mint officials.

Table 5.8: Salary Structure and Officials of the Mint[300]

Sr.No. (1)	*Officials* (2)	*Salary per month in rupees* (3)
1.	*Huwaldar*	15
2.	*Gumasta*	10
3.	Dier	7
4.	Servant	4
5.	Weighman	2
6.	Storekeeper	10

Like the Mughal system, in Bikaner state also, the wealthy bankers or *sahukars* were allowed to cast their own coins in the government mint on payment of service and other charges.[301] When a *sahukar* brought to the mint 1,025 *mashas* of silver then 100 rupees were minted, each *rupya* weighing 10 *mashas*. Out of the 1,025 mashas 25 mashas of silver were taken extra for every 100 rupees which was equivalent to 2½ rupees.[302] For minting Rs. 100 following charges were taken in the mint of Bikaner.

No alloying was done for the copper coins. One *maund* of copper costed Rs. 32 and *annas* 13. The copper coins struck of 1 *maund* copper costed Rs. 43 *As.* 4 and *Pai* 9, whereas its value was taken as Rs. 50. The margin was the net profit of the state.[303]

Table 5.9: Minting Charges of Silver Coins in Bikaner[304]

Sr. No.	*Charges head*	*Charges*		
		Rs.	*As.*	*Pai*
(1)	*(2)*	*(3)*	*(4)*	*(5)*
1.	Wastages of 7½ *mashas* in melting	0	12	0
2.	Custom duty	1	8	9
3.	Cleaning	0	2	0
4.	Alloying	0	0	11
5.	Cutting/dyeing	0	0	3
6.	Weighing	0	0	1
	Total	2	8	0

Sometimes the state gave full or partial concession to *sahukars* to their minting of coins.[305] Lala Ajodhya Prasad, an influential *sahukar* was granted full exemptions of *Hasil* on the minting, when he minted the coins of Rs. 2,000 in 1824 AD[306], Whereas 50 per cent concessions were provided to Daga Vinay and Tater Sultan Mal Baktawal Mal on their respective coins for minting.[307]

The work of minting was also given on *muqata* (*Ijara*) and received a fixed income during the period.[308] It was given on *muqata* to Kochar Anadu son of Balchand in 1810 AD. His remuneration was decided at Rs. 11 per month.[309]

The *sahukars* felt the shortage of coins in the market, so they requested the state administration to institute another copper *Taksal* (mint) at Rajgarh town in 1829 AD. The *Darbar* issued the direction to establish the same if it was beneficial to the state.[310] The process of monetization was correlated with the growth of trade and commerce in the state. As pointed out by modern scholars,[311] it is a noteworthy phenomenon that the demand of another mint to be established at Rajgarh in 1829 AD, despite one already functioning at the capital city Bikaner not only suggests a measure of an administrative convenience but also an index of growth of trade and commerce and rise in some new commercial centres in Bikaner during the period of study. We find the state issuing *Takka* (coins of copper) in 1797 AD.[312] It distributed them in the *qasbas* of Deshnoke and Bidasar for circulation, which were initially not accepted by the subject or concerned (presumably for inferior quality or under weight). So, an order to this effect was executed on them that the new *takkas* should be honoured and used, otherwise a penalty would be imposed on the refusal. Bidawat Jalim Singh Keshri Singhot, *Thakur* of Bidasar was simultaneously requested to convince the traders and concerned for the same.[313] We have also mentioned the *Challani* (debased) coins in vogue in Churu[314] for practical purposes/transactions.[315]

The metallic currency had significance of its own, as money could be accepted instead of goods as well as it had contained greater value of metal.[316] But the crude and simple minting could help a skilled rogue to tamper or counterfeit the coinage.[317] We have references to Gaj Singh being prescribed penalties for counterfeiters, but he failed to check the practice.[318] Further in Bikaner *Mandi* Re. 1 and takka 4 were found to be fake.[319] and Gaj Singh penalized Dewa Kandoi with Rs. 2 in 1779 AD[320] and Rs. 11 in Rajgarh i 1782 AD for illegally discounting the *Gajshahi* Rupee and *Takkas*.[321]

Moreover, on the fluctuation of the prices of metal the value of the coins could also vary as the metal contents varying in them accordingly.[322] Consequently, in days of war or shortage of metal *chalani* (debased) coins were issued in which silver contents were reduced to an extent that 100 debased coins could purchase hardly 30 to 35 current rupees.[323] G.N. Sharma observes that in this manner the money refused to discharge the primary duty of a standard currency.[324] Since, the supply of the bullion was received in India mainly from Europe and the Middle East[325] its supply to the state also fluctuated and in the short supply of bullion the debased coins might have been struck in the local mint.

Exchange of Coins and Discounting

Owing to the trade relations of Bikaner with other states of Rajputana the traders brought currency of their own state and those were accepted and exchanged after giving some discount known locally as *Batta* (discount), on the basis of metal contents and weight of the coin.[326]

The rate of discount varied from coin to coin depending on

weight and the metallic contents. The *sarrafs* engaged in this job of *parkhai* (testing) earned sizeable profits in it. The general rate of discount as mentioned in *Bahis* was Rs. 10 and 6 *As.* per 100 rupees.[327]

As much as 30 varieties of coins were in circulation in Rajputana at that time and each of them acording to the trade usage were acceptable and liable to different rates of discount.[328]

In 1864 AD while Deputy Commissioner Ajmer submitted a report to the Commissioner, Ajmer-Merwara about 26 kinds of coins were current in Rajasthan.[329] They were enumerated with their respective weights in *masha* and *ratti* in Table 5.10 and which could be taken to be used in common exchange in the early 19th century.

Table 5.10: Exchange Value of Silver Coins[330]

Sr.No.	*Coins of the State*	*Weight in Masha & Ratti*		
		Gross	*Silver*	*Alloy*
(1)	*(2)*	*(3)*	*(4)*	*(5)*
1.	Bikaneri	12 - 0*	11 - 6	0 - 2
2.	Chittori	11 - 4	8 - 7½	2 - 4½
3.	Kishangarhi	11 - 4	9 - 4½	1 - 7½
4.	Kota	11 - 7	11 - 4¾	0 - 2¼
5.	Vijaishahi	12 - 0	11 - 5	0 - 3
6.	Kuchamani	11 - 4	7 - 7	3 - 5
7.	Jaipuri	12 - 0	11 - 6	0 - 2

* :1 *Masha* comprised 8 *Rattis*.

We have a reference of exchange of *Ahmedshahi* coins of Rs. 1,625 with *Gajshahi* of Bikaner for Rs. 1,617. Thus Rs. 7 and 9*As*. were charged as discount the rate being ½%.[331] Rs. 900 *Ratanshahi* (coins of Ratan Singh, 1828-1851 AD) were exchanged for Rs. 948 of *Chehrashahi* coins. The difference (Bagha (बाघा - as literally the difference was termed)of Rs. 48 were credited in the *mandi* account.[332] The discount rate of *Chehrashahi* mentioned was 1 *takka* per rupee. The exchange rate of Calcutta coins was mentioned as four per cent.[333] The *Karanshahi* Rs. 1,609 were discounted in Rs. 134.[334] Thus, the discount rate varied as per the intrinsic value, its depreciation and its weight.

However, it appears that it depended to a great degree on the skills of a *sarraf* to mention the value of exchange of a particular coin. This led them to earn sizeable profits. Thus, the *sarrafs* were in a position to lend money to the state.[335]

(6) WEIGHTS AND MEASUREMENTS

Weight

The locally prevalent weights and measurements varied from village to village and town to town during the second half of the 18th century.[336] The references of *baat* (weights), *takri* (weighing balance) and *tolawatias* (a group of traders who occupied business of weighing) in *bahis* evince that things were weighed.[337] There were two types of weights prevalent in Bikaner state. They were *kaccha maund* and *pacca maund*.[338] The standard or a *pacca maund* (one maund) consisted uniformly of 40 *seers*, and one *seer* had 16 *chhataks*. A unit of 5 seers was known as a *Dhadi*. Other weighing units were known as *Tola, Masha* and *Ratti*. Their relationship is as mentioned below:

5 *Tolas* = 1 *Chhataka,* and
80 *Tolas* = 1 *Seer*[339]

But the wight of a *kaccha maund* differed from place to place in the state indicated below :

Table 5.11: Weight of Local *Kaccha Maund*

Sr. No.	*Place*	*1 maund (kaccha) consisted of seers*
1.	Suratgarh	28 seers[340]
2.	Churu	19 seers[341]
3.	Bikaner city	28 seers[342]
4.	Nohar	19 seers[343]
5.	Anupgarh	32 *seers*[344]

The contemporary record also provides information about other methods of weighing. A *Payli* was a popular and simple device of an earthern, metallic or wooden pot for weighing. By this method the *dhan* (grains), pulses, opium and clay were weighed uniformly through this container. Since the *Payli* method was simple so it was used commonly by the people to avoid any kind of controversy in regard of weights. In Bikaner one *Payli* was equivalent to 2 and ½ seers while in other places one *Payli* was 2 seers.[345]

The expensive items like gold, silver and gems were weighed in *tola, masha* and *ratti*.[346] They were used by jewellers, *sarrafs* (money changers) and vaidyas for weighing respectively precious metals, gems and medicines.[347] One *tola* was equal to 12 *mashas* and one *masha* to 8 *ratti*. In Bikaner one standard gold *mohar* usually consisted of 12 *mashas*.[348]

As it has been observed that weighing units differed from village to village and town to town. Therefore, these weights were known by the place names as well. For instance, it was specified *'Nohar re Tol ra'* (weight of Nohar), *'Bhensli re Tol ra'* (weight of village Bhensli in Rajgarh) and *'Sadau re Tola ra'* (weight of village Sadau in Rajgarh).[349] Owing to non-uniformity in the system, there was difficulty in transaction and the state got the advantage while collecting the revenue in kind. Often, the *bahis* record the excess grains as *'Badhotar ra'* (excess in collection).[350] It was due to difference in weight units and the collection by the state officials of land revenue in kind used to be higher.

We find the state administration was conscious enough against the under-weighing practices in the market. It imposed penalties on the shopkeepers for the defaults of under weighing. All the shopkeepers of the Rajgarh markets were penalized @ 2½ rupees per shop for keeping sub-standard weights in 1809 AD. They were directed to maintain uniformity in the weight units.[351]

It further tried to streamline the weights in the entire state in 1818 AD. It issued an order directing that earlier *kaccha tol* was practised in the state but from now onwards only the *pacca tol* would be followed.[352]

Interestingly, the weighing of the fodder had other distinctive units. They have been quoted in the *Bahis* as *Dhigli* (heap of fodder), *Bora* or *Chhanti* (sack made of goats hair) *Lada* (two sacks on either side of the camel) and *Jhal* (cartload) have been mentioned.[353]

Measurement

The general unit for linear measurement was called *gaj* (yard); which consisted of 2 feet for measuring land and 3 feet for general use subdivided into 16 girah[354] (गिरह). The length of a scroll of cloth (थान) was generally 24 *gaj*[355] Measurements through body parts like fingers, *balisth*, hand length, elbow length, *paondas* (double paces of legs), the primitive signs, were in vogue. Twelve fingers constituted I *balisth* (length stretched from point of thumbs to smallest finger), 24 fingers formed 1 hand length and 84 fingers were equal to 1 *purus*[356] (used for measuring the depth of wells). Paper was measured in *Dasta* and *Gaddi*, 1 *Gaddi* consisted of 11 *Dasta*.[357]

To measure the land units of *Gaj, Paonda, Dori, Biswa, Kos* and *Bighas* were used. A *paonda* was about 5½ feet long (i.e. the double paces of legs), *Dori* had 70 hand length (equivalent to 20 *purus*). Powlett remarks that *Bigha* was 70 cubits square, the *Kos* consisted of 2000 *Paondas* of 5½ feet each, *Biswa* being the 1/20 part of *Bigha*.[358] There used to be minor differences in the measurement of *Bighas* being the difference in the length of *Dori* or hand lengh or *Paondas*. Interestingly, Deshnoke was a place of religious sanctity where land was not measured by *Dori* but by *Paondas*, the reason was the respect for the place of the local deity *karniji*.[359]

Thus, the weights and measuring units differed from place to place resulting in inconvenience to people. In this situation its accuracy was doubtful. More so, we do not find any impact of the Mughal units of weight and measurement and the units of local use were in vogue.

REFERENCES

1. *Suba Re Sarkaran ne Pargana Re Vigat*, No. 226/3, A.S.L., Bikaner, *Mandi re Jagat ri Bahi*, No. 81, V.S. 1807/1750 AD, R.S.A., Bikaner; Col. Tod, *Annals* op. cit., pt. II, pp. 1248-50.
2. *Kagad Ri Bahi*, No. 3, V.S. 1827/1770 AD, R.S.A., Bikaner; *Sanad Parwana Bahi*, Jodhpur Records, No. 25, V.S.1838/1781 AD f. 77, R.S.A., Bikaner.
3. *Mandi Re Jagat Ri Bahi*, No. 81, V.S. 1807/1750 AD, R.S.A., Bikaner.

4. Powlett, Capt. P.W., *Gazetteer of Bikaner State, 1874,* (Bikaner, 1935), Appendix I.
5. *Kagad Bahi,* No. 12, V.S. 1859/1802 AD; No. 15, V.S. 1866/1809 AD; *Byav Bahi,* No. 158, V.S. 1827/1770 AD; *Sawa Bahi Mandi Sadar, Bikaner,* No. 8, V.S. 1815-16/1758-59 AD; No. 3, V.S. 1805/1748 AD, *Jagat Bahi,* No. 81, V.S. 1807/1750 AD, R.S.A., Bikaner.
6. The state was prone to recurrent scarcities and famines and the income from land revenue was fluctuating and uncertain because the peasants were used to migrating out of the state during the calamity.
7. See chapter, 'Geographical and Historical Background'.
8. See map of the trade routes (Figure 5.1).
9. Sarnath Insciption, V.S. 1010/953 AD; Bhavnagar Inscription, No. 1, pp. 67-69; Pali Inscription, V.S. 1213/1156 AD, Barmer Inscription, V.S. 1362/1305 AD. These inscriptions mention that *Madhyadesh* (the mid-land country) lying between the Himalayas on the north, Vindhya mountains in the south, Sindhu on the west, Prayag on the east, Agra and Delhi on the north-east were connected with various parts of Rajasthan. Cf. Sharma, G.N., *Social Life in Medieval Rajasthan*, 1st edition, Agra, p. 322.
10. The route from Delhi to Gujarat passed through Narayana, Narhad, Reni (Bikaner), Nagaur and Ajmer and then proceeded to Gujarat by way to Eklingji and Udaipur or by way of Pali, Bali, Abu Road and Palanpur. Sharma, Dashrath, *Rajasthan Through the Ages*, Part 1, Bikaner, 1966, pp. 492, 740.
11. Goetz, Herman, *Art and Architecture of Bikaner State*, pp. 40-50; Agrawal, Govind, *Churu Mandal ka Shodhpurna Itihas*, Ajmer, 1974, p. 477; Sharma, Girija Shankar, *Marvari Vyapari*, Bikaner, 1988, p. 20.
12. Agrawal, Govind, op. cit., p.148 (footnote). The city of Bikaner was a meeting point of traders from different directional routes from Sindh, Hissar, Nagaur and Phalodi in the 15th century. Devra, G.S.L., 'A Study of the Trade Relations Between Rajasthan and Sindh-Multan (1650-1800 AD)' in *Socio-Economic Study of Rajasthan*, (ed.) Devra, G.S.L., Jodhpur, 1986, p. 36-37.
13. Devra, G.S.L., op. cit., p. 37.
14. In Bikaner state many old commercial centres like Bikaner, Pugal, Churu were further developed but Rajgarh, Suratgarh, Ratangarh, Rajaldesar, Anupgarh, Nohar and Bhadra emerged as some new commercial centres. See chapter '*Mandis* (Commercial Centres)'.
15. Sharma, G.N., op. cit., p. 319.
16. This was a branched route of the Mughal highway of Delhi-

Marwar-Pali and was a busy one from the commercial traffic point of view. It is evident from *Kagad ri Bahi*, No. 47, V.S. 1897/1840 AD; *Desh Re Jagat Ri Bahi*, No. 68, V.S. 1858/1801 AD, R.S.A., Bikaner. It is surprising to note that no route passing through Bikaner has been shown in *An Atlas of the Mughal Empire* (ed.) Irfan Habib, Delhi, 1982. See sheet no. 6A and 6B, whereas we find from the *Bahis* that in the late 18th century many trade routes passed through the state territory.

17. Gaj Singh (1746-87) and Surat Singh (1787-1828) both encouraged the traders to initiate their trade activities in the state. See for detail, 'State: Trade and Commerce' in this chapter.
18. The introduction of the railway and the participation of the Englishmen in the trade activities and some other factors brought about the changes in the routes. See for detailed study Sharma, Girija Shankar, *Marwari Vyapari*, op. cit., pp. 21-22.
19. *A Descriptive List of Bikaner Bahis (17th-19th century)*, Part I, Bikaner, 1982, pp. 120-138, 142-173, 78-119.
20. Capt. Powlett in his *Gazetteer of Bikaner State* has provided the distances of some of the principal routes as under:

Bikaner to Ajmer	-	150 miles
Bikaner to Bhiwani	-	180 miles
Bikaner to Sirsa	-	160 miles
Bikaner to Bahawalpur	-	150 miles

Powlett, op. cit., p. 109.

21. The external and internal routes of the state have been drawn out on the information of the following *Bahis* and works as under– *Sawa Bahi Mandi Sadar*, Bikaner, No. 3, V.S. 1805/1748 AD; No.4, V.S. 1807-10/1750-53 AD; *Kagad Bahis* No. 3, V.S. 1827/1770 AD; No. 5, V.S. 1838/1781 AD; No. 11, V.S. 1857/1800 AD, No. 13, V.S. 1861/1804 AD; *Jagat Bahi*, No. 81, V.S. 1807/1750 AD; *Jama Kharach ri Bahi*, No. 240, V.S. 1776/1719 AD; *Byav Bahis*, No. 159, V.S. 1827/1770 AD Powlett, op. cit., (Appendix-I); Col. Tod, *Annals*, op. cit., Part II, pp. 1154-56; Munshi, Sohan Lal, *Tawarikh Rajshri Bikaner*, Bikaner, p. 69, R.S.A., Bikaner.
22. Ibid.
23. In Shekhawati area *Jagirdars* levied duties on goods in their respective areas. Capt. Powlett, pp. 157-58; Sohan Lal, op. cit., pp. 69-74.
24. Sharma, G.N., op. cit., p. 326.
25. *Kagdon Ri Bahi*, No.10, V.S. 1854/1797 AD, BIkaner.
26. Ibid., No. 2, V.S. 1859/1802 AD, *Baisakh badi* 14, R.S.A., Bikaner.
27. Ibid., No. 14, V.S. 1863/1806 AD, *Baisakh badi* 3, R.S.A., Bikaner.

28. The *Bhattis* and *Raths* were the converted Muslims and were not friendly to the state. They subsisted on either animal husbandry or took recourse to plundering in the vicinity of the trade routes passing in the north-west. See Ojha, G.H., op. cit., pp. 21-22 (footnote).
29. *Barothia* was a self-deserted person from the native place or expelled from the state in punishment usually a thief or a dacoit or any disgruntled noble. Lalas, Sita Ram, *Rajasthani Hindi Sankshipt Sabdakosh*, No. 157, Jodhpur, 1987, p. 207.
30. Surat Singh (1787-1828) realized heavy *Peshkashi* amount from his *Jagirdars* and converted the *Chakri* (military services) into cash in 1794 AD which caused a dissatisfaction among the nobility.
31. *Kagad Bahi*, No. 18, V.S. 1854/1797 AD, *Phalgun Sudi* 3, *Asoj Sudi* 7; No. 12, V.S. 1859/1802 AD, *Baisakh sudi* 4, R.S.A., Bikaner.
32. *Kagad Bahi*, No. 9, V.S. 1851/1794 AD, *Phalgun Sudi* 3, No. 10, V.S. 1854/1797 AD, *Mingsar Sudi* 13, R.S.A., Bikaner.
33. *Kagad Bahi*, No. 1, V.S. 1811/1754 AD, No. 3, V.S. 1827/1770 AD, f. 25(b), R.S.A., Bikaner.
34. Ibid.
35. *Sawa Bahi Rajgarh*, No. 1, V.S. 1828/1771 AD, f. 105(a).
36. Ibid., No. 4, V.S. 1839-42/1782-85 AD
37. *Kagad Ri Bahi*, No. 6, V.S. 1839/1782 AD
38. Tod, op. cit., Part I, p. 554.
39. *Desh Re Jagat Ri Bahi*, No. 68, V.S. 1858/1801 AD; Sharma, Girija Shankar, op. cit., p. 37.
40. *Jagat Bahi*, No. 81, V.S. 1807/1750 AD, R.S.A., Bikaner.
41. A *Rebari* of village Kapursar offered his services on payment @ Rs. 5. per camel per month for a period of 3 months to the state administration. *Kagad Bahi*, No. 14, V.S. 1864/1807 AD, *Jyestha Badi* 3, R.S.A., Bikaner.
42. Col. Tod, op. cit., pp. 554-55.
43. Remuneration for the work. *Sawa Bahi Bikaner*, No. 3, V.S. 1805/1748 AD
44. Ibid.
45. Ibid.
46. *Jama* included the income of *Kasoor* (default), *Sawa Bahi Mandi Bikaner*, No. 3, V.S. 1805/1748 AD, R.S.A., Bikaner.
47. *Sawa Bahi Anupgarh*, No. 14, V.S. 1901/1844 AD, R.S.A., Bikaner.
48. *Sawa Bahi Mandi Reni*, No. 1, V.S. 1815/1758 AD, f. 13(b).
49. *Sawa Bahi Nohar Mandi*, V.S. 1822-23, ff. 67b-68a.
50. *Sawa Bahi Mandi Anupgarh*, No. 1, V.S. 1904/1847 AD, No. 15, f. 92.

51. *Kagad Bahi*, No. 13, V.S. 1861/1804 AD, *Asadh Badi* 13, R.S.A., Bikaner.
52. *Kagad Bahi*, No. 13, V.S. 1861/1804 AD, *Shrawan Badi*, 6, R.S.A., Bikaner.
53. *Kagad Bahi*, No. 13, V.S. 1861/1804 AD, *Asoj badi*, 5, R.S.A., Bikaner.
54. *Bohra* and *Sahukar* also provided financial loans to peasants and artisans. *Kagad Bahi*, No. 13, V.S. 1861/1804 AD, ff. 58, 237.
55. *Pothia* was one who carried packload or head load of goods and sold it from place to place. *Kagad Bahi*, No. 14, V.S. 1863-64/ 1806-07 AD, f. 252; *Sawa Bahi Mandi Churu*, No. 1, V.S. 1828/1771 AD, f. 35b, R.S.A., Bikaner.
56. Sharma, G.N., *Social Life in Medieval Rajasthan (500-1800 AD)*, Agra, 1965, p. 316.
57. *Sawa Bahi Mandi Churu*, No. 1, V.S. 1828/1771 AD, f. 35b, R.S.A., Bikaner.
58. Ibid.
59. *Gawan Ri Jagat Ri Bahi*, No. 84/A, V.S. 1865/1808 AD, R.S.A., Bikaner.
60. Ibid.
61. *Kagad Bahi*, No. 14, V.S. 1863/1806 AD, f. 252, *Posh badi, 15,* R.S.A., Bikaner.
62. Local term for the seasonal gatherings on religious fairs or festivals.
63. In the desert there is a special significance of these *melas* and festivals. The people rejoice and wear colourful dresses and attend them with family. Traders usually brought the necessary items for sale from distant places and paid duties to the state. Therefore, these fairs had assumed commercial significance for state.
    (a) *Sawa Bahi Mandi Churu*, No. 1, V.S. 1829/1772 AD, f. 45(b).
    (b) *Sawa Bahi Mandi Sadar*, Bikaner, No. 39/b, V.S. 1877-80 1820-23 AD, f. 86(b).
    (c) *Sawa Bahi Mandi Nohar*, No. 1, V.S. 1823/1766 AD, f. 33(a).
64. Powelett, op. cit., p. 120.
65. *Sawa Bahi Mandi Bikaner*, No. 28, f. 176(b).
66. Ibid., f. 177.
67. Ibid., No. 29, f. 52(b).
68. Ibid., No. 39/B.
69. Ibid., No. 39/B.
70. *Rajputana Gazetteers*, Vol. III(a), p. 346.
71. Sharma, G.N., op. cit., p. 316.
72. *Gawan Ri Jagat Bahi*, No. 84/A, V.S. 1865/1808 AD
73. *Sawa Bahi Mandi Churu*, No. 1, V.S. 1829/1772 AD, f. 35(b).

74. *Sawa Bahi Rajgarh Mandi*, No. 14, V.S. 1880, f. 239(a), Rampuria collection, R.S.A., Bikaner.
75. *Adhatiya* is also a *dalal*, who usually sold goods of farmers or other goods at his own level and charged *Adhat*, i.e. the commission. The word *Adhat*, implies the work of selling goods of others at his own level for commission. See Lalas, Sita Ram, op. cit., Part 1, p. 97.
76. *Dalal* is an Arabic world. *Dalal*, is a middleman or mediator in between a seller and a buyer. *Dallal* is he who "directs the purchaser to the merchandize, and the seller to the price". He takes commission for his role from the either parties. A.J. Qaiser has very vividly discussed the categories and role of the *Dallals* in India. He has broadly categorized the *Dallals* into four categories, viz. Firstly, the regular employees of companies, secondly, those who worked for more than one client simultaneously; thirdly, those who took his assignment on an ad hoc basis (broker-contractors) and lastly, were the state appointed brokers at the commercial centres. See for detailed study Qaiser, A.J., 'The Role of Brokers in Medieval India' in *Facets of a Marwar Historian*, (ed.) B.L. Bhadani and D. Tripathi, Jaipur, 1996, pp. 147-79.
77. *Kagad Bahi*, No. 13, V.S. 1861/1804 AD, *Asadh badi*, 13, *Shrawan Badi 6* and *Asoj Badi* 5, R.S.A., Bikaner.
78. *Sawa Bahi Churu Mandi*, No. 1, V.S. 1828/1771, f. 32, R.S.A., Bikaner.
79. *Katār* literally means sequence or line. The group of camels were called *katar*. Traders used to convoy their goods on the camels in the desert. Therefore, the word *Kataria* has frequently been used for the caravans of traders.
80. The '*Bāladia*' term is used in the archival records for the *Banjaras*. Some of them were also called *Lakhi Banjara* as they had maintained around one lakh of bullock with them. They had their own paraphernalia of security force laded with arms and ammunitions. See for detail—*Sobhagya Singh Sekhawat—'Rajasthan Baat Sahitya Mai Binaj Vyapaar'* (Article) *Jagti Jot* (Magazine) Vol. 2, May-July, 1992, Bikaner, pp. 13-14; *Binjaro*, Manohar Sharma, *Vishwambhara*, Bikaner, July-September, 1997, yr. 29, No. 3, pp. 16-22.
81. *Kagad Bahi*, No. 10, V.S. 1854/1797 AD, f. 34. Instructions were issued to the *Banjara* carriers of village Suwai to pay the tax on such transactions.
82. Banjara Rehmat Khan kept his 421 bullocks on rent in the army

of Kumehdan Ganga Singh in 1807 AD, *Kagad Bahi*, No. 14, V.S. 1863-64/1806-07 AD, f.226.

83. *Kagad Bahi*, No. 14, V.S. 1863-64/1806-07 AD, f. 225, *Magh sudi* 15, R.S.A., Bikaner.
84. *Kagad Bahi*, No. 14, V.S. 1864/1807 AD,f. 325, R.S.A., Bikaner.
85. *Sawa Bahi Mandi Sadar Bikaner*, No. 3, V.S. 1805/1748 AD, No. 4, V.S. 1807-10/1750-53 AD, R.S.A., Bikaner.
86. This is evident from the directions issued in 1810 AD to the villagers of village Goplana.
"गाँव गोपलाणों रो चौधरीयो रैत समसुतो जोग्य-धोन वा दुजी जीनस आपरे मतै बीछायतो ने तोल देवो वा. गोंवो में बेच आवे जगाती री चीठी भोलावणीयों सामी करावो नही सु आछो काम कीयो नही। हमें भोलावणीयों कनै माल तोलावजो जगाती कने चीठी करावजो जगात री चीठी बीना उठ लदीया तो जगात गुनेगारी सुधा लागसी जगात रा हुवालदार सावण वद ९" *Kagad Bahi*, No. 16. V.S.1867/ 1810 AD, *Shrawan Badi*, 9.
87. The *zamindars* and some affluent peasants usually sold their productions in the nearby smaller town and through *Dalals* it could reach the bigger *Mandis*.
88. Sharma, G.C., *Administrative System of Rajputana*, New Delhi, 1979, p. 167.
89. *Kagad Bahi*, No. 1, V.S. 1811, *Kartik Sudi* 13, R.S.A., Bikaner.
90. Ibid.
91. Sharma, G.C., op. cit., p. 316.
92. *Kagad Bahi*, No. 15, V.S. 1866/1809 AD, *Jestha Badi* 4, R.S.A., Bikaner.
93. Sharma, G.C., op. cit., p. 167.
94. *Kagad Bahi*, No. 1, V.S. 1811/1754 AD, R.S.A., Bikaner.
95. *Kagad Bahi*, No. 13, V.S. 1861/1804 AD, Baisakh *badi*, 5.
96. *Kagad Bahi*, No. 14, V.S. 1863-64/1806-07 AD, *Chetra badi*, 12.
97. *Shri Mandi Re Jama Kharach Ri Bahi*, No. 54, V.S. 1846/1789 AD ff. 2-3. R.S.A., Bikaner.
98. *Sawa Bahi Mandi Sadar Bikaner*, No. 11, V.S. 1822, No.13, V.S. 1824, No. 33, V.S. 1861-63/1804-06 AD, and V.S. 1864-65/1807-08 AD; *Churu Re Thana Ri Bahi*, No. 141, V.S. 1881/1824, f. 63, R.S.A.B.
99. *Sawa Bahi Churu Mandi*, No. 1, V.S. 1829, f. 45.
100. *Shri Mandi Ro Jama Kharach*, No. 93, V.S. 1856/1799 AD, f. 1; *Sawa Bahi Mandi Sadar Bikaner*, No. 11, V.S. 1822/1765 AD, R.S.A.B.
101. *Shri Mandi Ri Golak Ro Lekho*, No. 61, V.S.1855, ff. 1-2, R.S.A.B.
102. This fact is evident from an instance that in 1826 AD Rs. 501 were fixed of *Sahukari Bhanchh* to be realized from the *Dalals* of woollen cloth in the state, instead, they voluntarily offered to pay Rs. 751

and the very next year the state increased the *Sahukari Bhanchh* in 1827 AD upto Rs. 900. This shows that the *Dalals* were earning profits and were in capacity to pay as required. *Kagad Bahi,* No. 33/1, V.S. 1884/1827 AD, f. 47(a), R.S.A., Bikaner.

103. In some literacy sources like *Varsha Ritu Ra Doha* of the 17th century descriptions are made that after the close of the rainy season the traders went in groups to neighbouring areas. Sometimes they would go to distant parts also and return after a very long period. *Varsha Ritu Ra Doha*, No. 183, V. 29, f. 88a (SBLU) cf. Sharma, G.N., op. cit., p. 319.
104. Saxena, A.N., 'Economic Condition of Bikaner State during the 16th Century' (article) *Journal of the Rajasthan Institute of Historical Research*, Jaipur, Vol. XVII, No. 3, September-December 1979, pp. 11-12.
105. Gupta, B.L., *Trade and Commerce in Rajasthan*, Jaipur, 1987, pp. 83-88.
106. *Kagad Bahi*, No. 20, V.S. 1871/1814 AD, f. 375, *Jestha Badi* 12, R.S.A., Bikaner.
107. Nensi in his *Khyat,* quotes that cloth, tobacco, grains and salt were articles of inter-state trade. See *Nensi's Khyat*, ff. 47a, 98a, 134a.
108. The state regularized the import or export of specific commodities whenever needed. It issued a ban on export of foodgrain towards Marwar and instructed officials of various *chowkis* of such direction. *Kagad Bahi*, No. 10, V.S. 1854/1797 AD f. 39, *Mingsar Sudi* 3, R.S.A., Bikaner.
109. *Kagad Bahi*, No. 17, V.S. 1867/1810 AD, f. 191, R.S.A., Bikaner.
110. Sharma, G.N., op. cit., p. 322
111. Mughal Emperor Akbar's *firman* to Rai Singh, dated 12 *Razab-ul-Murazzab 990 Hizri* year. Corresponding to 25 April, 1592 AD, R.S.A., Bikaner.
112. *Kagad Bahi*, No. 34, V.S. 1885/1828 AD, f. 106,(a)
113. Ibid., f. 77(a)
114. Tod, *Annals and Antiquities of Rajasthan*; Bhadani, B.L., *Tod ke Arthik Ankre Ek Sankhyakiya Adhyayan, Itihaskar James Tod Vyaktitva Evam Krititva* (Hindi) (ed.), Bhati, Hukum Singh, Udaipur, p. 107.
115. *Kagad Bahi*, No. 26, V.S. 1877/1820, *Chetra sudi* 2, R.S.A., Bikaner.
116. *Sawa Bahi Mandi Sadar Bikaner*, No. 4, V.S. 1807-10, Bikaner.
117. *Kagad Bahi*, No. 22, V.S. 1873/1816 AD, *Magh Sudi* 9.
118. Sharma, G.C., *Administrative System of Rajputs*, p. 154.
119. Agrawal, Govind, *Churu Mandal ka Shodhpurna Itihas*, pp. 462, 481 Sharma, G.C., op. cit., New Delhi, 1979, pp. 154-55.
120. See Chapter 'The Role and Activities of Commercial Groups'.

121. Agrawal, Govind, *Churu Mandal Ka Shodhpurna Itihas* (in Hindi), Ajmer, 1974, p. 148 (F.N.); Devra, G.S.L., 'A Study of the Trade Relations between Rajasthan and Sindh-Multan (1650-1800 AD)' in *Socio-Economic History of Rajasthan*, Jodhpur, 1986, p. 37; Zaidi, Sunita, 'Akbar's Annexation of Sind: An Interpretation' in *Akbar and His India*, (ed.) Irfan Habib, OUP, Delhi, 1997, pp. 25-33.
122. Tod, *Annals and Antiquities of Rajasthan*, Vol. II, pp. 1154-55; Erskine, *Gazetteer of Rajputana*, pp. 351-52; Singh, Karni, *The Relations of the House of Bikaner with the Central Powers*, Delhi, 1974, p. 10.
123. *'Chhand Rao Jetsiro – Vitho Suje ro kiyo'*, lines 63-64, 99, 218-20, *Bibliothika Indica*, A.S.B. New Series, No. 1439, Calcutta.
124. Morkhana Inscriptions, V.S. 1573, vide Tessitory, L.P. Report (1916), Rajasthan State Archives, Bikaner, Vol. XIII, pp. 214-16.
125. In the 18th century's second half new commercial towns like Rajgarh, Suratgarh, Rajaldesar, Gajsinghpur and Sujangarh could emerge and also *Mandis* were established there. *Mandi Re Jama Kharch Ri Bahi*, No. 78,V.S. 1783/1726 AD; No. 79, V.S. 1799/1742, Bikaner *Bahiyat* section,R.S.A., Bikaner; Sohan Lal, *Tawarikh Raj Shri Bikaner*, Bikaner, 1890, p. 242; Sharma, G.N., *Social Life in the Medieval India* (1500-1800 AD), Agra, 1965, p. 319-21.
126. There are a number of references of state protection and concessions, for instance, see *Kagad Bahi* No. 1, V.S. 1811/1754 AD *Chhoot Ra Kagad; Kagad Bahi,* No. 3, V.S. 1827/1770 AD, *Kartik sudi* 14, No. 6, *Sanad magh Sudi*, 14, V.S. 1839/1782 AD, No. 7, *Sanad*,V.S. 1840/1783 AD bear explicit references of invitations, concession and protection to traders.
127. The goods coming into the state for sale were termed locally in the *Bahis* as *pesar* (import), and goods going out of the territory for sale was called *Nekal* (export), and the goods passing through the state territory without sale was called *Vahtivon* (the *Mughal rahdari*).
128. *Magre Khari Patti Re Jagat Ro Lekho*, No. 108, V.S. 1858/1801 AD; *Jagat Bahi*, No. 61 - *Mandi Re Golak Ri Bahi*, V.S. 1855/1798 AD, *Sri Rajgarh re Thana Ro Jama Kharach Ro Saho*, No. 62, V.S. 1855-60/1798-1803 AD, *Bahi Baharli Chowki re Jagat ri*, No. 108, V.S. 1869/1812 AD, *Jagat Bahi*, No. 81, V.S. 1807/1750 AD are some *Jagat Bahis;* There are *Sawa Bahis* for each *Mandi* providing detailed accounts of income and expenditures of the *Mandis* situated at Bikaner, Churu, Anupgarh, Suratgarh, Sujangarh, Rajgarh, etc. See *A Descriptive List of Bikaner Bahis* (17-19 century) Part I, for details pp. 142-178, published from R.S.A., Bikaner, 1982.

129. *Byav Bahi* and *Kagad Bahi* of different years have been very useful for the information regarding export and important as well for the transit trade of Bikaner. *Byav Bahi*, No. 167 - *'Bai Sardar Kunwar ji re Biha wa Naler Melo Teri'*, V.S. 1827/1770 AD; No. 159, *Bai Udai Kanwarji re Byav ri Jeenas ri Khata Bahi*, V.S. 1839/1782 AD, R.S.A., Bikaner.
130. *Sawa Bahi Rajgarh Mandi*, No. 4, V.S. 1839/1782 AD, f. 23a.
131. *Kagad Bahis*, No. 3, V.S. 1827/1770 AD, ff. 22, 24, 45; No. 7,V.S. 1839/1782 AD, f. 41; No. 11, V.S. 1857/1800 AD, f. 130, No. 17, V.S.1867/1810 AD, f. 89. Powlett, P.W., *Gazetteer of Bikaner State, 1874*, Bikaner (1935), pp. 142-44; *Bahi Navi Jagat ro Lekho*, No. 74, V.S. 1859; (*Jagat Bahi*) and *Oon re Lunkara ri Jagat ri Bahi*, No. 53, V.S. 1844-1787 AD, ff. 1-7, R.S.A., Bikaner.
132. *Pallans* (पलाण) were wooden saddles for camels.
133. *Chhagal* was a flat device made of straw sticks for winnowing the grains or to sort out the grains from the grass and husk.
134. *Kagad Bahis*, No. 9, V.S. 1851/1794 AD; No. 10, *Prachoon Kagad*, V.S. 1854/1797 AD, No. 11, V.S. 1857/1800 AD; f. 137; *Sawa Bahi Mandi Sadar Bikaner*, No. 3, V.S. 1805/1748 AD; No. 4, V.S. 1807-10/1750-53 AD *Churu re Jagat ri Bahi*, No. 33, V.S. 1831-32 ff. 1-8, *Jagat Bahi*, No. 81, V.S. 1807/1750, R.S.A., Bikaner.
135. Ibid.
136. *Jagat Bahi*, No. 4, V.S. 1805/1748 AD, *Oon re Lunkara re Jagat ri Bahi*, No. 53, V.S.1844/1787 AD ff. 1-7, R.S.A., Bikaner.
137. *Bahi Navi Jagat ro Lekho*,No. 74, V.S. 1859/1802 AD, Jagat Bahi Bikaner, No. 143, V.S. 1887/1830 AD ff 1-7, *Kagad Bahi*, No. 3 V.S. 1827/1770 AD, f. 46.
138. *Sawa Bahi Mandi Sadar Bikaner*, No. 29, V.S. 1856-57/1799-1800 AD, f. 64(b), R.S.A., Bikaner.
139. Goats and sheep were exported to Sindh on a large scale. *Sawa Bahi Mandi Sadar Bikaner*, No. 3, V.S. 1805/1748 AD, Asoj badi *12*, *Kagad Bahi*, No. 3, V.S. 1827/1770 AD, *Posh Sudi* 12, R.S.A., Bikaner.
140. *Sawa Bahi Mandi Sadar Bikaner*, No. 29, V.S. 1856-57/1799-1800 AD, f. 64(b), R.S.A., Bikaner.
141. *Sawa Bahi Mandi Sadar Bikaner*, No. 5, V.S. 1810/1753 AD, f. 15b.
142. *Sawa Bahi Mandi Sadar Bikaner*, No. 3, V.S. 1805/1748 AD, f. 56b, R.S.A., Bikaner.
143. *Magre Khari Patti ri Jagat Bahi*, No. 66, V.S.1858/1801 AD, ff. 7-10, *Sawa Bahi Mandi Bikaner*, No. 20. V.S. 1832/1775 AD ff. 1-3, R.S.A., Bikaner.
144. *Rajaldesar ri Jagat Bahi*, No. 64, V.S. 1857/1800 AD, *'Lekho Chowki*

Hardesar ri', Jagat Bahi Bikaner, No. 25, V.S. 1829/1772 AD, R.S.A.,Bikaner.

145. *Sawa Bahi Mandi Sadar Bikaner,* No. 4, V.S. 1807-10/1750-53 AD, f. 126A.
146. *Suratgarh ri Jagat ro Lekho,* No. 87, V.S. 1862/1805 AD, ff. 2-10, *GajSinghpura re Jagat ri Bahi,* No. 10, V.S. 1815/1758 AD ff. 1-5, R.S.A., Bikaner.
147. *Sawa Bahi Mandi Sadar Bikaner,* No. 21, V.S. 1835-36/1778-1879 AD, f. 89b. Rs. 83 and As. 15 were realized at *Bikaner Mandi* as *Nekal Jagat* for sending indigo from Churu to Pali in the year 1778-79 AD.
148. *Kagad Bahi,* No. 12, V.S. 1859/1802 AD.
149. *Parwana Bahi,* No. 1, V.S. 1700-1800, f. 629b; No. 4, V.S. 1800-1900/1743-1843 AD, *Chiti Diwani,* V.S. 1823, *Phalgun Badi* 5, Camp. Chandasar, R.S.A., Bikaner.
150. *Sawa Bahi Mandi Sadar Bikaner,* No. 11, V.S. 1822/1765 AD, ff.1-2, *Jagat Bahi,* Bikaner, No.7, V.S. 1807 ff. 1-6, *Bahi Mahajana Re Peedhiyon Ri, miscelleneous Bahi,* V.S. 1926/1869 AD, ff. 39-41, R.S.A., Bikaner.
151. *Jagat Bahi Bikaner,* No. 69, V.S. 1858/1801 AD, ff. 1-12, *Jagat Bahi Ratangarh Ri,* No. 81, V.S. 1860/1803 AD,ff. 1-9 R.S.A., Bikaner.
152. *Jagat Bahi Bikaner,* No. 17, V.S. 1821/1764 AD, ff. 3-8. *Churu Re Jagat Ri Bahi,* No. 33, V.S. 1831-32/1774-75 AD, ff. 1-8, R.S.A., Bikaner.
153. *Sri Mandi ri Jama Kharach ri Bahi,* No. 35, V.S. 1834/1777 AD, ff. 1-2, *Jasrasar ri Chowki ro Lekho - Bahi Desh re Jagat ri,* No. 77, V.S. 1859/1802 AD, R.S.A., Bikaner.
154. *Sanad Parwana Bahi,* V.S. 1840/1783 AD, f. 65, Jodhpur records, R.S.A., Bikaner. Cf. Sharma, G.S., *Marwai Vyapari,* Bikaner (1988), p. 21.
155. *Kagad Bahis,* No. 12, V.S. 1859/1802 AD; No. 15 V.S. 1866/1809 AD, *Byav Bahi,* No. 159, V.S. 1827/1770 AD, *Sawa Bahi Mandi Sadar Bikaner,* No. 8, V.S. 1815-16/1758-59, R.S.A., Bikaner.
156. *Sawa Bahi Mandi Sadar Bikaner,* No. 21, V.S. 1835-36/1778-79 AD, f. 103b, R.S.A., Bikaner.
157. *Sawa Bahi Mandi Sadar Bikaner,* No. 2, V.S. 1802-03/1745-46 AD, f. 10b, R.S.A., Bikaner.
158. *Sawa Bahi Mandi Sadar Bikaner,* No. 2, V.S. 1802-03/1745-46 AD, f. 32-b, No.3, V.S. 1805/1748 AD; f. 56b; No. 4, V.S. 1807-10/1750-53 AD, ff. 55-a, 126-a; No. 17, V.S. 1829-30/1772-23 AD, f. 59b, R.S.A., Bikaner.
159. *Sawa Bahi Mandi Anupgarh,* No. 14, V.S. 1899/1842 AD, f.154, *Sawa*

Bahi Mandi Bikaner, No. 3, V.S. 1805, ff. 2a, 63a, No. 16, V.S. 1827/1770 AD, f. 48b; No. 21, V.S. 1835-36/1778-79 AD, f. 10a; No. 22, V.S. 1837/1780 AD, f. 32b, R.S.A., Bikaner.

160. *Sawa Bahi Mandi Bikaner*, No. 4, V.S. 1807-10/1750-53 AD, f. 83a.
161. *Sawa Bahi Mandi Sadar Bikaner*, No. 2, V.S. 1804/1747 AD, f. 27b, No. 3, V.S. 1805/1748 AD, f. 56b, No. 15, V.S. 1826/1769 AD, f. 8a; No. 17, V.S. 1829-30/1772-23 AD, f. 140b, No.19, V.S. 1832/1775 AD f. 22a, No. 9, V.S. 1818-21/1761-64 AD, f. 46b, R.S.A., Bikaner.
162. *Sawa Bahi Churu Mandi*, No. 1, V.S. 1828/1771 AD, ff. 20; 25a.
163. *Sawa Bahi Suratgarh Mandi*, No. 3, V.S. 1860/1803 AD, ff. 48-49, Large quantities of tobacco was brought into Suratgarh by the traders from Ajmer and in exchange they took away *sajji* and sindhi salt from Suratgarh.
164. *Sawa Bahi Mandi Sadar Bikaner*, No. 3, V.S. 1805/1748 AD, f. 122a, No. 4, V.S. 1807-10/1750-53, f. 3a; No. 10, V.S.1821-22/1764-65 AD, ff. 4(b), 39(a), R.S.A., Bikaner.
165. *Sawa Bahi Mandi Bikaner*, No. 3, V.S. 1805/1748 AD, f. 56b.
166. Ibid, No. 21, V.S. 1835-36/1778-79 AD, ff. 10b, 84b. *Sawa Bahi Rajgarh Mandi*, No. 11, V.S. 1864/1807 AD, f. 65, R.S.A., Bikaner.
167. *Sawa Bahi Mandi Bikaner*, No. 4, V.S. 1807-10/1750-53 AD, f. 109b, R.S.A., Bikaner.
168. *Sawa Bahi Reni*, No. 15, V.S. 1815/1758 AD, f. 38, R.S.A., Bikaner.
169. Sharma, G.S., op. cit., p. 21.
170. See trade routes discussed in the chapter.
171. The various *mandis* were working at Bikaner, Reni, Churu, Rajgarh, Sujangarh, Ratangarh, Anupgarh, Hanumangarh, Nohar, and Lunkaransar. The *Sawa Bahis* and *Jagat Bahis* of these *Mandis* are procured in the Raj. State Archives, Bikaner. See *A Descriptive List of Bikaner Bahis*, op. cit., pp. 142-178.
172. The *Mandis* were supplemented by the *Chowkis*. Some mentionable *Chowkis* were *Chowkis* of Jasrasar, Punrasar, Gandheli, Rawatsar, Rajaldesar, Kharbara, Jhajhu, Kalu, Mehsar, Bhensli, Hardesar, Karanpur, Bigga, Sandwa, Budhnuo, Kumbhana etc. *Bahi Yaddast Chowki mein Jagat Liya Teri*, No. 92, V.S. 1869/1812AD, ff. 1-10, R.S.A., Bikaner.
173. *Bholawania* was an appointed personnel responsible for collection of *Jagat* from traders who bypass the check points. Sometimes, out of the merchant class a person was appointed for it, who along with his business performed this duty as well. They were paid a fixed rate of remuneration, and while submitting their accounts of the village collection of Jagat they deducted their

payments. *Sawa Bahi Suratgarh*, No. 4, V.S. 1881-84/1824-27 AD, ff. 189-90 No. 5, V.S. 1888/1831 AD; *Sawa Bahi Churu*, No. 1, V.S. 1828/1771 AD, ff. 11-12, R.S.A., Bikaner.

174. *Barothias* were the punished and deserted persons who lived outside the state. Village Jeevandesar was completely deserted on account of a wholesale loot by the *Barothias*. The state attempted to rehabilitate them in 1811 AD *Kagad Bahi*, No. 18, V.S. 1868/1811 AD, *Adalat ra Kagad*, in 1814 village *Berasar Padiharon ro* was plundered four times by dacoits. *Kagad Bahi*, No. 20, V.S. 1871/1814 AD, *Migsar badi* 11, R.S.A., Bikaner.
175. Franklin, William, *Military Memoirs of George Thomas*, Cf. Sharma, G.S., op. cit., p. 21.
176. *Sawa Bahi Suratgarh*, No. 5, V.S. 1880-89/1823-32 AD, (Year 1823).
177. Sharma, G.S., op. cit., p. 22.
178. *Sawa Bahi Mandi Bikaner*, No. 22, V.S. 1837/1780 AD, f. 32b.
179. *Sawa Bahi Anupgarh*, No. 15, V.S. 1906, f. 137.
180. Ibid., *Mandi* Bikaner, No. 4, V.S. 1807-10, f. 113a, No. 20, V.S. 1833/1776 AD, f. 42(b).
181. *Sawa Bahi Mandi Sadar Bikaner*, No. 3, V.S.1805/1748 AD, f. 55(b); *Sawa Bahi Reni*, No. 1, V.S. 1823/1766 AD, ff. 239, 243.
182. Ibid., No. 21, V.S. 1835-36, f. 11(a).
183. *Sawa Bahi Mandi Sadar*, No. 4, V.S. 1807/1750 AD, f. 45(a).
184. *Sawa Bahi Mandi Bikaner*, No. 20, V.S. 1833-34/1776-77 AD, *Mandi Suratgarh*, No. 5, V.S. 1881-89/1824-28, f. 100, R.S.A., Bikaner.
185. The birth of a male horse child was rejoiced and the sixth day bath was given to the mother of the colt, also heavy transit duty in Bikaner was taken on the horse. The total amount of Rs. 21 for 3 horses was realized in Suratgarh for three check points of Suratgarh, Anupgarh and Hanumangarh respectively in 1790 AD, *Sawa Bahi Suratgarh*, No. 1, V.S. 1847/1790 AD, f. 71.
186. *Kagad Bahi*, No. 1, V.S. 1811/1754 AD
187. *Sawa Bahi Mandi Sadar Bikaner*, No. 3, V.S. 1805/1748 AD, f. 74-b, R.S.A., Bikaner.
188. Ibid., No.16, V.S. 1827, f. 6b.
189. Ibid., ff. 11a.
190. *Sawa Bahi Bikaner*, No. 3, V.S. 1805, f. 74b, No. 16, V.S. 1827, f. 11(a), No. 22, V.S.1837-38/1780-81, f. 1a; No. 28, V.S. 1853/1796 AD, f. 45-b.
191. *Sawa Bahi Bikaner*, No. 16, V.S. 1827, f. 6b, No. 21, V.S. 1835-36, f. 103a, R.S.A., Bikaner.
192. Ibid., No. 21, V.S. 1835-36, ff. 10a, 85a.
193. Ibid.

194. Pelsaert in his *Remonstrentai,* mentions that Multan was a producing centre of opium, sulphur, Gallnut and the camels of good breed were sent all over the country. Cf. Jahangir Kalim Bharat (Tr.) B.L. Bhadani, Jaipur (1996), pp. 50-51.
195. *Sawa Bahi Mandi Bikaner*, No. 22, V.S. 1837-38/1780-8. f. 5b, R.S.A., Bikaner.
196. *Sawa Bahi Anupgarh*, No. 15, V.S. 1907, f. 173.
197. *Sawa Bahi Mandi Bikaner*, No. 3, V.S. 1805, f. 93 a.
198. Ibid., No. 5, V.S. 1810-12 (V.S. 1810) f. 58b.
199. Ibid., No. 4, V.S. 1807-10, f. 25b.
200. Ibid., No. 23, V.S. 1838-40, f. 3a.
201. *Sawa Bahi Churu Mandi*, No. 1, V.S. 1828, f. 27.
202. *Bandedo* literally meant packload of goods, like wet fruit, water melon or spices, etc. When it could be carried on a person's head it was called *Seervo*, i.e. the load carried on the head. See *Sawa Bahi Churu*, No. 1, V.S. 1828, f. 37b, R.S.A., Bikaner.
203. There are innumerable references in the *Kagad Bahis* showing such interests. Almost every *Kagad* (order) contains the following concluding lines for the merchant class – 'बसता रहजो बीणज वोपार करजो थांरी पीठ रहसी' (Do reside in the state and continue the commercial activities, the state would support you) See *Chhoot ra Kagad* appended in the various *Kagad Bahis*. *Kagad Bahi*, No. 1, V.S. 1811/1754 AD, No. 2, V.S. 1820/1763 AD, No. 15, V.S. 1866/ 1809 AD, R.S.A., Bikaner.
204. The state was hostile to Jodhpur state during this period. It attacked Bikaner many times. The *Thikanedars* of Bikaner also revolted against the state and hatched conspiracies. See Ojha, G.H., *Bikaner Rajya Ka Itihas*, 2nd ed., Jodhpur, 1999, Part I, pp. 323, 26, 42, 44, pt. II, pp. 372-73, 385, 68, 78, 91 & 97.
205. Such honours were also conferred upon the local merchants while granting a *muqata* or for rendering any outstanding services to the state by them like encouraging settlement in any village. *Sawa Bahi Suratgarh*, No. 8, V.S. 1898/1841, f. 133, R.S.A., Bikaner.
206. *Sawa Bahi Nohar*, No. 1, V.S. 1822/1765 AD, f. 23, R.S.A., Bikaner.
207. *Sawa Bahi Sujangarh*, No. 7, V.S. 1914/1857AD, f. 422(b), R.S.A., Bikaner.
208. *Kagad Bahi*, No. 33/1, V.S. 1884/1827AD, f. 82(a); *Potedar Sangrah ke Aprakashit Kagzat* by Govind Agrawal, pp. 45-46; 'Marushri', Ajmer, 1976 AD, Yr. 5, Vol. 1-2.
209. Sharma, G.C., *Administrative System of the Rajputs*, New Delhi, 1979, pp. 155-58; the artisans were also favoured by bestowing upon them certain financial favours. For instance, Rs. 130 as state

help was provided to *Usta* artisans Sahu Mohd. Biram Abu and Sultan on the marriages of their wards. *Kagad Bahi*, No. 18, V.S. 1868/1811 AD, R.S.A., Bikaner.

210. *Kagad Bahi*, No. 13, V.S. 1861/1804 AD, *Bhadwa sudi* 6, R.S.A., Bikaner.
211. *Kagad Bahi*, No. 30, V.S. 1881/1824AD, *Bhadwa Sudi* 6, R.S.A., Bikaner.
212. *Kagad Bahi*, No. 10, V.S. 1854/1797AD, f. 39, R.S.A., Bikaner.
213. *Kagad Bahi*, No. 22, V.S. 1873/1816 AD, *Magh Sudi* 9, R.S.A., Bikaner.
214. *Kagad Bahi*, No. 30, V.S. 1881/1824 AD, ff. 1(a), 16(a) and 106(b); No. 14, V.S. 1863-64/1806-07, ff. 225 & 240; No. 13, V.S. 1861/ 1804 AD, *Bhardrapad Badi* 4, R.S.A., Bikaner.
215. Sharma, G.C., op. cit., pp. 155-56.
216. *Kagad Bahi*, No. 13, V.S. 1861/1804 AD, *Shravan Badi* 11.
217. Ibid., *Bhadrapad Badi*, No. 4, R.S.A., Bikaner.
218. *Sawa Bahi Lunkaransar*, No. 1, V.S. 1889/1832 AD, f. 38(a), R.S.A., Bikaner.
219. *Sawa Bahi Suratgarh*, No. 3, V.S. 1877/1820 AD, f. 176, R.S.A., Bikaner.
220. *Sawa Bahi Rajgarh*, No. 1, V.S. 1828/1771 AD, R.S.A., Bikaner.
221. Rs. 1,026 and *Annas* 14 in 1748 AD were loaned to the Multani traders in Bikaner. *Sawa Bahi Mandi Bikaner*, No. 3, V.S. 1805/ 1748 AD, f. 55 (b).
222. *Sawa Bahi Reni*, No. 1, V.S. 1823/1766 AD, ff. 239, 243.
223. 'The policy of the Rajput rulers of Rajasthan towards the commercial class in the 18th century', by Gupta, B.L. (Summary), pp. 344-45, PIHC, 46th Session, Amritsar, 1985; Gupta, B.L., *Trade and Commerce in Rajasthan*, Jaipur, 1987, pp. 233-34.
224. *Kagad Bahi*, No. 1, V.S. 1811/1754 AD, R.S.A., Bikaner.
225. Ibid., No. 23, V.S. 1874/1817 AD, *Bhadrapad badi* 1.
226. *Chhoot Ra Kagad, Kagad Bahi*, No. 1. V.S. 1811/1754 AD, No. 3, V.S. 1827/1770 AD, f. 8(a); *Prachun Kagad, Kagad Bahi*, No. 10, V.S. 1854/1797 AD, f. 8; No. 20, V.S. 1871/1814 AD
227. Village Kumbhana (near the capital city of Bikaner) was dominated by Khatri merchants.
228. *Kagad Bahi*, No. 26, V.S. 1877/1820 AD, *Chetra Sudi* 2, R.S.A., Bikaner.
229. Ibid., No. 20, V.S. 1871/1814 AD, *Kartik Badi* 3, R.S.A., Bikaner.
230. Ibid.
231. *Kagad Bahi*, No. 1, V.S. 1811/1754 AD, *Jyestha Badi* 8, R.S.A., Bikaner.

232. *Prachum Kagad, Kagad Bahi,* No. 10, V.S. 1854/1797 AD, f. 8, R.S.A., Bikaner.
233. Orders were issued in 1797 AD regarding 2 camels of traders to be grazed in the pasture land of village of *Magra, Kagad Bahi,* No. 10, V.S. 1854/1797 AD, f. 20, R.S.A., Bikaner.
234. *Kagad Bahi,* No. 1, V.S. 1811/1754 AD, order for the escorting goods and necessary security was given.
235. *Kagad Bahi,* No. 19/2, V.S. 1870/1813 AD, *Baisakh Sudi* 6, R.S.A., Bikaner.
236. Ibid.
237. *Sawa Bahi Churu,* No. 1, V.S. 1829/1772 AD, f. 25b, R.S.A., Bikaner.
238. Kagad Bahi, No. 3, V.S.1827/1770 AD, f. 13a.
239. Ibid.
240. *Sawa Bahi Rahgarh,* No. 4, V.S. 1840/1783 AD, f. 576, R.S.A., Bikaner.
241. *Kagad Bahi,* No. 10, V.S. 1854/1797 AD
242. Letter of Maharaja Gaj Singh to Maharaja Sawai Madho Singh, dtd. *Jyestha Badi,* 10, V.S. 1819/1762 AD; Draft *kharita and parwana,* Jaipur records, Cf. Gupta, B.L., op. cit., pp. 232-36.
243. *Miscellaneous Bahi,* No. 190, V.S. 1861-67/1804-10 AD *Asoj Sudi* 4, V.S. 1862/1805 AD, Cf. Gupta, B.L., op. cit., pp. 232-36, *Sawa Bahi Rajgarh,* No. 1, V.S. 1828/1771 AD f. 3a. The looted camels of a trader of Rajgarh were recovered and returned to him in 1771 AD, *Sawa Bahi Rajgarh,* No. 4, V.S. 1839/1782 AD There are more examples available to us in the bahis. In 1774 AD a *katar* carrying *Pashmina* and cotton cloth from *Pithod* to Bikaner was looted at Rajpura by Mian Qammauddin. On the request of the traders the state instructed the officials of Churu, Bhadra and Nohar that none should purchase the looted items and the goods should be recovered soon. *Kagad Bahi,* No. 10, V.S. 1854/1797 AD The many references of looting shows the gross insecurity at the trade routes.
244. *Kagad Bahi,* No. 22, V.S. 1873/1816 f. 182, *Kartik Sudi* 12, R.S.A., Bikaner.
245. *Sawa Bahi Nohar,* No. 1, V.S. 1822/1765 AD, f. 16b, R.S.A., Bikaner.
246. Ibid., f. 23.
247. *Sawa Bahi Rajgarh,* No. 1, V.S. 1828/1771 AD, f. 105a, R.S.A., Bikaner.
248. *Kagad Bahi,* No. 10, V.S. 1854/1797 AD, *Phalgun Sudi* 3, *Asoj Sudi* 7, No. 12, V.S. 1859, *Baisakh Badi* 4, R.S.A., Bikaner.
249. *Kagad Bahi,* No. 3, V.S. 1827/1770 AD, *Posh badi* 1, No.1, V.S. 1811/1754 AD, R.S.A., Bikaner.
250. *Kagad Bahi,* No. 30, V.S. 1881/1824 AD, ff. 183, a and b. R.S.A., Bikaner.

251. *Sawa Bahi Anupgarh,* No. 14, V.S. 1898/1841 AD, f.151. There were two agents Lunia Parsa Ram and one other in Anupgarh area. At the rate of Rs. 15 p.m. comes to Rs. 90 only. It is not known why Re. 1 is in excess.
252. Nawal Ram Daga, a *Sahukar* of Bhadra, when he was subjected to pay some amount to the state under '*Attak*' (arrest), he took shelter of Mirza Mal in Bhadra in 1827 AD He wrote letters to Mirza Mal Potedar for his security (Letter - S. 172, S. 651 and S. 301. Potedar collection of Churu). There were some more incidents recorded in the collection cited, that Mirza Mal was approached to abstain from the '*Attak*' incidences. The '*Attak*' was a kind of an arrest by the state of a particular *sahukar,* shop, *katar* or a person in which he was subjected to pay the required amount out of his accumulated wealth or to fulfil the demand of any type. It was more or less a forced raid. For details see 'Papers relating to *attak*' by Govind Agrawal, pp. 6-17. *Marushri,* Yrs 11-12, Vol. 4-1, July-December, 1982, Churu, Rajasthan.
253. When he was departing from the *Darbar* (court) he was honoured with his fellowmen or *Gumastas* (agents) with *Siropaos, Motiyon ro chowkdo* and shawls worth Rs. 3,800 in 1827 AD *Kagad Bahi,* No. 33/1, V.S. 1884/1827 AD, f. 82(9); '*Potedar Sangrah ke Aprakashit Kagad*', Govind Agrawal, pp. 45-46, *Marushri,* Yr. 5, Vol. 1-2, Churu, 1976 AD
254. *Khas Rukka* of Maharaja Surat Singh dated *Asadh Badi* 5, V.S. 1884. Quoted in *Potedar Sangrah ke Aprakashit Kagzat,* Govind Agrawal, op. cit., p. 34.
255. *Chaar Lakh ki Aitihasik Hundi* (Hindi) Govind Agrawal, *Maru Bharti,* Yr. 18, No. 4, (ed.) Kanhiyalal Sahal, January 1971, Pilani; *Potedar Sangrah ke Aprakashit Kagzat,* Govind Agrawal, op. cit., pp. 34-45.
256. *Kagad Bahi,* No. 10; *Potedar Sangrah ke Arakashit Kagzat,* Govind Agrawal, op. cit., p. 34. 1854/1797 AD, f. 50, *Asadh Badi* 3.
257. *Kagad Bahi,* No. 19/1, V.S. 1870/1813 AD, *Mingsar Sudi* 4; *Potedar Sangrah ke Arakashit Kagzat,* Govind Agrawal, op. cit., p. 34. 1870/1813 AD, *Mingsar Sudi* 4.
258. *Sawa Bahi Anupgarh,* No. 14, V.S. 1901/1844 AD, *Potedar Sangrah ke Arakashit Kagzat,* Govind Agrawal, op. cit., p. 34. 1901/1844 AD.
259. *Kagad Bahi,* No. 3, V.S. 1827/1770 AD, f. 10b, *Kartik Sudi* 2. *Potedar Sangrah ke Arakashit Kagzat,* Govind Agrawal, op. cit., p. 34.
260. The Mughal emperors Jahangir, Shahjahan and Aurangzeb participated into the overseas trade and the queens also invested

in trade and even had junks of their own. The monopoly rights were created for important commodities like saltpetre, indigo and lime coming from Bhroach; Satish Chandra, 'Commercial Activities of the Mughal Emperors during the 17th Century', pp. 163-169 in *Essays in Medieval Indian Economic History,* Congress, Golden Jubiliee Year Publication Series, Vol. III, New Delhi, 1987.

261. The mention of '*Reni Rupya*' in circulation in the *Churu Mandal* is available in '*Dravya-pariksha*' by Thakkar Feru of 1718 (V.S. 1775). The book deals with the technology of alloying and minting of coins. Cf. Govind Agrawal, *Churu Mandal ka Shodhpurna Itihas*, pp. 469-70. The *Morkhana* inscription further contains that six *takkas* were levied as tax for a Jain temple from goods carried passing through *Morkhana* in Bikaner region. (*JAS Bengal*, Vol. XIII, pp. 214-15; Tessitory Report, 1916, Jain Inscription, II, p. 70). Cf. Sharma, G.N., *Social Life in the Medieval Rajasthan*, op. cit., p. 333.

262. The *Dam* was a marine copper coin weighing normally 323.5 grains. 40 *Dams* were recognized as an equivalent to a silver rupee of 172.5 grains. Chopra, P.N., *Some Aspects of Social Life During the Mughal Age* (*1526-1707 AD*), Agra (1963), 1st ed. (Glossary).

263. For the detailed study of the Mughal currency and the imperial mints see "Currency Output of the Mughal Empire and the Extension of the Price Revolution to India", PIHC Mysore Session, December, 1966 and 'Mints of the Mughal Empire (A Study in Comparative Output)' Both articles by Aziza Hasan; *Essays in Medieval Economic History*, (ed.) Satish Chandra, Vol. III, New Delhi, 1987. Also Irfan Habib's, *Currency System of the Mughal Empire, Medieval India. Quarterly-IV*, Nos. 1-2, Aligarh, 1960.

264. Brown, C.J., 'Some Remarks on the Mughal Currency', *The Journal of the U.P. Historical Society*, Vol. 1, p. 152; Mishra, K.P., *The Role of the Banaras Bankers in the Economy of the 18th Century India*, PIHC, 1973, Vol. II, Chandigarh Session, p. 67.

265. Powlett, Capt. P.W., *Gazetteer of the Bikaner State*, pp. 117-18, Gupta, B.L., op. cit., pp. 169-70.

266. The process of monetization accelerated in whole of the country after the decline of the Mughal empire. However, it had least correlation with the decline of the empire. Frank Perlin, *Mint Technology and Mint Output in an Age of Growing Commercialization*, pp. 292-302, Indian History Congress Golden Jubilee Series—*Essays in Medieval Economic History*, Vol. III, New Delhi, 1987.

267. Web, W.W., *The Currencies of Hindu States of Rajputana, 1893*, Translated in Hindi by Mayank, Mangilal, entitled *Rajputana ke*

Hindi Rajwade ke Sikke, Jodhpur, pp. 69-82. The Hindi translation has been used. Powlett, op. cit., pp. 117-18.

268. However, it is only believed so there is no document available to substantiate the fact. Web, op. cit., pp. 69-82; Powlett, op. cit., pp. 117-18. *Rajasthan District Gazetteer - Bikaner*, Jaipur, (1972), pp. 197-98.
269. *Kagad Bahi*, No. 1, V.S. 1811, *Jyestha Sudi* 5, Rampuria Records, R.S.A., Bikaner.
270. Web, op. cit., pp. 69-82.
271. Ibid.
272. Ibid.
273. Ojha, G.H., *Bikaner Rajya ka Itihas*, Vol. I, p. 38.
274. *Juhari* is a ceremonial gift being given to the bridegroom usually while departing after the marriage or his visit to the in-laws' house.
275. *Byav bahi*, No. 158 and 159, *'Bai Sardar Kunwar re Byav ri Bahi'*, R.S.A., Bikaner. The value of a golden *mohar* varies from Rs. 13¾ to Rs. 15; *Akhateej ri Bahi*, (miscellaneous bahis), R.S.A., Bikaner.
276. Web, op. cit., pp. 69-82.
277. Ibid.
278. Ibid., Powlett, p. 118.
279. Web, pp. 69-82; *Byav ri Bahi*, No. 159, V.S. 1827/1770 AD, R.S.A., Bikaner.
280. Ibid., Powlett, p. 118.
281. *Byav Bahis*, No. 158 and 159, V.S. 1827/1770 AD, R.S.A., Bikaner.
282. *Sawa Bahi Anupgarh*, No. 1, V.S. 1753-54/1696-97 AD, ff. 2, 9a, 10, 13, 18 and 19; No. 5, V.S. 1902/1845 AD, f. 12; No.15, V.S. 1902-03, f.12. *Sawa Bahi Mandi Sadar Bikaner*, No. 2, V.S. 1804/1747 AD, f. 43b; R.S.A., Bikaner.
283. *Chitti Khaton ri Bahi*, No. 6, V.S. 1869/1812 AD, *Hundiyon ri Vigat ri Bahi*, No. 241, V.S. 1726/1669 AD, R.S.A., Bikaner; *Sawa Bahi Rajgarh*, No. 21, V.S. 1901-02/1844-45 AD, f. 134, R.S.A., Bikaner; Web, W.W., op. cit., pp. 69-82; Powlett, p. 118.
284. *Sawa Bahi Mandi Bikaner*, No. 3, V.S. 1805/1748 AD, *Sawa Bahi Anupgarh*, No. 15, V.S. 1902/1845 AD, R.S.A., Bikaner.
285. Ibid.
286. Ibid., No. 15, V.S. 1902-03/1845-46 AD, f. 12, R.S.A., Bikaner.
287. *Sawa Bahi Anupgarh*, No. 1, V.S. 1753-54/1696-97 AD, f. 13, R.S.A., Bikaner.
288. Cf. Gupta, B.L., op. cit., pp. 169-70.
289. *Sawa Bahi Bikaner Mandi*, No. 3, V.S. 1805/1748 AD, *Kagad Bahi*, No. 1, V.S. 1811/1754 AD, *Phagun Badi 7*, Web, op. cit., pp. 69-82,

R.S.A., Bikaner.

290. Cf. Gupta, B.L., op. cit., pp. 169-70.
291. *Byav ri Bahis*, No. 159, V.S. 1827/1770 AD, R.S.A., Bikaner.
292. Shah, P.R., 'Introduction of British Indian Currency in Jodhpur State'– A Case Study in Economic Reforms and its Execution', p. 108, PRHC, Vol. VI, Beawar Session, 1973.
293. Web, W.W., op. cit., pp. 69-82.
294. Ibid.
295. Ibid., *Kooch Muqam ri Bahi*, No. 1, V.S. 1886/1829, f. 102, R.S.A., Bikaner.
296. Web, op. cit., pp. 69-82.
297. *Jagat ro Chopaniyo*, No. 42, V.S. 1840/1783 AD, *Bahi Mahajana re Peedhiya ri*, V.S. 1926 (miscellaneous *Bahi*) see *'Taksal ri Yaad'*, *Bikaner Bahiyat* Section, R.S.A., Bikaner.
298. Web, op. cit., pp. 69-82.
299. *Bahi Peshkashi re Lekhe ri*, No. 1, V.S. 1833/1776 AD; Web, op. cit., pp. 69-82.
300. Ibid.
301. *Kagad Bahi*, No. 30, V.S. 1881/1824 AD, f. 1029, R.S.A., Bikaner.
302. Web, op. cit., pp. 69-82.
303. Ibid.
304. Ibid.
305. *Kagad Bahi*, No. 19/1, V.S. 1870/1813 AD, f. 11, R.S.A., Bikaner.
306. Ibid., and *Kagad Bahi*, No. 30, V.S. 1881/1824 AD, f. 109, R.S.A., Bikaner.
307. *Kagad Bahi*, No. 19/1, V.S. 1870/1813 AD, f. 11.
308. *Kagad Bahi*, No. 16, V.S. 1867/1810 AD, *Shrawan Sudi* 1, Rs. 24 were collected in Bikaner in 1798 AD from *taksal* of copper, *Bahi Jama Kharach ri*, V.S. 1855/1798 AD, R.S.A., Bikaner.
309. Ibid.
310. *Kooch Muqam ri Bahi*, (Muqam Rajgarh), No. 1, V.S. 1886/1829 AD, f. 102, R.S.A., Bikaner.
311. Aziza Hasan, 'Mints of the Mughal Empire (A Study in Comparative Currency Output)' in *Essays in Medieval Economic History*, (ed.) Satish Chandra, Vol. III, New Delhi, 1987, p.183.
312. *Kagad Bahi*, No. 10, V.S. 1854/1797 AD, *Jyestha Badi* 9, f.10, R.S.A., Bikaner.
313. Ibid.
314. *Sawa Bahi Churu*, No. 1, V.S. 1828/1771 AD, f. 11a (चलणी).
315. *Sarab Takka Bahi*, V.S. 1828/1771 AD V.S. 1840/1783 AD, R.S.A., Bikaner. Cf. G.S. Sharma, op. cit., p. 337.
316. Sharma, G.N., op. cit., pp. 336-37.

317. Ibid., *Sawa Bahi Mandi Sadar Bikaner*, No. 9, V.S. 1818-21/1761-64 AD, f. 30b, R.S.A., Bikaner.
318. Ibid.
319. *Sawa Bahi Mandi Bikaner*, No. 9, V.S. 1818/1761 AD, f. 30b, R.S.A., Bikaner.
320. *Sawa Bahi Rajgarh Mandi*, No. 3, V.S. 1836/1779 AD, f. 80a, R.S.A., Bikaner.
321. *Sawa Bahi Rajgarh Mandi*, No. 4, V.S. 1839/1782 AD, f. 23b.
322. Sharma G.N., op. cit., pp. 336-37.
323. *Sarab Takka Bahi*, V.S. 1828/1771 AD, V.S. 1840/1783 AD, *Sawa Bahi Churu*, No. 1, V.S. 1828/1771 AD, f.11a, R.S.A., Bikaner.
324. Ibid.
325. Aziza Hasan, op. cit., pp. 170-198.
326. Sharma G.S., *Marwari Vyapari*, Bikaner (1988), p. 24.
327. *Sawa Bahi Mandi Bikaner*, No. 3, V.S. 1805/1748 AD, f. 55b, R.S.A., Bikaner.
328. Sharma, G.N., op. cit., p. 335.
329. Ajmer currency files, 1-a, letter No. 429, 1864 AD, Cf. Sharma, G.N., op. cit., p. 335.
330. Ibid.
331. *Byav ri Bahi*, No. 159, V.S. 1827/1770 AD, R.S.A., Bikaner, Gupta, B.L., op. cit., p. 173.
332. *Sawa Bahi Rajgarh*, No. 22, V.S. 1903-05/1846-48 AD, f. 146. We have some more examples of exchange of *Ratanshahi* with *Chehrashahi* coins as under –

Sr. No.	*Ratanshahi*	Exchange with *Chehvashahi*	*Bagha* paid (difference)
1.	Rs. 1,000	Rs. 1,012 *As.* 8	Rs. 12 *As.* 8
2.	Rs. 300	Rs. 302 *As.* 13	Rs. 2 *As.* 13

Sawa Bahi Rajgarh, No. 23, V.S. 1906/1849 AD and V.S. 1907/1850 AD, f. 12a, 43a, R.S.A., Bikaner.

333. *Sawa Bahi Rajgarh*, No. 20, V.S. 1899/1842 AD, f. 165b, R.S.A., Bikaner.
334. *Sawa Bahi Anupgarh*, No. 1, V.S. 1753-54/1696-97 AD, f. 13, R.S.A., Bikaner.
335. *Sarrafon re Lekhe ri Bahi*, V.S. 1940/1883 AD, R.S.A., Bikaner. Account of *Sarraf* Sindhi Shiv Lal Rughnath and Sarraf Dammani Nand Lal were maintained. They used to lend money on interest to the state.
336. Agrawal, Govind, *Churu Mandal ka Shodhpurna Itihas*, pp. 465-67.
337. *Sawa Bahi Mandi Rajgarh*, No. 4, V.S. 1839/1782 AD, f. 23b; *Sawa Bahi Mandi Sadar Bikaner*, No. 29, V.S. 1856-57/1799-1800 AD, ff.

130a, 142a, R.S.A., Bikaner.

338. Agrawal, Govind, op. cit., pp. 465-67.
339. *Banika Shikshak*, by Dammani, Makkhan Lal, Bikaner, 1943, pp. 7-8, *Sawa Bahi Suratgarh*, No. 1, V.S. 1844/1787 AD, f. 54a, R.S.A., Bikaner.
340. *Sawa Bahi Mandi Suratgarh*, No. 1, V.S. 1844/1787 AD, f. 549; R.S.A., Bikaner.
341. *Byav ri Bahis*, No. 159, V.S. 1827/1770 AD, R.S.A., Bikaner.
342. Ibid.
343. Ibid.
344. *Sawa Bahi Mandi Anupgarh*, No. 9, V.S, 1874/1817, f.240, R.S.A., Bikaner.
345. *Sawa Bahi Suratgarh*, No. 1, V.S, 1844/1787 AD. It has been mentioned that 'मण 126 पायली रो मण 56, 2¼ सू'.
346. Agrawal, Govind, op. cit., pp. 465-67.
347. Gupta, B.L., op. cit., pp. 182-84.
348. *Bai Sardar Kanwar re Byav ri Bahi*, No. 159, V.S. 1827/1770 AD, R.S.A., Bikaner.
349. *Sawa Bahi Nohar*, No. 1, V.S. 1824/1767 AD, f. 79b; *Sawa Bahi Mandi Rajgarh*, No. 1, V.S. 1828/1771 AD, ff. 1(b)& 2(b), R.S.A., Bikaner.
350. The *Nohar Modikhana* earned Rs. 11 from the excess grains collected in this way. *Sawa Bahi Nohar*, No. 1, V.S. 1824/1767 AD, f. 334, R.S.A., Bikaner.
351. *Kagad Bahi*, No. 15, V.S. 1866/1809 AD, *Asadh Badi* 9, f. 138, *Sawa Bahi Rajgarh*, No. 4, V.S. 1839/1782 AD, f. 23b. A *Totawatia* (weigh man) was penalized for Rs. 150 on under weighing in Rajgarh.
352. *Kagad Bahi*, No. 24, V.S. 1875/1818 AD, *Mingsar sudi* 12, R.S.A., Bikaner.
353. *Sawa Bahi Rajgarh*, No. 1, V.S. 1828/1771 AD, ff. 61-62; *Sawa Bahi Suratgarh Mandi*, No. 8, V.S. 1898/1841 AD, f. 137; R.S.A., Bikaner.
354. Agrawal, Govind, op. cit., pp. 465-67.
355. Gupta, B.L.. op. cit., p. 180.
356. Agrawal, Govind, op. cit., pp. 465-67.
357. *Sawa Bahi Rajgarh*, No. 3, V.S. 1835/1778 AD, f. 20; R.S.A., Bikaner.
358. Ibid., Powlett, p. 107. 1 mile is equal to 2.588 squire kilometeres.
359. *Kagad Bahi*, No. 11, V.S. 1857/1800 AD, f. 210, '... पण देशनोक में डोरी कदैई ना घाती...', R.S.A., Bikaner.

6

Mandis (Commercial Centres)

(1) THE *MANDIS* IN THE STATE

(a) Old *Mandis*

The state policy of encouragement led to the re-opening and development of old commercial centres as well as the emergence and growth of some new commercial centres in the state, where wholeseller markets locally called *'Mandis'* were established with their infrastructure during the second half of the 18th century.

The literary and historical evidences of the 16th & 17th century testify that Bikaner, Pugal, Morwana, Derawar, Reni and Churu were some old and important commercial centres of this region. Important trade routes connecting them were passing through the state for south and eastern provinces from the north-west.[1] These centres were considered important in western *Rajputana* as *caravans* of the traders used to bring goods from distant places to these centres (*mandis*) and the rulers of Bikaner also earned good transit and trade duties.[2] The Imperial *Farman* issued to Rai Singh by the Mughal Emperor Akbar also confirmed the fact.[3]

The following were some old *mandis* (commercial centres) in the state:

Bikaner

Bikaner, the state capital city was an old centre of commercial significance where commercial activities were carried out sufficiently.[4] Traders and *Banjaras* brought and sold cloth, *gur*, horses, opium, sugar and salt from distant places over here and carried away in exchange wool, woollen blanket, *multani-mitti*, *sajji*, etc.[5] Besides the trade and commerce, the banking and '*Hundi*' trade was actively done. '*Leni hundiyan kiwi teri vigat*'– a *lekha wa jama kharch ri bahi* of 1669 AD mentions that the local *sahukars* had their agents and branches at Delhi, Agra, Burhanpur, Ahmedabad and Aurangabad and *Hundis* were sent from Bikaner for discounting at these places.[6] The centre was well connected by inter-regional and provincial trade with Pali, Marwar, Sindhi, Multan, Delhi, Agra, Jaipur and Kota.[7]

Churu

Churu, a town in the eastern part of the state was also one of the important and old centres. It had some small commercial townships within it, viz. Reni, Dronpur, Bhadag and Sindhmukh known in the olden days of Churu *mandal*.[8] Churu was considered to be the Emporium of Medieval times[9] as goods of different places were available over here. Jagdish Singh Gahlot remarks that in medieval *Rajputana*, Churu was connected with Rajgarh in Bikaner, Malpura in Jaipur and Pali in Marwar and these were among important trade centres and functioned as intermediary *mandis* between the western ports and north India. Goods of northern India, Kashmir and China were exchanged at these places with the goods of Europe, Persia and Africa brought through traders. *Caravans* of *Banjaras* from ports of Kachha and Gujarat reached here.[10] The commercial activities were done at Churu which is further confirmed from the description of commercial shops available in the old record of Potedar Mirza Mal of Churu.[11]

Pugal

Pugal was another old commercial town of western Rajasthan.[12] Roads to Multan and Sindh passed through it. Since, it was located in the desert, it had become a midway place of exchange of commodities for traders in indigenous products like sheep and goats, *ghee*, wool, *sajji* and *khaar* reaching distant places by inter-regional trade. It earned a substantial amount in the form of transit duty.[13]

Reni

The routes from Delhi and the Punjab to Bikaner passed through Reni. It earned as noted in the source Rs. 12,365 as transit duty in V.S. 1839 (1782 AD)[14]

Apart from these old *mandis,* some new *mandis* were also founded which later acquired commercial significance.

(b) Foundation and Emergence of Some New *Mandis*

We notice that side by side some new commercial trade centres emerged and later grew in the state under the state protection. The state established wholesale markets (*Mandis*) in these centres to accelerate the mercantile activities. The following some new commercial centres (*Mandis*) came up during the second half of the 18th century:

(1) Rajgarh

Maharaja Gaj Singh (1746-1787 AD) established this town in 1766 AD in the name of his son Raj Singh. Mehta Bakhtawar Singh built a strong fortress over here. It was situated 135 miles north-east of Bikaner.[15] Gradually, Rajgarh became a wholesale commercial mart of Bikaner in the eastern part and was the rendezvous for the *caravans* from all parts of northern India.[16] It became the gateway to Delhi-Agra and the provinces of eastern India from the west. The produce of the Punjab and Kashmir reached directly through Hansi and Hissar and from the eastern parts consisting of silk, fine cloth, indigo, sugar, iron, tobacco, etc. through Delhi, Rewari and Dadri, etc.; from the Haroti and Malwa side came opium which was supplied to all the Rajputana states, and from Multan and Sikarpur came dates, wheat, rice, *loongees* (silk vestments for women) and fruit. From Pali goods from maritime countries such as spices, tin, drugs, coconuts and ivory reached to this place. The greater part of the trade was a mere transit trade which yielded revenue.[17] To encourage trade and commerce in Rajgarh, some influential traders were honoured with grants of shops. Potedar Juhari mal Bahader Mal, Potedar Ram Ratan Mirzamal and Agrawal Lahori Ram, Fateh Chand Ugresen, Harnarain and Preetam Das were the recipients. They were assured of all support and also the debts due in them were postponed for time being.[18]

(2) *Sujangarh*

Sujangarh was another town founded and developed as a *Mandi* (commercial centre) by Gaj Singh at the village identified as *'Kharbooji ka kot'* in 1778 AD in the name of Maharaja Sujan Singh.[19] Sujangarh mandi was important because it was a border town and served as the exit gate to Shekhawati and marwar region. It was located on the branch highways of Delhi-Marwar. It was also known for availability of salt and copper mines. *Kagad Bahi* of 1822 AD mentions that the state provided shops to merchants and traders of Ladnu (Marwar) and Laxmangarh (Sikar) to start their business in Sujangarh and realized *Bhada* (rent) of these shops @ Rs. 25 in all, annually. About 12 merchants were provided with these shops and they were permitted to trade. The list of shpkeepers is appended in the *bahi*.[20]

(3) *Anupgarh*

Anupgarh emerged as one of the important *mandis* after the suppression of the recalcitrant *Bhattis* in the region.[21] It gained commercial significance and it was the entry gate of Bikaner state from Multan and Bahawalpur in the north-west and it had a strong fortress to watch and ward the territories of the state. Due importance was given to it in developing a commercial town its being a bordering town. It has abundance of *sajji* and *khaar*, sheep and goats.[22]

(4) *Suratgarh*

Suratgarh was another important commercial town and *mandi* that emerged at village Sodhal. It was established by Surant Singh in 1805 AD. It is situated at 113 miles north-west of Bikaner.[23] This town and *mandi* was situated on the trade route passing from Multan to Delhi and Hansi-Hissar. It connected Anupgarh and Hanumangarh (Bhatner) and in the south to Bikaner. A *thana* and fortress were established to provide complete security to the traders.[24] We are informed from the

Kagad ri Bahi of 1810 AD that traders and merchants of Ajmer were asked to carry goods from Suratgarh as well as bring required commodity to this town. They were assured of all support.[25] The state constructed several of shops in the *mandi.* Rupees 109 and *Annas* 8 were incurred on the construction of these shops.[26] For construction of some shops half the cost was borne by the allottees of the shops.

(5) Hanumangarh (Bhatner)

Hanumangarh was another important commercial town 144 miles away from Bikaner in the north-east of the state. However, it was not a new town but was, then captured from Bhattis and annexed into Bikaner state in 1805 AD.[27] It was historically and popularly known as Bhatner but it was renamed as Hanumangarh by Surat Singh.[28] It assumed importance for the state on being a border town and located on the route leading to Hissar and Hansi, a British occupied territory after 1818 AD. It had a strong fort which many times previously, it changed hands between Bikaner and *Bhattis.*[29] Being a fertile part of the state the agrarian production was available for commercial use.

(6) Ratangarh

Ratangarh was another commercial centre established by Surat Singh, some 80 miles east of Bikaner.[30] It was situated on the branch highway of Delhi-Marwar via Rajgarh and Churu. It was developed as a commercial town by both Surat Singh and Ratan Singh.[31] The state constructed a fortress to secure it. For the construction of *Shahar-kote* (fortress) the state administration levied additional *jagat* on the commodities from the *sahukars* which ranged from 4 *Annas* to Re.1.[32] When goods from Charkhi Dadri and other distant places were imported by the *sahukars* of Ratangarh, they were subjected to pay an additional duty of Rajaldesar check point on their good.[33] The food grain was exported towards Sikar from Ratangarh. When an additional duty of Rajaldesar was demanded from *sahukars* on the export of grain it was opposed and the state favourably conceded to the request of *sahukars* not to levy the same.[34] The state seems to be concerned to promote Ratangarh as a commercial centre that on requests of *sahukar* and it ordered not to levy any type of *begar* from *sahukars* from 1811 AD onwards.[35]

There were some more small townships having local markets at Rajaldesar and Bidasar in the east, Deshnoke and Jhajhu in the south-west, Lunkaransar, Kumbhana, Jaitpur, Kharbara[36] were in the north of Bikaner which have been busy and small trading centres.

(2) THE *MANDI* : FUNCTIONS AND ADMINISTRATION

Functions

As already discussed that in various commercial towns *Bade bazars*[37] (wholesale markets) were established by the state which were called locally as *mandis*. These *mandis* were bigger markets for the wholesale transactions by the traders and merchants who brought and sold their goods. The regional commodities and the goods from outside reached these *mandis* for sale and commercial exchange. The state could realize the *jagat*[38] (common term assigned for import, export and the transit duty) on their transactions. Thus, these *mandis* were established with following the motives:

(i) To augment and accelerate the commercial activities and help exchange of goods into these centres.

(ii) To collect the maximum possible *jagat* and other commercial taxes from it.

(iii) And also the income, other than *jagat* was realized and accounted into the *mandi* offices.[39] This way, it functioned as an important revenue collection centre of the respective area.

Like the commercial towns, these *mandis* could be developed on the main trade routes or their birfurcations[40] and also on those places where there an administrative centre or security *thana* already existing.[41] The *mandis* of Suratgarh[42] and Rajgarh[43] and the *chowkis* of Dadrewa and Dhaba villages[44] were preceded by respective *thanas* which continued to protect them.[45] The *jagidars* were likewise instructed to secure the *jagatis* and help their functioning in their areas.[46] The *mandis* could also grow in such places which served as the entrances into the state in the bordering regions due to their viable contacts with the neighbouring states. The *mandis* of Rajgarh, Sujangarh, Anupgarh and Bhatner (Hanumangarh) fell into this category.[47]

Mandi Organisation

With the increase in the commercial activities in the state during the second half of the 18th century, many *mandis* with their infrastructure were created to collect the commercial income. Consequently, a widespread network of *mandis* and *chowkis* came into being in the state.

The central *mandi,* known as the *Shri Sadar Mandi Bikaner,* was at capital city Bikaner[48] but other *mandis* were functioning in the different parts of the state. The other *mandis* were located at Bhatner (Hanumangarh), Nohar, Rajgarh, Churu, Sujangarh, Ratangarh, Reni and Lunkaransar.[49] The *bahis* entitled as *Sawa bahis*[50] contain detailed accounts of each *mandis* and are available in Rampuria collection of the Rajasthan State Archives, Bikaner, for the period.[51]

Each *mandi* had its subordinate *chowkis* called as *baharli chowkis* (out posts) located on the junctions of routes in the state. For instance, under *mandi* Churu, there were *chowkis* of Hardesar, Budhnao, Loonch Girad, Suwai and Rajaldesar in 1802 AD.[52] The prominent *chowkis* in the state were *chowki* Jasarasar, Punrasar, Gandheli, Rawatsar, Rajaldesar, Kharbara, Jhajhu, Kalu, Mensar, Mahajan, Bhensli, Karanpura, Jaitpura, Biggha, Sodwa, Budhnao, Ruhi, Kurman, etc.[53]

Bholawanias (persons entrusted with the work of collection of *Jagat* in village) were working in the villages around *chowki* to collect the *Jagat* from those who were not subjected to pay the due Jagat.[54] Reference of mobile checkpost is also available (बैठी जगात चालती जगात चौकी) in the bahis.[55]

Thus, we find a three-tier system of *mandi* structure for collection of *jagat*/commercial income. *Bholawania* at village level, *jagatia* (officer at *chowki*) at minor townships and *mandis* at the town level. These segments constituted the *mandi* network and the units were well interlinked. All *mandis* and their constituents functioned under the central administration.

Administration

The *mandis* and its units were in themselves serving the purpose of markets on the one hand and were responsible for revenue collection on the other. The *mandi daftar* (office) was staffed with many officials and servants both administrative and technical.[56] In *mandis*, the *Huwaldar*[57] was the chief officer with a *Daroga* to run the administration. The state orders have been addressed to *Huwaldar* in the *Kagad bahis*.[58] He was assisted by *Khajanchi* (cashier), *Mussarrf* (clerk), *Lekhanias* (writers/scribes), *Tolawatia* (weigh man), *Batwal* (*jagat* collection), *Sarraf* (money changer) and many other servants including *chowkidars*.[59] All rendered their services on monthly salaries. For instance, these employees were paid salaries at varying rates and also in cash or *Jinsi* (Kind) as per details below: *Huwaldar* and *Sarraf* were paid Rs. 10 and Rs. 3 p.m. in cash. Similarly, *Chhapedar* was paid Rs. 5 and *Annas* 4 per month. It is interesting to note that the *Chakar* was paid in kind. His salary seems to have been fixed in cash but he was paid in kind (i.e. *Jinsi*). He was given the *Jins* costing Rs. 3 per month.[60] *Jagatia* or *Jagatidar* (in charge of *chowkis*) and *Bholawania* discharged their duties at *chowkis* and villages respectively. All the appointments were made by the *Diwan* office Bikaner on the basis of ability and integrity.[61] Inspections of Chief *Huwaldar* of *Sri Mandi Sadar Bikaner* to subordinate *chowkis* were also undertaken sometimes.[62]

The detailed accounts of *mandis* and *chowkis* were kept by *Khazanchi* with the help of *Lekhanias*[63] (scribes). *Jagatiyas* and *Bholawanias* were to remit their monthly income statement to the concerned *mandis*.[64] However, it is noted that if they failed to submit the accounts in time, a penalty was imposed upon them. For example, a *Jagatia* of Rajgarh *mandi* had to pay a fine along with the actual *jagat* collection. Occasionally, income accruing from *chowkis* have been shown separately in the accounts in the *bahis*.[65] For instance, it was mentioned in the account of *Churu mandi* as under.

Table 6.1: Income Break-up of *Mandi* and *Chowkis* in *Mandi* Churu in 1802 AD[66]

Sr.No.	*Name of Mandi/Chowki*	*Period of Collection*	*Jagat Collection*			
			Rs.	*As.*	*Takka*	*Dam*
(1)	*(2)*	*(3)*	*(4)*	*(5)*	*(6)*	*(7)*
1.	Churu *Mandi*-Proper	6 months (*Asoj Sudi* 3 to *Chetra Badi* 15)	650	3	1	0
2.	*Chowki* Hardesar	"	560	3	0	25
3.	*Chowki* Budhnao	"	214	11	0	00
4.	*Chowki* Loonch Girad	"	172	7	1	0
5.	*Chowki* Suwai	"	169	6	1	0
6.	*Chowki* Rajaldesar	"	17	0	0	0
		Total Rs.	1,783	14	3	25

The trend of receipt of *jagat* shows that it was comparatively higher at *chowkis* instead of *mandi* Churu headquarters. This further shows the larger activities of traders in the internal posts of the area. Financial adjustments of income of respective *mandis* were done on receipt of monthly accounts from check posts.[67]

Revenue Collection at *Mandis*

Revenue of both commercial and non-commercial nature were collected at the *Mandi* office through two separate agencies, i.e. through state officials and private individuals under the following systems as evinced from the *Sawa Bahis* of *Mandis*.[68]

(a) Huwala Soapa

Under it, the work of revenue collection was handed over to *Huwaldars*. The *Huwaldars*, *Jagatiyas* and *Bholawanias* collected the *Jagat* on approved tariffs (*jagat* rates). The other income also remitted to the revenues of *Mandis* by the *Huwaldars* from his jurisdiction. Sometimes an additional *Huwaldar* was provided to realize other income.[69]

(b) Muqatis or Ijaredars

But under the other system contrary to the former, private *Ijaredars* (*muqatis*) were authorized to collect the specific sources of income (called *thod*) or the revenue of any *mandi/chowki* through highest bidding.[70] In *Bikaner mandi*, at least 11 *thods* (heads of income) were given on *muqata* to a *sahukar* Gumane Dammami of Bikaner in the year 1781 AD. The bidder was termed as *muqati* (*Ijaredar*) and his assignment as *muqata* (*Ijara*). This *muqata* rights were given usually for one year to three years[71], however, it could be terminated even earlier on still higher bidding by some other *Sahukar*. In that case the due compensation was to be paid by the new incumbent[72] to the former.

The *sanads* of *muqata* contained in the *Kagad bahis* show the rights and obligations of the *muqati* as well as the details of amount to be remitted to the states in advance or in instalments. The *muqatis* were directed to restrict themselves to only the dues of *jagat* or taxes and to encourage the people to settle down in the concerned area as well as to pay the salaries of the officials deputed in the area under him.[73]

A competitiveness could be initiated among the *sahukars* to bid for higher rates for such *muqatas* and thereby increased the state income from the source. We see that during the second half of the 18th century *muqatas* of sources of income of *mandis* were given on larger scales. The *muqatis* were also frequently changed due to the higher biddings. The prominent *mandis* were let out on *muqata* to the *sahukars*. For instance, we see that the *chowki* of Reni was on *muqata* in 1770 AD for Rs. 8,101[74], after one month it was let out to another *muqata* for Rs. 9,301[75] and after another 3 months it was shiffted to another on Rs. 10,301[76]; finally in 1782 AD it was let out for Rs. 12,633 annually for three years to a different *muqati*.[77] Although, it increased the state revenue from a source but was not at all beneficial for the inhabitants of the area and were left to the mercy of the *muqati*.

(3) INCOME AND EXPENDITURE OF A *MANDI* : A FOCUS ON THE *SHRI MANDI SADAR* BIKANER (1750-1800)[78]

We have undertaken *Shri Mandi Sadar* Bikaner as a representative *mandi* for the detailed study of its nature and pattern of income and expenditure during the second half of the 18th century. For it was an old and central *mandi* of the state located in the capital. The details of statistical data are also available.[79]

Income of *Shri Mandi Sadar Bikaner*
(a) Nature of Income in the *Mandi*

The income of *Shri Mandi Sadar* comprised mainly of the following–

(i) Income accrued from *jagat*, etc.
(ii) Income accrued from various other sources.

***(i) Income Accrued from* jagat**

The word *Jagat* was a common and indigenously assigned term for the tax/duty levied on merchandise in nature of *Nekal* (export), *Pesar* (import) and *Vahtivon* (goods in transit in the state territory) at different rates and on various commodities. The share of *jagat* in the total *jama* of *Shri Mandi* was significant and ranged from 39.51% in 1750 AD to 53.75% in 1800 AD. This amount of *jagat* also included miscellaneous charges of *kiyali* (weighing charges), *panchayati* (seeking decision from *panchayat*) and *moharano*[80] (putting seal on papers). The *jagat* income in the period has been drawn out in the following table.

Table 6.2: *Jagat* Proportion of *Shri Mandi Sadar* Bikaner

Sr. No.	*Years AD/V.S.*	*Jagat of Shri Mandi Sadar (in Rs.)*	*Percentage of jagat in the total jama of Shri Mandi Sadar*	*Source*
(1)	*(2)*	*(3)*	*(4)*	*(5)*
1.	1750/1807	70,821+	39.51	*Sawa bahi*, No.4
2.	1761/1818	77,886	55.16	*Sawa bahi*, No.9
3.	*1771/1828	59,222	44.59	*Sawa bahi*, No.16
4.	1781/1838	58,751	50.99	*Sawa bahi*, No.23
5.	1794/1851	54,725	48.19	*Sawa bahi*, No.27
6.	1797/1854	51,396	55.51	*Sawa bahi*, No.28
7.	1800/1857	39,362	53.75	*Sawa bahi*, No.29

+ : Rupees rounded off for convenience to the next rupee.
* : Leap years, Average of twelve months have been taken.

The table shows that although, the share percentage of *jagat* has increased compared with the other sources of income of

Shri Mandi (Table 6.3) in absolute terms, the *jagat* reduced from Rs. 70,821 in 1750 AD to Rs. 39,362 in 1800 AD, except in the year 1761 when it increased slightly. This indicates a gradual reduction in the total income of *Shri Mandi* as shown in Table 6.5.

(ii) Income Accrued from Other Micellaneous Sources

Besides the collection of *jagat* there were many other sources of income of *Shri Mandi Sadar* Bikaner, i.e. the income accrued from various taxes being imposed and realized on merchants, traders, artisans and other occupational groups working under the jurisdiction of the *mandi*. Besides, income also accrued from the religious fairs (organized in the state), mines, rent of the state-owned building, fines and penalties, perquisites (*lajmas*) of the state officials and from the fees charged upon the registration of re-marriages and adoption of son (*Khola*) in the state. The *Peshkashi* and *Nazrana* received for the chief of the state was also credited into the *mandi's* account. The details of these sources of income have already been discussed in the Chapter—'Non-Agricultural Sector: Sources of Income'.[81]

The income accruing from these taxes was also realized through the *Muqatis* and the state officials as well.[82] We see the income from these sources, compared to *jagat* income, also has declined in proportion, gradually (with some exceptions) both in share percentage and in an absolute terms. This is evident from the given Table 6.3.

Table 6.3: Table to Show Income from Other Sources (Other than *Jagat*)

Sr. No. (1)	*Years AD/V.S.* (2)	*Amount (in Rs.)* (3)	*Percentage in the total jama of Shri Mandi* (4)	*Source* (5)
1.	1750/1807	1,08,417	60.49	*Sawa bahi*, No. 4
2.	1761/1818	63,303	44.84	*Sawa bahi*, No. 9
3.	1771/1828	73,603	55.41	*Sawa bahi*, No. 16
4.	1781/1838	56,470	49.01	*Sawa bahi*, No. 23
5.	1794/1851	58,836	51.81	*Sawa bahi*, No. 27
6.	1797/1854	41,196	44.49	*Sawa bahi*, No. 28
7.	1800/1857	33,875	46.25	*Sawa bahi*, No. 29

The Expenditure of *Shri Mandi Sadar Bikaner*

(a) Nature of Expenditure[83]

The income of *Shri Mandi* thus, collected from various sources, was incurred on the following different heads of expenditure, as recorded in the *Sawa Bahis*.

(1) ***Raj Lok Kharch*** (The royal family and household) included expenditure on payments of their maintenance allowance and meeting their personal needs and demands.

(2) ***Punyarth Kharch*** (The religious activities) included expenditure on charity by royal members, usual grants to the various temples for maintenance dresses and offerings to the deities and gods, celebration of festivals and also the salaries to the persons employed in various temples.

(3) ***Shri Mandi Aur Jagaton Talke Kharch*** (expenditure of *Shri Mandi* and *chowkis*) covered wages and salaries of the various officials of *mandi* and *chowki* besides stationery expenses, etc.

(4) ***Kohar Talab Kharch*** (The public utility work) covered construction of wells and reservoirs, maintenance of city walls and forts.

(5) ***Byaj Udhara Hundawana Kharch*** (The repayments of debts, interest and *Hundi* expenses) Loans are borrowed to meet the various needs of *Shri Mandi* and that was repaid in instalments with interest. The charges for *hundis* were also paid.

(6) ***Siropaw and Bija Kharch*** (The robe of honour and misc. expenditure) was incurred on encouraging the merchants, traders and other officials by honouring them through *Siropaw*, turbans and shawls besides other miscellaneous and contingent expenses.

(b) The Proportion of Expenditure

To appreciate the expenditure proportions an attempt has been made to compare the expenditure as incurred in the year 1761 (V.S. 1818) and year 1800 (V.S. 1857) pertaining respectively to the period of Gaj Singh (1746-87 AD) and Surat Singh (1787-1828 AD). The results are shown in the Table 6.4.

Table 6.4 : Comparison of Expenditure Proportions of Year 1761 AD and 1800 AD[84]

Sr. No.	*Head of Expenditure*	*Yr. 1761 (V.S.1818) (Gaj Singh)*		*Yr. 1800 (V.S.1857) (Surat Singh)*	
		Amt. incurred (in Rs.)	*Percentage of the total expenditure*	*Amt. incurred (in Rs.)*	*Percentage of the total expenditure*
(1)	*(2)*	*(3)*	*(4)*	*(5)*	*(6)*
1.	*Raj lok kharch*	85,276	59.36	36,467	52.89
2.	*Punnyartha kharcha*	7,696	5.36	5,482	7.95
3.	*Shri Mandi* jagaton talke *kharcha*	40,632	28.28	17,073	24.76
4.	*Kohar talab Kharcha*	1,472	1.02	2,023	2.93
5.	*Byaz udhara hundawana kharcha*	2,270	1.58	5,619	8.15
6.	*Siropaw and bija kharcha*	6,318	4.40	2,291	3.32
	Total Expenditure Rs.	1,43,664	100%	68,955	100%

A major part of expenditure was consumed in the maintenance and livelihood of the royal family, household and other personnel attached in their service. It was 59.36% in 1761 which decreased to to 52.89% in 1800 AD. It is evident that more than 50% of the income of *Shri Mandi* was spent by the rulers on themselves and household. These rulers employed a large numbers of persons for their own service and who were called *khidmatgujars*.

The establishment of *Shri Mandi* and *chowkis* and its running consumed a significant portion of 28.28% in 1761 AD and 24.76% in the 1800 AD. Religious activities of the royal family ranged between 5.36% to 7.95%. The public work expenditure was confined to an insignificant proportion varying between 1.02% to 2.93%. It is worth mentioning that the percentage share of the repayment of debt and interest there on increased from 1.58% to 8.15% significantly, which shows that in the second phase the ruler resorted to raising loans for meeting the increasing needs.

The Pattern of Income and Expenditure of *Shri Mandi Sadar* (1750-1800 AD)

During this period, in all, four rulers, i.e. (1) Gaj Singh (1746-1787), (2) Raj Singh (1787), (3) Pratap Singh (1787) and (4) Surat Singh (1787-1828) ruled the state. In fact, in an interim period of nearly five months of Raj Singh and Pratap Singh is insignificant[85] and only under Gaj Singh and Surat Singh a major change seems to have taken place. For better understanding of the pattern of income and expenditure the period under study can be divided into two phases (i) 1750-1787 AD (ii) 1787-1800 AD

Table 6.5: Pattern of Total Income and Expenditure of *Shri Mandi* Bikaner (1750-1800 AD) (in Rs.)

Sr. No. (1)	*Year AD/V.S.* (2)	*Total jama* (3)	*Total kharch* (4)	*Difference deficit/surplus* (5)	*Source* (6)	*Remarks* (7)
1.	1750/1807	1,79,238	1,83,115	(-) 3,877	*Sawa bahi*, 4	**Phase-1**
2.	1761/1818	1,41,189	1,43,654	(-) 2,465	*Sawa bahi*, 9	Gaj Singh
3.	1771/1828	1,32,825	1,41,808	(-) 8,983	*Sawa bahi*, 16	(1746-87)
4.	1781/1838	1,15,221	1,44,335	(-) 29,114	*Sawa bahi*, 23	
5.	1794/1851	1,13,561	1,21,302	(-) 7,741	*Sawa bahi*, 27	**Phase-II**
6.	1797/1854	92,592	94,662	(-) 2,070	*Sawa bahi*, 28	Surat Singh
7.	1800/1857	73,237	68,955	(+) 4,282	*Sawa bahi*, 29	(1787-1828)

The above table evinces that there was a gradual declining trend in the income in both phases. In the first phase it decreased from Rs. 1,79,238 in 1750 AD to Rs. 1,15,221 in 1781 AD. Likewise in the second phase it came down from Rs. 1,13,561 in 1794 AD to Rs. 73,237 in 1800 AD.

Though both the rulers, Gaj Singh and Surat Singh made efforts to raise income by providing favourable conditions to the traders through their protection, security and various incentives[86] for the expansion of trade and commerce to which traders also responded favourably to some extent. The rulers invited the traders to come and settle down in the state,[87] provided escort facility[88] and security of the merchandise[89], gave compensation to the lost goods in transit[90] and also the exemption in tax and its rates[91] besides, honouring them to encourage trade activities through *siropaws*, turbans and shawls, etc.[92]

Despite the fact, the income of *Shri Mandi* could not be increased or even sustained during the period, and the deficit increased sharply during the first phase from Rs. 3,877 in 1750 AD to Rs. 29,114 in 1781 AD as the decrease in income was sharper than the reduction in expenditure.

As the process of consolidation and stability attempted by Gaj Singh in phase I (1750-87) was marred by the disturbances of *Bhattis, Johiyas* and *Daodputras* in the region coupled with his engagements in animosity of Jaipur and Jodhpur throughut his reign, kept him busy.[93] It also resulted in a general inefficiency of administration and feudal-aristocratic dominance and rivalry. This had an adverse impact on the trade-commerce and also increased his expenditure as a whole.

When Surat Singh in phase II (1787-1800) succeeded to re-establish the authority on the administration and also brought out innovation in the tax structure in general,[94] even the impact of these measures is not visible in the income of *Shri Mandi*. Of course, there was a significant reduction in the expenditure of the *Shri Mandi* which is depicted in the breakup of various heads of expenditure as shown in Table 6.4.

The net effect of a relatively marginal decline in income and a more significant reduction in expenditure is reflected in the deficit coming down sharply from Rs. 29,114 in 1781 (i.e. the end of phase I) to Rs. 2,070 in 1797 AD to a tentative surplus of Rs. 4,282 in 1800 AD.

Despite the marginal surplus, there was a general deficit phenomenon in the *Mandi* income seen in the second half of the 18th century as evident from the trend of income and expenditures of various *Mandis*. A table to show, it is set out as follows:

Details of *jagat* and income/expenditure of various *mandis* of the state (figures have been rounded off to the nearest rupees).

Table 6.6: Figures of Income and Expenditure of *Mandi* Ratangarh

Year V.S./AD	*Jagat collection*	*Total jama realized*	*Expen-diture*	*Differ-ence*	*Reference*
(1)	*(2)*	*(3)*	*(4)*	*(5)*	*(6)*
1858/1801	1,200	13,206	21,816	(-) 8,610	*Sawa Bahi Ratangarh* No.1, V.S. 1858-61/1801-1804 AD
1859/1802	266	3,773	4,279	(-) 505	Ibid
1860/1803	2,650	6,325	2,647	(+)3,678	Ibid
1870/1813	3,422	11,726	14,182	(-)2,456	Ibid., No. 3, V.S. 1867-75/1810-1818 AD
1871/1814	2,752	10,483	11,739	(-)1,256	Ibid
1875/1818	2,871	8,185	15,121	(-)6,936	Ibid

Table 6.7: Figures of Income and Expenditure of *Mandi* Suratgarh

Year V.S./AD	*Jagat collection*	*Total jama realized*	*Expen-diture*	*Differ-ence*	*Reference*
(1)	*(2)*	*(3)*	*(4)*	*(5)*	*(6)*
1855/1798	363	6,946	12,830	(-)5,884	*Sawa Bahi Suratgarh* No.2, V.S. 1855/1798
1856/1799	N.A.*	4,550	10,356	(-)5,806	Ibid, No.3, V.S. 1856-1881/1800-1824 AD
1873/1816	63	4,565	4,982	(-)417	Ibid
1875/1818	50	NA	NA	NA	Ibid
1876/1819	172	NA	NA	NA	Ibid
1877/1820	224	NA	NA	NA	Ibid

* N.A. : Not available

Table 6.8: Figure of Income and Expenditure of *Mandi* Rajgarh

Year V.S./AD (1)	*Jagat collection* (2)	*Total jama realized* (3)	*Expenditure* (4)	*Difference* (5)	*Reference* (6)
1828/1771	NA	25,433	25,890	(-)457	*Sawa Bahi Rajgarh* No.1, V.S. 1828-30
1829/1772	NA	46,777	49,360	(-)2,583	Ibid.
1830/1773	NA	31,964	33,931	(-)1,967	Ibid.
1838/1781	1321 (नवजगात रामंडीसु)	30,843	32,130	(-)1,287	Ibid., No. 3 V.S. 1835-38
1840/1783	NA	35,480	35,480	Nil	Ibid., No. 4, V.S. 1839-42
1842/1785	NA	17,864	24,418	(-)6,554	Ibid., No. 5, V.S. 1842-44
1843-44/1786-87	53	24,460	27,758	(-)3,298	Ibid.
1844-45/1787-88	1,205	22,904	22,922	(+)18	Ibid., No. 6, V.S. 1844-46
1848/1791	2,145	30,967	32,785	(-)1,818	Ibid., No. 7, V.S. 1846-49
1849/1792	1,337	30,757	34,813	(-)4,056	Ibid.
1864/1807	6,136	17,713	36,412	(-)18,699	Ibid., No. 11, V.S. 1864-67
1865/1808	3,227	20,553	47,470	(-)26,917	Ibid.
1866/1809	7,361	23,093	56,218	(-)33,125	Ibid.
1867/1810	5,554	19,162	49,140	(-)29,978	Ibid.
1868/1811	NA	26,554	55,877	(-)29,323	Ibid., No. 12, V.S. 1868-71
1870/1813	NA	30,847	76,873	(-)46,026	Ibid.
1871/1814	NA	25,262	86,411	(-)61,149	Ibid.
1872/1815	3,725	18,202	54,360	(-)36,158	Ibid., No. 13, V.S. 1872-77
1873/1816	NA	36,010	80,651	(-)44,641	Ibid.
1874/1817	NA	25,527	83,262	(-)57,735	Ibid.
1875/1818	NA	97,397	1,40,996	(-)43,599	Ibid.
1876/1819	NA	98,613	1,65,132	(-)66,519	Ibid.
1877/1820	13,006	1,31,949	1,97,856	(-)65,907	Ibid.

Contd...

Contd...

1879/1822	NA	58,410	1,08,270	(-)49,860	Ibid., No. 14, V.S. 1879-80
1881/1824	NA	44,797	57,122	(-)12,325	Ibid., No. 15, V.S. 1881-84
1884/1827	6,058	60,522	78,467	(-)17,945	Ibid.
1885/1828	NA	62,909	69,494	(-)6,585	Ibid., No. 16, V.S. 1885-89
1887/1830	7771	59,289	82,092	(-)22,803	Ibid

Table 6.9: Figure of Income and Expenditure of *Mandi* Hanumangarh

Year V.S./AD	*Jagat collection*	*Total jama realized*	*Expen-diture*	*Differ-ence*	*Reference*
(1)	(2)	(3)	(4)	(5)	(6)
1864/1807	8,061	22,871	35,329	(-)12,458	*Sawa Bahi Han-mangarh* No.1, V.S.1862-67/ 1805-1810 AD
1865/1808	2,611	30,046	39,237	(-)9,191	Ibid.
1866/1809	5,604	25,967	34,398	(-)8,431	Ibid.
1883/1826	7,450	14,942	19,322	(-)4,380	*Sawa Bahi Han-mangarh* No.3, V.S.1879-84/ 1822-1827 AD
1884/1827	9,405	16,648	20,392	(-)3,744	Ibid.

The state attempted to make up deficiency of income temporarily to meet the expenditures through many ways as follows.

(i) By seeking loans from the *sahukars* at interest.
(ii) By realizing sometimes the state dues in advance in lump sums.
(iii) And by deferring the payments of the debts of the people in the state to future dates.[95]

The statistical accounts show that they faced a difficult situation on account of shortage of finances after their detachment from the Mughal empire and they made serious efforts to create fresh financial resources and avenues through trade and commerce and therefore, provided various facilities and security to the trading community. The increase in the *Mandis* and *Chowkis* was also an outcome of the state policy. However, the period of the second half of the 18th century was a transitory phase for Bikaner state and it was struggling hard to survive and surmounting this difficulty.

REFERENCES

1. (i) Morwana inscription of V.S. 1573 (1516 AD) vide L.P. Tessitory's report, 1916, *JSAB*, Vol. XIII, pp. 214-15. Morwana and Derawar were important trade centres enroute to Multan and Sindh.
   (ii) Col. Tod, op. cit., p. 152.
   (iii) Agrawal, Govind, *Churu Mandal ka shodhpurna Itihas* (Hindi), Ajmer (1974), pp. 476-78.
2. Saxena, A.N., 'Economics condition of Bikaner state during 16th century', pp. 10-13, *Journal of Rajasthan Institute of Historical Research* (ed.) M.L. Sharma, Vol. XVIII, No. 3, Jaipur (1979).
3. Imperial *Farman* of Mughal Emperor Akbar to Rai Singh of Bikaner dated 12, *Rajjab-ul-Murazzab*, 990, *Hizri* year; corresponding to 25 April, 1592 AD.
4. Dhari, Alakh, *The Life and Exploits of Raja Rai Singh of Bikaner*, Bikaner (1934), pp. 175-76. The author remarks that the state of Bikaner possessed and exercised the rights of levying import and export duty on commodities from beginning of its establishment and has through the ages levied such duties.
5. Saxena, A.N., op. cit., pp. 10-13.
6. *Leni hundiyan kiwi teri Bahi*, No. 241, V.S.1726/1669 AD, R.S.A., Bikaner.
7. Dutta, R.C., *Rambles of India*, Calcutta, 1895, p. 50.
8. Agrawal, Govind, *Churu Mandal ka Shodhpurna Itihas*, pp. 476-78.
9. Ibid.
10. Gahlot, Jagdish Singh, *Rajputana ka Itihas*, Vol. I, pp. 177-18, Cf. Govind Agrawal, op. cit., p. 477.
11. *Churu Mein Pracheen Hatan ki Vigat* by Agrawal, Govind, Bahi of Potedar Mirza Mal, V.S. 1884/1827 AD, Potedar Collection, Churu), *Marushri*, Year 2-3, Vol. 4-1, Churu, 1973, pp. 43-47.
12. Pugal was under the dominance of *Bhati* Rajputs under Shekha Bhati before the establishment of Bikaner state. The influence of *Bhatis* was spread over an area from Jaisalmer to Punjab in the

north west. *Bhatis* of Pugal in the west were Rajputs where as *Bhatis* of the north around Bhatner were the converted Muslims known as Bhattis. Rao Bika's increasing power and his area of dominance, later in the year 1478 AD made *Bhatis* of Pugal to accept the suzerainty of Bika. Henceforth, Pugal became the part of Bikaner state. Ojha, G.H., *Bikaner Rajya ka Itihas*, Part 1, pp. 73-74, 93-96.

13. Muhnot, Nensi, *Nensi ki Khyat*, Vol. II, p. 500, *Kagad Bahi*, No. 1, V.S. 1811/1754 AD, *Posh Sudi 5*, Sharma, G.C., *Administrative System of Rajputs*, New Delhi, 1979, p. 161.
14. *Kagad Bahi*, N. 6, V.S. 1839/1782 AD.
15. (i) *Desh Darpan*, Das, Sidhayach Dayal, Published by Rajasthan State Archives, Bikaner, 1989, edited by J.K. Jain, p. 56.
    (ii) Ojha, G.H., *Bikaner Rajya ka Itihas*, Part 1, p. 63.
16. Tod, *Annals and Antiquities of Rajasthan*, Vol. II, pp. 1154-55, Erskine, *Rajputana Gazetteer*, Vol. III B, Allahabad, 1908, pp. 351-52.
17. (i) *Kagad Bahi*, No. 6, V.S. 1839, *Baisakh Badi 1*,
    (ii) Tod, op. cit., Vol. II, p. 1154-55.
    (iii) Erskine, op. cit., pp. 352-53
    (iv) Banerjee, A.C., *Rajput States and the East India Company*, Calcutta, 1944, pp. 183-84.
18. *Kagad Bahi*, No. 28, V.S. 1879/1822 AD, ff. 184-85.
19. Ojha, G.H., Part 1, op. cit., pp. 60-61.
20. *Kagad Bahi*, No. 28, V.S. 1879/1822 AD, f.22(a).
21. Ojha, G.H., Part II, p. 374.
22. Ibid.
23. *Desh Darpan*, Das, Sidhayach Dayal, op. cit., 65, Ojha, G.H., op. cit., Part II, p. 686.
24. Ibid.
25. *Kagad ri Bahi*, No. 17, V.S. 1867/1810 AD, first *Baisakh Badi* 14.
26. Sawa Bahi Suratgarh, No. 3, V.S. 1877/1820 AD, f. 176.
27. Ojha, G.H., op. cit., Part I, p. 64.
28. Ibid.
29. Ibid., p. 64.
30. Ojha, G.H., Part I, op. cit., p. 60.
31. Ibid.
32. *Kagad Bahi*, No. 20, V.S. 1871/1814 AD, f. 116(a).
33. *Kagad Bahi*, No. 17, V.S. 1867/1810 AD, *Jyestha Badi* 11.
34. Ibid, *Shrawan Sudi* 6.
35. *Kagad Bahi*, No. 19/1 V.S. 1870/1813 AD, *Mingsar Badi* 8, R.S.A., Bikaner. Many towns of commercial significance emerged during

the 18th century specially at the eastern border of Bikaner. For details see my research article entitled 'Urbanization and Trade Routes: A Case Study of the Eastern Region of Bikaner State: 1750-1828 AD' published in Proceedings of U.G.C. Sponsored National Seminar in 2009, Jodhpur. The seminar was organized by the History Department of J.N.V. University, Jodhpur, pp. 122-132.

36. *Bahi Yaaddast Chowki Jagat ri*, No. 92, V.S. 1865; *Jagat bahi Bikaner*, No. 7, V.S. 1807/1750 AD, *Nohar re Thana re Jama Kharach ri Bahi*, No. 8, V.S. 1814/1757 AD, R.S.A., Bikaner.
37. The *mandi* located at capital city is still identified as *Bada bazar* in Bikaner - Description of the main market of Rajgarh is available which contain 27 shops constructed besides other temporary hutments which gave a substantial amount as shop rents to the *mandi*. *Sawa Bahi Rajgarh*, No. 1, V.S. 1828, f. 16(b).
38. *Jagat* is an indigenously assigned term for combined income of custom and transit duty, etc. *Jagat* is a vernacular corruption of *zakat*. Wilson, H.H., *A Glossary of Judicial and Revenue Terms of British India*, p. 481.
39. The account manuals of the *mandis* record the income of *jagat* and commercial taxes as well the other non-commercial income of the area. Therefore, all types of income pooled into the *mandi* account. See *Sawa Bahi Mandi Sadar Bikaner*, No. 2, V.S. 1802-04/ 1745-47 AD, R.S.A., Bikaner.
40. Devra, G.S.L., *Rajasthan ki Prashashnik Vyavastha* (*1574-1818 AD*) Bikaner, 1981, pp. 132-33, Shrma, G.C., *Administrative System of Rajputs*, New Delhi (1979), pp. 153-59. The important trade route passing through Bikaner, besides Delhi-Marwar-Pali via Bikaner, was Dera Gazi Khan - Bikaner-Nagaur-Sikar-Jaipur. It could be termed as the *Ghora Marg* (route for horses) because horse, silk, dry and wet fruit were passing profusely from it. *Sawa Bahi Mandi Sadar Bikaner*, No. 2, V.S. 1835-36.
41. Ibid.
42. *Sawa Bahi Mandi Suratgarh*, No. 1, V.S. 1844-54/1787-97 AD, R.S.A., Bikaner.
43. *Sawa Bahi Mandi Rajgarh*, No. 1, V.S. 1828, R.S.A., Bikaner.
44. Ibid., No.22, V.S. 1905/1848 AD, f. 354b, R.S.A., Bikaner.
45. The *thanas* (the security station) were to help realization of *jagat* by the *mandis*. A *thana* was usually preceded before establishing a *mandi*. The initial account of *mandi* of Rajgarh has been mentioned as *Rajgarh re Thana ro Lekho* (the account of Rajgarh *thana*) *Sawa Bahi Mandi Rajgarh*, No. 1, V.S. 1828/1771 AD, ff. 1-2.
46. Rawat Bhagat Singh of village Bilaniasar was directed to keep

secure the *jagatis* deputed in his area and help their functioning in 1770 AD *Kagad Bahi*, No. 3, V.S. 1827/1770 AD, f. 12, R.S.A., Bikaner.

47. Rajgarh, Sujangarh, Bhatner and Anupgarh were located on the borders of the state, and on the main trade routes. Rajgarh and Sujangarh on the Delhi-Marwar branch highway and Bhatner on the route leading to Hansi and Hissar. Anupgarh was the gateway to Multan and Bahawalpur.
48. This was an old and prominent *mandi* of the state and was located inside the old city. It included Biggha, Gajsinghpura, Kharipatti, Magra, Lunkaransar, Jaitpura, Sodwa, etc. as its jurisdiction including Bikaner city. *Sawa Bahi Mandi Sadar*, No. 2, V.S. 1802-04, R.S.A., Bikaner.
49. The detailed accounts of these *mandis* are available in the Rajasthan State Archives, Bikaner in the Rampuria section. See *A Descriptive List of Bikaner Bahis, Part I (17-19th c.)*, Bikaner (1982), R.S.A., Bikaner, pp. 142-178.
50. *Sawa Bahi* is a corrupt form of *Siah-bahi* which implied the ledger or daily book in which daily receipts and disbursements are entered. It is sometimes applied to a journal or diary in which the orders of a court of justice are recorded. Wilson, op. cit., p. 481.
51. See A Descriptive List of Bikaner *Bahis*, Part I (17-19th c.) R.S.A., Bikaner, 1982, pp. 142-178.
52. *Baharli Jagaton ro Lekhon - Bahi Rajaldesar re Jagat ri*, V.S. 1859/1802 AD, R.S.A., Bikaner. The *chowkis* of Suratgarh mandi were - *Chowki Kishanpura*, Rang Mahal, Albone, Bhagwansar, Karnisar, Rampura and Nekone in 1803 AD *Sawa Bahi Mandi Suratgarh*, No. 3, V.S. 1860/1803 AD.
53. *Jagat ri Bahi*, No. 92, V.S. 1869/1812 AD, ff. 1-10, R.S.A., Bikaner.
54. *Desh re Jagat ri Bahi*, Bikaner, No. 70, V.S. 1858, Bikaner *Bahiyat*, R.S.A., Bikaner.
55. *Kagad Bahi*, No. 24, V.S. 1875/1818 AD, f. 190. The order mentions the exemption in deduction in their salary.
56. *Sawa Bahi Mandi Sadar Bikaner*. No. 21, V.S. 1835-36/1778-79 AD, R.S.A., Bikaner.
57. *Huwaldar* was a state appointed revenue and administrative officer. Devra, G.S.L., op. cit., pp. 121.
58. *Huwala ra Kagad, Kagadon ri Bahi*, No. 3, V.S. 1827/1770 AD, R.S.A., Bikaner.
59. Devra, G.S.L., op. cit., pp. 120-23.
60. *Sawa Bahi Mandi Sadar Bikaner*, No. 21, V.S. 1835-36/1778-79 AD, Their prime duty was to safeguard the state's interest through

mutual cooperation.

61. Devra, G.S.L., op. cit., pp. 111, 118-23.
62. *Sawa Bahi Mandi Sadar Bikaner*, No. 4, V.S. 1807/1750 AD, R.S.A., Bikaner, G.S.L. Devra, op. cit., p. 121.
63. The detail of officials and *Khajanchis* are entered in the opening lines of the respective *Sawa Bahis*. The monthly account are maintained in these *Bahis*. *Sawa Bahi Mandi Sadar Bikaner*, No. 9, V.S. 1818/ 1761 AD, and No.29, V.S. 1857/1800 AD, R.S.A., Bikaner.
64. *Sawa Bahi Rajgarh*, No. 14, V.S. 1880/1823 AD, f. 210, R.S.A., Bikaner.
65. *Sawa Bahi Rajgarh*, No. 16, V.S. 1887/1830, contains breakup *jugat* collection is as follows in *Rajgarh Mandi-*

Mandi jagat	*Chowki jagat*	*Village jugat*
Rs. 1,573-4	Rs. 3,131-0	Rs. 3,067-4

Sawa Bahi Rajgarh, No. 13, V.S. 1877/1820 AD, also contains the breakup of *Jagat* in *Mandi* and *Chowki* - as Rs. 3,736-4 and Rs. 9,269-12 respectively in 1829 AD, R.S.A., Bikaner.

66. *Bahi Rajaldesar re Jagat ri*, V.S. 1859/1802 AD, R.S.A., Bikaner.
67. Rs. 40 *Annas* 4 were adjusted into the *mandi* account of Reni from *Rajgarh mandi* in V.S. 1863/1806 AD *Sawa Bahi Rajgarh*, No.11, V.S. 1863/1806 AD, f. 35.
68. *Sawa Bahi Mandi Sadar Bikaner*, No.2, V.S. 1802-4/1745-47 AD; No.22, V.S. 1837-38/1780-81 AD; *Sawa Bahi Mandi Suratgarh*, No. 5, V.S. 1881-89/1824-32 AD; *Sawa Bahi Ratangarh*, No. 1, V.S. 1858-61/1801-04 AD.
69. *Huwaka Kagad, Kagad ri Bahi*, No. 2, V.S. 1820/1763 AD, *Bhadwa Sudi* 10.
70. *Kagad ri Bahi*, No. 3, V.S. 1827/1770 AD, *Mingsar Sudi* 12, *Posh Sudi* 8, *Chetra Badi* 14, No. 6, V.S. 1839/1782 AD, *Posh Badi* 10, R.S.A., Bikaner; *Sawa Bahi Mandi Sadar Bikaner*, No. 23, V.S. 1838-40 (Year 1781 AD) f. 44a, R.S.A., Bikaner.
71. Ibid.
72. Ibid.
73. Ibid., *Kagad Bahi*, No. 7, V.S. 1840/1783 AD, No. 11. V.S. 1857/ 1800 AD, R.S.A., Bikaner.
74. *Kagad Bahi*, No. 3, V.S. 1827/1770 AD, *Mingsar Sudi* 12, R.S.A., Bikaner.
75. Ibid., *Posh Sudi* 8, R.S.A., Bikaner.
76. Ibid., *Chetra Badi* 14, R.S.A., Bikaner.
77. Ibid., *Kagad Bahi*, No. 6, V.S.1839/1782 AD, *Asoj Badi* 8.
78. The *mandi* of Bikaner was the central *mandi* at Bikaner. It had the

advantage of being located on the place where trade routes linking Multan, Delhi, Marwar, Mewar and Jaipur passed. Also a larger area was put under its jurisdiction including capital. *Sawa Bahi Nohar*, V.S. 1849/1792 AD *Jagat Bahi*, No. 84, V.S. 1822/1765 AD, R.S.A., Bikaner; Sohan Lal, *Tawarikh Rajshri Bikaner*, pp. 69-74, Bikaner, Powlett's *Gazetteer*, pp. 157-58, Bikaner.

79. A research paper has been presented in the 60th Diamond Jubilee Session at proceedings of Indian History Congress. K.L. Mathur, 'Pattern of Income and Expenditure in *Sadar Mandi Bikaner* During the Second Half of the 18th Century', PIHC, Calicut Session, 1999, p. 1165.
80. *Sawa Bahi Mandi Sadar Bikaner*, No. 2, V.S. 1802-04, f.1, R.S.A., Bikaner. *Moharano* was realized from traders on goods while passing through a *pargana*. Besides *Sri Mandi*, it was levied at *chowkis* of Sodwa, Phithod, Rajaldesar and Hardesar.
81. *Sawa Bahi Mandi Sadar Bikaner*, No. 5, V.S. 1810-12, No. 8, V.S. 1815-16. No. 10, V.S. 1821-22, R.S.A., Bikaner.
82. *Sawa Bahi Mandi Sadar Bikaner*, No. 4, V.S. 1807-10. For details of *Muqata* institution, see Devra, G.S.L., *Rajasthan ki Prashashnik Vyavashtha* (Hindi), pp. 140-46, Bikaner, 1981, and Sharma, G.S., op. cit., p. 29.
83. *Sawa Bahi* of *Sri Mandi Sadar*, No. 9, V.S.1818/1761 AD, and No. 29, V.S. 1857/1800 AD other *Bahis* also contain these expenditures.
84. Ibid.
85. Raj Singh ruled from 4.4. 1787 t0 25.4.1787 AD and Pratap Singh from April, 1787 to four months onwards only.
86. *Kagad Bahi*, No. 10, V.S. 1854/1797, *Posh Badi* 13, Rampuria records, R.S.A., Bikaner. Messrs Gopal Das Khatri, Sant Ram Khatri and Bhinva Das Arora of Multan settled in Bikaner and carried out brisk trade. *Sawa Bahi Mandi Sadar Bikaner*, No. 4, V.S. 1807-10, *Kagad Bahi*, No. 6, V.S. 1839.
87. Agrawal, Govind, *Potedar Sangrih ke Aprakashit Kagad* (Hindi), Ajmer, 1976, p. 19.
88. *Kagad Bahi*, No. 13, V.S. 1861/1804 AD, *Shrawan Badi* 11.
89. *Kagad Bahi*, No. 10, V.S. 1854/1797 AD.
90. Ibid., No. 3, V.S. 1827/1782 AD.
91. Ibid., No. 7, V.S. 1840/1783 AD Half the rate of *jagat, nekal* and tax were levied from the traders of Mewar, Haroti and Malwa.
92. *Sawa Bahi Mandi Sadar Bikaner*, No. 10, V.S. 1821-22, R.S.A.B.
93. Ojha, op. cit., Part I, pp. 323-334.
94. Tax rates were increased and was realized with more alertness.
95. *Sawa Bahi Mandi Sadar Bikaner*, No. 16, V.S. 1885-89/1828-32 AD, f. 15b, R.S.A., Bikaner.

7

Price Structure in Bikaner

The study of general price level helps us to understand the economic condition of the state. As the economy of Bikaner was basically an agricultural economy, therefore, it were mainly the agricultural prices which affected the general price level. An attempt in this section, has been made to study and put up a comparative analysis of the prices of various commodities available in Bikaner during the period from 1687 AD to 1820 AD.

The official price data surviving in the *Bahis* for the aforesaid period is of immense help in studying the economic history of the state. The state *Bahis* specially the *Byav Bahis*[1] provide us the details of the purchases of various commodities during different years in the span of 1687 to 1820 AD (133 years) in Bikaner. From these availabe prices[2] of the normal days one can estimate the price level of commodities and its emerging trends.

But the difficulty in analysing the available raw data of prices is that they are available in the contemporary fractional value of *maunds, seers* and *Chhatang* weights[3]; the value of a rupee then, also varied in *Takka* and *Dam*. Moreover, there was prevalence of a *Kachha maund* and *Pacca maund* in the state, which too varied from place to place, as has already been discussed earlier.[4] Another significant limitation of price data to which we are referring, pertains to different dates in different years and they do not belong to strictly comparable points each year for which they are available. This has to be kept in mind while examining the tables of prices for commodities we offer ahead. Therefore, to dispense with these difficulties and convert the available prices into per unit in rupees following methodology has been followed to compare prices and also to show a trend, through price index number.

Methodology: Estimation of Prices and Prices' Index Number

For imparting uniformity and the clear understanding of the comparison, the available raw data of prices of various commodities in these *Bahis* of Bikaner State, have been converted into, rupees per *maund* assuming a *maund* to be standard *maund* comprising of 40 *seers* and a rupee equal to 100 *paisa*[5], because there used to be variation in the *maunds* and value of rupee.

To compare the prices and observe their trends, prices' indices are measured as per the categories of the commodities with change in base year. These indices show the percentage of increase or decrease in the prices during the period under study.

Formula for the measuring of price index number is the following–

$$P_{01} = \frac{P_1}{P_0} \times 100$$

Where P_{01} indicates price index number, P_1 is the current year price and P_0 is the base year price. With this methodology prices have been analysed as under. In the case of summation of prices the formula for price index number is–

$$P_{01} = \frac{\Sigma P_1}{\Sigma P_0} \times 100$$ here, Σ (sigma) indicate summation.

Table 7.1 reveals the comparative prices of *gur*-sugar, *ghee*-edible oil, rice and red chilly. It is observed that prices of all commodities have been increased except edible oil and red chilly from 1687 to 1820 AD. Price of edible oil reduced from Rs. 11.24 per *maund* in 1687 AD to Rs. 2.5 per *maund* in 1820. There was a sharp decline in the prices of red chilly from Rs. 16.81 per *maund* to Re. 1 per *maund*. The decrease in prices indicates that gradually the supply of imported edible oil and red chilly was increased.

Table 7.1: Comparative Price of *Gur*-Sugar, *Ghee*-Edible Oil, Rice and Red Chilly in Bikaner during 1687-1820 AD (Prices per *maund* in Rupees)

Commodity *(1)*	*1687AD* P_0 *(2)*	*1770AD* P_1 *(3)*	*1782AD* P_2 *(4)*	*1820AD* P_3 *(5)*
Gur	0.638	2.758	4.210	-
Sugar (*Khand*)	12.195	-	9.412	13.072
Ghee	2.031	7.797	8.888	14.545
Oil	11.235	-	3.404	2.500
Rice				
(a) Rajgarh quality	4.338	-	24.540	40.000
(b) Pali-thick	4.154	-	22.857	-
(c) Pali-thin	4.197	-	22.857	-
Red chilly	16.806	8.000	1.000	-

Source: Appendix No. 1

Table 7.2: Price Index Number of *Gur*-Sugar, *Ghee*-Oil, Rice and Red Chilly in Bikaner during 1687-1820 AD

Commodity *(1)*	*1687AD* P_0 *(2)*	*1770AD* P_1 *(3)*	*1782AD* P_2 *(4)*	*1820AD* P_3 *(5)*	*(+)Increase* *(-)Decrease* *(6)*
Gur	100	432.28	659.87	-	(+)659.87
Sugar (*Khand*)	100	-	77.18	107.19	(+)107.19
Ghee	100	383.90	437.62	716.15	(+)716.15
Oil (edible)	100	-	30.298	22.25	(-)22.25
Rice					
(a) Rajgarh quality	100	-	565.70	922.08	(+)922.08
(b) Pali-thick	100	-	550.24	-	(+)550.24
(c) Pali-thin	100	-	544.60	-	(+)544.60
Red chilly	100	47.60	5.95	-	(-)5.95

Table 7.2 shows the price index number of the prices quoted in Table 7.1 assuming 1687 AD as base year. Index numbers indicate that during the period 1687 to 1820, there was a significant rise in the prices of various commodities, such as,

prices of *gur* increased by more than six and a half times, and *ghee* by more than seven times, prices of different qualities of rice showed a hike by 5.44 to 9.22 times. Price index number of sugar (*khand*) shows a more or less constant trend which is 107.19 for the year 1820 AD. Index number of oil (22.25) in 1820 and of red chilly (5.95) in 1782 indicate a significant decline in prices of these commodities as stated above and shown in graph 7.1.

Graph 7.1: Comparative Prices of *Gur*, Sugar, Ghee, Oil, Rice and Red Chilly in Bikaner during 1687-1820 AD

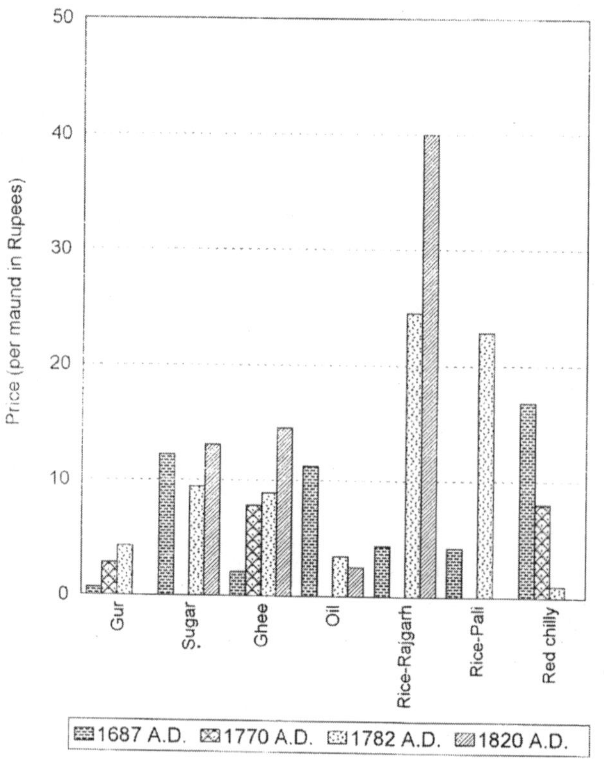

Values of Rice-Pali is the average of thick and thin quality of rice

Table 7.3: Comparative Prices of Floor, Pulses and Intoxicants in Bikaner during 1687-1820 AD (Prices per *maund* in rupees)

Commodity *(1)*	*1687AD* P_0 *(2)*	*1770AD* P_1 *(3)*	*1782AD* P_2 *(4)*	*1820AD* P_3 *(5)*
Maida	5.000	-	2.286	5.714
Besan	5.000	-	2.500	-
Moong Dal	4.672	-	11.834	-
Tobacco	12.307	5.00	-	-
Opium	170.940	-	-	634.920

Source: Appendix No.2

Likewise Table 7.3 include comparative prices of floor, pulses and intoxicants during 1687-1820 AD, and except *Besan* and Tabacco records a general hike in prices of floor, pulses and opium during the period. Prices of *Besan* reduced from Rs. 5 per *maund* in 1687 to just half i.e. Rs. 2.5 per *maund* in 1782 AD; whereas prices of tobacco declined from Rs. 12.31 per *maund* in 1687 to Rs. 5 in 1770 AD. The decline in the prices of *Besan* seems to be the outcome of good supply of gram in 1782 AD.[6] Tobacco, which was also produced at Rajgarh, Sujangarh and Bhadra area, was available in market.[7] Besides, the improvement in supply of tobacco due to import from Malwa and Sindh led to the decline in prices.[8]

Table 7.4: Price Index Number of Floor, Pulses and Intoxicants in Bikaner during 1687-1820 AD

Commodity *(1)*	*1687AD* P_0 *(2)*	*1770AD* P_1 *(3)*	*1782AD* P_2 *(4)*	*1820AD* P_3 *(5)*	*(+)Increase* *(-)Decrease* *(6)*
Maida	100	-	45.72	114.28	(+)114.28
Besan	100	-	50.00	-	(-)50.00
Moong Dal	100	-	253.30	-	(+)253.30
Tobacco	100	40.63	-	-	(-)40.63
Opium	100	-	-	371.43	(+)371.43

The relevant price index number shown in Table 7.4 for floor, pulses and intoxicants assuming base year in 1687 AD, records accordingly a general rise in *Moong Dal* (pulses) by about 2.5 times from Rs. 4.67 in 1687 to Rs. 11.83 in 1782; Opium by more than 3.71 times from Rs. 170.94 in 1687 to Rs. 634.92 in 1820 AD *Besan* recorded a steep decline by 50% from Rs. 5 per *maund* in 1687 to Rs. 2.5 in 1782, and tobacco by 60% from Rs. 12.31 in 1687 to Rs. 5 in 1770. *Maida* showed more or less a constant trend which was 114.28 for the year 1820 AD except a short fall by 45.72% in 1782 AD, the reasons are not clear for this eventual decrease. It is mentionable that there was a negligible production of opium in the state and the overall

Graph 7.2: Comparative Prices of Floor, Pulses and Intoxicants in Bikaner during 1687-1820 AD

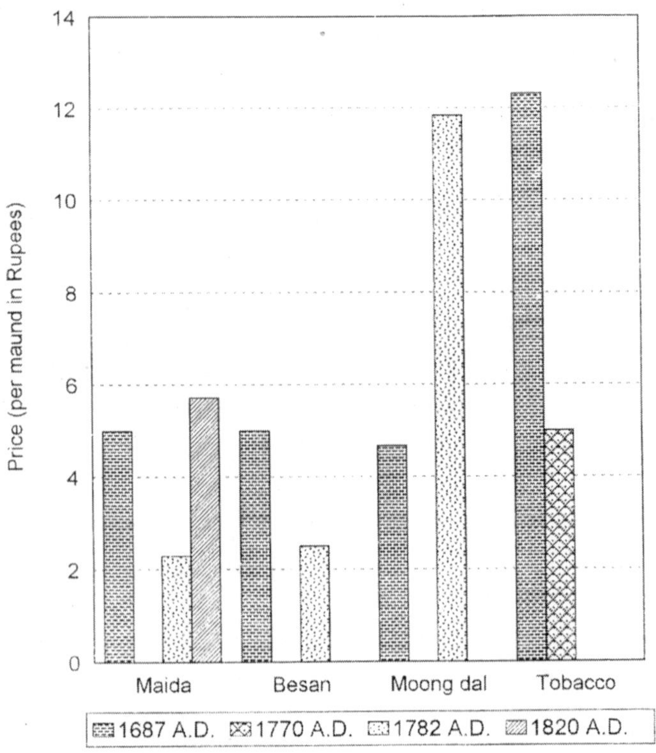

demand was satisfied by importing it from Kota and Malwa.[9] Since, Kota and Malwa were the chief producers and suppliers of opium in the country there used to be a shortage in supply, which in turn, led to price escalation. *Moong* (for *Moong Dal*) was also produced in a very limited fertile part of the north-east and in the north of the state and the additional demand was to be met out by the supply received from Marwar and Kota.[10] The imbalance in regular supply raised the prices. The graph 7.2 exhibits the trends of the prices.

Table 7.5 exhibits the prices of spices and food grain during 1770 to 1820 AD. In the table, except the *Sunth*, all other commodities like wheat, *bajra, moth, dhania* and turmeric showed a considerable increase in prices. The prices of *sunth* decreased from Rs. 9.31 per *maund* in 1770 to Rs. 8.0 per *maund* in 1820 AD. In fact, this marginal decline in the prices of *sunth* in the span of some 50 years was because of the short supply of *sunth* through the import trade from Sindh and Multan in the state but is insignificant.[11]

Table 7.5: Comparative Prices of Spices and Food Grains in Bikaner during 1770-1820 AD (Prices per *maund* in rupees)

Commodity (1)	*1770AD* P_0 (2)	*1782AD* P_1 (3)	*1820AD* P_2 (4)
Dhania	2.254	3.077	-
Turmeric	4.332	7.273	6.563
Sunth	9.308	-	8.000
Wheat	6.416	10.322	-
Bajra	0.571	0.629	0.952
Moth	0.615	0.800	0.851

Source: Appendix No. 3.

The corresponding price index number has been shown in Table 7.6 with assumed base year in 1770 AD. It also represents accordingly and register a gradual increase in prices of spices like turmeric by 1.5 times (approximately 51%) from Rs. 4.33 per *maund* in 1770 to Rs. 6.56 in 1820; wheat, a food grain, increased by more than 1.5 time (60.88%) from Rs. 6.42 per

Table 7.6: Price Index Number of Spices and Food Grain in Bikaner during 1770-1820 AD (Prices per *maund* in rupees)

Commodity (1)	*1770AD* P_0 (2)	*1782AD* P_1 (3)	*1820AD* P_2 (4)	*(+)Increase (-)Decrease* (5)
Dhania	100	136.51	-	(+)136.51
Turmeric	100	167.89	151.50	(+)151.50
Sunth	100	-	85.95	(-)85.95
Wheat	100	160.88	-	(+)160.88
Bajra	100	110.16	166.73	(+)166.73
Moth	100	130.08	138.37	(+)138.37

maund in 1770 to Rs. 10.32 in 1782, whereas *bajra* also followed the same trend and rose more than 1.5 times (66.73%) from Rs. 0.57 per *maund* in 1770 to Rs. 0.95 in 1820 AD. The price trend for *dhania* and moth also showed a moderate hike respectively by 36.51% in 1782 and 38.37% in 1820 AD. The wheat production in the state was very low and there was a general shortage and often the state imposed restrictions upon its *nekal* (export) or transportation anywhere.[12] However, the necessary requirements of wheat was fulfilled by the supply from Sindh, Marwar, Kota which was often hampered for resons like insecurity of routes.[13] This carried an adverse impact and the prices rose gradually. *Bajra* and *moth* were, though, the chief crops of the state but were the main ingredient of their staple diet also and were chiefly grown for the consumption.[14] Since, the chiefs of Bikaner during the period from 1770 to 1820 encouraged fresh settlements in the villages and towns,[15] the population also seems to have increased, whereas the crop was still dependent on the natural rainfall. Therefore, this was one of the factors for the rise in the prices of *moth* and *bajra*. *Dhania,* which also increased moderately was not produced in the state and was imported from Marwar and Nagaur, caused the price rise.[16] Graph 7.3 represents this trend of prices.

Graph 7.3: Comparative Prices of Spices and Food Grains in Bikaner during 1770-1820 AD

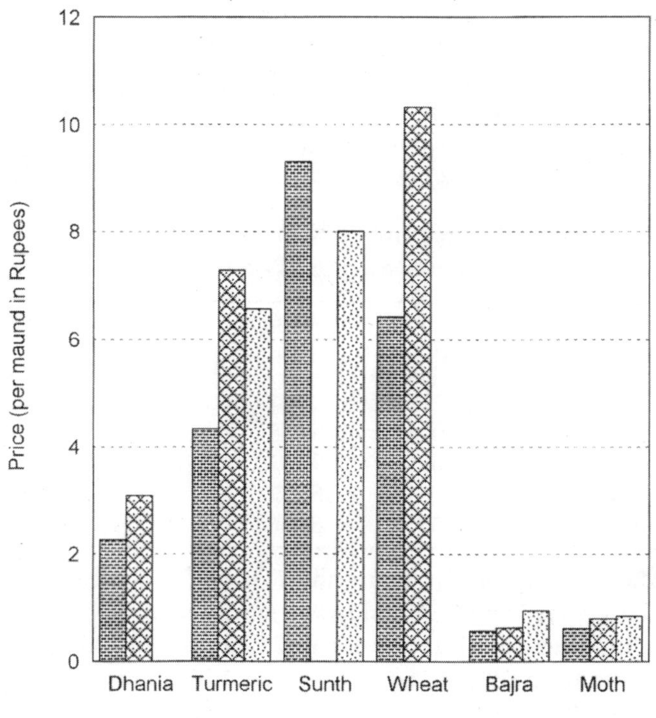

Table 7.7: Comparative Prices of Dry Fruits in Bikaner during 1770-1816 AD (Prices per *maund* in rupees)

Commodity (1)	*1770AD* P_0 (2)	*1782AD* P_1 (3)	*1816AD* P_2 (4)
Pistachio	8.45	13.51	22.00
Almond	12.16	11.84	22.00
Dry Gota (Coconut)	13.30	24.62	-
Currant	8.45	7.50	16.12

Source: Appendix No.4

Likewise, the Table 7.7 enlists the prices of dry fruits in Bikaner from 1770 to 1816 AD. The dry fruits listed in the table 7.7 have been increased in prices in the period. The Pistachio increased from Rs. 8.45 per *maund* in 1770 to Rs. 22 in 1816 AD; Almond increased from Rs. 12.16 per *maund* to Rs. 22 in 1816, the *Currant* from Rs. 8.45 per *maund* in 1770 to Rs. 16.12 in 1820. Accordingly, prices for dry *Gota* (coconut) also raised from Rs. 13.30 per *maund* in 1770 to Rs. 24.62 in 1782.

Table 7.8: Price Index Number of Dry Fruits in Bikaner during 1770-1816 AD

Commodity (1)	*1770 AD* P_0 (2)	*1782 AD* P_1 (3)	*1816 AD* P_2 (4)	(+)*Increase* (–)*Decrease* (5)
Pistachio	100	159.88	260.36	(+)260.36
Almond	100	97.37	180.92	(+)180.92
Dry Gota (Coconut)	100	185.11	-	(+)185.11
Currant	100	88.76	190.77	(+)190.77

The related price index number (Table 7.8) of the dry fruits with base year in 1770 AD shows a significant rise in 1816 AD. Pistachio increased by more than 2.5 times (260.36%) in 1816 AD, Almond and *Gota* by more than 1.75 times respectively (Almond 80.92% in 1816 and *Gota* 85.11% in 1782), whereas the prices for *Currant* gone up by around 2 times (90.77%) in 1816. The cause of this increase seems to be imminent as the supply of dry fruits was chiefly adjunct with the horse trade from Sindh and Multan, the chief suppliers. The demand for the dry fruits and horses, in the period in Rajputana was higher because these two things were largely required by the ruling classes.[17] The supply from the north-west too was, often, hampered due to the disturbances and plundering activities on the trade routes in the north-west by the *Raths, Bhattis*, and *Johiyas*.[18] This led to a price hike in the dry fruits and is also shown graphically in Graph 7.4.

Graph 7.4: Comparative Price of Dry Fruits in Bikaner during 1770-1816 AD

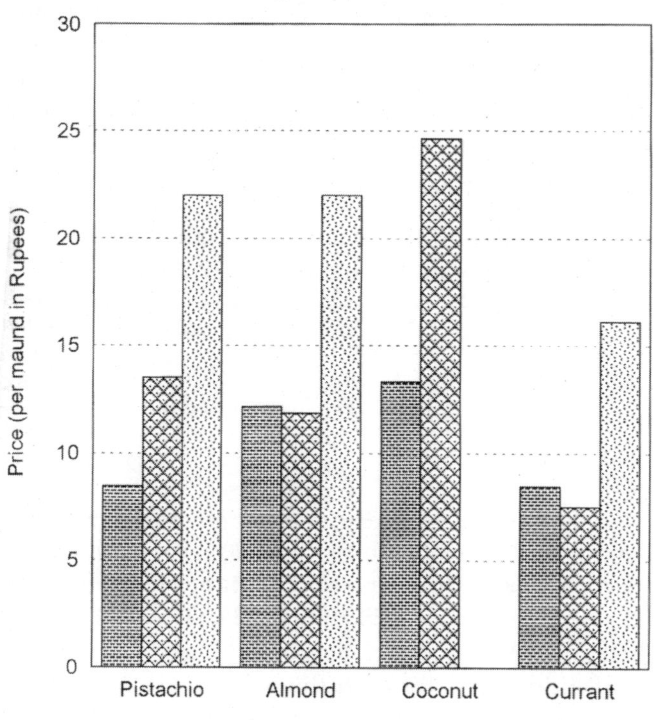

Table 7.9: Comparative Prices of Gold and Silver in Bikaner during 1687-1852 AD (Prices per 10 gram in rupees)

Commodity (1)	*1687AD* P_0 (2)	*1770AD* P_1 (3)	*1852AD* P_2 (4)
Gold	11.5	14.70	16.90
Silver	-	0.86(P_0)	1.93(P_1)

Source: Appendix No. 5

The general phenomenon of the price hike was not restricted to only the essential commodities enumerated uptil, but also enclaved, the precious metals as well, i.e. the gold and silver. The prices for gold and silver also shot up significantly during the period which also bore a relative impact upon the purchasing power of a silver rupee. Table 7.9 is set out to show the prices per 10 gram in rupees. The prices in the table 7.9 evince that gold marked a gradual rise in its prices from Rs. 11.5 per 10 gram in 1687 AD to Rs. 16.90 in 1852 AD; also the bullion which was Rs. 0.86 per 10 gram in 1770 rose upto Rs. 1.93 in 1852 AD.

Table 7.10: Price Index Number of Gold and Silver in Bikaner during 1687-1852 AD

Commodity (1)	*1687 AD* P_0 (2)	*1770 AD* P_1 (3)	*1852 AD* P_2 (4)	*(+)Increase (–)Decrease* (4)
Gold	100	127.83	146.96	(+)146.96
Silver	-	100 (P_0)	224.42 (P_1)	(+)224.42

The measured index number (Table 7.10) exhibits that the gold prices shoot up to near about 1.5 times (146.96%) and the bullion significantly by 2.25 times (224.42%). The rise in the prices was exclusively dependent on the supply of these metals from the Middle East through the north-west[19] and like other commodities the prices also gone considerably high. The rising trend in the prices of gold and silver is shown in graph 7.5.

Interestingly, we could have an access to the prices of some essential commodities available in the *Bahis* for different years, i.e. for Suratgarh in 1787[20] AD and for Anupgarh in 1817[21] AD shown in Table 7.11. Despite the difference in weights and period, an attempt to match the prices of these two *qasbas* was ventured to ascertain the price level in these two *qasbas*. The prices available have been converted into rupees per *maund* first (considering the prevailing of actual *seers* in a *maund* at the places) and then to prices in rupees per 100 seers.

Graph 7.5: Comparative Prices of Gold and Silver in Bikaner during 1687-1852 AD

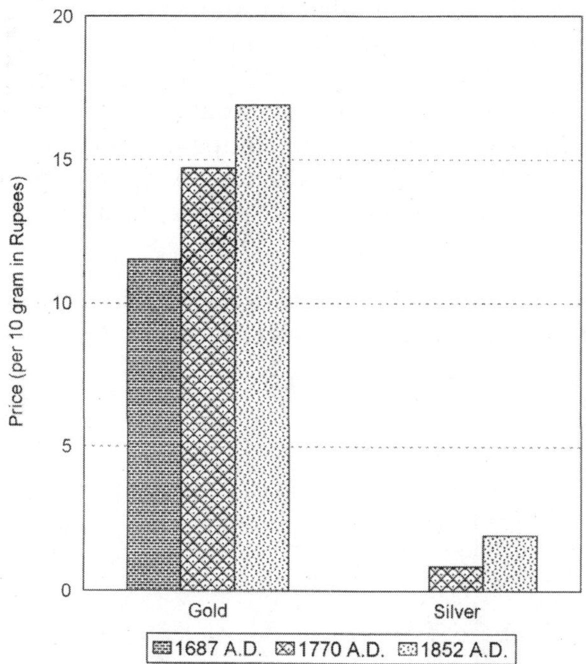

Table 7.11: Price Comparison between Suratgarh and Anupgarh *Qasbas* of *Ghee*, Edible Oil, Wheat, *Moth* and Red Chilly (Prices per unit in rupees)

Commodity	*Suratgarh (1 maund = 28 seers) 1787 AD Prices*		*Anupgarh (1 maund = 32 seers) 1817 AD Prices*	
	Per maund	*: per 100 seers*	*Per maund*	*: per 100 seers*
(1)	*(2)*	*(3)*	*(4)*	*(5)*
Ghee	3.830	13.679	5.016	15.675
Oil	2.871	10.254	3.200	10.000
Moth	0.553	1.975	0.717	2.243
Wheat	0.818	2.921	1.333	4.166
Red chilly	2.154	7.693	2.667	8.334

Source: Appendix No. 6

The results are interesting and does not show any drastic change in price structure in different years in these two *qasbas*. Generally, the prices prevailing in Anupgrah in 1817 AD show a slight increase over the price level of 1787 AD in Suratgarh. The prices of wheat was cheaper at Suratgarh in comparison to Anupgarh. The reason is explicit. Suratgarh had a fertile zone and produces wheat more than Anupgarh. Further, there is a difference of about 30 years for the margin of prices which seems justified for the difference in prices. Graph 7.6 shows comparative prices of these two *qasbas*.

Graph 7.6: Comparative Prices of Suratgarh and Anupgarh *Qasbas* of *Ghee,* Oil, Wheat *Moth* and Red Chilly

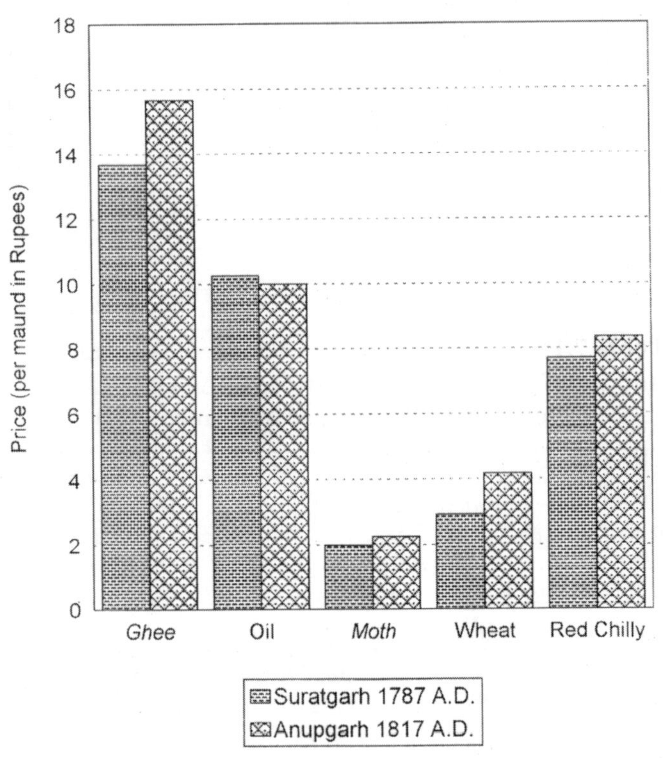

Thus, the prices, in general show a gradual trend of increase in price level in a long span of time. However, these prices have been of normal days, but during the time of famine, war and political instability showed a hike in prices for which supply of the commodities was badly affected due to failure of crops and insecurity of routes.

Capt. Powlett in his *Gazetteer*[22] of Bikaner quotes that the famines generally affected the price of grains in Bikaner. He quotes an instance (However of as late as 1873 AD) that "the price of grain in Bikaner went gradually upto 6 seers in a rupee, and there was little difference between the prices of different kinds....Just before the famine *bajra* was 35 *seers* and *moth* at 45 *seers*. The people consider that a famine has begun when *bajra* was at 15 *seers*." So, at the times of famine and scarcities, the prices usually shoot up three times and also alike in the political instability when the supply was scanty. The incidental expenses on transportation of commodities and transit duties further added to the cost and made them still dearer.

Apart from the prices of essential commodities, the *Bahis* also quote, sparingly, prices of various other general items, imported cloth, golden ornaments, silver utensils and animals, etc. But their analysis can not be offered, at present, for want of comparative prices in the sources. However, they are being reproduced to evince the price level in the period:

Prices of General Items in Bikaner in 1770 AD

Byav Bahi of 1770 AD quoted prices of following items as follows–

Roap leather @ Rs. 8 per *maund*, cloth for making *Kosh* (water bucket) @Rs. 2.5 per scroll, *Kori* (unwashed coarse cloth) costed 0.28 paise per hand length. A *Jaipuri golden Varaq* and *Multani Golden Varaq* each costed per piece simultaneously @ Rs. 0.083 and Rs. 0.012. A local made woolen blanket costed in Rs. 1.13, whereas sugar candy was Rs. 10 per *maund*. An imported sword was of Rs. 41 and a carved golden handle of sword was of Rs. 14 per piece.[23]

Prices of Variety of Imported Cloth in 1770 AD

A variety of cloths was imported for the royal family, therefore, its prices per scroll have been quoted[24] as under:

A scroll of *Burhanpuri pagh* (Turban) in Rs. 10, a scroll of printed cloth of *Khimkhab* in Rs. 58.5, scroll of *Banarsi Dupatta* in Rs. 29, scroll of *Gujrati* Turban (*Kiramchi*) of 16 *Gaj*[25] in Rs. 500, one scroll of Multani *Chintz* is Rs. 12, one scroll of *Jaipuri Khimkhab* in Rs. 20, one scroll of *Farrukhshahi* turban in Rs. 40, one scroll of *Mehtabi Chira* in Rs. 12, one scroll of *Mehtabi Kurta* in Rs.30, one piece of *Balabandi* in Rs.16, one scroll of *Zari* in Rs. 25, one scroll of *Malmal* in Rs. 3, were available.

Price of Golden Ornaments and Silver Utensils in 1770 AD

One necklace (*Chandrahaar*) of weight 5 *Tola* 1½ *Masha* costed Rs. 91, one *Kilangi* jewelled costed Rs. 801. Whereas a *Sirpech* jewelled was of Rs. 701. One *Bajubandh's* pair of weight 5 *Tola* 5½ *Masha* costed Rs. 97 and a pair of jewelled *Hasth-Phool* costed Rs.65.[26]

The prices of some silver utensils have also been mentioned as under in the same year–one *Gangajali* (water jug) plain costed Rs. 220.61, and a *Jhari* with four legs (water container) was for Rs.270. One *Lota* costed Rs.22, a *Kalash* Rs. 395, a *Chari* (water container) Rs. 301 and a *Peekdani* costed Rs.29.[27] The *Bahis* do not mention the weights of these commodities, therefore, it would be difficult to compare even if we come across the prices of these items in the pre and post period of our study.

Prices of Animals

A horse (breed not known) was available from Rs. 33 to 275, an elephant in Rs. 4,000 to Rs. 8,000 and an ox was available for Rs. 15.50 to Rs. 22.50. A camel was also available in Rs. 30 to 65.[28] It is worthwhile to mention that the prices of these animals also varied on their breed and age.

Thus, these prices exhibit the price level of various commodities and general increasing trend in Bikaner from 1687 to 1820 AD.[29]

REFERENCES

1. *Byav Bahis* of Bikaner State contain the details of marriages, ceremonies, and the income and expenditure pertaining to it and the details of the purchases of required items. The prices (per

rupee) have been recorded there-in, of variety of goods purchased by the *Modikhana* and *Karkhana*. Following *Byav Bahis* have been consulted:
Bai Ram Kanwar Ro Byav Anup Singh Ji Kiyo Teir Bahi - Byav Bahi, No. 143, V.S.1744/1687 AD; *Bai Sardar Kanwarji Re Byav wa Naler Melo Teri Bahi - Byav Bahi* No. 159, V.S. 1827/1770 AD; *Bai Shri Udai Kanwar Ji Re - Byav Re Jeemus Ri Khata Bahi - Byav Bahi*, No. 167, V.S. 1839/1782 AD; *Bahi Maharaj Kanwar Shri Ratan Singh Ji Re Byav Ri - Byav Bahi*, No. 170, V.S.1877/1820 AD

2. The rates quoted in the *Bahis* seems to be retail prices as the goods purchased were not in larger quantities.
3. See Appendices, No. 1-6.
4. See Chapter 'Trade and Commerce' for the details.
5. Method adopted for converting 'per-rupee-prices' into 'per-*maund*-price' (in rupees) is setout below for convenience -
   Gur purchased in 1687 AD in 1 rupee = 62 *seers* and 11 *chhatang*
   To convert 11 *chhatang* into *seers* - 11/6 = 0.69 *seers*
   62 Seers + 0.69 *seers* = 62.69 *seers*
   To convert 62 seers into per *maund* prices in rupees = (100/ 62.69)×40 *seers* = 63.80/100 = 0.638 paise per maund
6. *Sanad Parwana Bahi*, V.S. 1840/1783 AD, f. 65, Jodhpur Records; *Bhandar*, No. 14, *Basta* No.13, V.S. 1887, Kota records, Cf. Gupta, B.L., op. cit., p. 44.
7. Ojha, G.H., *Bikaner Rajya ka Itihas*, Part I, p. 13.
8. *Byav Bahi*, No. 159, V.S. 1827/1770 AD Tobacco found way into the state in good quantity from Sindh, Multan, Ajmer, Kota and from eastern provinces of India. *Sawa Bahi Mandi Bikaner*, No. 11, V.S. 1822/1765 AD, ff. 1-2, *Jagat Bahi Bikaner*, No. 69, V.S. 1858/ 1801 AD, ff. 1-12.
9. *Byav Bahi*, No. 143, V.S. 1744/1687 AD, No. 170, V.S. 1877/1820 A.D, R.S.A., Bikaner, Sharma, G.S., *Marwari Vyapari*, op. cit., p. 21.
10. *Sanad Parwana Bahi*, V.S. 1840/1783 AD, f. 65, Jodhpur Records, *Bhandar* No. 14, *Basta* No. 13, V.S. 1887, Kota Records, Cf. Gupta, B.L., op. cit., p. 46.
11. *Sawa bahi Mandi Bikaner*, No. 16, V.S. 1827/1770 AD, f. 48(b); No. 22, V.S. 1837/1780 AD, f. 32(b), R.S.A., Bikaner.
12. *Kagad Bahi*, No. 12, V.S. 1859/1802 AD
13. The routes had become unsafe and the *Bhattis*, *Raths* & *Johiyas* were used to plunder the carvans carrying goods on the routes passing from the north-west region. Ojha, G.H., op. cit., Part I, pp. 21-22. Also see section 'Trade Routes' in Chapter 'Trade and Commerce.'

14. See Chapter 'Agriculture Economy'.
15. Ibid.
16. *Parwana Bahi*, Bikaner Records, No. 1, V.S. 1700-1800, f. 629(b); No. 4, V.S. 1800-1900/1743-1843 AD, *Chitti Diwani*, V.S. 1823, *Phagun Bahi* 5, Camp. Chandasar village, R.S.A., Bikaner.
17. *Sawa Bahi Mandi Bikaner*, No. 3, V.S. 1805/1748 AD, ff. 2(a), 63(a); No. 21, V.S. 1835-36/1778-79 AD, f. 10(a), *Sawa Bahi Mandi Anupgarh*, No. 14, V.S. 1899/1842 AD, f. 154; *Sawa Bahi Mandi Suratgarh*, No. 1, V.S. 1847/1790 AD, f. 71, R.S.A., Bikaner.
18. See section, 'Trade routes' in Chpater 'Trade and Commerce'
19. Hasan, Aziza, 'Mints of the Mughal Empire', op. cit., p. 180.
20. *Sawa Bahi Suratgarh*, No. 1, V.S. 1844/1787 AD, f. 33, R.S.A., Bikaner.
21. *Sawa Bahi Anupgarh*, No. 143, V.S. 1874/1817 AD, f. 67, R.S.A. Bikaner.
22. Capt. Powlett, P.W., *Gazetteer of Bikaner State*, op. cit., p. 107.
23. *Byav Bahi*, No. 159, V.S. 1827/1770 AD, R.S.A., Bikaner.
24. Ibid.
25. 1¼ hand length was equal to 1 *Gaj* (Yard) *Byav Bahi*, No. 159, V.S. 1827/1770, R.S.A., Bikaner.
26. Ibid.
27. Ibid.
28. Ibid.
29. Also see Research article of K.L. Mathur, 'Change and Continuity in the Prices in Bikaner from Close of the Sventeenth to the Early Nineteenth Century' published in *Medieval India 2: Essays in Medieval Indian History and Culture* (ed.) Shahbuddin Iraqi; Centre of Advanced Study, Department of History, Aligarh Muslim University, Aligarh, Published by Manohar, New Delhi, 2008, pp. 97-107.

Appendix-1

Prices of *Gur*, Sugar, *Ghee*, Edible Oil, Rice and Red Chilly in Bikaner during 1687-1820 AD (Prices per rupees availabe in the *Bahis*)

Commodity	*1687 AD*[1] *M - S - C*[*]	*1770 AD*[2] *M - S - C*	*1782 AD*[3] *M - S - C*	*1820 AD*[4] *M - S - C*
Gur	0-62-11	0-13-0[#] to 0-16-0	0-9½-0	-
Sugar(*Khand*)	0-3-4½	-	0-4¼-0	0-3-1
Ghee	0-19-11	0-5-0 to 0-5¼-0	0-4½-0	0-2¾-0
Oil	0-3-9	-	0-11¾-0	0-16-0
Rice				
(a) Rajgarh quality	0-9-3½	-	0-1½-2	0-1-0
(b) Pali-thick	0-9-10	-	0-1¾-0	-
(c) Pali-thin	0-9½-½	-	0-1¾-0	-
Red chilly	0-2-6	0-5-0	1-0-0	-

* M- *Maunds*, S-*Seers*, C- *Chhatang*

In the case of two prices the average prices have been considered

Appendix-2

Prices of Flour, Pulses and Intoxicants in Bikaner during 1687-1820 AD (Prices per rupee available in the *Bahis*)

Commodity	*1687 AD*[5] *M - S - C*[*]	*1770 AD*[6] *M - S - C*	*1782 AD*[7] *M - S - C*	*1820 AD*[8] *M - S - C*
Maida	0-8-0	-	0-17½-0	0-7-0
Besan	0-8-0	-	0-16-0	-
Moong Dal	0-8½-1	-	0-3¼-2	-
Tobacco	0-3¼-0	0-8-0	-	-
Opium	0-0-3¾	-	-	0-0-1

* M - *Maunds*, S - *Seers*, C - *Chhatang*

Appendix-3

Prices of Spices and Food Grain in Bikaner during 1770-1820 AD (Price per rupe available in *Bahis*)

Commodity	*1770 AD*[9] *M - S - C*	*1782 AD*[10] *M - S - C*	*1820 AD*[11] *M - S - C*
Dhania	0-17¾-0	0-13-0	-
Turmeric	0-9-3¾	0-5½-0	0-6-1½
Sunth	0-4¼-¾	-	0-5-0
Wheat	0-6-3¾	0-3¾-0 to 0-4-0	-
Bajra	1¾-0-0	1½-3½-0	1-2-0
Moth	1½-5-0	1¼-0-0	1-7-0

* M - Maunds, *S - Seers*, C - *Chhatang*

Appendix-4

Prices of Dry Fruits in Bikaner during 1770-1820 AD (Price per rupees available in *Bahis*)

Commodity	*1770 AD*[12] *M - S - C*	*1782 AD*[13] *M - S - C*	*1816 AD*[14] *M - S - C*
Pistachio	0-4-11¾	0-2-15½	0-1-13
Almond	0-3-4.7 (4*Ch*.11*As*)	0-3-6	0-1-13
Dry Gota (Coconut)	0-3-0	0-1½-2	-
Currant	0-4-11¾	0-5-5½	0-2-7¾

* M - *Maunds*, S - *Seers*, C - *Chhatang*

Appendix-5

Prices of Gold and Silver in Bikaner during 1687-1852 AD (Price per *Tola* in rupees available in *Bahis*)

Commodity	*1687 AD*[15] *M - S - C*	*1770 AD*[16] *M - S - C*	*1852 AD*[17] *M - S - C*
Gold (Hem)	13-6	17-8 to 18-0	19-12
Silver (Rupa)	-	1-0	2-4

* Rs.- *Rupees*, *As - Annas*

Appendix-6

Prices of *Ghee*, Edible Oil, Wheat, *Moth*, and Red Chilly, in *Qasbas* of Suratgarh in 1787 AD and in Anupgarh in 1817 AD (Prices per rupees available in *Bahis*)

Commodity	*Suratgarh*[18] *1687 AD* *M - S - C*	*Anupgarh*[19] *1817 AD* *M - S - C*
(1)	*(2)*	*(3)*
Ghee	0-7¼-1	0-6¼-2
Oil	¼-2¾-0	¼-4-0
Moth	1½-8½-2	1-7-0
Wheat	1-6¼-0	½-8-0
Red chilly	¼-6-0	¼-4-0

* M - *Maunds*, S - *Seers*, C - *Chhatang*

REFERENCES

1. *Byav Bahi*, No. 143, V.S.1744/1687 AD, R.S.A., Bikaner
2. *Byav Bahi*, No. 159, V.S.1827/1770 AD, R.S.A., Bikaner
3. *Byav Bahi*, No. 167, V.S.1839/1782 AD, R.S.A., Bikaner
4. *Byav Bahi*, No. 170, V.S.1877/1820 AD, R.S.A., Bikaner
5. *Byav Bahi*, No. 143, V.S.1744/1687 AD, R.S.A., Bikaner
6. *Byav Bahi*, No. 159, V.S.1827/1770 AD, R.S.A., Bikaner
7. *Byav Bahi*, No. 167, V.S.1839/1782 AD, R.S.A., Bikaner
8. *Byav Bahi*, No. 170, V.S.1877/1820 AD, R.S.A., Bikaner
9. *Byav Bahi*, No. 159, V.S.1827/1770 AD, R.S.A., Bikaner
10. *Byav Bahi*, No. 167, V.S.1839/1782 AD, R.S.A., Bikaner
11. *Byav Bahi*, No. 170, V.S.1877/1820 AD, R.S.A., Bikaner
12. *Byav Bahı*, No. 159, V.S.1827/1770 AD, R.S.A., Bikaner
13. *Byav Bahi*, No. 167, V.S.1839/1782 AD, R.S.A., Bikaner
14. *Bikaner Mandi re Jama Kharach ri Bahi*, No.117, 1872-73/1815-16 AD R.S.A., Bikaner
15. *Byav Bahi*, No. 143, V.S.1744/1687 AD, R.S.A., Bikaner
16. *Byav Bahi*, No. 159, V.S.1827/1770 AD, R.S.A., Bikaner
17. *Byav Bahi*, No. 178, V.S.1889/1852 AD, R.S.A., Bikaner
18. *Sawa Bahi Mandi Suratgarh*, No. 1, V.S. 1844/1787 AD, f. 33, R.S.A., Bikaner
19. *Sawa Bahi Mandi Suratgarh*, No. 143, V.S. 1874/1717 AD, f. 67, R.S.A., Bikaner

8

Role and Activities of the Commercial Groups

The state patronage and protection to trade and commerce on a larger scale and consequential active participation of the *Vyaparis* and *Sahukars* into the commercial and financial activities, as such, led to the economic growth in the state in the second half of the 18th century. The *Vyaparis* and *Sahukars* constituted the most influential and dynamic class in the economic structure as the distribution of agricultural and industrial goods and the work of moneylending was handled by them.[1] The state could realize extra revenue from their commercial activities particularly in a period when it had to part with the income which they received from the Mughal *Jagirs* as the Mughal *Mansabdars*.[2] Therefore, an attempt has been made in this chapter to analyse and ascertain their role and activities in the state economy during the period under review.

The state *Bahis*, specially *Kagad Bahis*, *Sawa Bahis* and the *Jagat Bahis* have been useful in ascertaining their activities as these *Bahis* record their financial and commercial transactions as well as the state orders relating to them.[3]

While quoting the *Jagat* rates or otherwise the merchants and traders have been addressed by the terms *Byopari*, *Bonia* or *Mahajan*.[4] Thus, the terms did not stand for caste but for the profession as a whole which included the castes of *Mahajans* (Agrawal, Oswal and Maheshwari) as well as *Brahmins* and other. The term *Sahukar* has been used in the *Bahis* for the money-lender but somtimes also used for all the other merchants and traders as well.[5] Besides, specific terms for various groups like

Bichhayati, Dalal, Sarraf, Pothia (peddler) *Bohra* and *Shah* have been used.[6]

(1) THE CASTES (Merchants as a Heterogeneous Class)

Though the social base of the commercial community was not confined to a single caste or religion but was more or less a combination of Hindu, Jain and Muslim religions, but still mainly dominated by the *Vaishya* community of which *Oswal Maheshwari* and *Agrawal* formed the main constituents.[7] Many sub-castes[8] of them operated in the multifarious commercial ventures/functions in the state. *Maheshwaris* included the sub castes of Daga, Damani, Pugalia, Mantri, Bagri, Ladha, Mohta, Sadani, Mundhra, Kothari, Sethia, Surana, Sawansukha, Abhani, Banthia, Golecha, Kochar and Khazanchis and Agrawals included Baghlo, Lohiyo, Agrawal and Dhanuka. These castes were highly professional and well-versed in the business transactions.[9]

It is noticed in the *Bahis* that Ratansi, Dharanji, Shrikishan of Mahajan community extensively traded in Bikaner-Jaipur,[10] Devchand, Raychand and Udai Chand Golecha were prominent wool traders[11] and Daga Gokul Chand, Raja Ram, Kothari Gumana, Lakhotiya Rup Ram were the reputed grocery merchants.[12]

Apart of the Vaishyas, the Khatris and Modis, immigrants from the Punjab (as even today they are called Punjabi-Khatri and Modi because of their original habitat in the Punjab), were also actively participating in the trade and commerce in those days. *Sawa Bahi Suratgarh* of 1850 AD, besides the Vaishya community records various sub-castes of Khatris as Midha, Nagpal, Sinwat, Sethia, Gidar, Narang and Khatri.[13] They had earned a good reputation and served in the state stores and *Modikhanas* and also settled in and around Bikaner. Kumbhana village, Kharbara and Anupgarh were dominated by them.[14] They were operating in Anupgarh, Phuleda and Kharbara in grain trade.

Besides Mahajans and Khatris, Brahmins were also engaged in mercantile and financial business and also in taking *Muqatas* of sair-jagat (contracts of realizing commercial taxes). The principal castes of Brahmins engaged in such activities were Acharaj, Vyas, Ojha, Purohit, Paliwal and Gusai (Mahant). Nathu Purohit, Meghraj Vyas, Kishan Das Bhatt, Chaturbhuj Acharaj and Gusai Nirbongirji (Mahant) were known traders and money lenders in Bikaner.[15] Jagroop Brahmin was a known cloth merchant of *qasba Bidasar* of Sujangarh and used to participate in the fair of Mundawa.[16] Gosains were a wealthy community and advanced loans to the state handsomely.

Yet there were some more castes engaged in transportation work. They were Charans, Bhats, Raika, Rebari, Gusai, Sikh and Kayamkhanis, besides the *Banjaras*. Some Muslim traders were engaged in the sale of animal and leather works.[17]

It is thus, evident that the social composition of the merchant class in Bikaner was not confined to one caste only, but was heterogeneous.

(2) CATEGORIES

The towns of the state in the later half of the 18th century had become places of considerable mercantile activities and a set pattern of marketing had emerged in them. So that the merchant class can be categorized according to their types of occupation or the nature of their work as under–

(i) **Wealthy merchants/wholeseller:** *Seth, Shah, Sahukar,* etc. dealt in *Hundi,* moneylending, export and import. Even lent money to the state. The state borrowed Rs. 4,00,001 in 1827 AD[18] from Seth Mirza Mal Potedar of Churu who had shops in various *mandis*.[19] The wholesellers came in this category.

(ii) **Small merchants/retailers:** Known as *Bichayats* (commodity dispayer in the market), *Pothias* (peddlers), retailers, etc. who were operating within a restricted area and specialized in specific commodities.[20] They were transacting with very small capital. They can be categorized as the retailers.

(iii) **Others:** Transacting in moneylending, banking, *hundis, dalali, sauda,* money changing, insurance of goods, transportation, *huwala, muqata,* etc.[21] Can be kept in the other category.

(3) ROLE AND ACTIVITIES OF COMMERCIAL GROUPS

(a) Marketing, Importing and Exporting of Commodities

The merchants and traders procured and marketed the agricultural and industrial products into the *bazars* and *mandis* both at wholesale and retail levels. The work of import and export of required goods and the functions of sale and purchase were done by them. *Bikaner Gazal* and *Prachin haton ki vigat* testify to the existence of various shops at Bikaner and Churu and discharging of their market functions.[22] Thus, important market functions and supply of essential commodities were managed by them.

(b) *Huwala-soapa*[23] and *Muqatas* (*Ijaras*)

Among the various commercial pursuits discharged by the merchants the system of *Huwala-soapa* and the *muqatas* were very significant as the state largely depended on these two systems of revenue collection during the period. The *huwala kagads* appended in the *kagad bahis* show that the income of various sources were being realized through these systems.[24] A large group of merchant class engaged themselves in these popular methods under the *huwala-soapa* system in which a few *khalisa* villages were entrusted to a person for revenue realization. The work was called *huwala-soapa* and the allottee was known as the *huwaladar*. An instance of *huwala-soapa* used in the year 1774 is set out in the following table below–

Table 8.1: Revenue Realization under the *Huwala-Soapa* System[25]

Sr. No.	*Year V.S./AD*	*Caste & name of kamdar to whom huwala was given for realization*	*Nos. of Khalisa villages given for realization*	*Rozgar (remuneration)given (in Rs.)*
(1)	*(2)*	*(3)*	*(4)*	*(5)*
1.	1831/1774	Kothari Udai Ram	05	200
		Dhannani Gumane	02	100
		Kothari Har Rai	01	125
		Shah Daulat Ram	07	200

Contd...

Shah Ajab Ram Mali	07	25
Kothari Khinvsi & Mali Bharani Das	05	100
Kothari Pratapsi & Mali Megha	06	200
Kothari Jethmal	06	100

The *rozgar* payments varied with the volume of work in a village or with the size of the villages concerned.

The state revenue was also collected through the *muqatas* (*Ijaras*). The source of income was auctioned to the highest bidder for collection in a specified period. Th *muqata* rights usually, were auctioned to the bidder for 4 months to 3 years. The grantee of the *muqata* was called *muqati* and the allotment as *muqata*.[26] A list of *muqatas* contracted in different years is appended which shows the prevalence of *muqata* in the 18th century.

Table 8.2: Revenue Realization under the *Muqata* System

S.N.	*Year V.S./ AD*	*Amount of Muqata (in Rs.)*	*Period of Muqata*	*Mode of Payment*	*State source of income given on Muqata*	*Name and Caste of Muqati*
(1)	*(2)*	*(3)*	*(4)*	*(5)*	*(6)*	*(7)*
1.	1811/ 1754[27]	4,601	6months	–	*Nekal* ri *Jagat*	Kothari Maluk Chand, Acharaj Kishandas
2.	1827/ 1770[28]	51	1 year (360 days)	–	Income of gambling and dice playing in Bikaner (*Juve ro Feto Ro Muqato*)	Jalu
3.	1827/ 1770[29]	800	1 year	–	Rajaldesar Ri *Jagat*	Dhannani Gumane
4.	1827/ 1770[30]	151 (*Gajshahi*)	4 months	Full payment	Income of *Jagat* on watermelon (*Kakdo Ro Pato*)	Vyas Jeevan & Kachu Fathoni
5.	1827/ 1770[31]	10,301	1 year (360 days)	Instalment	*Jagat of Reni Mandi* and its outposts	Duggal Inde
6.	1831/	125	1 year	-	*Jagat* of stone	Chuhan Jeevan

Contd...

Contd...

	1774[32]		(360 days)		mines at Khari and Saatsar in Bikaner	
7.	1833/ 1776[33]	7,201	1year (360 days)	Instalment with partly advance	*Jagat* income of *Desh*, Kharipatti & Berasar *Chowki*	Duggad Sawai Daga Bhau Acharaj Jeev and others
8.	1835/ 1778[34]	14,501	13 months (390 days)	Instalment of Rs.500/-	*Jagat* income of *Desh*, Kharipatti, Berasar, Rajaldesar, Hardesar.	Bardia Gujarmal
9.	1835/ 1778[35]	290	1 year	Instalment	*Dalali* income from *Dalals* dealing in cotton and woollen cloth	Bardiya Mehrajya, Tulsi Mishra
10.	1837/ 1780[36]	18,001	1 year (390 days)	Instalment	*Muqata* of income of out checkposts of Berasar, Lunkaransar, Rajaldesar, *Desh* & Kharipatti	Golecha Gopa
11.	1837/ 1780[37]	9,003	3 years (1080 days)	Instalment	Income of mine of *Multani mitti*	Chouhan Jeevan Das
12.	1838/ 1781[38]	11,004	1 year (360 days)	Instalment	11 heads of Income being collected at *Mandi* Sadar (of various taxes)	Acharaj Som Datt Mohta Gulaba Bardia Mehraj Kochar Sambhu & Kothari Kushal Chand
13.	1843-44/ 1786-87[39]	24	1year (360 days)	-	*Takri Ri Tolai*	Kochar Seru
14.	1839/ 1782[40]	8,402	2 years (720 days)	-	Income of Nohar *Mandi* and its outer checkposts	Kochar Udaichand
15.	1855-57/ 1798-1800[41]	4,601	2 year	Annual	*Ropata* Income tax on sale of camels and on shopkeepers	Mundhra Chaturbhuj, Daga Bhop Singh and others

Contd...

Contd...

16. 1857/ 1800[42]	4,901	1 year	Annual	-do-	-do-
17. 1854/ 1797[43]	401 (Surat-shahi)	1 year (360 days)	Annual	Income of Orchards of Gajpat Vilas at Gajsinghpur	Acharaj Bijai Moti Gun Dhar Mula Khatri
18. 1856-57/ 1799-1800[44]	801	3 years (1110 days)	-do-	-do-	-do-

It seems, the state was assigning land on *muqata* because of the uncertainty of income. These were revised frequently and at increased rates. The system appeared to be beneficial to the *muqatis* as large profits accrued to them. The *huwaldars* had become the *muqatis*. They tried to realize more than the bid amount in specified period for their profit.[45] The system largely helpd the state in revenue realization but became instrumental in exploitation of the common people.

Distinction between the *Huwala-soapa* and *Muqata* System

On the surface these appear to be the same but in fact, differed substantially. Under *huwala-soapa* the work of revenue collection was generally entrusted to a state-appointed *kaamdar* or others on certain *rozgar* (remuneration) in a stipulated preiod. They were restricted to only revenue realization. Whereas, in a *muqata* (*Ijara*) the work of collection of any source of income was auctioned to the highest bidder with certain conditions to be followed. The state officials who were hitherto, paid their salaries by the state treasury were now to be reimbursed by the *muqatis*.

Moreover, we do not find reference of the former being withdrawn from the allotment as in the case of the latter. The *muqatas* were very frequently terminated and substituted with another *muqati* with the increased amount of *muqata*.

The state encouraged the *muqatis* to enhance the bidding amount as high as possible. *Motiyon ro chowkdo* (costing Rs. 200) was bestowed upon Shah Shivdan Bardia for enhancing the amount of *muqata* by Rs. 3,000 in 1778 AD.[46] The *muqata* was not confined to collection of income of land revenue of *khalisa* villages or the commercial taxes only but also extended upto raising a contingent (*paltan*) of the army for the state. Agrawal Behari Lal with certain conditions to be followed, was to raise a small army contingent in Rajgarh in 1802 AD. The monthly expenses of Rs. 382 *Annas* 8 were paid for that.[47]

Sometimes, the due balance of the *muqata* amount was exempted ex-gratia to a *muqati*. Rs. 25 were exempted to Bafna Budha Dhola, the *muqati* of weighing (*takri ro muqato*) in 1833 AD in Lunkaransar due to poor conditions of *muqati*. His request for exemptions was conceded.[48] This was a sort of concession which was extended by the state sympathetically to the *muqatis*. All disputes arising among the old and new *Muqatis* were resolved by the state.[49]

(c) Moneylending and the *Hundi* Business

The moneylending and the *hundi* business were another important banking functions undertaken by a specialized group of merchants known as *Sahukars* and *Bohras*. Generally, they belonged to the *Bania* community but *Mahant* or *Gusains* and some *Brahmin* castes also adopted this business.

The *Sahukars* known as *shahs* and *seths* were affluent money-lenders and had branches of their firms at commercial centres being looked after by their *Munims* and *Gumastas*. The *Bohras* were financiers with small capital in rural and urban areas providing moderate loans to peasants, artisans and shopkeepers. The *Sahukars* had to pay a tax on their profession known as *Sahukari Bhanchh*. *Gusains* or *Mahants* were religious saints known as '*Pashminawale gusain*'[50] and were engaged in money-lending.

(i) Loans to State

The *Sahukars* and *Gusains* advanced heavy loans to the state government during the second half of the 18th and early decades of the 19th century at high rates of interests.[51] The state had to pay a large amount every month as interest against these loans. Various sources of income of state including revenue of villages (*khalisa*) or *mandis* and *chowkis* were assigned to debtors for their recovery of loans. The debtor was allowd to recover it with the help of state employees. Till the loan was fully repaid the assigned source of income was kept by the debtor as a guarantee.[52] We see that sometimes, golden ornaments were also mortgaged with the *Sahukars* for loans.[53]

Tables showing state borrowings (Table 8.3) and payments of interest in one month in 1812 (Table 8.4) have been set out to show the evidence and magnitude of interest.

Table 8.3: Loans Borrowed by the Rulers of Bikaner

S.N.	*Year V.S./ AD*	*Amount borrowed (in Rs.)*	*Rate of interest (p.a.)*	*Moneylenders' caste and name*	*Security*	*Mode of payment*
(1)	*(2)*	*(3)*	*(4)*	*(5)*	*(6)*	*(7)*
1.	1840/ 1783 Bikaner[54]	516	N.A.	Ojha, Radhakishan	Kilangi-one	Cash
2.	1804. 1747 Bikaner[55]	650	N.A.	Modi	N.A.	Cash
3.	1826/ 1769 Bikaner[56]	15,000	N.A.	Banthia ManakChand Bijai Chand, Khushal Chand, Saheb Singh, Ratan Chand, Parakh Mokham Singh, Swaroop Chand, Abhay Raj	Golden ornaments	Partly cash partly through *hundi.*
4.	1814/ 1757 Reni[57]	400	24%,Re.1 additional as *Tikko Oak*	Gusain Arjangir	N.A.	Cash
5.	1831/ 1774 Rahgarh[58]	400	12%	Kothari Raichand	N.A.	Cash
6.	1851/ 1794 Rajgarh[59]	401 125 233	36% 18% 12%	Acharaj Gumani Ram Fatehpuria, Shrikishan Lahoti Kashi Ram	- - -	- - -
7.	1851/ 1794 Rajgarh[60]	114	24%	Fatehpuria, Shrikishan	-	Cash
8.	1861/ 1804 Rajgarh[61]	100	12%	Vyas Anand Ram	*Kara Ri Jodi* (one pair of *Kara*)	-

Contd...

Contd...

9. 1863/ 1806 Rajgarh[62]	100	36%	Sikh Ganda Singh	N.A.	Cash
10. 1850/ 1793 Surat-garh[63]	100 80	30% 24%	Swami Laxman Das Sandu Govind	N.A.	Cash
11. 1884/ 1827 Bikaner/ Churu[64]	4,00,001	24% 12%	Partly Potedar Mirzamal Partly Purohit Harlal	Source of income of *Jagat*	Cash

Table 8.4: Sampling of Payment of Interest on Loans in the Month of '*Chetra*' V.S. 1869/1812 AD by the State (Broadly Calculated on the Basis of *Chitti-khat Bahi* V.S. 1869)

S.N.	*Date of Month of the payment*	*Total amount of interest paid Rs.-As.*	*Rate of interest (per annum)*	*Loaning caste/ community*	*Purpose of borrowing loan*
1.	*Chetra badi* 15 (*Amavasya*)[65]	204-2	36%	Acharaj Purohit, Ojha, Vyas	–
2.	*Chetra badi* 15[66]	11-8	36%	Mahant-Gusain	–
3.	*Chetra badi* 15[67]	3-0	36%	–	Celebration of Ram Navami
4.	*Chetra badi* 15[68]	34-4	-	Bohra, Gusain, Vyas	–
5.	*Chetra badi* 15[69]	4-0	-	Vyas	On petty requirement of ruler
6.	*Chetra sudi* 4[70]	2-2	-	Acharaj & Modi	–
7.	*Chetra sudi* 6[71]	4-0	-	-	–
8.	*Chetra sudi* 7[72]	10-8	-	-	–
9.	*Chetra sudi* 10[73]	149-5½	30%	Gusain	–
10.	*Chetra sudi* 10[74]	10-0	-	Purohit	Navratra Puja
11.	*Chetra Sudi* 14[75]	40-0	-	Gusain	
	Total	472-13½	For chetra month (the first month of the Hindi calendar)		

From these tables it is evident that the Brahmin sub-castes Ojha, Purohit, Vyas, Acharay and Mahant (*Gusains*) were among the moneylenders who advanced loans to the state. The rate of interest on state loans varies from time to time and ranged between 12% to 36% p.a.[76] Obviously, the merchants practised usury. Fluctuation in interest rates depended on the risk involved in lending to the state because of frequent failures on the part of the state and the stability of the state's political condition. When Surat Singh borrowed a large loan of Rs. 4,00,001 from Potedar Mirza Mal of Churu and Harlal in 1827 AD the rate of interest was 24% on Rs. 25,600 (the part loan) and 12% on the 14,400, but we see that despite the assignment of income of various *mandis*. The whole income of Bhadra *qasba* was assigned to him for recovery including *mandi*. It could not be repaid fully.[77] Thus, the moneylenders abstained usually from lending money to the state.[78]

(ii) The Rural Moneylending and Commercial Credit

The state *bahis* generally do not cover the cases of rural money-lending or the commercial credit, but some stray references are sometimes found. We find that *Bohras* and *Sahukars* gave loans to the rural people as well as commercial credit to the merchants for business purposes.

In the rural loans on a secure basis were given and some items of use or sometimes children were used as security for loans.

In 1806, Lalchand, a menial, of village Balrajsar handed over his son Pramil to Barath (Charan) Kirti of his village as a security against a loan of 25 *maunds* of grain. The mortgage of a child in security was called *Bhogalia* practice in which a loan was given without interest and the child in question would be serving his new master.[79] The same year Sankhla Kone mortgaged his *bandook* (rifle) with Deedwania Hanumant.[80] In 1810 AD Dhadi-Jalu's father of village Jhadeli took a loan of Rs. 8 and mortgaged 1 *dhol* (drum) of worth Rs. 12, 1 *nadh* (trumpet) of Rs. 5 and 2 *maunds* of grain against the loan from Choudhary Purkha, Aja and Devraj Malani in his village. Rupees 5 were repaid by him against the debt of his father, even then the items which were mortgaged were not returned till the loan was not fully repaid. Ultimately, the state interfered and settled the case in Jalu's favour.[81]

This suggests that generally the secured loans were given and the items put under mortgage were not returned till the loan was not fully repaid. The torture of the loanee by the debtor this way, could not be ruled out. The rates of interest were not quoted but we presume that they should not be very high in the secured loans.

In the commercial loans to the merchants we find that merchants were also mortgaging their houses, shops and the storage of grains to obtain loans from the *sahukars*. In 1807, AD Kothari Sultan Mal put his house in mortgage with Modi Tekchand for a loan.[82] Whereas in 1809 AD Parakh Dhane Pansari kept his shop partly with Ojha Girdhari and partly with Sarwan Gadhi for Rs. 100 at 12% p.a. interest rate in Bikaner.[83] In 1801 Choudhary Kushle of village Likhmidesar mortgaged his storage of grains (khawdo) weighing 93 *maunds* with Sidha Ram[84] and in 1810 AD Gordhan Daftari a storage of *moth* with Gusain Fatehgir in his village which was later sold by the state to realize his *dhan ri chowthai* tax.[85]

Thus, we find that in secured loans 12% p.a. rate of interest was in practice in commercial loans which was not as high as taken in the state loans.[86]

The loans to the loanee were provided after executing an agreement called '*khat*'. The state usually borrowed loans through *khats*. The *khats* were the *miyadi* (termed) agreements and it included witnesses of loans, mode and sources of repayment of loans. After the expiry of the given terms/period the interest was to be compounded.[87]

Hundi Business (Bills of Exchange)

The practice of issuing and discounting *hundi* or bill of exchange was an important indigenous system prevailing then. It is evident by the *Chitti Khaton ri Bahis* and *Bahi Hundiyon Kiwi Teri Vigat ri* V.S. 1726/1669 AD available in the archival collection of *Bahis* in the Bikaner Archives.[88]

A *hundi* or bill of exchange was an undertaking promising

payments to the desired place after a specified period mentioned therein allowing a discount[89] which included interest, insurance charges[90] (*jokha*) *adhat* or *dalali*[91] and the cost of transmission of money.[92] During the period under review the *hundis* were issued for two purposes.[93]

(i) for transaction of money from one place to another, and

(ii) for moneylending.

Out of the available references a comprehensive table has been prepared by recording the transactions of *hundis* to analyse and understand the system of *hundi* prevailing in the period.

Table 8.5: *Hundi* Transaction and the Rate of *Hundawan* in Bikaner

S. N.	*Date & Year of Hundi*	*Place of firm issuing Hundi*	*Drawn at Place & drawee agency*	*Amount of Hundi (in Rs.)*	*Type & period of payment of Hundi*	*Rate of Hundawan (inRs.)*
1.	*Bhadwa sudi* 8 VS 1726/ 1669 AD[94]	Bikaner Pat Rai Bhinvsi	Malpura (kota) Shah Sadul Daga	294	*Muddati* (21 days)	-
		Bikaner Sarang Dhar	Malpura (Kota) Shah Sadul Daga	200	*Muddati* (21 days)	-
2.	*Kartik sudi* 1 VS 1726/ 1669 AD[95]	Bikaner Thirani Chod Das Udai Singhvi	Ahmedabad Jagjeevan Das Udai Singh	300	*Muddati* (61 days)	-
3.	*Phalgun sudi* 15 VS 1726/ 1669 AD[96]	Bikaner Narain	Aurangabad Shah Kapoor Banthia	100	*Muddati* (46 days)	4%
4.	*Baisakh badi* 10 VS 1726/ 1669 AD[97]	Bikaner	Burhanpur	400	*Muddati* (37days)	3%
5.	*Mingsar badi* 2 VS 1726/ 1669 AD[98]	Bikaner Shah Sukha	Agra Shah Som Singh Kishan Feteh-puria	111	Muddati (31days)	-
6.	*Mingsar badi* 11 VS 1726/ 1669 AD[99]	Bikaner Shah Thirpal	Jaisalmer Shah Uttam Chand	1,200	*Muddati* (45 days)	-
7.	VS 1805/ 1748 AD[100]	Bikaner	Jehanabad	900	*Darshani*	4%
8.	VS 1807/ 1750 AD[101]	Bikaner	Hissar	14,425	*Darshani*	9½%
9.	VS 1828/ 1771 AD[102]	Rajgarh Surat Ram	Bikaner Jethmal Daftari	300	*Darshani*	1¼%

Contd...

Contd...

10. *Shrawan badi* 5 1848/ 1791 AD[103]	Jaipur	Bikaner Laloo Mitri	450	*Darshani*	1%
11. *Chetra badi* 5 VS 1853/ 1796 AD[104]	Churu	Rajgarh	100	*Darshani*	3/4%
12. *Baisakh Sudi* 6 VS 1869/ 1812 AD[105]	Ratangarh	Bikaner	300	*Darshani*	2%

The transactions in the table shows that the *hundi* business in Bikaner was well established and was largely followed by the state both for transacting and borrowing money within the state territory and outside the state. A *hundi* rather than cash, increasingly became the standard form of payments in major commercial transactions; specially in long distance trade this form of payment not only met the requirements of an expanding demand for credit but also reduced the risks involved in the transmission of cash to distant places.[106]

Through various references quoted in the *Bahi Lashkaran-nu-Neni-Hundiyan meli-Teri Vigat* of 1669 AD and some other *Bahis* like *Sawa Bahis* of *Mandis*, we are informed that the *kothiwals* styled as *shahs*[107] mostly operated the *hundi* business all over through their agents at distant places, while some *Bohras* and *Sarrafs* also arranged payments of *hundis* through mutual exchange. The *hundi* merchants mostly belonged to *Vaishya* community. The *dalals* were also of *Vaishya* castes operated in this business and worked on their commission. They often sold and purchased the *hundis* and arranged the payments. A specialized group of *hundi* merchants had emerged among the commercial classes.

The *Bahi Hundiyan Kiwi Teri Vigat* of 1669 AD shows that from Bikaner *hundis* were issued and discounted for distant places like Burhanpur, Ahmedabad, Aurangabad, Agra, Nagaur, Jaipur and Jaisalmer along with places within the state territory.[108] This *Bahi* mentions that Messers Sarang Dhar and Patrai Bhinvsi wrote two *hundis* of Rs. 200 and 294 respectively on their agents Sah Sadul Daga in Malpura, Kota.[109] Thirani Chod Das Udai Singhvi issued a *Hundi* upon Jagjeevan Das Udai Singh in Ahmedabad in 1669 AD. Likewise, Narain wrote a *hundi* of Rs.100 in the same year upon the Shah Kapur Banthia at Aurangabad.[110]

The either types of *hundis*, viz. the *Darshani* and the *Muddati* (*miyadi*) were issued and discounted by merchants, *Bohras* and *Sarrafs* here.[111] The former was payable on demand while the latter was payable on the expiry of the stipulated period mentioned in the *hundi*. The *Muddati hundi* could be encashed prematurely subject to some additional charges, and likewise interest was paid on the delayed payments of a *Muddati hundi*. Normally, payments were arranged after the due dates. In the *Shahjog hundis* the payments were only to be made to the addressee of the *hundi* in person.[112] The *hundis* were generally sent through a messenger but if the original *hundi* was lost a duplicate (*peth*) was written[113], quoting the reference of the previous one. Very occasionally the payments of any *hundi* was refused without specific ground or on suspect of falseness.[114] The *hundis* could be sold many times before it could reach the destination for payments.[115]

For issuing a *hundi* to a customer the moneylender charged his commission for his services known as *hundawan*. The charges of *hundawan* ranged for places from Rs. 1% to 9.5% which appeared to be high; but it varied on the distances of the desired places for *hundi* or due to the agency arrangements at a particular place.[116] When a *hundi* is executed through a *dalal* the charges of *hundawan* were comparatively higher than charged by a merchant himself. It is interesting to note that specific currency payments were also mentioned in some *hundis*. In a *hundi* of Malpura (Kota) Shahjahani coins were specifically mentioned to be paid. The *hundis* were generally sent through the messengers whose expenses were to be borne by the customers.[117]

Therefore, apart from the moneylending and discounting (exchanging) the currency, the *Sahukars* and *Bohras* were issuing and discounting *hundis* as well which had become a most characteristic credit institution in itself.

(d) Insurance Business

Some reference of insurance cover, *Bima* or *Jokhas* (called in local language) are available in the state *Bahis*[118] in which we find that a group of merchants were involved in insuring the consignments of goods or produce against theft, loot or dacoity; and arranged to reach their destinations safely. For this they charged commissions.[119]

Because of the political instability and insecurity over various trade routes due to plundering of *Barothias* (deserted people) and *Dhadvees* (groups of raiders) in the late 18th century, the traders had difficulty in convoying their goods or produce to various places. This stimulated a group of affluent and influential merchants to owe the responsibility in arranging to send the goods to the destinations safely.

Some firms had taken to this business on different routes. On the Bahawalpur-Bikaner route Messers Jagmohan Pratap Sadani used to take *jokhas*.[120] These *jokhas* were also called the *hunda bhada* in the local language.[121] Messers Banthia was another firm in insurance taking contract at Bikaner-Marwar route. *Sawa Bahi Mandi Bikaner* of 1750 AD mentions that it purchased a *jokha* of a Multani trader's goods in transit from Mewar to Bikaner.[122] Messers Ghanshyam Das and Mesers Nanag Ram Mirza Mal were also firms working at Churu and taking larger contracts of consignments with insurance. The Potedar collections of Churu testify to it.[123]

The general rate of insurance was *Annas* 7 for Rupees 100; however[124] it differed at times. On routes with risks of loot and on adverse conditions, the rates would be higher. The *Raznawa ri Bahi* of Messers Nanag Ram Mirza Mal mentions the rates of *pacca bima* as Re 1% for Rs. 25,000 and *Annas* 12% for Rs. 12,000 for *kaccha bima*.[125] The charges of *Dharmada* (expenses for philanthropic works) were also realized along with the insurance charges. The state had a substantial income from the insurance business. It used to realize a tax on the insurance business as *chowthai* of *jokhas* (1/4 of insurance charges).[126]

If the insured goods were lost/looted in transit the merchant undertaking the insurance had to give the compensation. When goods of *multani* traders were seized by Raj Singh at Merta in transit from Mewar to Bikaner, the *Banthia* firm had to compensate the loss.[127] Persons with enough resources of men and money used to obtain the contract of safe convoying the goods. The system or such contract were called *cholai* or *bolai* in local language. In lieu of a certain amount they guarded the goods upto the destinations.[128]

(e) *Dalali* and *Sauda* Business

It has been mentioned elsewhere that the market activities were intensified by the brokers known as *dalals*. They played a role of intermediary between the seller and purchaser in finalizing transactions. *Adhatiyas* who were also commission agents, were instrumental in procuring and selling goods for others and charged commission for the services rendered. The business of *dalals* and *Adhatiyas* were therefore very significant at *mandis* and *bazars*. The state realized a tax on their occupation known as *Dalalon-ri-bhanchh*.[129]

These *dalals* operated in various commodities, viz. wool, woollen clothes, precious metals like gold and silver, fodder, weighing work, sale of animals, sale of immovable properties, opium and groceries. It seems that *dalas* played a pivotal role and dealt in almost all commodities.[130]

Besides *dalali* they were also engaged in *satta* or *sauda* of prices of opium, silver and gold and also for the probability of rains.[131]

(f) Transporting Business

The transportation of goods were done mainly through camels oxen and pony. The *Banjaras* mainly executed this work with their paraphernalia, but in the state some specific castes of *Charans, Gusai, Rebari* and *Kayamkhani* were occupied with this work of transportation. The Sikhs known as *Diwana fakir* did this work on the Bahawalpur-Bikaner route, whereas Mullar Brahmins were engaged in carrying the goods on the routes leading to Phalodi and Sirsa from Bikaner.[132] The *Charans* who were considered a respectable caste and largely piloted the caravans sometimes involved in business activities.[133]

The role of the traders cannot be ignored in organizing the commercial activities in the *melas* (fairs) of the state. Animals and other useful items of daily life were brought and sold at the fairs.[134]

Therefore, apart from the role in the administrative hierarchy and military expedition, the manifold commercial role of the mercantile class was of paramount importance in the period. The discharge of various pursuits testify to the expansion of trade and commerce in the state.

(4) THE MIGRATION OF *SAHUKARS*

In the later part of our period of study (mainly in the early 19th century), we come across a few cases of migration of some *Sahukars/Vyaparis* to distant places.

The *bahi Bikaner ri Mandi re Jama Kharach ri* of 1820 AD mentions that Kothari Dwarka Das, a trader of Bikaner had migrated to Mirzapur and was running a shop there.[135] Sojiram of Churu had also gone to Mirzapur in the late 18th century, the descendants of whom were running a firm there and were dealing in money exchange and insurance business.[136] *Kagad Bahi* of 1816 AD refers that Chachan Shivji Mohonani of Reni had left for Hansi in 1810 AD because he had failed in his business. The debtors were pressing hard for their debt. However, the state assured him of all support and assistance against the debtors.[137] *Kagad Bahis* of 1828 AD quotes that Maloo Ladi Ram Lichhman Das of Bikaner migrated to Lucknow with his family in 1828 AD[138], likewise Jhanwar Jethmal of Bikaner also migrated to Mirzapur. Seth Gajraj of Churu in 1823 reached Calcutta via Mirzapur and adopted the business of dalali.[139]

As for the cause of migrations, there is a possibility that the state's high demand of taxes and cesses (*Sahukari Bhanch* and other taxes) and loans upon the commercial classes might have been the causes for such migration. The state, consequently granted large-scale concessions and remission in taxes to them.

But, as has already been pointed out that a few of them left the state once their business failed and were hard pressed by the debtors, and the state was ready to offer comport to them. However, from these stray references a general trend of migration is not established.

REFERENCE

1. Bhargava, B.K., 'Indigenous Banking in Ancient and Medieval India', Bombay, 1935, p. 25, Sharma, G.S., *Marwari Vyapari* (Hindi), Bikaner, 1988, pp. 9, 23-31, Sharma, G.D., '*Vyaparis* and *Mahajans* in Western Rajasthan During the 18th century' – *Essay in Medieval Economic History* (ed.) Satish Chandra, Vol. III, New Delhi, 1987, pp. 284-59. Bhadani, B.L., *Peasants, Artisans and Entrepreneurs*, Jaipur, 1999, pp. 338-59.
2. Income received by Rajput chiefs as Mughal *Mansabdars* in lieu of the salary many *Jagirs* were assigned to them.
3. *Kagad ri Bahi*, No.1, V.S. 1811 to No. 34 V.S. 1884 contain the orders, directions and the details of *Huwalas* and *Muqatas*. *Sawa Bahis* of different *Mandis* offer us the details of their commercial transactions and the income/expenditure of the *Mandis*, V.S. 1802 to 1885, and the *Jagat Bahis* provide us the details of the movement of the traders/merchants and import/export of various commodities. See A Descriptive List of Bikaner *Bahis*, Bikaner, (17-19C) 1982. Part I, R.S.A., Bikaner, pp. 78-119, 120-138, 142-173.
4. For instance an order runs as under – 'गा.सुवाई रो बोणियो बोपारीयो जोग्प तीथा अकरों रो माल थे लेवो छो वा. देवो छो तेरी जगात तल में सबखर लागै छै सु सबखर चुकाव देजो... । कातीसुद 15' *Kagad Bahi*, No. 4, V.S. 1831/1774, ff. 26-28, No. 10, V.S. 1854/1797 AD, ff. 20, 34, 51. Some other examples are quoted in *Sawa Bahi Mandi Sadar Bikaner*, No. 29, V.S. 1856-57/1799-1800 AD, ff. 3, 7, R.S.A., Bikaner.
5. *Bahi Sahukara Neni Hundiya Bheji Teri Vigat*, No. 241, V.S. 1726/1669 AD, *Sawa Bahi Mandi, Bikaner*, V.S. 1807-08/1750-51 AD, R.S.A., Bikaner.
6. Ibid., *Sawa Bahi Mandi Rajgarh*, No. 1, V.S. 1828, f. 2, *Sawa Bahi Sujangarh*, No. 7, V.S. 1909, f. 122, R.S.A., Bikaner.
7. Sometimes the merchants have been addrssed by their caste name as Oswal, Agrawal and Maheshwari. This suggests their dominance in mercantile activities. *Prachoon Kagad, Kagad ri Bahi*, No. 6, V.S. 1839, f. 43, R.S.A., Bikaner.
8. A *Sawa Bahi* of Bikaner of V.S. 1807-10 records following sub-castes of Oswal and Maheshwari in Bikaner-Singhvi, Daga, Sansukha, Kothari, Sihani, Dhannani Golecha, Pugalia, Sipani, Surana, Jaisalmeri Daga, Dungrani and Rathi Bothra, Sonawat, Bhopni, Asni, Mohnot, Rakhecha, Daswani, Ved Pugalia, Marothi Jhanwar, Saadni Pugalia, Medag, Muhta, Binnani, Rathi, Nathoni, Bagri, Daga Mashri, Lakhotia, Deghani and Dalal. *Sawa Bahi*

Mandi Sadar Bikaner, No. 4, V.S. 1807-10, ff. 135-39, R.S.A., Bikaner, Munshi, Sohan Lal, *Tawarikh Rajshri Bikaner*, Bikaner, 1898.

9. A 17th century traveller Ovington remarks, "The Banias are mainly addicted to prosecute their temproral interest and the amassing of treasure; and therefore will fly at securing of a pice, though they can command whole lakhs of rupees", Ovington, J., *A Voyage to Surat in the Year 1689* (ed.) Rawlinson, H.G., London, 1929, p. 165; When Banarasi Das (writer of '*Ardha Kathanak*') showed a punchant for scholarly pursuits, his "elders told him that too much study was meant for a Brahmin or a Bhat, the son of Vanik ought to sit in the shop." Cf. *The Cambridge Economic History of India* (ed.) Choudhary, T.R. and Habib, Irfan, Vol. I (C.1200-1750) (Reprint 1984), Orient Longman, Hyderabad, p. 343.
10. *Jagat Bahi,* No. 81, 1807/1750 AD, *Bikaner Bahiyat,* R.S.A., Bikaner
11. Ibid.
12. Ibid.
13. *Sawa Bahi Mandi Suratgarh,* No. 10, V.S. 1907/1850 AD, f. 25, R.S.A., Bikaner.
14. *Kagdon ri Bahi,* No. 3, V.S. 1827/1770 AD, *Desh re Jagat ri Bahi,* No. 7, V.S. 1858/1801 AD, RSAB.
15. *Chithi Khaton ri Bahi,* No. 6, V.S.1869/1812 AD, *Jagat Bahi,* No. 81, V.S. 1807/1750 AD; *Sawa Bahi Suratgarh,* No. 8, 1897/1840 AD, ff. 46-47.
16. *Sanad Parwana Bahi Jodhpur,* No. 2, V.S. 1822/1765 AD, Jodhpur records, R.S.A., Bikaner, Cf. Gupta, B.L., *Trade and Commerce in Rajasthan,* Jaipur, 1988, p. 32.
17. *Mandi re Amdani re Golak ri Bahi,* No. 146, V.S. 1889/1832 AD, f. 3, *Jagat ri Bahi,* No. 132, V.S. 1879/1822, f. 33, R.S.A., Bikaner. Capt. Powlett, *Gazetteer of Bikaner State,* p. 142.
18. Agrawal, Govind, *Potedar Sangrih ke Aprakashit Kagzaat* (Hindi), Bikaner, 1976, p. 13, In Bikaner some known *Sahukars,* were recorded in the *Bahi*-Lakho Singhvi, Bijay Ram Gandhi, Gopal Ram Purohit, Amarchand Singhvi, Sita Ram Purohit and Jadam Ram Ojha, *Sawa Bahi Mandi Sadar Bikaner,* No. 29, V.S. 1856-57, ff. 3, 7.
19. Agrawal, Govind, *Vanijya Vyapar Mein Muneem Gumaston ki Bhoomika* (Hindi), Churu, 1983, pp. 1-66, refers to multifarious and widespread commercial activities of the commercial house of Mirza Mal Poddar of Churu.
20. *Sawa Bahi Mandi Rajgarh,* No. 1, V.S. 1828/1771 AD, f. 2, *Sawa Bahi Mandi Sujangrah,* No. 7, V.S. 1909/1852 AD, ff. 94 & 122, R.S.A., Bikaner.

21. With the expansion of the trade and commerce in the state multifarious mercantile activities and pursuits were undertaken by different sections of the commercial classes during th second half of the 18th century and these continued up to 1828 AD in the state.
22. *Bikaner Gazal* (*Rajasthani*) Nahta, Agarchand collection, Bikaner (1709 AD) pp. 1-2; *Jain Kavi Udai Chand Rachit Bikaner Gazal,* Nahta, B.L., *Vaichariki*, Part I, Vol. 2-3. *Gazal* literature is also a good source of economic information. It is a poetic compostion in couplets describing the condition of trade-commerce, habitation and cultural heritage, composed by the Jain poets during Medieval Rajasthan. *Gazals* of different places have been traced and collected. '*Churu Mein Pracheen Haton ki Vigat*'– Govind Agrawal, 'Marushi', Year 2-3, Vol. 4-1, Churu, 1973, pp. 43-47.
23. '*Huwala soapa*' literally meant 'Handing over to somebody'. In fact, the work of revenue realization from villages were handed over to the state officials who were designated as *huwaladars.*
24. *Huwala Kagads* of *Kagad Bahis* testify it. *Kagad ri Bahis,* No. 2, V.S. 1820, ff. 2, 6, 8, 10; No. 3, V.S. 1827, f. 3-4; No. 6, V.S. 1839/1782 AD; No. 10, V.S. 1854/1797 AD; No. 11, V.S. 1859/1802 AD, R.S.A., Bikaner.
25. *Huwala Kagad, Kagad Bahi,* No. 4, V.S. 1831/1774 AD, R.S.A., Bikaner.
26. See *Muqata Kagad, Kagad Bahis,* No. 4, V.S. 1831/1774 AD, *Asadh Sudi* 3, No.7, V.S. 1840, *Kartik Bahi* 7, No. 10, V.S. 1854/1797 AD, ff. 2-3, *Sri Mandi ri Khata Teri Bahi,* No. 12, V.S. 1818 ff. 5-6; *Sawa Bahi Mandi Sadar Bikaner,* No. 20, V.S.1833, f. 40; *Sawa Bahi Mandi Rajgarh,* No. 5, V.S. 1843-44, f. 68(a), R.S.A., Bikaner.
27. *Kagad Bahi,* No. 1, V.S. 1811.
28. *Kagad Bahi,* No. 3, V.S. 1827, f. 8-b.
29. Ibid., f. 14-b.
30. Ibid., f. 50.
31. Ibid., f. 76.
32. *Kagad Bahi,* No. 4, V.S. 1831, f. 5.
33. *Sawa Bahi Mandi Sadar Bikaner,* No. 20, V.S. 1833, f. 40.
34. Ibid., No. 21, V.S. 1835-36, f. 18-b.
35. Ibid., f. 36-b.
36. *Sawa Bahi Mandi Sadar Bikaner,* No. 22, V.S. 1837, f. 43-b.
37. Ibid., f. 55(a).
38. Ibid., No. 23, V.S. 1838, f. 3(b).
39. *Sawa Bahi Rajgarh Mandi,* No. 5, V.S. 1843-44.
40. *Kagad Bahi,* No. 6, V.S. 1839, *Huwala Kagad,* f. 2.

41. *Sawa Bahi Mandi Sadar Bikaner*, No. 28, V.S. 1856-57, f. 36(b)
42. Ibid., f. 150.
43. *Kagad Bahi*, No. 10, V.S. 1854/1797 AD
44. *Sawa Bahi Mandi Bikanr*, No. 29, V.S. 1856-57, f. 124
45. Fagan, 'Report on the settlemnt of *Khalisa* villages of the Bikaner state', 1893, p. 16; *Bahi Sri Mandi re Jama Kharach ri*, No. 44, V.S. 1840/1783, ff. 2-3
46. *Sawa Bahi Mandi Sadar Bikaner*, No. 21, V.S. 1835-36/1778-79 AD, f. 118(b), R.S.A., Bikaner
47. *Kagad Bahi*, No. 12, V.S. 1859/1802 AD, ff. 12, 71-72, R.S.A., Bikaner.
48. *Sawa Bahi Lunkaransar*, No. 1, V.S. 1890/1833 AD, f. 45(b), R.S.A., Bikaner
49. *Prachoon Kagad, Kagad Bahi*, No. 9, V.S. 1851/1794, *Asadh Badi* 4, R.S.A., Bikaner
50. They generally wore the blanket of imported *pashmina* wool, therefore, they were called as *Pashmina wale Gusain*. See *Chitti Khaton ri Bahi*, No. 6, V.S. 1869/1812 AD
51. *Bahi Chitti Khaton ri*, No. 2, V.S. 1851/1794 AD No. 6, V.S. 1869/1812 AD, *Kagad Bahi*, No. 16, V.S.1867/1810 AD, ff. 18-19, Munshi, Sohan Lal, *Tawarikh Raj Shri Bikaner*, p. 248.
52. Ibid.
53. *Sawa Bahi Mandi Bikaner*, No. 2, V.S. 1802-03, f. 32(b). *Sawa Bahi Rajgarh Mandi*, No. 10, V.S. 1861-62, f. 24, R.S.A., Bikaner.
54. *Sawa Bahi Mandi Sadar Bikaner*, No. 2, V.S. 1802-03, f. 32(b).
55. Ibid., f.42(a).
56. *Sawa Bahi Mandi Sadar Bikaner*, No. 15, V.S. 1826, f. 89(a).
57. *Sawa Bahi Reni*, No. 1, V.S. 1814/1757, ff. 7, 15.
58. *Sawa Bahi Rajgarh*, No. 2, V.S. 1831-35, f. 45(b).
59. *Sawa Bahi Rajgarh*, No. 8, V.S. 1851-55, f. 4b.
60. Ibid., f. 106.
61. Ibid., No. 10, V.S. 1861-62, f. 24.
62. *Sawa Bahi Rajgarh*, No. 11, V.S. 1863, f. 11(b).
63. *Sawa Bahi Suratgarh*, No. 1, V.S. 1850, f. 119.
64. *Kagad Bahi*, No. 34; Marushri, Churu.
65. *Chitti wa Khaton Ri Bahi Samvat*, 1869, ff. 1-2.
66. Ibid., f. 3b.
67. Ibid., f. 5b.
68. Ibid., f. 6.
69. Ibid., f. 6b.
70. Ibid., ff. 2-3.
71. Ibid., f. 2.

72. Ibid., f. 3a.
73. Ibid., f. 2a.
74. Ibid., f. 4(a).
75. Ibid., f. 7.
76. In Marwar the rate of interest during 17th century ranged between 12% to 18% p.a. on state loans. Bhadani, B.L., *Peasants, Artisans and Entrepreneurs*, Jaipur, 1999, p. 324. But in Mewar in most cases the general rate of interest ranged between 10% to 30%, Sharma, G.N., *Social Life in Medieval Rajasthan*, Agra, 1965, p. 340.
77. *Kagad Bahi*, No. 34, V.S. 1885, f. 1, R.S.A., Bikaner.
78. A *Kagad* in this regard is available in the *Kagad Bahi* of 1813 AD runs as under– "श्री बीकानेर रे साहूकारों ओसवालों महेसरीयों समसुतों जोग्य तीथा जगात भरो ते उप्र आगे रुपीया उधार सदामद देवता हमें थे देवो नहीं सु देजो प्ररा न दीनों थोरे लेखो पासे मंडे छै सु कोई मंडसी सु हमें कागद बाचत पीण रुपीया देजो आधा काधण जुं म्हें दु.सी. हा. मुलतोणमल खंजोची मीगसर सुद 4 मु.रतनगढ।", *Kagad Badi*, No. 19/1, V.S. 1870/1813 AD R.S.A., Bikaner.
79. *Kagad Bahi*, No. 13, V.S. 1861/1804 AD, f. 58, R.S.A., Bikaner.
80. The rifle was not returned by the moneylender to the loanee till the interference of the state. *Kagad Bahi*, No. 13, V.S. 1861/1804, *Magh Sudi* 10, R.S.A., Bikaner.
81. *Kagad Bahi*, No. 16, V.S. 1867/1810 AD, *Phagun Badi* 9, R.S.A., Bikaner.
82. *Kagad Bahi*, No. 14, V.S. 1863-64/1806-07 AD, f.237, R.S.A., Bikaner.
83. *Kagad Bahi*, No. 15, V.S. 1866/1809 AD, R.S.A., Bikaner.
84. *Kagad Bahi*, No. 13, V.S. 1861/1804 AD, *Srawan Sudi 7*, R.S.A., Bikaner.
85. *Kagad Bahi*, No. 16, V.S. 1867/1810 AD, R.S.A., Bikaner.
86. In Marwar the rate of interest on commercial credit ranged between 9% to 18% p.a. in the 17th century, Bhadani, B.L., op. cit., pp. 321-323. In eastern Rajasthan, the rate of rural money lending ranged from 10 to 25% per annum in the 18th century. See Dilbagh Singh, 'The Role of Mahajans in the Rural Economy in the Eastern Rajasthan during the 18th Century', *Social Scientist*, No. 22, May, 1974, p. 24.
87. *Chitti Khaton ri Bahi*, No. 6, V.S. 1869/1812, R.S.A., Bikaner
88. Ibid, *Bahi Hundiyan Kivi Teri Vigat*, No. 241, V.S. 1726/1669 AD, R.S.A., Bikaner
89. *The Cambridge Economic History of India*. Vol. I (1200-1750 C.) (ed.) Choudhary, T.R. and Habib, Irfan, Delhi, 1982, pp. 346-47.
90. Charges for insurance cover charged by the merchant.

91. General commission charged by a firm that works as an intermediary in the transaction.
92. This was called *Hundawan*. It was charged by the *sahukar* for his services of transfer of money for a person to the place desired by him.
93. The *Bahis* refer both purposes for a *Hundi* writing. See "Bahi of Chithi and Khat of V.S. 1869 of Maharaja Surat Singh (1787-1828 AD) of Bikaner - A Study and an Annotation" by Kanti Lal Mathur (unpublished approved Dissertation for the degree of M.Phil. in 1989 by M.D.S. University, Ajmer, Rajasthan) p. 23.
94. *Bahi Lashkara Nu Neni Hundiyan Bheji Teri Vigat*, No. 241, V.S. 1726/1669 AD, *Bikaner Bahiyat*, R.S.A., Bikaner.
95. Ibid.
96. Ibid.
97. Ibid.
98. Ibid.
99. Ibid.
100. *Sawa Bahi Mandi Bikaner*, No. 3, V.S. 1805/1748 AD, f. 57(a).
101. Ibid., No. 4, V.S. 1807-10/1750-53 AD
102. *Sawa Bahi Rajgarh*, No. 1, V.S. 1828/1771 AD
103. Ibid., No. 7, V.S. 1848/1791 AD, f. 1126.
104. Ibid., No. 8, V.S. 1852/1795 AD, f. 141(b).
105. *Chitti Khatoon Ri Bahi*, No. 6, V.S. 1869/1812 AD, f.17(a).
106. *The Cambridge Economic History of India*, op. cit., pp. 346-47. 'The System of Bills of Exchange (*Hundis*) in the Mughal Empire', Habib, Irfan, PIHC, Muzaffarpur Session, 1972, pp. 290-303
107. *Hundis* generally were addressed to the *Shahs* called *Shahjog*, which were to be encashed by the concerned merchant. The *Shahs* were also called *Kothiwals* as the establishments of the affluent merchants were called *Kothis*.
108. *Hundiyan Kivi Teri Vigat*, No. 241, V.S. 1726/1669 AD, R.S.A., Bikaner.
109. Ibid.
110. Ibid.
111. Ibid. For detailed study see *Commercial Policy of the Mughals* by Pant, (Reprint), Delhi, 1978.
112. Ibid.
113. Ibid.
114. *Kagad Bahi*, No. 10, V.S. 1854/1797 AD, R.S.A., Bikaner.
115. Sharma, G.S., *Marwari vyapari*, Bikaner, 1988, p. 26.
116. See enclosed table.
117. Ibid.

118. Agarwal, Govind, *Samridha Bhartiya Beema Paddhati Unneesvi Sati Purvardh Mein*, (Hindi), Churu, 1987.
119. *Kagad Bahi*, No. 7, V.S. 1840/1783 AD, f. 17, Sharma, G.S., op. cit., p. 27.
120. *Kagad Bahi*, No. 20, V.S. 1871/1814 AD, f.71. Agrawal, Govind, *Churu Mandal ka Shodhpurna Itihas*, Ajmer, 1974, p. 481.
121. Ibid.
122. *Sawa Bahi Mandi Sadar Bikaner*, No. 4, V.S. 1807-10/1750-53 AD, f.45(a), R.S.A., Bikaner.
123. *Raznawa ri Bahi*, Nanag Ram Mirza Mal ki, V.S. 1883-87/1826-30 AD, ff. 184-85, 199-201; Cf. Sharma, G.S., *Marwari vyapari*, pp. 27-28.
124. *Sawa Bahi Mandi Rajgarh*, No. 1, V.S.1828/1771 AD, f. 6, R.S.A., Bikaner.
125. *Raznawa ri Bahi*, Nanag Ram Mirza Mal ki, V.S. 1883-87/1826-30 AD, Cf. Potedar collection, Churu. Regarding the types of *Bima* (Insurance) there ought to be a difference in the rates of the *Kaccha* and *Pacca Bima* as shown above. Because there was a difference in these two types of *Bimas*. In a *Pacca Bima* the insurance merchant was bound to deliver to his client the exact quantity and numbers of the goods insured at the destination, otherwise a compensation was to be paid. However, in a *Kaccha Bima* he was not liable to compensate for the damage caused to the insured goods in transit but he had to pay for the shortage if any.

    See for details, Agrawal, Govind, *Unnisavi Sati Purvardha men Samridha Bhartiya Bima Paddhati*, Chapter 3, Churu, 1987, pp. 27-38.
126. *Kagad Bahi*, No. 20, V.S. 1871, f. 71, R.S.A., Bikaner.
127. *Sawa Bahi Mandi Sadar Bikaner*, No. 4, V.S. 1807-10/1750-53 AD, f. 45(a), R.S.A., Bikaner.
128. Agarwal, Govind, *Churu Mandal ka Shodhpurna Itihas*, op. cit., p. 481.
129. *Shri Mandi ri Golak ro Lekho*, No. 61, V.S. 1855/1798 AD, ff. 1-2, R.S.A., Bikaner.
130. *Bikaner re Talake ri Mandi ro Jama Jod ri* (*Jagat Bahi*) No. 43, V.S. 1840, ff. 2-3, *Shri Mandi re Khata Teri Bahi*, No. 112, V.S. 1818/1761 AD, *Kagad Bahi*, No. 10, V.S. 1854/1797 AD, f. 3, R.S.A., Bikaner.
131. Powlett, p. 145; Agrawal, Govind, p. 476, Sharma, G.S., p. 31.
132. Powlett, p. 142.
133. Col. Tod., *Annals and Antiquities of Rajasthan*, Vol. II, (Reprint), Delhi, 1971, p. 1029.

134. *Shri Mandi re Jama Kharach ri Bahi,* No. 31, V.S. 1831, ff. 3-4, R.S.A., Bikaner.
135. *Bahi Bikaner ri Mandi re Jama Kharach ri,* No. 117, V.S. 1877/1820 AD, R.S.A., Bikaner.
136. Sharma, G.S., op. cit., p. 48.
137. *Kagad Bahi,* No. 22, V.S. 1873/1816, *Magh sudi,* R.S.A., Bikaner.
138. Ibid., No. 34, V.S. 1885/1828 AD
139. Sharma, G.S., op. cit., p. 48.

9

Crafts and Artisans

The craft production has been an important sector of the economy and the artisans played a significant role in satisfying the needs of different sections of rural and urban populations during the second half of the 18th and the early 19th century. The traditional village community crafts were not yet separated from the agriculture but was a complementary source of income to an agriculturist-craftsman, whereas in the towns it was becoming, more or less, an independent profession due to larger demands and commodity-money relations. These aspects have been vividly threshed out by modern scholars and researchers.[1]

The state *Bahis* testify to the existence and functioning of varied crafts at villages and at towns, on a varying level in Bikaner state. However, the nature and kind of information regarding crafts and artisans is very meagre and scattered too in the sources. The *Kagad Bahis*, *Sawa Bahis*, *Jagat* and *Byav Bahis*[2] do reflect some light on aspects related to the subject. The lack of proper information regarding the artisan class in the *Bahis* seems to be reflective of the contemporary caste discrimination and disparity in the social setup in Bikaner.

The Types of Craft Production

The craft production by artisans in Bikaner seems to have been organized largely into the following two forms–

(1) Rural-based village community crafts

(2) Urban-based small-scale commodity handicrafts

The first was the traditional form of rural community craft production adjunct with the agriculture. Secondly, in the towns (urban areas) crafts were not necessarily attached with agriculture but a full-fledged autonomous commodity production of crafts was done by the professional artisans. Evidences are available that some of the artisans like *Teli* (oilmen), *Sonar* (goldsmith), *Khati* (carpenter), *Kalal* (liquor distiller), *Chunpaz* (lime worker) and others were doing cultivation along with their crafts in village Jasarasar-Khariya Wati[3] and in Rajgarh town.[4] In Bikaner also, it is noticed that *Kumbhar* (potter) and *Khatis* had manufactured and sold their products.[5]

(1) RURAL BASED VILLAGE COMMUNITY CRAFTS

(a) Nature of Rural Crafts

The rural crafts were mainly based on the agricultural produce. They were closely connected with agriculture as the craftsmen also undertook the cultivation work. The artisans, grouped in castes, were discharging their hereditary caste occupations as community servants. The rural crafts were meant to cater for the elementary needs of the residents of the village. In spite of the outside contacts of the villages, during the period under study, more or less, were still functioning as self-sufficient units.[6]

(b) Rural Crafts

There used to be some traditional crafts in almost every village to meet the local demands.[7] Out of them some were seasonal and irregular crafts, while others were regular crafts undertaken by the artisans. The work of oil extraction by *Telis* (oilmen) and green grocery growing by *Malis* (gardeners) were quite seasonal. But *Suthar* (carpenter), *Luhar* (blacksmith), *Dhedh* (leather worker), *Mochi* (shoe-maker), *Kalal* (liquor distiller), *Kumbhar* (potter) and weavers were some other craftsmen available in villages of Bikaner working on a regular basis. They run their rural craft single-handedly and sometimes were assisted by their family members as well. Whatever was produced with the raw material being obtained from the village agricultural produce was crude, simple and rather unfinished in quality. Also, their scale of production was restricted to the village requirements only.

Edible oil extraction by a *Teli* (oil presser) through his *Ghani* (wooden press) was a useful and necessary seasonal rural crafts. By compressing the oil seeds of seasame (*til*) mustard (*sarson*) in his *ghani* (oil press) he could extract the unrefined edible oil for consumption. Evidence of oil extraction at Lunkaransar is available in *Kagad Bahi* of 1770 AD Muhta Jagroop of Bikaner was sent to get oil extracted from Lunkaransar of Rs. 101 for the need of the royal household.[8]

A *Khati* or *Suthar* generally repaired and manufactured cots, ploughs, *palans*, grills for well, the necessary domestic wooden wares and agricultural implements.[9] The village *Luhar* (blacksmith) manufactured agricultural implements and domestic items like knives, nails, plough-mouth and sickles. by smelting and moulding the iron.[10] *Balais* were engaged in tanning of animal skins, whereas a *Chamar* (cobbler) made shoes (*Jutiyan*), *Charas* (leather bucket for draining water out from a well) and leather ropes.

The village *Kumbhar* (potter) manufactured earthenware of different sizes for cooking food, drinking water and storing grains and seeds.

A group of small villages or a big village usually had one *Kalal* (liquor distiller) for selling and distilling liquor.[11] The liquor was sold outside the village boundary. A fine of Rs. 18 *Annas* 8 and *Dam* 25 were realized from Amariya Kalal in Nohar in 1757 AD for he extracted liquor on *Gyarsi,* i.e. the 11th day of every fortnight of a month.[12] It seems that the state discouraged extracting or distilling the liquor on certain auspicious days.

Chhajlas (the baskets of grass-sticks) were being manufactured for winnowing grains at fields, tailoring of bags of coarse cloth, spinning of cotton, and hairs of animals like camel and goats, preparation of *gur* (raw sugar) were some other crafts also being undertaken in the rural sector.[13]

The spare time of an agriculturist-artisan was used in making minor repairs of their agricultural appliances.[14] The rural women also took interest in the cottage crafts of spinning cotton and hairs on their spinning wheels or *Charkhas*[15] apart from their regular domestic works.

(c) Relations of Artisans with Village Community

(i) Maintenance of Village Artisans

Since, an artisan was working under a social obligation to the village community, therefore, responsibility of his maintenance was of the village society. Hence, on the basis of *Jajmani* system,[16] in lieu of his services, an artisan received remuneration in kind. Out of the village agricultural production and often in the exchange of commodities.[17] Sometimes, he was granted some piece of tax-free-agricultural land called *Muafi* land for maintenance. For instance, a Luhar Dedo son of Gidhe in *qasba* Reni was granted a tax free land in 1774 AD.[18]

(ii) Social Status of Artisan in Village Society

The artisan class as a whole carry a lower social status in the caste stratification of village communities and hence they were called village servants. Generally, a term is used for them in records i.e. *Karu-kamin*.[19] The *Karu* means artisan-worker and *Kamin* meant a menial (*Kamin*, a Persian word means small or insignificant). They though, formed an inalienable segment of the rural economic organization and acquired important place in social setup, were disparaged. Being village servants (generally of privileged castes of Brahmins, Rajputs and Vaishyas) they had some hereditary and customary rights. They received *Kansa*[20], *Petias*[21] and *Kharchi* (expenses) on occasions, like Holi, Diwali, marriages and other such occasions while they were supposed to offer their services. Rs. 31 was distributed by the state among artisans and others as *Kharchi* (for petty expenses) among *Potters, Suthar, Gandhi, Doom, Hamals, Tamboli* and *Chopdar* in 1747 AD[22] in Bikaner.

Similarly, the rural artisans as hereditary servants of the village community were often enlisted by the peasants for the auxiliary agriculture work.[23] For instance, a village barber offered his services as a healing worker, village veterinarian, a cook, a messenger in a marriage and also a dancer in a gathering.[24]

Apart from of this caste distinction between the artisan classes and the upper castes there used to be a caste distinction among artisans themselves. Some of the menials *Halalkhor* (cleaner), butcher, scavenger, *Dedh-Chamar* (leather workers), *Kalal* were usually considered still lower among the artisans themselves, perhaps due to their unclean occupations they were despised and offered lower status.[25]

Thus, the traditional village crafts were not many but meant to serve and satisfy the village needs. They were assigned a secondary status in the village community. However, they enjoyed some customary rights on festivals and special occasions.

(2) URBAN-BASED SMALL-SCALE COMMODITY HANDICARFTS

(a) Forms of Urban Handicrafts

The town-based small-scale commodity handicrafts was a new form of economic organization of crafts, a qualitatively new stage compared with the traditional village community crafts and the work of non-community artisans to the order of customers.[26]

During the period under review three forms of small-scale commodity handicraft production existed in Bikaner.

First, that was represented by a combination of handicraft production for the market in peasant households with practising agriculture work.

Second, that was carried on by the professional artisans—the commodity producers in towns[27] without practising agriculture.

And lastly, they worked in the state *Karkhanas* on a regular salary basis as the skilled artisans to satisfy the needs of the royal household.[28]

(b) Factors of Growth and Development of the Urban Craft

The growth and steady development of the urban craft/cottage industry and a consequently larger production as a commodity to meet the increasing demands was presumably due to the following factors–

(i) The decline and disintegration of the Mughal empire

in the mid-18th century diminished its grandeur and glory and accordingly reduced patronship to skilled artisans and craftsmen. Artisans and craftsmen, skilled in a variety of vocations, were out of Mughal employment and services leading to loss of subsistence. Being displaced from Delhi were now seeking employment at towns in Rajputana feudal states.[29] They were getting employment in towns of Bikaner also. The *Usta* painters, *Shoregars* (makers of explosives) and other skilled artisans received employment in the state. Usta Isso Kayam, Usta Hamid, Jeevan Sahu, Usta Abu Mehmad, Usta Hasan and some others were granted employment in Bikaner and they were granted land in village Rasisar and in Bikaner.[30] These artisans brought with them the new forms and designs and were now introducing the same in the state resulting in a synthesis of taste, arts and fashions in the later 18th century.[31]

(ii) The native chiefs of Bikaner had also witnessed for long, the Mughal grandeur and luxury on being their *Mansabdars*. They had developed a taste for clothes, food and luxury dwellings and now, therefore, imitating this luxurious life in their own state when they had become autonomous chiefs. They also adopted the system of *Karkhanas* (state establishment) of centre in their own principality.[32] In these *Karkhanas* they provided employment to those migrant artisans and other local skilled artisans for meeting their luxury and military requirements.

(iii) Moreover, the richer classes of feudals, merchants and traders might have developed a desire for more decorative products in wool, metal, stone, leather, etc.[33] Their demands for these items further increased growth and enlargement of the town-based cottage commodity crafts in the following areas–

(c) Various Urbans Crafts

The urban cottage industry consisted of various traditional and professional crafts as under–

(i) Wool Textile

Animal rearing being an important occupation in Bikaner territory the production and supply of finest wool in India have been possible.[34] Sheep are reared for wool in the desert area and owing to the most succulent grasses available here, the wool of good quality is obtained.[35] The most popular woollen articles of Bikaner have been the woollen blanket, *Lohis*, Shawls, carpets, flannels, and *Ghuggis* (rain covers). Col. Tod in his 'Annals' bears the testimony to the antiquity of the woollen industry. Erskine also corroborates it.[36] The wool of Bikaner was particularly of superior quality, therefore, it has a wider market in Sindh, Multan, Delhi, Ujjain and other parts of India.[37] *Jagat Bahi* Bikaner of 1750 AD records that 18 *maunds* of woollen cloth was carried away to Delhi from Bikaner by a trader Hansu Fatehpuria.[38] It was also famous for coloured blankets.[39]

(ii) Cotton Textile

Cotton cloth of low grade was produced which was called *Dowti* and *Khaddar* for the use of general masses as cotton was not profusely produced in the desert. The fine cloth like muslins from Bengal and *chintz* from Burhanpur and *Chanderi* were imported in Bikaner but their use was limited to richer people, its being expensive.

Sawa Bahi Sujangarh of 1851 AD mentions that cotton bags were prepared in Sujangarh to be carried away out by princess Chhoti Bai to Jaipur in 1851 AD and material like *Dowti* etc. were purchased for *Anna* 7 and *Takka* 1.[40]

(iii) Wood Work

In towns, there used to be many skilled *Suthars* (carpenters) engaged in manufacturing bullock carts, carts for carrying cannons, cots, wooden ladders, windows and doors, wheels for carts, *Raths*, palanquins, saddles, *pallans*, Scabbards for swords, grills of well (*Bhuwan*), lid covers of water tanks, the parts of *Ghani* (wooden press) of *Teli* and handles of agricultural implements.[41]

Sawa Bahi Lunkaransar of 1831 AD records that skilled carpenters of Bikaner were called to Lunkaransar to manufacture wooden ladders in 1831 AD and were paid Rs.26 *Annas* 4 for 2 ladders.[42]

Saddles and cartwheels were the famous works discharged at Rajgarh and Bikaner. In 1780 AD two cannon carts were manufactured at Rajgarh for Rs. 123 *Anna* 14 and *Dam* 19.[43] Wooden scabbards were being exported to *Bap* village in Jaisalmer from Bikaner.[44] Udai Prahlad and Ratno were popular carpenter in Rajgarh and material for the wooden articles were locally procured.[45]

(iv) Metal Works

Bikaner was also known for manufacturing fighting weapons like sword blades, match locks, daggers, iron lances, tin boxes & iron brass and copper wares.[46] The industry in sword handles had reached a high state of proficiency and the products were in great demand for local use and also for export to other parts of India.[47] Jatu Ratan Singh, Dungar Singh and others were entrusted the work of manufacturing under supervisors of *Karkhana* as many as 500 *Bandooks* (rifles) @ Rs.4 per *Bandook* without paying any taxes/cesses.[48]

The blacksmith also produced agricultural implements like spades, spikes (खूँटे), axis, pitch forks, sickles, weeding hoes, (गैंची) etc. *Sawa Bahi Rajgarh* of 1781 AD mentions that two iron locks costing Rs. 14 were purchased in Bikaner and sent to Rajgarh.[49] It seems that locks were also manufactured over here. Spades of iron were purchased in *Sujangarh Mandi* in 1851 AD[50] for clearing sand. Handcuffs of iron were manufactured locally in Anupgarh in 1753 AD for Takha 1½[51] Rifles were also repaired by *Lohars* in 1771 AD in *Rajgarh*.[52]

The goldsmith or silversmith also manufactured ornaments and wares skillfully in Bikaner. *Byav ri Bahi* of 1770 AD speaks that certain ornament like *kankan,* Ring *Nath* and necklace of gold and domestic wares of silver like *lota*, glass and plates were being prepared by Gumano and Prabhu, the goldsmith of Bikaner on the occasion of the marriage of Princess Suraj Kanwar.[53] Devchand was a known jeweller of Bikaner as records the *Sawa Bahi* of Bikaner of 1750 AD.[54]

(v) Leather Works

Sawa Bahi Bikaner of 1758-59 AD testifies that the artisans engaged in the leather work were *mochis* and *chamars.* Items like shoes, leather buckets, *Mashaqs* or *Pakhal* and leather cases for guns were manufactured and were in demand.[55] A *mashaq* of leather costed Rs. 2 *Annas* 12 and three sets of reins of horses costed *Annas* 12. A big drum was inlaid by leather in Rs. 3 in Rajgarh in 1774 AD.[56] Saddles originally made of cloth and stuffed with cotton were replaced by leather.

(vi) Bangle Works

Bikaner possessed expert artists for making ivory and *lac* bangles inlaid or barnished. *Churis* (Bangles) or ivory bracelets were popular here. The craftsmen engaged in this industry were known as *Churigar* (artist of ivory bangle) and *Lakhara* (artist of *lac* bangles).[57] The *lac* for *churis* was imported from Multan.[58] The *lac churis* were popular among common people whereas richer or royal family used ivory *churi. Sawa Bahi Bikaner* of 1745 AD quotes that Rs. 142 and *Annas* 6 and *Takka* 2 were paid for sets of *Chura* of ivory for royal family.[59] Danti Gopinath and Kabir were known *Churigar* of Bikaner.[60] Kabir made six pairs of beautiful ivory bangles costing Rs. 54 *Takka* 1 and *Dam* 15.[61] Col. Tod provides us cost of a set of ivory bangles between Rs. 15 to Rs. 35.[62] It is significant to point out that the ivory was reaching to Bikaner from Africa via Sindh and Gujrat.[63]

(vii) Printing and Dyeing Work

Printing and dyeing of cloth were done in Bikaner by *Chheepa* (printers) and *Rangara* or *Leelgar* (dyers) as they were called respectively. Rajaldesar was known for dyeing work.[64]

(viii) Building Industry

Building industry was also in a good prospects and skilled, semi-skilled artisans and labourers were largely engaged in it. They were called *Maimar*[65] (mason) and *majoor* (labourer). The lime worker were actively engaged in producing lime for construction and white washing work. He was called *Chunpaz*[66] (lime worker). A *Silawat* was an expertise in stone cutting and carving and engaged in creating beautiful edifices over here. The old buildings and palaces are evident of it in Bikaner.[67] Some *Karigar* (skilled mason) of Jaipur and south India (Deccan) were also worked over here in the construction work.[68]

(ix) Painting Work

Painting work and beautiful designs with golden and silver colours were being done in Bikaner. *Kuppis* (elliptical shaped flat container) of camel hide of typical designs with minute decorative golden painting and other lacquer work on them were admirably done by *Usta* painters.[69] They were among those migrants from Delhi after the decline of the Mughal empire who received employment in Bikaner.[70] They were very expert in decorative paintings, walls and ceilings of palaces and made unprecedented contributions in royal palaces by their *Usta Qalam* (brush or instrument for painting).

(x) Brick Industry

The brick making industry was also functioning in the state. Artisan of it was called *Pazabgir*. The necessary sticking mud for constructing bricks was unearthed at various places like Suratgarh, Hanumangarh and Bikaner.[71] The *Kacchi* (unbaked) and *Pacci* (baked) bricks of uniform size were manufactured for constructional work. A brick was made up through a certain process. The grinded wet mud was framed in a particular size and later stacked to dry-up. *Kamthana Bahis* have also the references of the use of *Kacchi* and *Pacci* bricks.[72]

(xi) Other Crafts

Apart from these crafts there were some more crafts undertaken in varying scales in Bikaner. Entwiners, *Manihars*, tailors and potters were earning their livelihood. The salt workers were also producing salt at Lunkaransar and Chhapar (Sujangarh).[73] The *sajji* extraction work at Anupgarh was also done by local people.

(d) The Nature of Urban Craft

The town handicrafts were more in nature of a commercial

production. They had a wider clientele as ruling classes, feudals and elites were living in the towns. Therefore, their output had to be large and was more improved and were also assisted sometimes by few apprentices on wages.

The skilled artisans and craftsmen, local and migrants were employed in the state *karkhanas*. These were owned by the chiefs of the state to meet out articles of luxury and military requiremtnts. Therefore, all these contributed to the steady growth in the period under study.

(e) Relations of Artisans with Urban Population

It is interesting to note that the craft production in the town was not a service but a commodity being produced for the money. We have evidences of marketing and exporting such commodities. The woollen products like blankets, *lunkaras,* etc. were sent out as stated above.[74] Potters of village Meghana have been found to have sold his earthen wares.[75] It shows that commodity-money relations and commercialization had emerged in the towns. So, artisans had no obligations towards the urban population as they had in the villages under the *Jajmani* system. It was a stage towards the separation of agriculture from crafts in towns.

(f) Changes in the Nature of Urban Craft

The urban crafts, thus, underwent a significant change both in quality and quantity as well as in the nature of production.[76] However, it is difficult to appreciate the degree of separation of craft (cottage industry) from agriculture[77] but certainly it was intensified during the late 18th and early 19th century resulting in seasonal unemployment of artisans and absence of the community maintenance system, i.e. *Jajmani* system[78] which led to occasional starvation in famines and droughts.

The change in itself was a cumulative impact of various elements like the population growth and urbanization process to some extent. The growth and development of trade and commerce further encouraged the process.

(3) STATE AND THE ARTISANS' CLASS

(1) Taxes and Cesses on Artisans

The relationship between the artisans and their consumers seems to have undergone a change in the urban centres. In the rural sector, the *Jajmani* system continued but in the urban social sector money-commodity relationship emerged. This is evident from the fact that in the urban centres, the state realized taxes from the income of the artisans.

Almost all occupational artisans were to pay professional taxes/cesses to the state. For instance, a carpenter was to pay Rs. 2 per annum known as *Bansole ki Bhanchh*.[79] A *Rangara* was to pay a tax @ Rs. 2 *Takka* 2 per *pata* (lot of dyeing) known as *Rangara Re Pate Ra*[80] in Rajaldesar. Likewise, *Kumbhar, Teli, Goldsmith, Silawat, Chheepas* and others were subjected to pay the taxes on their occupation. Details of these taxes have been provided in Chapter-4 - 'Sources of Income'. The potters and *Suthar* of village Madh (near Kolayat) were supposed to pay an annual regular levy of Rs. 3 for Kolayat fair (Rs.2 for fodder and Re.1 for fair).[81] The taxes were relaxed by the state whenever felt heavy by them.

(2) State Protection to Artisan Class

State administration, in turn, encouraged and provided protection to artisans, local or migrants and also employed in *Karkhanas*. State encouraged them with rewards and honours. *Dupatta* and *Pagh* were bestowed upon *Luhar* of Churu in 1746 AD while a *Phenta* (turban) and a pair of *Kara* (golden) were given to *Silawat* Imart in Bikaner.[82]

The state put its all efforts to persuade artisans to stay into their native places and to continue their vocations. When some *Telis* (oilmen) of Lunkaransar and adjacent villages were leaving villages due to excessive taxes and private debts, the state assured them that nothing other than the due would be realized and the private debt would be suspended for post dates.[83] *Luhar* families of Uvad Ahmed and Mehraju were leaving Nohar to migrate to Bithede (place near Patiala in the Punjab) were rehabilitated in Nohar and *Jagat* levied on grains, they had brought for sowing were exempted.[84] *Kumbhar* families of Suratgarh were paid Rs. 6 to rehabilitate while they were intending to leave the place in 1799 AD.[85] It seems that the state assured incentives to stay in native places.

Tax exemptions and remissions were also granted as an incentive to the artisans. The *Kumbhars* (potters) of villages Meghana were exempted of *Jagat* on their sale of earthen wares and the grains of seeds they brought for sowing.[86] The *Hazuria Suthars* of village Sujasar were exempted of *Bansole Re Bhanchh* being employed in state services.[87]

The interest free loans and state help was provided to a *teli* Wadhu of *qasba* Reni. An interest free loan of Rs. 15 was provided to him to rehabilitate in Rajgarh as his *Ghani* (wooden press) was set on fire and ox taxen away by Sikhs in loot in 1771 AD. He was provided with an ox and his *ghani* re-established at Rajgarh.[88] Some *Usta* artisans were granted state help ranging from Rs. 20 to 50 each on the occasion of the marriages of their wards.[89]

Apart from these favours, some land grants were also given to some of the artisans in lieu of their *Chakri* alongwith some special favours. *Parwana Bahi* of 1743-1843 AD mentions that various *Parwana* were issued in favour of some *Usta Karigar* assigning land grants. *Usta* Isso Kayam, *Usta* Hamid, *Usta* Abud Isso and *Usta* Hasan were assigned tax free land in Rasisar village near Bikaner for their services.[90] *Luhar* Dedo was granted land in Reni in 1774 AD[91] while *Suthars* Natho, Narain, Chataro and Ram Chand were given tax free land in villages Jagdewala, Balowala, Sihoni Ro Bas and in Kodamdesar respectively in different years 1773 to 1779 AD.[92] A *Silawat* Akho in 1791 AD was granted special favour while employing in state *Karkhana* at Rs. 7 as monthly salary. He was authorized to receive a *Mohar* at every delivery of a child in the royal household, a *Naler* (coconut) on every transaction of land in Bikaner city and a facility of using waters of Anupsagar well. A special permission to enter into the *Zanana Diodi* (female private apartment) in the royal palace was granted for his work.[93] Some old *Pattas* of land of *Kansaras* and *Rangaras* were revised.[94]

Apart from the encouragement, the state often took

customary *Begar* as usual from the artisans. Potters of Bikaner were subjected to provide clay wares on the Holi, Diwali and Teej festivals as *Begar*.[95]

(4) WAGES OF ARTISANS AND LABOURERS

The *Kamthana Bahis* mention daily cash wages for various types of artisans and labourers engaged in the construction work at the Bikaner fort. It helps us to understand the wage structure of the daily-wage earners in the second half of the 18th century. The available data of wages in the *Kamthana Bahi* of 1751 AD (V.S. 1808)[96] have been classified into two professional groups as superior and ordinary of the artisans and labourers as under:

Table 9.1: Wage Structure of Artisans and Labourers[97]

Year (1)		*Artisan/Labourer* (2)		*Wages (per day) Rs. As.-Pice* (3)
1751 AD (V.S.1808)	1.	Mason (*Karigar*)	Superior	0-4-0
			Ordinary	0-1-3
	2.	*Usta* (painter)		0-2-2
	3.	Labour (Male)	Superior	0-2-2
			Ordinary	-
	4.	*Chungar*	Superior	0-3-0
	5.	*Suthar*		0-3-3
	6.	*Luhar*		0-1-3
	7.	*Silawat* (Stone worker & carver)	Superior	0-4-0
			Ordinary	0-3-2
1754 AD[98] (V.S.1811)	8.	*Jaipuria* mason	Superior	0-10-0
			Ordinary	0-6-0
	9.	*Usta*		0-10-0
	10.	Deccani majoor	Superior	0-8-0
			Ordinary	0-2-2

The above Table 9.1 shows that with the number of working days in a month being 30 the rate of daily wages of artisans to labourers ranged as low as 4 *Annas* to 1.3 *Annas*. It seems that abundance of labour availability forced the wages to be low. Moreover, the artisans and labourers brought from Jaipur and Deccan must have specialized in specific jobs which possibly explain the higher wages being given to them compared to local artisans and labourers. It further shows that the required professional expertise was not available in Bikaner and hence brought from outside.[99] Presumably, these low wages to the local artisans and labourers were supplemented by the *petias* in kind. The practice of giving grains and its inclusion in the wages had became a common feature in those days.

(5) CONTRIBUTION OF ARTISANS IN THE ECONOMY

Being producers they had contributed significantly to the state economy and satisfied the requirements of different sections of population as well as met out the needs of the royal household. Their manufacturing supplemented further the growth of commercial activities to some extent. Apart of it, their artistic and architectural contribution was also worth noticeable. Buildings and palaces, fortress and *havelies* were constructed with prominent carving and paintings resulting in generation of the employment.

The foregoing descriptions enable us to draw following concluding points that Artisans both of rural and urban areas in their distinctive forms, i.e. community craft and commodity crafts played an important role in the feudal economy of Bikaner during the period of study. The rural craft was combined with agriculture while in town it began to be separated. The process became more acute in the late 18th and early 19th century resulting in changes in the traditional agrarian relations. The caste system played a decisive role in artisan's life. The source material at our disposal does not enable us presently, to determine, even approximately, the proportion of the craft production at rural or town level. It can be presumed that it was widespread, embracing a large sum of population before the colonial era began in the state.

REFERENCES

1. Chicherov, A.I., *India, Economic Development in the 16th-18th Centuries, Outline History of Crafts and Trade,* (Eng. Tr.) Lahore, 1976, Chapters II, III & IV. Habib, Irfan, *Agrarian System of Mughal India* (*1556-1707*), OUP, 2nd ed., 1999, pp. 62-68, 144-160.

2. *Kagad Bahis*, No. 2, V.S. 1820/1763 AD, No. 3, V.S. 1827/1770 AD, No. 4, V.S. 1831/1774 AD, No. 14, V.S. 1864/1807 AD, No. 18, V.S. 1868/1811 AD, No. 26, V.S. 1877/1820 AD, No. 28, V.S. 1879/1822; *Byav Bahi*, No. 159, V.S. 1827/1770 AD, *Sawa Bahi* of Bikaner, No.22, V.S. 1837-38/1780-81 AD, *Sawa Bahi Lunkaransar*, No. 1, V.S. 1890/1833 AD *Bahi Churu Re Sahe Ri- Jagat Bahi*, No. 114, V.S. 1877/1820 AD, *Bahi Dhan Re Nekal Ri-Jagat Re Chowko Navo Bethi Teri*, No. 71, V.S. 1858/1801 AD, R.S.A., Bikaner.
3. Details of their doing cultivation and paying *Beghedi* (cash land tax) to the state are mentioned in the *bahi*, See *Lekho Jasarasar Khariya Wati Ro - Bahi Churu Re Sahe Ri (Jagat Bahi)*, No. 114, V.S. 1877/1820 AD *Telis* also paid tax on their craft of oil extraction in that village.
4. *Bahi Punia Re Pargana Ri*, No. 123, V.S. 1827/1770 AD
5. *Kagad bahi*, No. 4, V.S. 1831/1774 AD, f. 41, R.S.A., Bikaner.
6. Habib, Irfan, op. cit., p.144.
7. In village Jasarasar Khariyawati (Churu) there were *Telis, Lohars, Sonars, Chungar, Khati, Mali, Nai, Kumbhar* and *Kalal* as well. *Lekho Jasarasar Khariyawati Ro - Churu Re Sahe Ri*, No. 114, V.S. 1877/1820 AD, R.S.A., Bikaner.
8. *Kagad Bahi*, No. 3, V.S. 1827/1770 AD, R.S.A., Bikaner.
9. *Sawa Bahi Rajgarh*, No. 1, V.S. 1828/1771 AD, f. 13(a), No. 9, V.S. 1837/1780 AD, f. 129(b), R.S.A., Bikaner.
10. Four and half maunds of iron costing Re. 1 and *Anna* 3 were used for making a gate of iron in Rajgarh in 1802 AD *Sawa Bahi Rajgarh*, No. 9, V.S. 1859/1802 AD, f. 141.
11. *Jagat Bahi Nohar*, V.S. 1814/1757 AD, R.S.A., Bikaner. Sharma, G.N., *Social Life in Medieval Rajasthan*, op. cit., p. 296.
12. *Ighyaras*, the 11th day of every month is one of the auspicious days when the liquor distilling was prohibited. *Ighyaras* falls twice in a month and therefore atleast for two days in a month distilling was prohibited. *Sawa Bahi Nohar*, No. 1, V.S. 1822/1765 AD, R.S.A., Bikaner.
13. *Sawa Bahi Sujangarh*, No. 7, V.S. 1908/1851 AD, ff. 107-08. *Sawa Bahi Suratgarh*, No. 1, V.S. 1850/1793 AD, f. 129. *Sawa Bahi Rajgarh*, No. 8, V.S. 1851/1794 AD, f. 110, No. 9, V.S. 1859/1802 AD, f. 141; No. 10, V.S. 1861/1804 AD, f. 41, R.S.A., Bikaner.
14. Sharma, G.N., op. cit., p. 297.
15. Ibid.
16. The *Jajmani* system was the traditional system of collective maintenance of the artisans by the village community and the payments to them of a remuneration in kind. It was wide spreadly

adopted in rural area in 17th-18th century, more or less, all over India and continued in early 19th century also. Chicherov, A.I., op. cit., pp. 25, 28.

Choudhary, T.R., *Cambridge Economic History of India*, op. cit., p. 279. Habid, Irfan, *Agrarian System of Mughal India*, The system has been discussed in detail. See pp. 157-58.

17. Usually, the peasants of a village got the items of an artisan in exchange of grains in the village under *Barter* system.
18. *Parwana Bahi*, No. 4, V.S. 1800-1900/1743-1843 AD, R.S.A., Bikaner.
19. *Kagad Bahi*, No. 4, V.S. 1831/1774 AD, R.S.A., Bikaner.
20. *Kansa* is a prepared food.
21. *Petia* is raw material of food for a staple diet.
22. *Sawa Bahi Mandi Bikaner*, No. 2, V.S. 1804/1747 AD, f. 47(a), R.S.A., Bikaner.
23. Chicherov, A.I., op. cit., p. 20, *Cambridge Eco. History of India*, op. cit., p. 279.
24. Chicherov, A.I., op. cit., p. 20.
25. Choudhary, T.R. in *Cambridge Economic History of India* remarks in this regards that "It was virtually impossible for an artisan to aspire to a higher social status and one imagines like the untouchable who had accepted the untouchability as a part of God given order, the manufacturer accepted his economic and social situation as unalterable facts." See p. 278.
26. Chicherao, A.I., op. cit., p. 44.
27. Ibid.
28. *Sawa Bahi Bikaner*, No. 2, V.S. 1804/1747 AD, f. 47(a), R.S.A., Bikaner.
29. After Farrukhsiyar (1719) the artists and craftmen of Delhi began to migrate to the *Subas* (provinces) and states to seek patronage from the Governors or the *Rajput Rajas* of Rajputana. This exodus was complete during the reign of Mohd. Shah. A number of such skilled craftsmen were employed by the rulers of Rajputana. Saxena, Malti, op. cit., p. 99.
30. *Parwana Bahi Bikaner*, No. 4, V.S. 1800-1900/1743-1843 AD, R.S.A., Bikaner.
31. Saxena, Malti, op. cit., pp. 99-100.
32. *Karkhanas* were the royal establishments to fulfil various types of needs of the royal household. Sultan Firoz Tughlaq had 36 *Karkhanas* for his needs. Later, the Mughals also followed this pattern and had many *Karkhanas* for the Imperial requirements. In Rajputana the chiefs of *Amber* and then other chiefs adopted

the Imperial pattern of *Karkhanas*. In Bikaner there were various *Karkhana* viz. *Modikhana, Gangajal Karkhana, Kirkirkhana, Farrashkhana, Sutarkhana, Peelkhana, Toshakhana* etc. The *Bahis* pertaining to these department are available in the Rajasthan State Archives, Bikaner.

33. Saxena, Malti, op. cit., pp. 99-100.
34. Dhari, Alakh, *Life and Exploits of Raja Rai Singh of Bikaner*, Bikaner, 1934, pp. 180-81. *Jagat Bahi Bikaner*, No. 81, V.S. 1807/1750 AD, Col. Tod, op. cit., Vol. II, p. 1158.
35. Ibid.
36. Tod, op. cit., Erskine, p. 211.
37. *Jagat Bahi Bikaner*, No. 81, V.S. 1807/1750 AD, R.S.A., Bikaner.
38. Ibid.
39. *Sawa Bahi Mandi Bikaner*, No. 4, V.S. 1807-10/1750-53 AD
40. *Sawa Bahi Sujangarh*, No. 7, V.S. 1908/1851 AD
41. *Sawa Bahi Rajgarh*, No. 1, V.S. 1828/1771 AD, ff. 12, 181; No. 2, V.S. 1831-35/1774-79 AD, f. 67; No. 9, V.S. 1855-60/1798-1803 AD, f. 33, *Sawa Bahi Lunkaransar*, No.1, 1888/1831 AD
42. Ibid., f. 18(b).
43. *Sawa Bahi Rajgarh*, No. 3, V.S. 1837/1780 AD, f. 129; No. 2, 1831-34/1774-77 AD, f. 38; No. 9, V.S. 1855-60/1798-1803 AD, f. 33.
44. *Sawa Bahi Mandi Bikaner*, No. 4, V.S. 1807-10/1750-53 AD f. 3
45. Ibid.
46. Tod, op. cit., Vol. II, pp. 126-127.
47. Ibid.
48. *Bhaiya* records, Non-Archival Section Bikaner, *Basta* No.1, *Parwana-Rukka* etc., *Likhant-Parwana* Dated *Bhadwa Sudi* 10, V.S. 1873/1816 AD, R.S.A., Bikaner.
49. *Sawa Bahi Rajgarh*, No. 3, V.S. 1838/1781 AD, f. 154; R.S.A., Bikaner.
50. *Sawa Bahi Sujangarh*, No. 7, V.S. 1908/1851 AD ff.107-108, R.S.A., Bikaner.
51. *Sawa Bahi Anupgarh*, No. 1, V.S. 1810/1753 AD R.S.A., Bikaner.
52. *Sawa Bahi Rajgarh*, No. 1, V.S. 1828/1771 AD, f. 79(a).
53. *Byav Ri Bahi*, No. 159, V.S. 1827/1770 AD, R.S.A., Bikaner.
54. *Sawa Bahi Mandi Bikaner*, No. 4, V.S. 1807-10/1750-53 AD, R.S.A., Bikaner. A Research Paper was presented and approved for the publication in the proceedings of the National Seminar on the *Science and Technology in Rajasthan: In the Historical Perspective* sponsored by I.C.H.R., New Delhi and organised by Department of History, J.N.V. University, Jodhpur during Febrary 10-12, 2012; by Dr. K.L. Mathur entitled *Metal Technology in the Mughal*

Successive State of Bikaner: 1750-1818 AD.

55. *Sawa Bahi Mandi Bikaner*, No. 8, V.S. 1815-16/1758-59 AD, R.S.A., Bikaner.
56. *Sawa Bahi Rajgarh*, No. 2, V.S. 1831-35/1774-78 AD, ff. 44-45, R.S.A., Bikaner.
57. *Sawa Bahi Bikaner*, No. 11, V.S. 1822/1765 AD; Powlett, op. cit., pp. 97-98.
58. *Jagat Bahi Bikaner*, No. 81, V.S. 1807-10/1750-53 AD, R.S.A., Bikaner.
59. *Sawa Bahi Bikaner*, No. 2, V.S. 1802-04/1745-47 AD, f. 33.
60. Ibid.
61. Ibid., No. 11, V.S. 1822/1765 AD.
62. Tod, op. cit., Vol. II, p. 229.
63. Ibid.
64. *Kagad Bahi*, No. 4, V.S. 1831/1774 AD, f. 56, *Baisakh Badi* 1, R.S.A., Bikaner.
65. *Kamthana Bahis*, V.S. 1727; V.S. 1749, V.S. 1807, V.S. 1808, V.S. 1812, V.S. 1812-13, ff. 2, 3, 13, 14, 64 R.S.A. Bikaner.
66. Ibid.
67. Ibid.
68. Ibid.
69. *Rajasthan District Gazetteer*, Bikaner, Jaipur, 1972, p. 170.
70. *Parwana Bahi*, No. 4, V.S. 1800-1900/1743-1843 AD, record *Parwanas* of land grants and *Chakri* of these *Ustas*.
71. Powlett, op. cit., pp. 150-51.
72. *Bade Kamthana Ri Bahi*, No. 16, V.S. 1860/1803 AD The baked bricks costed @ Re.1 for 3,500 bricks.
73. *Byav Ri Bahi*, No. 159, V.S. 1827/1770 AD, R.S.A., Bikaner.
74. *Jagat Bahi Bikaner*, No. 81, V.S. 1807/1750 AD, R.S.A., Bikaner.
75. *Kagad Bahi*, No. 4, V.S. 1831/1774 AD, f.41.
76. Chicherao, A.I. op. cit., p. 58, Chicherao has highlighted the process of change and separation of craft and agriculture and from community craft to commodity crafts, particularly it intensified throughout 17th and 18th century India.
77. Habib, Irfan, op. cit., p. 67.
78. Ibid.
79. *Sawa Bahi Rajgarh*, No. 1, V.S. 1828/1771 AD, f. 13(a); No. 9, V.S. 1837/1780 AD, f. 129(b), R.S.A., Bikaner.
80. *Kagad Bahi*, No. 4, V.S. 1831/1774 AD, f. 54, R.S.A., Bikaner.
81. Ibid, No. 5, V.S. 1838/1781 AD, f. 49, R.S.A., Bikaner.
82. *Bakshish Ri Bahi Gaj Singhji Ri*, V.S. 1803/1746 AD, Lallgarh Museum Records, Lallgarh Palace, Bikaner.

83. The *Telis* were of villages Brahmsar, Mokalsar, Chahadwas, Kumbhana, Ranehar and Lunkaransar. Kagad Bahi, No. 3, V.S. 1827/1770 AD f. 10(b).
84. *Kagad Bahi,* No. 4, V.S. 1831/1774 AD, f. 52.
85. *Sawa Bahi Suratgarh,* No. 3, V.S. 1856-81/1799-24 AD (Year 1799 AD), f. 9.
86. *Kagad Bahi,* No. 4, V.S. 1831/1744, f. 41.
87. *Kagad Bahi,* No. 7, V.S. 1840/1783 AD, f. 43. *Parchoon Kagad,* R.S.A., Bikaner.
88. *Sawa bahi Rajgarh,* No. 1, V.S. 1828/1771 AD, ff. 2, 77.
89. *Kagad Bahi,* No. 18, V.S. 1868/1811 AD, f. 318.
90. *Parwanas,* V.S. 1814; First *Asoj Sudi* 9, V.S. 1823, *Jyestha Sudi* 3, V.S. 1835, *Posh Sudi* 8, V.S. 1836, *Chetra Sudi* 12, *Parwana Bahi,* No. 4, V.S. 1800-1900/1743-1843 AD, R.S.A., Bikaner.
91. *Parwana,* V.S. 1831, *Mingsar Badi* 1, *Parwana Bahi,* op. cit., R.S.A., Bikaner.
92. *Parawana,* V.S. 1840, *Asoj Badi* 5, V.S. 1830, *Chetra Sudi* 13, V.S. 1821, *Asoj Badi* 1, V.S. 1853, *Jyestha Sudi* 4, *Parwana Bahi,* op. cit., R.S.A., Bikaner.
93. *Parwana,* V.S. 1848, *Bhadwa Badi* 12, *Parwana Bahi,* op. cit., R.S.A., Bikaner.
94. *Parwanas,* V.S. 1874, *Bhadwa Sudi* 1, V.S. 1821, *Posh Badi* 6, *Parwana Bahi,* op. cit., R.S.A., Bikaner.
95. *Kagad Bahi,* No. 3, V.S. 1827/1770, ff. 41-42.
96. *Kamthana Bahi,* V.S. 1808-12/1751-55 AD, R.S.A., Bikaner.
97. Cf. Chatterjee, Anjali, *Wage Structure of Artisans and Labourers Engaged in Constructional Work in Medieval Rajasthan (1670-1761 AD): A Case Study of Bikaner State.* PIHC, Amritsar, 1985, pp. 316-25. These wages have been converted into rupees and *Anna*-paise by Dr. Chatterjee from original wages in *Takka* and *Dam* considering the 16 *Takka* per rupee value (standard).
98. Ibid.
99. Ibid.

10
Conclusion

The erstwhile state of Bikaner, known by its capital town which came into existence in 1488 AD, has gone through various vicissitudes during its history from its inception to final integration into Rajasthan in 1949 AD. It has been a Rathore principality and was included in the Mughal empire in the *Subah* of Ajmer and categorized as a *Sarkar*.

Our survey of the economy of the period 1746-1828 AD is to ascertain the continuity and changes after its separation from the Mughal empire and leads us to following results–

It is noticed that geographically it was completely a desert area and nature has acted niggardly in the economic resources, as such, it proved a significant determinant in the economic resources, and played an important role in its economy. Famines and droughts affected its economy to a larger extent. After coming out of the Mughal hegemony, feudal polity with more rigour developed here with dire consequences. Socially, it has a heterogeneous society of which some artisan castes bear an impact of the Central Asia probably through the Mughal contacts.[1]

The state grappled with the shortage of population throughout the period on account of calamities and migrations. Owing to these facts, sometimes, the entire village was deserted. The density of population in the year 1877 AD was as low as only 10 people per sq. mile.[2]

The agricultural production during the period continued to remain uncertain and uneven in the state, mainly because of lack of irrigational facilities and rainfed cultivation. The average area under cultivation, as surveyed and estimated by P.G.Fagan in 1893 and some scholars,[3] by and large, was not more than 15% of the total land and it varied greatly from 34% in *Pargana* Hanumangarh to only 3% in *Chira* Anupgarh. Most part of the state still formed an area of single *Kharif* crop and the cash crop was negligible.[4]

There was, more or less continuance of the Mughal land revenue system in the state with some variations as the situation demanded. All the methods of land revenue assessment suited to local conditions were followed. The state had to make certain changes in respect of collection of land revenue which was often farmed out to the highest bidder called *Muqati*. Of course, this term *Muqati/Muqata* has been in use in the Mughal system, but it had assumed much significance in Bikaner that during the period of financial hardships the state borrowed loans from moneylenders (*Seth, Sahukars*) and mortgaged the state sources of income with them to pay off this loan. Though it had reduced its burden of paying it off, but the peasantry had to bear its brunt.[5]

To increase income the state also made efforts to extend the area of cultivation by providing some incentives and adopting various methods to rehabilitate the depopulated villages during and after calamities. Such concessions were also extended during the Mughal period, but the significant change is that no facilities were given to the peasants in the Mughal period for rehabilitation in a new place. On the contrary, in Bikaner a peasant who returned to his native village even after a period of 40 years, was restored with his original land, house and privilege held previously by him,[6] without a distinction of *Asli* and *Dakhli* peasants. Thus, his status as *Asli* was restored to him.

Since income through the land revenue was very low, the state had to resort to other cash taxes known by *Rokad Raqams* (cash taxes) and *Bija Raqams* (other taxes), over and above the land tax. No doubt, the peasantry was heavily taxed and sometimes migrated from *Khalisa* to *Jagir* areas or sheltered in the sacrosanct place of Deshnoke to escape from it. Sometimes, the state then had to relax the taxes to retain them in *Khalisa* land or induced to return back.

The realization of land revenue was in either cash or kind. Again the pattern of the Mughal system had seen no change. The Mughals preferred cash payments, the same continued in Bikaner state and it was left to the convenience of the peasants to pay in kind or cash. If the realization was in kind it was marketed by the officials. Owing to the 'desert economy' some peasants were given concessions and they were called *Pasayati* which are not known in the Mughal system.[7]

The finance being an important ingredient in the 'desert economy', the state taxation system presumably, underwent a thorough change. Apart from, the adoption of the Mughal taxes in the state, some new taxes and cesses of commercial and non-commercial nature, were imposed and realized from different sections of the society. It was to cope with the increasing expenditures and the loss of income from the Mughal *Tankhwa-i-Jagir* being accrued to the state chief. Out of these taxes *Jagat* (custom duty) and commercial levies were of significant proportions in the state income. These taxes, different from Mughal taxes which included taxes like providing of safety (*Rukhwali and Khusali* taxes), *Khola* tax (adoption tax), *Neota* (cess for invitation of marriage), *Dharti Ri Chouthai* (tax on transaction of land), *Reeth* (tax on remarriage), *Phirangiyon Re Sartan Ri Bhanchh* (tax to recoup the expenses of the British). Bidawat *thakurs* had also to pay a regular levy to the state called *Bidawation Ri Bhanchh*. The military *Chakri* being realized from *Thakurs* and sub-assigness were converted into cash. Moreover, for realization of these taxes the *Muqata* system was resorted to largely. Evidently, it increased the tax net and its burden, the *Muqatis* added to the general discontentment among the masses.[8]

To augment more financial resources still more, the chief of the state laid a greater stress on the expansion of trade and commercial activities. This is manifested in the state's policy of encouragement to traders and merchants by way of tax exemptions, security to merchandize and other inducements,[9] and also in the growth of some trade routes in the territory. Some recognized external trade routes and minor internal routes improved here. The state could use the routes in realizing *Jagat* and transit duties on the movements of the commodities passing through these routes. However, these routes were not free from loot and plundering. In the field of communication and transportation no significant change is noticed from that of the Mughal period. However, besides *Banjaras,* some other castes like *Charans, Brahmins, Sikhs,* etc. began to participate in this field.[10]

The internal as well as the external trade seems to be well organized in the period. It is worth mentioning that the state organized religious fairs at places to arrange sale-purchase of the required commodities and this was an additional source of income to the state. So far as the export trade is concerned it was insignificant because of low productivity. Only woollen products, animals, *multani mitti,* and *sajji* were generally exported. But to meet the daily needs of the people, import trade was resorted to and items like sugar, *gur,* iron, cloth, horses, opium, grains, tobacco and luxury items were imported profusely and therefore, the balance of trade due to larger imports than the exports, was not in favour of the state.[11]

Another significant change was that the chief of Bikaner were allowed to have their own coins minted and a mint at Bikaner was established. Silver and copper coins were minted indigenously and circulated. This suggests that this period noticed the rise of the money economy and gradually replaced the barter system prevalent in the villages. This resulted in the increased demand of coins. Apart from the working of a mint at Bikaner there was a demand for another mint at Rajgarh town. But a significant change is noticed that during the Mughal period, the Mughal silver coin had equal face and intrinsic value due to the nominal minting charges and the fixed alloying ratio. But Bikaner's indigenous coins lacked in either respect. Furthermore, there used to be a number of coins of different states in circulation, creating a problem of exchange. The expertise of a *sarraf* was the sole agency who could determine the exchange value. Therefore *sarrafs* gained considerably. Some debased coins in Bikaner, also in circulation due to short supply of bullion, were refused to be accepted in some corners of Bidasar and Deshnoke.[12]

There was no uniformity in weight and measurement. There was a difference in standard and local and also in *Kachha* and *Pacca* weights causing inconvenience in commercial transaction and the accuracy was doubtful. There is the possibility that excess land revenue from the peasantry might have been realized on this count. The primitive methods of measurements of using limbs of the body were in vogue. It is presumed that the chief of Bikaner, for reasons not known, could not apply the standard weights and measurements prevalent in the Mughal times.[13]

The growth and emergence of some commercial centres locally called '*Mandi*' was another distinct feature of the post-Mughal period in the state. These *Mandis,* like Mughal *Mandis,* had grown up as commercial centres. For the state these were primarily the *Jagat* collection centres and interestingly, these developed on the trade routes also. The Subordinate *Chowkis* for the same purpose were also established. The small villages where these were located grew into bigger commercial towns. Their growth suggests the relative expansion of commercial activities and commercial traffic through the state. It also suggests the increase of the state income. However, the detailed study of the balance sheets of the *Sadar Mandi Bikaner* and some other *Mandis* during the period evidently show their expenditure being higher than the income putting them into deficits. The direct beneficiaries were the commercial classes rather than the state.[14]

The tables, indices and graphs of prices of the general consumable items prepared from the Mughal times to the early 19th century, i.e. 1687 to 1820 AD, showed a general trend of price rise. In this respect the position of Bikaner state was not different from that of the Mughal empire where scholars have noticed a continuous price rise.[15] Since, most of the commodities were imported from outside and often the supply being irregular a gradual price hike was imminent. It is also noticed that the prices fluctuated and increased during the period of war, famine, droughts and other calamities, but resumed normal level when the calamities were over. The general hike in prices during normal days caused inconvenience to the masses and the merchants exploited the situation. They hoarded the items and sold them at higher rates during normal days.

The merchant class played an important role in trade and commerce. They had a heterogeneous class composition and discharged diversified commercial function during the period under review. With the predominance of the *Bania* community, other castes of *Khatris* (migrants of the Punjab), *Modis*, Brahmins and some others actively participated in various pursuits. Their nature of work allow us to categorize them into affluent whole sellers, petty retailers and others, viz. intermediaries and bankers.[16]

Besides marketing, importing and exporting commodities, they also obtained *Huwala* and *Muqatas* (contracts of state revenue realization) of the state. During the period the state revenue was largely auctioned to these *Muqatis* bidding highest. The system appeared to be beneficial to the *Muqatis* because large profits accrued to them as they tried to extract more than the bid amount in the *Muqata* area in the specified period. The system also helped the state in revenue realization but it became instrumental in exploitation of common people.

Moneylending and *Hundi* transaction were frequent in the state. *Sahukars* and *Bohras* lent money to borrowers with or without securities. The rate of interest varied accordingly and marked a difference in the state loans, rural lending and in the commercial loans. The state borrowed heavy loans and paid fair amount every month, as interest to *Sahukars* at a high rate of interest ranging from 12% to 36% p.a. The state source of income were usually mortgaged with the debtors till it was fully repaid. The rate of interest largely depended on the necessity of the borrower. The *Bohras* in the rural society, advanced loans to the peasants on mortgaging their belongings, crops and sometimes their offsprings. They took full advantage of the rural poverty and exploited heavily. The state had to interfere in some cases to save them from exploitation.[17]

The commercial credit was also available to merchants from the money lenders and it is noticed that merchants borrowed credit on mortgaging shops, godowns and stored grains. The rate of interest was comparatively lower than the loans given to the states.

The execution and discounting of *Darshani* and *Miyadi Hundis* were in practice here both for transferring money to the places inside and outside of the state and also for borrowing loans from *Sahukars* through their branches at places. In this respect there was no change from the practice prevailing in the Mughal empire and thus, *Hundis* continued to be an important credit institution. The rate of *Hundawan* ranging from 1% to 9% varied on factors of distance, risk, and the nature of the *Hundi* as well.[18]

The practice of insuring the goods against loss, theft and plunder during Mughal times was also adopted by the specialized group of merchants in the state. It is noticed that the insurance (*Bima*) was becoming popular with growing insecurity on the routes. This gave rise to another contractual service known as *Bolai* under which safer passage of goods was arranged by some high profile people or *zamindars* on high consideration of money. This was not the case in the Mughal empire. The *Kachha* and *Pacca Bimas* with difference in rates were also in practice. In the former, damage of goods was not compensated, but in the latter, it was obligatory. The rate of insurance was 7 *annas* per 100 rupees but varied on risk, distance and like factors.

The intermediaries—*Dallals* and *Adhatiyas* working as middlemen, were also actively participating in the town's market and earning good profits along with the speculators. The state, therefore, charged taxes on these commercial groups. We do not find any established trend of migration in the state during the period despite some stray references.[19]

Another development marks changes in the field of craft productions. Artisans, both of rural and urban areas in their distinctive forms, i.e. community craft and commodity craft played an important role in the feudal economy of Bikaner during the period of study. The rural craft was combined with agriculture while in town it began to be separated. The process became more acute in the late 18th and 19th century resulting in changes in the traditional agrarian relations. It seems that it was because of the larger demands in towns and requirements of luxury items by the royalty, feudals and the elites residing in the towns. The relationship between the artisans and their consumers seems to have undergone change in the urban centres. In the rural sector the *Jajmani* system continued but in the urban social sector, money-commodity relations emerged. This is evident from the fact that in the urban centres the state realized taxes from the income of the artisans. The caste played a decisive role in artisans life and was responsible for class disparity, and distinction within themselves.The state also employed them in the state *Karkhanas* to satisfy their needs. The material condition of a town artisan and labourers was not good due to the low wages they received. However, the state took a keen interest in growth of small-scale handicrafts and it was because of the interest, some new crafts like *Usta* painting, bricks industry, carving by *Silawat,* etc. had developed in the state.[20]

Thus, in case of Bikaner as a successor state the implication of the decline of the Mughal empire was not positive and precisely it had unfavourable consequences, viz. (a) it lost the income being received from the Mughals (*Tankhwah-i-Jagir*) and, (b) it succumbed to internal distrubances and revolts and the external attacks, for which it had to incur larger amounts for safety. The depleting financial resources and increasing expenditures created difficult situation.

To get out of it, it imposed and realized heavy taxes with sternness. Further the realization of state revenue was very often subjected to *Muqatas* (contractual realization) who exploited the assigned sources for their profits. This resulted in gross incovenience to peasantry and often migrations with complaints of excessive tax burden. The state had to mollify them with certain remissions and exemptions in taxes.

To generate alternative revenue state keenly encouraged commercial activities. Consequently, trade developed in the state, commercial centres emerged with infrastructure of *Mandis* and *Chowkis*, many commercial pursuits were carried out by heterogeneous commercial class. Apparently, it showed a positive growth but virtually the merchant class, bankers and intermediaries gained profits and the state was at a loss. This is borne out by the balance sheets of the *mandis*. The state expenditure were more on the maintenance of the infrastructure of the *mandis*. The public welfare was undermined. Apparently, there was no substantial growth in agriculture and in population. The pattern of expenditure as *Bahis of Sadar Mandi*, Bikaner show, was also not conducive with 50% on royal household and 24% on royal establishment and only 2% on the developmental works of the total *Mandi* income.[21]

This unconstructive pattern of expenditure and insufficient income led them to borrow larger loans from the *Sahukars* at high rates of interest, which ultimately put them into a vicious circle of continuous borrowings per month aggravating the financial conditions. Thus, the political instability coupled with the financial crisis bound the chief to opt for another subordination under the British East India Company in 1818 AD.

REFERENCES

1. Chapter 2, Sec (1) & (2).
2. Ibid.
3. Fagan, P.G., *The Settlement Report of Khalisa Village of Bikaner*, Bikaner, 1893; Devra, G.S.L., *Rajasthan Ki Prashashnik Vyavashtha*, Bikaner; See Chapter 3, Section (1).
4. Chapter 3, Section (1).
5. Ibid., Section (2).
6. Ibid., Section (4).
7. Ibid., Section (2).
8. Chapter 4, Section (1) & (2).
9. Chapter 5, Section (4).
10. Chapter 5, Section (1) and Map 5.1.
11. Ibid., Section (2) & (3).
12. Ibid., Section (5).
13. Ibid., section (6).
14. Chapter 6.
15. Chapter 7. The trend of the upward prices has continued further in the later period, i.e. 1860-1947 AD; See *The Cambridge Economic History of India (1557-1947)*, Vol. II (ed.) Dharma Kumar, Delhi, Reprint 1984, pp. 878-904.
16. Chapter 8, Section (1) & (2).
17. Chapter 8.
18. Ibid.
19. Chapter 8, Section (3).
20. Chapter 9.
21. Chapter 6, Section (3).

Glossary

Adhatiyo	:	A commission agent to whom custody of saleable goods is handed over
Adhiyo	:	A tax at ½ rate
Asāmi	:	Cultivator
Asan Petio	:	Halting allowance
Attak	:	Seizure or arrest to realize demand
Badarki	:	Tax for escorting caravans to destination
Badi Bhānchh	:	A common term for three taxes collectively realized, viz. *Dhunwa*, *Pāgh* and *Ango*
Bāgar	:	Semi-arid area
Baghechi	:	A water body surrounded by greenery
Bāghru	:	Peasant tilling fallow land on lump sum rent
Bāharli Chowki	:	Out checkpost for collection of *Jagāt*/ transit duty
Bahi	:	Ledger or account book
Bālad	:	Herd of oxen cart owned by *Banjārās*
Bāladia	:	*Banjārās*, carriers of merchandize, especially foodgrain and salt
Bāndedo	:	Pack load, unit of tax realization
Bansole-ri-Bhānchh	:	Anuual tax from carpentor
Bārothiā	:	Expelled on punishment or self-exiled/ deserted with resentment from the native place
Battā	:	Discount
Begār	:	Compulsory service without payment
Betalab Pattā	:	Tax exempted-grant of land (*Muāfi*)
Bhānchh	:	Cess

Bhog	: Land tax in kind (synonymous to Māl) considered at par with sacred offerings to God
Bhoglāwā	: Interest free pawned item to be used in lieu of interest
Bhogtā	: Assignee of land enjoying *Bhog* i.e. land tax in lieu of his services
Bholāwaniā	: *Jagāt* Collector in village on certain remuneration
Bhombāb	: Rent paid by *Bhumiā*
Bhumiā	: Hereditary right holder on land or *Zamindār*
Bhuraj	: Tax for storage
Bichhāyati	: Pavement dealer
Bighedi	: Land revenue on the basis of measurement of land, a system of land revenue assessment
Bija Raqam	: Other cash taxes
Boliyār	: Type of cultivator tilling land on contractual rent
Bohrā	: Rural moneylender
Chadas	: Water bucket used for draining water from well
Chākri	: Military obligation and personal attendance to chief realized from sub-assignees
Chauhātiya	: Cultivators paying land revenue @ ¼ rate
Chhatāk	: 1/16 part of a *seer*
Chhoot-ra-Kāgad	: Remission papers
Chirā	: Administrative and revenue unit
Chithi	: Letter of payment or credit letter
Chunpaz	: Lime worker
Dallāl	: Middle man between seller and purchaser working on commission
Dām	: 1/50 part of a *takkā*
Darbār	: Term used for ruler of the princely state
Deshprath	: Tax on animal
Dez	: Land revenue due from *Hāli* cultivator
Dhādvi	: Raider or plunderer
Dori	: A rope for measuring land of about 20 hand length

Gaiwāl income : Property forfieted of heirless deceased person
Gairvilla : Lost or displaced
Gawādi : Family
Ghāni : Wooden oil press
Ghughri : Boiled preparation of wheat and *Bājrā*
Gugghi : Thick woollen raincoat made of goat hairs
Halgat : Cultivator of per plough method in desert and also its payments
Hāli : Cultivator of *kankut* method of revenue assessments
Harkārā : Official news carrier
Hem : Gold
Hundāwan : Charges for *Hundi* transmission
Hundā-bhārā : Charges for insurance
Hundi : Bill of exchange
Huwaladār : State-appointed official for realization of revenue or working in state office
Huwāla soapā : A system of revenue realization on remuneration
Jagāt : Corrupt form of *Zaqāt;* term used for custom duty and transit duty
Jagātiyā : *Jagāt* collector
Jāgir : A fief
Jajmāni system : Traditional system of collective maintenance of artisans by village community and payment to them of a remuneration in kind
Jinsi : In kind
Jokhā : Insurance
Juhāri : Gift/cash in honour
Kachhā Bimā : Insurance of goods without responsibility of damage of goods in transition
Kāgad : State order or document
Karbi : Stalk of *Jawār* used as fodder
Kāru-Kamin : Term used for artisans and workers (*Kāru*-worker and *Kamin*-Menial or insignificant)
Katār : Camels in row (caravan)
Katāria : Carriers of *Katār* (camel traders)
Khat : Deed for termed loan

Kholā : Adoption tax
Khusāli : Tax for protection and welfare
Korad : Leaves of *moth* and *til* used as fodder for horses
Kuppi : Elliptical shaped flat container of *ghee*
Laag-bāg : Traditional taxes and cesses
Lunkārās : Woollen *Khesh*
Magrā : Rocky area
Mālba : Tax for villages' expenses
Mandi : Wholesaler market/Commercial centre
Māpā : Sales tax
Māshā : Equivalent unit of 15 grains or 8 *Ratti*
Maund : Unit of 40 *seers* for weighing
Mela-Magariā : Fairs and seasonal social gatherings on festivals
Mohrāno : Cess for putting a seal on papers at checkpost certifying payments of *Jagāt* or transit duty
Muqāta : Contract through auction for revenue realization (*Ijārā*)
Muqāti : Contract holder
Naudā : Salt pit
Neotā : Invitation tax realized on marriage in royal household
Paat : Flat surface in desert
Paccā Bimā : Insurance of goods with compensation of damage in transition, if any
Pallān : Saddle for camel
Panchāyati : Cess for soliciting *Panchāyat's* decision
Pani peev ra : Water tax
Paondā : Pairs of legs - one *paondā* consisted of 5½ ft. length
Parkhāi : Test of purity of coins by *sarrāf*
Pasāyati : Privileged cultivator who enjoyed tax exemptions or village headman
Pattāyat : *Jagirdār* or *Pattā* holder
Pāyli : Device to weigh grains usually of 2 seers
Pazābgir : Brick maker artisan
Pesār : Import of goods
Pokhān : Mines of stones

Poonchhadi : Camel tale, unit for tax
Pothiā : Small peddler
Qāsid : Messenger
Raibāri : A caste of camel breeders and domesticators of camels
Reeth : Tax for remarriage
Rokad Raqam : Cash taxes, over and above land tax
Rozgār : Employment or remuneration
Rukhwāli Bhānchh : Protection tax
Rupo : Silver/bullian
Sadāmad : Perpetually
Sahukār : Moneylender, also term used in general for merchants of all types
Sar : Pond, water body formed by rain water in depressions
Sarrāf : Money changer
Sāsan : Tax free-land in charity
Satoriā : Speculator
Seer : 1/40 part of *maund*
Seervo : Headload of commodity
Siropāo : Robe of honour
Sohnā : Village revenue official expert in assessing cultivation by conjecture
Suin area : Flat and fertile area
Takkā : Equivalent of an Anna - 1/15 or 1/16 part of rupee
Takini : Customary cesses
Tihaliyā : Cultivators paying land revenue @1/3 rate
Tolā : 1/80 part of a *seer*
Tolāwatiā : Weighing man
Ustā : Urban artisan painter specialized in laquer work on camel hyde with gold and silver liquids
Vahtivon : Goods in transit and transit duty
Watan : Ancestral estate or hereditary *Jāgir*

Bibliography

The Rajasthan State Archives, Bikaner preserves the unique and ample collection of archival records in the forms of *Bahis*, letters, *choupanias* (account manuals), *farmans, nishans* and other official documents. They are unique because of their being contemporary and indigenous state official records created in the course of official activities. More so, they cover various aspects of history of the erswhile state of Bikaner specially the economic and social history. Hitherto, very little of them have been utilized for the research purpose. Some of these *Bahis* are the copies of the original one and the rest are in original, covering the period from the 17th to 19th centuries. The script of the *Bahis* is Devnagri and is in *Marwari* dialect. The Persian and Urdu words have also been used apart from the hundreds of local terms of the area.

These *Bahis* have been classified and captioned under various heads as per their nature of information available in them. Maximum possible numbers of *Bahis* relating to the subject have been utilized for evidences and understanding of the economy of the period as arranged in different sections of the archives as follows: (a) Rampuria section (b) Bikaner *Bahiyat* section. The Rajasthan State Archives, Bikaner also holds in its collection some of the private Archieal records as well. Among them *Bhaiya* records and *Mohta* records have been chiefly consulted. Apart of it, some of the Archival collection in the form of *Bahis* which are in the custody of the State Royal family and preserved in the Maharaja Sadul Singh Museum, Lallgarh Palace, Bikaner have been for the first time consulted and used. In the formulation of the work many more works of references, both in English and Hindi have been used for corroborating the facts and data. Apart from it, the scholarly works of the relevant subject published in journals, proceedings, survey reports have been gainfully utlisized.

I. UNPUBLISHED ARCHIVAL RECORDS

The Rajasthan State Archives, Bikaner (Rajasthan)

(a) Rampuria Section

(1) ***Kāgdon ri Bahis:*** The word *Kagad* literally means an order or document of state. The series contains 52 *Bahis* in all covering a period from 1754 to 1843 AD. The *Bahis* have the collection of state orders, circulars and directions issued at times and the material has been arranged and classified under different sub-heads, viz. *Chhoot ra Kagad, Huwala Kagad, Prachoon Kagad, Sanadi Kagad, Reeth Ra Kagad,* etc. providing information regarding a variety of subjects like land system, taxation, trade-commerce, administration, etc. and hence, are the prime part of the Rampuria section. Following *Bahis* have been used–

1. *Kagdon Ri Bahi,* V.S. 1811/1754 AD No. 1
2. *Kagdon Ri Bahi,* V.S. 1820/1763 AD No. 2
3. *Kagdon Bahi,* V.S. 1827/1770 AD No. 3
4. *Kagdon Ri Nakal Ri Bahi,* V.S.1831/1774 AD No. 4
5. *Kagdon Ri Nakal Ri Bahi,* V.S.1838/1781 AD No. 5
6. *Kagdon Ri Nakal Ri Bahi,* V.S.1839/1782 AD No. 6
7. *Kagdon Ri Bahi,* V.S. 1840/1783 AD No. 7
8. *Kagdon Ri Bahi,* V.S. 1849/1792 AD No. 8
9. *Kagdon Ri Bahi,* V.S. 1851/1794 AD No. 9
10. *Adalat Re Kagdon Ri Bahi,* V.S. 1854/1797 AD, No. 10
11. *Kagdon Ri Bahi,* V.S. 1857/1800 AD No. 11
12. *Kagdon Ri Bahi,* V.S. 1859/1802 AD No. 12
13. *Kagdon Ri Bahi,* V.S. 1861/1804 AD No. 13
14. *Kagdon Ri Bahi,* V.S. 1863-64/1806-07 AD No. 14
15. *Kagdon Bahi,* V.S. 1866/1809 AD No. 15
16. *Kagdon Wa Rajoo Re Chithan Re Nakal Ri Bahi,* V.S. 1867/1810 AD, No. 16
17. *Kagdon Re Nakal Ri Bahi,* V.S. 1867/1810 AD No. 17
18. *Kagdon Ri Bahi,* V.S. 1868/1811 AD No. 18
19. *Kagdon Ri Bahi,* V.S. 1870/1813 AD No. 19/1 (w.e.f. *Asoj Sudi* 11)
20. *Kagdon Ri Bahi,* V.S. 1870/1813 AD No. 19/2
21. *Bahi Kagdon Ri,* V.S. 1871/1814 AD No. 20

22. *Bahi Kagdon Ri*, V.S. 1872/1815 AD No. 21
23. *Bahi Adalat Re Kagdon Ri*, V.S. 1873/1816 AD No. 22
24. *Prachoon Kagdon Ri Bahi*, V.S. 1874/1817 AD No. 23
25. *Bahi Kagdon Ri Nakal Ri*, V.S. 1875/1818 AD No. 24
26. *Bahi Kagdon Ri Nakal Ri*, V.S. 1876/1819 AD No. 25
27. *Bahi Kagdon Ri Nakal Ri*, V.S. 1877/1820 AD No. 26
28. *Bahi Kagdon Ri*, V.S. 1879/1822 AD No. 28
29. *Prachoon Kagdon Ri Bahi*, V.S. 1881/1824 AD No. 30
30. *Bahi Kagdon Ri*, V.S. 1884/1827 AD No. 33/1
31. *Bahi Kagdon Ri*, V.S. 1885/1828 AD No. 34

(2) *Sāwā Bahis*: The word *Sāwā* is the corrupt form of *Siah* which meant the ledger of daily receipts and disbursements. These *Bahis* provide a vivid account of income and expenditure of the different areas pertaining to various *Mandis*. *Mandi* area wise *Bahis* cover also other information of taxation, commercial and non-commercial income and the rates thereof–

(A) *Sāwā Bahi Mandi Sadar, Bikaner*

32. *Sawa Bahi Mandi Sadar, Bikaner*, V.S. 1802-04, No. 2
33. *Sawa Bahi Mandi Sadar, Bikaner*, V.S. 1805, No. 3
34. *Sawa Bahi Mandi Sadar, Bikaner*, V.S. 1807-10, No. 4
35. *Sawa Bahi Mandi Sadar, Bikaner*, V.S. 1810-12, No. 5
36. *Sawa Bahi Mandi Sadar, Bikaner*, V.S. 1818-21, No. 9
37. *Sawa Bahi Mandi Sadar, Bikaner*, V.S. 1821-22, No. 10
38. *Sawa Bahi Mandi Sadar, Bikaner*, V.S. 1826, No. 15
39. *Sawa Bahi Mandi Sadar, Bikaner*, V.S. 1827, No. 16
40. *Sawa Bahi Mandi Sadar, Bikaner*, V.S. 1829-30, No. 17
41. *Sawa Bahi Mandi Sadar, Bikaner*, V.S. 1831-32, No. 18
42. *Sawa Bahi Mandi Sadar, Bikaner*, V.S. 1833-34, No. 20
43. *Sawa Bahi Mandi Sadar, Bikaner*, V.S. 1835-36, No. 21
44. *Sawa Bahi Mandi Sadar, Bikaner*, V.S. 1837-38, No. 22
45. *Sawa Bahi Mandi Sadar, Bikaner*, V.S. 1838-40, No. 23
46. *Sawa Bahi Mandi Sadar, Bikaner*, V.S. 1841-43, No. 24
47. *Sawa Bahi Mandi Sadar, Bikaner*, V.S. 1843, No. 24
48. *Sawa Bahi Mandi Sadar, Bikaner*, V.S. 1843-48, No. 25
49. *Sawa Bahi Mandi Sadar, Bikaner*, V.S. 1853-55, No. 28
50. *Sawa Bahi Mandi Sadar, Bikaner*, V.S. 1856-57, No. 29

(B) *Sāwā Bahi Mandi Rajgarh*–

51. *Sawa Bahi Mandi Rajgarh*, V.S. 1828-31, No. 1
52. *Sawa Bahi Mandi Rajgarh*, V.S. 1831-35, No. 2
53. *Sawa Bahi Mandi Rajgarh*, V.S. 1835-38, No. 3

54. *Sawa Bahi Mandi Rajgarh,* V.S. 1839-42, No. 4
55. *Sawa Bahi Mandi Rajgarh,* V.S. 1842-44, No. 5
56. *Sawa Bahi Mandi Rajgarh,* V.S. 1844-46, No. 6
57. *Sawa Bahi Mandi Rajgarh,* V.S. 1846-50, No. 7
58. *Sawa Bahi Mandi Rajgarh,* V.S. 1851-55, No. 8
59. *Sawa Bahi Mandi Rajgarh,* V.S. 1855-58, No. 9
60. *Sawa Bahi Mandi Rajgarh,* V.S. 1861, No. 10
61. *Sawa Bahi Mandi Rajgarh,* V.S. 1863-67, No. 11
62. *Sawa Bahi Mandi Rajgarh,* V.S. 1868-71, No. 12
63. *Sawa Bahi Mandi Rajgarh,* V.S. 1872-77, No. 13
64. *Sawa Bahi Mandi Rajgarh,* V.S. 1878-80, No. 14
65. *Sawa Bahi Mandi Rajgarh,* V.S. 1881-84, No. 15
66. *Sawa Bahi Mandi Rajgarh,* V.S. 1885-89, No. 16

(C) *Sāwā Bahi Mandi Sujangarh*

67. *Sawa Bahi Mandi Sujangarh,* V.S. 1865-69, No. 1
68. *Sawa Bahi Mandi Sujangarh,* V.S. 1875-84, No. 2
69. *Sawa Bahi Mandi Sujangarh,* V.S. 1884-87, No. 3
70. *Sawa Bahi Mandi Sujangarh,* V.S. 1887-94, No. 4
71. *Sawa Bahi Mandi Sujangarh,* V.S. 1895-1900, No. 5
72. *Sawa Bahi Mandi Sujangarh,* V.S. 1901-06, No. 6
73. *Sawa Bahi Mandi Sujangarh,* V.S. 1908-14, No. 7

(D) *Sāwā Bahi Mandi Anupgarh*

74. *Shri Anopgarh Re Jama Kharach Ri Bahi,* V.S. 1753-54, No. 1
75. *Anopgarh Re Sawa Ri Bahi,* V.S. 1818-21, No. 2
76. *Sawa Tehsil Anupgarh,* V.S. 1821-28, No. 3
77. *Sawa Bahi Mandi Anupgarh,* V.S. 1828-34, No. 4
78. *Sawa Bahi Mandi Anupgarh,* V.S. 1834-43, No. 5
79. *Sawa Bahi Mandi Anupgarh,* V.S. 1843-54, No. 6
80. *Sawa Bahi Mandi Anupgarh,* V.S. 1855-68, No. 8
81. *Shri Anopgarh Re Thana Ro Jama Kharach Ro Saho,* V.S. 1868-74, No. 9
82. *Sawa Thana Anupgarh Ro,* V.S. 1885, No. 11

(E) *Sāwā Bahi Mandi Suratgarh–*

83. *Sawa Bahi Mandi Suratgarh,* V.S. 1844-54, No. 1
84. *Sawa Bahi Mandi Suratgarh,* V.S. 1855, No. 2
85. *Sawa Bahi Mandi Suratgarh,* V.S. 1856-81, No. 3
86. *Sawa Bahi Mandi Suratgarh,* V.S. 1896-1900, No. 8

(F) *Sāwā Bahi Mandi Ratangarh*

87. *Sawa Bahi Mandi Ratangarh,* V.S. 1858-61, No. 1
(*Ratangarh Re Thana Ro Jama Kharach*)

88. *Shri Ratangarh Re Mandi Ro Jama Kharach*, V.S. 1868-75, No. 3

(G) *Sāwā Bahi Mandi Hanumangarh*

89. *Sawa Bahi Mandi Hanumangarh*, V.S. 1862-67, No. 1
90. *Sawa Bahi Mandi Hanumangarh*, V.S. 1879-84, No. 3

(H) *Sāwā Bahi Mandi Reni*

91. *Reni Ri Mandi Ro Jama Kharach*, V.S. 1814-23, No. 1

(I) *Sāwā Bahi Nohar*

92. *Sawa Bahi Nohar Ri*, V.S. 1822-25, No. 1

(J) *Sāwā Bahi Mandi Lunkaransar*

93. *Sawa Bahi Mandi Lunkaransar*, V.S. 1887-1891, No. 1

(K) *Sāwā Bahi Mandi Churu*

94. *Bahi Churu Re Thana Re Saho Ri*, V.S. 1828-29, No. 1

(3) *Khālisa Gāwān Ri Bahis*: These *Bahis* enlist the details of '*Hasil*' and '*Jama*' of land revenue and other taxes in the *Khalisa* villages–

95. *Basta* No. 2 - *Bahi Khalisa Ra Gawan Ri*, V.S. 1808
96. *Basta* No. 2 - *Bahi Khalisa Ra Gawan Ri*, V.S. 1809
97. *Basta* No. 2 - *Bahi Khalisa Ra Gawan Ri*, V.S. 1810
98. *Basta* No. 2 - *Bahi Khalisa Ra Gawan Ri*, V.S. 1811
99. *Basta* No. 2 - *Bahi Khalisa Ra Gawan Ri*, V.S. 1812/2
100. *Basta* No. 3 - *Bahi Khalisa Ra Gawan Ri*, V.S. 1817
101. *Basta* No. 3 - *Bahi Khalisa Ra Gawan Ri*, V.S. 1819
102. *Basta* No. 3 - *Bahi Khalisa Ra Gawan Ri*, V.S. 1907

(4) *Bahi Chithi Wā Khaton Ri:* These *Bahis* record the agreements of termed loans and detail of their daily transaction of petty amounts through *chitthis*.

103. *Bahi Prachoon Chitthi Ri Nakal*, V.S. 1851, No. 2
104. *Chitthi Wa Khaton Ri Bahi*, V.S. 1869, No. 6

(5) *Pattā Parwāna Bahi*: It is an important series of *Bahis* and has mention of *Parwanas* and *Sanads* issued in favour of the concerned.

105. *Parwana Bahi*, V.S. 1800-1900, No. 4

(6) *Kamthānā Bahis*: These *Bahis* provide useful information about the wages and salaries of workers and labourers deputed in various constructional works along with the material, implements used therein.

106. *Bade kamthana Ri Bahi*, V.S. 1808-14, No. 2

107. *Bahi Shri Kot Re Kamthana Ri*, V.S. 1812-13, No. 3
108. *Bahi Shri Bade Kamthana Ri*, V.S. 1860, No. 16
109. *Bahi Bade Kamthana Ri*, V.S. 1885, No. 25

(7) *Kooch Muqaam, Marzaad, Peshkashi* and *Sāsan Bahi*: These *Bahis* provide information regarding royal camps on visit, state declarations, *Peshkashi* collection and religious grants.

110. *Bahi Kooch Muqaam Re Kagdon Ri*, V.S. 1886-98, No. 1
111. *Bahi Kooch Muqaam Ri*, V.S. 1910-14, No. 2
112. *Bahi Marzaad Ri Kagdon Ri*, V.S. 1934, No. 1
113. *Bahi Peshkashi Re Lekhe Ri*, V.S. 1833-38, No. 1
114. *Sasan Bahi*, V.S. 1671, No. 1

(8) *Bahi Talbāna Ri*

115. *Bahi Kagdon Ri Talbana Ri*, V.S. 1896-99, No. 1

(9) Miscellaneous *Bahis*

116. *Bahi Mahajana Re Peedhiyon Ri*, V.S. 1933
117. *Sambhala Bahi*, V.S. 1754, No. 1

(b) Bikaner *Bahiyāt* Section

1. *Jagāt Bahis*: The word is corrupt of *Zaqat*. *Jagat* included taxes on *Nekal*, *Pesar* and *Vahtivon* merchandize. They provide useful information about the commercial products, trade routes and activities of traders and merchants at the *Mandis* and *Chowkis*.

118. *Bahi Mandi Re Golak Ri (Kharde Ri)*, V.S. 1855, No. 61
119. *Shri Rajgarh Re Thane Re Jama Kharch Ro Saho*, V.S. 1855-60, No. 62
120. *Bahi Shri Mandi Re Jama Kharach Ri Bikaner Ri*, V.S. 1855, No. 63
121. *Bahi Rajaldesar Re Jagat Ro Lekho*, V.S. 1859, No. 64
122. *Bahi Rajgarh Re Mandi Ro Saho Utaran Ri*, V.S. 1843-44, No. 65
123. *Magre Re Kharipatti Ri Bahi Jagat Chowki Ro Lekho*, V.S. 1858, No. 66
124. *Magre Kharipatti Re Jagat Ri Bahi*, V.S. 1858, No. 67
125. *Bahi Desh Re Jagat Ri*, V.S. 1858, No. 68
126. *Shri Bikaner Mein Jagaton Ro Lekho*, V.S. 1858, No. 69
127. *Desh Ri Jagat Ri Bahi*, V.S. 1858, No. 70
128. *Bahi Dhan Nekal Ri Jagat Ri, Nawa Chowka Betho Teri*, V.S. 1858, No. 71
129. *Mandi Re Jagat Ri Bahi*, V.S. 1807, No. 81
130. *Bahi Baharli Chowki Ri Jagat Ri*, V.S. 1809, No. 108
131. *Shri Rajgarh Ri mandi Re Jagat Ro Lekho*, V.S. 1869-73, No. 109
132. *Girad Re Chowki Ro Lekho*, V.S. 1869, No. 110
133. *Lunkaransar Re Jagat Ri Bahi*, V.S. 1869, No. 111

134. *Lunkaransar Re Jagat Ri Bahi,* V.S. 1869, No. 112
135. *Shri Bade Jagat Re Rokad Re Khata Ri Bahi,* V.S. 1870, No. 113
136. *Bahi Saho Churu Ri,* V.S. 1877, No. 114
137. *Reni Re Mandi Ro Saho,* V.S. 1872, No. 116
138. *Bahi Bikaner Re Mandi Re Jama Kharach Ri,* V.S. 1872-73, No. 117
139. *Lunkaransar Re Jagat Ri Bahi,* V.S. 1872, No. 118
140. *Bahi Ranisar Re Jagat Ro Lekho,* V.S. 1872, No. 119
141. *Bahi Mandi Re Jama Kharach Ri,* V.S. 1875, No. 120
142. *Uwarja Re Bahi,* V.S. 1875, No. 121
143. *Uoon Re Lunkara Re Jagat Ri Bahi,* V.S. 1844, No. 53
144. *Sahukaran Ro Khata Bahi,* V.S. 1861, No. 84
145. *Met Ri Jagat Ri Bahi,* V.S. 1900, No. 186
146. *Jagat Ro Choupaniyo,* V.S. 1844, No. 42

2. *Bahi Lekhā Wā Jamā Kharach Ri*

147. *Bahi Khalisa Ri Gawan Ri,* V.S. 1826-30, No. 1
148. *Bahi Khazane Ri,* V.S. 1803, No. 3
149. *Sarrafon Re Lekha Ri Bahi,* V.S. 1840
150. *Bahi Jama Kharach Ri,* V.S. 1855
151. *Lashkaran Nu Leni Hundiyon Melie Teri Vigat,* V.S. 1726, No. 241
152. *Bahi Sahukaran Re Shri Golak Mein Bharijia Teri,* V.S. 1861

3. *Hāsil Bahis* : State revenue realization has been recorded in these *Bahis*. They are in a very poor condition. The papers are torn and in a brittle state.

153. *Bahi Gaon Jodhasar Re Hasil Ri,* V.S. 1747, No. 6
154. *Bahi Dhunwa Deshprath Re,* V.S. 1761-63, No. 41
155. *Bahi Chira Re Bharti Mein Khat Baqi Teri Vigat Ri,* V.S. 1809, No. 66
156. *Bahi Khalisa Wa Pargana Re Jama Jod Ri,* V.S. 1750
157. *Bahi Halgat Ri,* V.S. 1802-07, No. 63
158. *Bahi Halgat Ri,* V.S. 1809-22, No. 67
159. *Bahi Dhunwa Deshprath Ri,* V.S. 1810, No. 68
160. *Bahi Punia Re Pargana Ro Khato,* V.S. 1824
161. *Bahi Punia Re Pargana Ri,* V.S. 1884-87, No. 123
162. *Bahi Punia Pargana Shri Rajgarh Re,* V.S. 1846

4. *Byāv Bahis* : They quote details of ceremonies of marriages and the prices of commodities purchased at the occasions–

163. *Shri Gaj Singhji Parneejia Teri Kharach Ri Bahi,* V.S. 1808, No. 146
164. *Akhai Singhji Re Beti Re Byav Re Kharach Re Bahi,* V.S. 1808, No. 147
165. *Bai Shri Ram Kanwar Ro Byav Shri Anup Singhji Kiyo Teri Bahi* (V.S. 1744), V.S. 1816, No. 9 (No. 143)

166. *Bahi Byav Wa Naler Melo Bai Sardar Kanwar Re Byav Ri,* V.S. 1827, No. 159
167. *Bai Shri Udai Kanwarji Re Byav Ne Jeenus Re Khato Ri Bahi,* V.S. 1839, No. 167
168. *Maharaja Kanwar Shri Ratan Singhji Re Byav Ri Bahi,* V.S. 1877, No. 170

5. *Dhunwā Bahi*

169. *Dhunwa Deshprath Ri Bahi,* V.S. 1786, No. 9

6. *Habub Bahi*

170. *Rukhwali Bhanch Ri Bahi,* V.S. 1879, No. 10

Private Collections - R.S.A., Bikaner

(1) *Bhaiyā Records*: Bhaiya Nathmal and Jethmal Mathur were two brothers serving the state on various important positions as *Huwaldars*. Their personal correspondence, *Sanads, Bahis, Chitthis, Rukkas* are some important collections preserved in the Rajasthan State Archives, Bikaner.

171. Letters of Bhaiya Alam Chand, V.S. 1802-1830. Bhaiya Nathmal and Jethmal, V.S. 1866-73
172. *Pattas, Parwanas, Khas Rukkas, Chitthi, Sanads,* etc. collected in *Basta* Nos. 1 to 6
173. *Bahi Kharipatti Magra Re Rukhwali Ri,* V.S. 1859
174. *Nohar Re Thane Re Jama Kharach Re Bahi,* V.S. 1874

(2) *Mohtā Records*

175. Some *Parwanas* of the Bikaner rulers addressed to the Mohta family of Bikaner (21 *Parwanas*)

(3) Maharaja Bikaner's Personal Collection (Preserved in Sadul Singh Museum, Lallgarh Palace, Bikaner)

176. *Bagshish Ri Bahi Shri Gaj Singhji Ri,* V.S. 1803
177. *Bahi Halgat, Korad, Bhuraj, Jakhiro, Charo-Sehtaro Ro Lekho Ri,* (*Hasil Bahi*), V.S. 1855
178. *Bahi Khāto Tāzimi Sardāran Ro Wā Pattedāron Ro,* V.S. 1902
179. *Bahi Shri Kārkhāna Re Jamā Kharach Ri,* V.S. 1821
180. *Bahi Shri Ratangarh Ri Dhān Ri Chouthai Ro Lekho,* V.S. 1894
181. *Gāwān Ri Bhānchh Bahi,* V.S. 1889
182. *Rokad Khātā Bahi,* V.S. 1815
183. *Shastrā Ri Bahi,* V.S. 1834

Published Non-Archival Sources

(A) Persian Sources

184. *Ain-i-Akbari*, Abul Fazal (Eng.Tr.) Col. Jarett, Vol. II, Reprint, Delhi, 1989.
185. *Akbarnamah*, Abul Fazal (Eng.Tr.) H.Beveridge, 3 Vols., Delhi, 1989.
186. *Muntakhab-ul-Tawarikh*, Badaoni (Eng.Tr.), Vol. II, W.H. Lowe, Delhi (Reprint), 1973.
187. *Tuzuk-i- Jahangiri*, (Eng. Tr.) Rozers and Beveridge, 2 Vols., 2nd ed., Delhi, 1968.
188. *Maasir-ul-umara*, Shah Nawaz Khan (Eng. Tr.) Molvi Abdur Rahim, *Bib. Indica*, 3 Vols., 1885.
189. *Tarikh-i-Firuzshahi*, Shams Siraj Afif (ed.) Wilayat Hussain, Calcutta, 1891.
190. Imperial *Farman* of Mughal Emperor Akbar to Rai Singh of Bikaner, Dated 12 *Rajjab-ul-Murazab*, 990 *Hizri* year (April 25, 1592 AD).
191. *Farman* of Shah Alam to Maharaja Gaj Singh, 1762 AD

(B) *Rajasthani* Sources

192. *Desh Darpan*, Sidhayach, Dayal Das, (ed.) J.K. Jain, R.S.A., Bikaner, 1989.
193. *Dayal Das Ri Khyat*, Sidhayach, Dayal Das, Part II (ed.) Sharma, Dashrath, Bikaner, 1948.
194. *Marwar Re Pargana Ri Vigat*, Muhnot Nensi, (ed.) Bhati, N.S., Vol. I, Jodhpur, 1968.
195. *Nensi Ri Khyat*, Nensi, (ed.) Sakariya, Badri Prasad, 4 Vols., Jodhpur.
196. *Chhand Rao Jetsiro-Vithoo Suje Ro Kiyo*, Bibliothica Indica, A.S.B., New Series, No. 1439, Calcutta.

(C) English Sources

197. *Census of India, 1891, Vol. XXVI, Rajputana*, Part I, Col. Abbott, Calcutta, 1892 (Bikaner).
198. Erskine, K.D., *The Western Rajputana States Residency and the Bikaner Agency*, Allahabad, 1908.
199. Fagan, P.G., *Reports on the Settlement of the Khalisa Villages of Bikaner State*, Bikaner, 1893.
200. Hunter, W.W., *Imperial Gazetteers of India-Rajputana*, Oxford, 1921.
201. *National Atlas of India, Part I, Physical*, Calcutta, 1981.
202. Powlett, Capt. P.W., *Gazetteer of Bikaner State*, (1874), Bikaner, 1935.
203. *Reports on Administration of Bikaner State*, 1934.

204. Sehgal, K.K., *Rajasthan District Gazetteer-Bikaner District*, Jaipur, 1972.
205. *Techno-Economic Survey of Rajasthan*, 1963.

III. Works of Reference

206. Jain, J.K. (ed.) *A Descriptive List of Bikaner Bahis*, (17-19 C.), Part I, R.S.A., Bikaner, 1982.
207. Jain, J.K. (ed.) *A Descriptive List of Farmans, Manshoor* and *Nishans*, R.S.A., Bikaner, 1962.
208. Lalas, Sita Ram, *Rajasthani-Hindi Sanskshipt Sabdakosh*, 2 Vols., RORI, Choupasni, Jodhpur, 1986-87.
209. Munshi, Sohan Lal, *Tawarikh Rajshri Bikaner*, Bikaner, 1890.
210. Wilson, H.H., *A Glossary of Judicial and Revenue Terms*, Delhi, (Reprint), 1968.

IV. Secondary Works

211. Aggrawal, Govind, *Churu Mandal ka Shodhpurna Itihas*, Ajmer, 1974.
212. __________, *Vanijya Vyapar Mein Muneem Gumaston Ki Bhoomika*, Churu, 1983.
213. __________, *Samridha Bhartiya Beema Paddhati Unneesvi Sati Purvardha Mein*, Churu, 1987.
214. Alam, Muzaffar, *The Crisis of Empire in Mughal North India: Awadh and the Punjab (1707-48)*, Delhi, 1986.
215. Banerjee, A.C., *Rajput States and the East India Company*, Calcutta, 1944.
216. Bhadani, B.L., *Peasants, Artisans and Entrepreneurs*, Jaipur, 1999.
217. __________, (ed.) *Facets of Marwar Historian*, Jaipur, 1996.
218. __________, (Tr.) *Jahangir Kalin Bharat*, (Hindi Tr. of Pelsaert's, 'Remonstrentai'), Jaipur, 1996.
219. Bhargava, B.K., *Indigenous Banking in Ancient and Medieval India*, Bombay, 1935.
220. Chandra, Satish, *Medieval India: From Sultanate to the Mughals, Part II, Mughal Empire (1526-1748)*, Delhi, 1999.
221. __________, *Medieval India: Society, the Jagirdari Crisis and the Village*, Macmillan, Delhi (Reprint), 1997.
222. Chicherov, A.I., *India, Economic Development in the 16th-18th Centuries: Outline History of Crafts and Trade*, (Eng. Tr.) Lahore, 1976.
223. Chopra, P.N., *Some Aspects of Social Life During the Mughal Age (1526-1707 AD)*, Agra, 1963.
224. Choudhary, T.R. and Habib, Irfan, *Cambridge Economic History of*

India (1200-1750 C), Vol. I, Hyderabad, 1984.

225. Devra, G.S.L., *Rajasthan Ki Prashashnik Vyavastha*, Bikaner, 1981.
226. __________, (ed.) *Socio-Economic Study of Rajasthan*, Jodhpur, 1986.
227. Dhari, Alakh, *The Life and Exploits of Raja Rai Singhji of Bikaner*, Bikaner, 1934.
228. Goetz, Herman, *Art and Architecture of Bikaner State*, Oxford, 1950.
229. Gupta, B.L., *Trade and Commerce in Rajasthan*, Jaipur, 1987.
230. Habib, Irfan, *Agrarian System of Mughal Empire*, Bombay, 1963, 2nd Rev. ed., New Delhi, 1999.
231. __________, (ed.) *Akbar and His India*, Delhi, 1997.
232. __________, (ed.) *Medieval India-I, Researches in History of India (1200-1750)*, Delhi, 1982.
233. __________, *An Atlas of the Mughal Empire*, Delhi, 1982.
234. __________, *The Economic History of Medieval India—A Survey*, Delhi, 2001.
235. J.S., Gehlot, *Rajasthani Krishi Kahawaten*, Jodhpur, 1941.
236. Kachhawah, O.P., *Famines in Rajasthan*, Jodhpur, 1988.
237. Lal, Makkhan, *Banika Shikshak*, Bikaner, 1943.
238. Nizami, K.A. and Habib, M., *Comprehensive History of India—Delhi Sultanate*, PPH, Delhi, 1992.
239. Ojha, G.H., *Bikaner Rajya Ka Itihas*, 2 Parts, Ajmer, 1936.
240. __________, *History of Rajputana*, Vol. V, Ajmer, 1939.
241. Pant, D., *Commercial Policy of the Mughals* (Reprint), Delhi, 1978.
242. Rajvi, Amar Singh, *Medieval History of Rajasthan - Western Rajasthan*, Vol. I, Bikaner, 1992.
243. Sarkar, J.N., *Fall of the Mughal Empire*, 4 Vols., Calcutta, 1953.
244. __________, *History of Aurangzeb*, III, Calcutta, 1916.
245. Saxena, Malti, *Impact of the British Sovereignty on the Economic condition of Rajasthan* (1818-1947), Delhi, 1984.
246. Sharma, Dashrath, *Rajasthan Through the Ages*, Part I, Bikaner, 1964.
247. Sharma, G.N., *Social Life in the Medieval Rajasthan* (1500-1800), 1st ed., Agra, 1968.
248. Sharma, G.C., *Administrative System of Rajputs*, New Delhi, 1979.
249. Sharma, G.S., *Marwari Vyapari*, Bikaner, 1988.
250. Sharma, R.C., *Settlement Geography of the Indian Desert*, New Delhi, 1972.
251. Siddiqi, N.A., *The Land Revenue Administration under the Mughals (1700-1750 AD)*, Bombay, 1970.
252. Singh, Dilbagh, *The State, Landlords and Peasants*, Delhi, 1990.
253. Singh, Karni, *The Relations of the House of Bikaner with the Central Powers*, Delhi, 1974.

254. Tod, Col. James, *Annals and Antiquities of Rajasthan*, Vol. II, Reprint, Delhi, 1971.
255. __________, *Rajasthan Through the Ages* (1300-1761), Part II, Bikaner, 1970.
256. Web, W.W., *Currencies of the Hindu States of Rajputana*, 1893, (Hindi Tr.) Mangilal Mayank, *Rajputana Ke Hindu Rajwade Ke Sikke* Jodhpur.

V. Articles

257. Aggrawal, Govind, 'Potedar Sangrih Ke Aprakashit Kagzat', *Marushri* (ed.) Govind Aggrawal, yr. 5, Vol. 1-2, Ajmer, 1976.
258. __________, 'Papers Relating to *Attak*', *Marushri*, (ed.) Govind Aggrawal, yrs. 11-12, Vol. 4-1, July-December, 1982, Churu (Raj.).
259. __________, 'Chaar Lakh Ki Aitihasik Hundi' (Hindi) *Marushri* (ed.) Kanhiya Lal Sahal, Yr. 18, No. 4, Jan. 1971, Pilani (Jhunjhunu).
260. __________, 'Churu Mein Pracheen Haton Ki Vigat - Bahi of Potedar Mirzamal - V.S. 1882', '*Marushri*', (ed.), Govind Aggrawal, Yrs. 2-3, Vol. 4-1, Churu, 1973.
261. Ali, M. Athar, 'The Eighteenth Century– An Interpretation', *Indian Historical Review*, Vol. V, No. 1-2, (ed.) A.R. Kulkarni, Delhi, 1979.
262. Bhadani, B.L., 'Tod Ke Arthik Ankre - Ek Sankhyikiya Adhyayan', *Itihaskar James Tod - Vyaktitva Evm Krititva* (Hindi), (ed.) Hukum Singh Bhati, Udaipur.
263. Brown, C.J., 'Some Remarks on the Mughal Currency', *Journal of U.P. Historical Society*, Vol. I, Lucknow.
264. Chandra, Satish, 'Commercial Activities of the Mughal Emperors during the 17th Century', *Essays in Medieval Indian Economic History*, Vol. III, New Delhi, 1987.
265. Chatterjee, Anjali, 'Wage Structure of Artisans and Labourers Engaged in Constructional Work in Medieval Rajasthan (1670-1761 AD) - A Case Study of Bikaner State', PIHC, Amritsar, 1985.
266. Devra, G.S.L., 'Nature of Incidence of *Rokad Raqam* in the Land Revenue System of Bikaner State (1650-1750 AD), PIHC, 1976.
267. __________, 'A Study of the Trade Relations Between Rajasthan and Sindh/Multan', *Socio-Economic History of Rajasthan*, Jodhpur, 1986.
268. __________, 'Cropping Pattern of Rural Settlement in Bikaner State (1650-1700 AD)', PRHC, Bikaner Session, 1984, Vol. XIV, Jodhpur, 1986.
269. __________, 'Rajasthani Khshetra Mein (Bikaner State) Krishi Yogya Bhoomi Wa Uska Vargikaran', PRHC, IX, Kota, 1976.
270. 'Fullers Earth and its Uses', *Bikaner Bulletin*, Vol. VI, No. 6, Bikaner, January, 1949.

271. Gupta, B.L., 'The Policy of the Rajput Rulers of Rajasthan Towardds Commercial Class in the 18th Century' (Summary) PIHC, 46th Session, Amritsar, 1985.
272. Gupta, S.P., 'The System of Rural Taxation', PIHC, 1972.
273. Habib, Irfan, 'Currency System of the Mughal Empire' *Medieval India Quarterly*, IV, No. 1-2, Aligarh, 1960.
274. __________, 'The System of Bills of Exchange (*Hundis*) in the Mughal Empire' PIHC, Muzaffarpur Session, 1972.
275. __________, 'The Eighteenth Century of Indian Economic History', NIAS, Wassenaar, Netherlands, June, 1993.
276. Hasan, Aziza, 'Mints of the Mughal Empire (A Study in Comparative Currency Output)', *Essays in Medieval Economic History*, Vol. III, ed. Satish Chandra, New Delhi, 1987.
277. Jain, Anjula, 'Rukhwali Bhanchh', PRHC, Bikaner Session, Jodhpur, 1986.
278. Kachhawaha, O.P., 'A Study in the Famine Relief Policy of Maharaja Ganga Singh', *Ganga Singh Centenary Volume* (ed.) G.S.L. Deora, Bikaner 1980.
279. Mathur, Kanti Lal, 'Pattern of Income and Expenditure in *Sadar Mandi Bikaner* During Second Half of the XVIII Century', (Summary), PIHC, Calicutt Session, 1999, p. 1165.
280. __________, 'The Rate of Land Tax and Its Economics Pressure on the Peasantry in Bikaner during the Second Half of the 18th and Early 19th Century', PRHC, Jodhpur Session, February, 2001, pp. 36-42.
281. __________, 'A Note on the Malba Cess in the 18th Century Bikaner State', *The Jats*, Vol. 2 refered Journal, ed. by Dr. Vir Singh, Originals, Delhi, 2006. This paper has been presented at the Surajmal Jat Research Institute, Janakpuri, New Delhi, as the M.G.S. University Nominee in 2005-06.
282. __________, 'Change and Continuity in the Prices in Bikaner from the Close of the 17th to Early 19th Century', *Medieval India-2*, Journal of Aligarh Muslim University, Aligarh, Department of History, Aligarh, 2008.
283. __________, 'Fiscal Pattern of Bikaner *Mandi* in the Second Half of the 18th Century', Proceedings of Rajasthan History Congress, Sujangarh Session, March, 2008.
284. Mishra, K.P., 'The Role of the Banaras Bankers in the Economy of the 18th Century India,' PIHC, Vol. III, Chandigarh Session, 1973.
285. Nahta, B.L., 'Jain Kavi Udai Chand Rachit Bikaner Gazal', *Vaichariki*, Bhartiya Vidya Mandir Shodh Pratishthan, Bikaner,

January, 1972.

286. Perlin, Frank, 'Mint Technology and Mint Output in an Age of Growing Commercialization', *Essays in Medieval Economic History*, Vol. III, (ed.) Satish Chandra, New Delhi, 1987.
287. Qaiser, A.J., 'The Role of Brokers in Medieval India', *Facets of a Marwar Historian* (eds.) B.L. Bhadani and D. Tripathi, Jaipur, 1996.
288. Sharma, G.D., '*Vyaparis* and *Mahajans* in Western Rajasthan During 18th Century', *Essays in Medieval Economic History*, Vol. III (ed.) Satish Chandra, New Delhi, 1987.
289. Sharma, Manohar, Binjaro, *Vishawambhara* yr. 29, No. 3, July-Sept., 1997, Bikaner.
290. Saxena, A.N., 'Economic Conditions of Bikaner State During 16th Century', *Journal of the Rajasthan Institute of Historical Research* (ed.) M.L. Sharma, Vol. XVII, No. 3, September-December, Jaipur, 1979.
291. Shah, P.R., 'Introduction of British Indian Currency in Jodhpur State–A Case Study in Economic Reforms and its Execution', PRHC, Vol. VI, Beawar (Raj.) Session, 1973.
292. Shekhawat, Sobhagya Singh, 'Rajasthan Baat Sahitya Mai Binaj Vyapaar', *Jagti Jot*, Vol. 2, May-July, Bikaner, 1992.
293. Singh, Abha, 'Irrigating Haryana: The Pre-Modern History of the Western Yamuna Canal', *Medieval India-I, Researches in the History of India (1200-1750)*, ed. Irfan Habib, Delhi, 1992.
294. Siddiqi, Iqtadar Hussain, 'Social Mobility in the Delhi Sultanate' *Medieval India-1, Researches in the History of India (1200-1750)*, ed. Irfan Habib, Delhi, 1992.
295. Singh, Dilbagh, 'The Role of *Mahajans* in the Rural Economy in the Eastern Rajasthan During the 18th Century', *Social Scientist*, No. 22, May, 1974.
296. _________, 'Peasant's Indebtedness in the State of Bikaner 1887-1943', *Ganga Singh Centenary Volume*, (ed.) G.S.L. Devra, Bikaner, 1980.
297. Zaidi, Sunita, 'The Qayamkhani Shaikhzada Family of Fatehpur-Jhunjhunu', PIHC, Hyderabad, 1978.
298. _________, 'Akbar's Annexation of Sindh–An Interpretation', *Akbar and His India* (ed.) Irfan Habib, Delhi, 1997.

VI. Proceedings, Journals and Magazines

299. *Bikaner Bulletin*, Bikaner.
300. *Indian Historical Review*, New Delhi.
301. *Jagti Jot*, Bikaner.
302. *Journal of Rajasthan Historical Studies*, Jaipur.
303. *Journal of U.P. Historical Society*, Lucknow.

304. *Khyat, Dungargrah*, Bikaner.
305. *Maru Bharti*, Pilani.
306. *Marushree*, Churu.
307. *Medieval India Quarterly*, Aligarh.
308. Proceedings of Indian History Congress (Volumes cited by place and year of annual session).
309. Proceedings of Rajasthan History Congress (Volumes cited by place and year of annual session).
310. *Shodhak*, Jaipur.
311. *Social Scientist*, New Delhi.
312. *Vaichariki*, Bikaner.
313. *Vishwambhara*, Bikaner.

Index